Bipin Chandra Pal

It is difficult to say how far, if at all, Sir Ashutosh represents that rare combination of superior statesmanship and high administrative efficiency which have occasionally been found in the great administrators of free countries. His field of work has, so far, been much too limited, his opportunities too few, and even these in a subordinate sphere of public life, to give full play to any high statesmanlike qualities that he may possibly have. This is the universal tragedy of our present public life. One thing, however, is absolutely undeniable. Even the most careless student of Sir Ashutosh's career cannot deny that all appearances and outer impressions to the contrary notwithstanding, he has his visions, like the rest of his educated countrymen and his inner soul is as sensitive to our existing actualities, as the most vocal, or — may I say it without offence — even the most extremist of our patriots and politicians; and that his one aim and intention, in all his public labours, has been, as he himself once declared, to:

> Draw new furrows beneath the healthy morn
>
> And plant the great Here-After in the Now.

People's Spokesman

Sir Ashutosh is not the "tribune" of his people, has never aspired to that honour. But, as a member, first of the Bengal Legislative Council, then of the Indian, he has been as loyal and courageous a defender of popular rights as the most aggressive of our patriots and politicians. Of course, his style is his own. He never indulged in strong language, and has never appeared on any of our political platforms that offer so much temptation to it. But neither has he trained himself in the courtier's art of saying pleasant things only. His public utterances have always been measured and therefore moderate, in the true sense of the term, but always without any suspicion of falsehood or flattery in them. Sir Ashutosh's speeches both in the Bengal and the Imperial Council would fully bear this out. Discussing certain charges preferred by the Government of India in a letter to the Government of Bengal in connection with the Calcutta Municipal Bill (1899) then before the Council, he said that "Assuming, as indeed it is assumed, in the 13th paragraph of the letter from the Government of India, that the allegation is well-founded, that the existing Corporation

BIPIN CHANDRA PAL

Editors

M.A. Shewan

A.C. Akela **N.P. Sharma**

hbpl

Himalaya Books Pvt. Ltd.

'Ramdoot', Dr. Bhalerao Marg, Girgaon, Mumbai - 400 004
Tel : (022) 23863863. Fax : (022) 23877178
Email : himpub@vsnl.com

Edition : 2013

Published by : **H.B.P.L.**
"Pooja Apartments", 4-B, Murari Lal Street, Ansari Road,
Darya Ganj, New Delhi-110 002
Phones : 23270392, 23278631 Reliance : 30180392 to 396
Fax : 011-23256286 Email : hphdel@vsnl.com

Sole Distributers : HIMALAYA PUBLISHING HOUSE PVT. LTD.

Branch Offices

Mumbai : "Ramdoot", Dr. Bhalerao Marg, Girgaon, Mumbai-400 004.
Phones : 23860170/23863863 Fax : 022-23877178
Email : himpub@vsnl.com
Website : www.himpub.com

Nagpur : Kundanlal Chandak Industrial Estate, Ghat Road, **Nagpur - 440 018.**
Phone: 2738731, 3296733 Telefax : 0712-2721215

Bengaluru : No. 16/1 (Old 12/1), 1st Floor, Next to Hotel Highlands,
Madhava Nagar, Race Course Road, **Bengaluru - 560 001.**
Phone : 22281541, 22385461, Telefax: 080-22286611

Hyderabad : No. 3-4-184, Lingampally, Besides Raghavendra Swamy Matham,
Kachiguda, **Hyderabad - 500 027.** Phone: 040-27560041, 27550139,
Mobile:- 09848130433 Telefax: 040-27560041

Chennai : No. 85/50, Bazullah Road, T. Nagar, **Chennai - 600 017.**
Phone: 044-28344020, 32463737, 42124860

Pune : No. 527, "Laksha" Apartment, First Floor, Mehunpura, Shaniwarpeth,
(Near Prabhat Theatre), **Pune - 411 030.**
Phone: 020-24496323/24496333/32326733

Lucknow : House No. 731, Sehkhupura Colony, Near B.D. Convent School,
Lucknow - 226 024. Mobile : 09307501549

Ahmedabad : No. 114, "SHAIL", 1st Floor, Opp. Madhu Sudan House, C.G.Road,
Navrang Pura, **Ahmedabad – 380 009.**
Phone: 079-26560126, Mobiles: 09327324149, 09314679413

Ernakulam : No. 39/104 A, Lakshmi Apartment, Karikkamuri Cross Rd.,
Ernakulam, **Cochin – 682011**, Kerala.
Phone: 0484-2378012, 2378016, Mob.: 09344199799

Bhubaneswar : 5 Station Square, **Bhubaneswar (Orissa) - 751 001.**
Mobile: 9861046007, E-mail:- orissa@himpub.com

Indore : Kesardeep Avenue Extension, 73, Narayan Bagh.Flat No. 302,
IIIrd Floor, Near Humpty Dumpty School, Narayan Bagh,
Indore (M.P.) 452 007 Mobile: 09301386468

Kolkata : 108/4, Beliaghata, Main Road, Near ID Hospital, Opp. SBI Bank
Kolkata - 700 010.
Mobile: 09910440956, E-mail:- nkmitra@himpub.com

Guwahati : House No. 15, Behind Prajjyotish College, Near Sharma
Printing Press, P.O. Bharalumukh, Guwahati - 781009 (Assam)
Mobile: 07439040301; 07439040302

Printed by : Sri Prints & Sales, Delhi

Preface

Biography, is now a form of literature, very much in vogue. In fact, biography is a description or account of someone's life and the times, which is usually published in the form of a book. A biography is more than a mention of personal facts (life, education, work, relationships and death), it also portrays the subject's experience of events. Technically speaking, a work is biographical, if it covers, all of a person's life. Biography writing has a long history. A biography is real. Ancient Greeks developed the biographical tradition, which we have inherited, although until the 5th century AD, when the word 'biographia' first appeared, in Damascius' "Life of Isodorus," biographical pieces were called simply "lives". It is quite likely that the Greeks were drawing on a pre-existing eastern tradition. Certainly Herodotus' "Histories" contains more detailed biographical information on Persian kings and subjects. The earliest surviving pieces, which we would identify as biographical are Isocrates' "Life of Evagoras" and Xenophon's "Life of Agesilaos," both from the fifth century BC. "Parallel Lives" by Plutarch, a Greek writing under the Roman empire, is a series of short biographies of eminent men.

The Golden Age of English biography emerged in late eighteenth century, the century in which the terms "biography" and "autobiography" entered English lexicon. The classic works of the period were Samuel Johnson's "Critical Lives of the Poets" and James Boswell's "Massive Life of Johnson". Generally American biography followed English model. By World War I, cheap hardcover reprints had become popular. The decade of the 1920s witnessed a biographical 'boom'. Later, biographical writings developed a lot and today biographies are written and compiled in the finest form of the genre. In India too, biography, as a form of literature has been evolved, cultivated and polished over the years. Here is an effort to promote this tradition further.

This series of biographies of great men, great women and celebrities in all walks of life is an adventurous academic endeavour, in its own right. A team of researchers and compilers has worked for a good period of time to accomplish the project. For this purpose, hundreds of books by eminent authors and editors have been consulted and referred to. We have benefited from various works, liberally, in order to illustrate and enrich this effort of ours. Present book is devoted to the great personality of Bipin Chandra Pal.

Bipin Chandra Pal was a noted politician, journalist and an eminent orator. He had a remarkable literary competence and studied various books extensively. He was one of the three famous patriots, known as the trilogy of Lal-Bal-Pal. The other two being, Lala Lajpat Rai and Bal Gangadhar Tilak. He was one of the main architects of the Swadeshi movement. He firmly stood against the partition of Bengal. He preached the ideal of Swadeshi through himself in the non-cooperation movement, due to his difference of view points, with other leaders of the movement. Pal had a 'never say die' attitude and he lived by this principle. He revolted against the evils and ill practices of Hinduism. He was a member of the Brahmo Samaj and believed in the equality of men and women. He encouraged widow marriages and female education.

This is a compact and comprehensive account of the above mentioned great life, which is bound to attract the attention of scholars, researchers, students and the general readers, alike. Let's hope this humble effort would receive a warm welcome and due applause.

— ***Editors***

Contents

people only by his measured but therefore nonetheless straight and fearless criticism of official acts and policies. Indeed, opportunities for this criticism were closed to him by his appointment as a judge of the Calcutta High Court, almost immediately he had taken his seat in the Imperial Legislative Council. But the whole outlook is radically wrong. Opposition to the Government may proceed from various motives of different or indifferent moral values. The disappointed placeman is an opponent of Government all the world over.

In India, social disappointments of Europe[illegible]ed gentlemen who wanted to, but could not get adm[illegible] society, have occasionally ended in such [illegible] these have landed the disappointed ind[illegible] platforms. There have been others, a much [illegible] whose patriotism has been inspired by [illegible] ideas and whose aim and intention in all their [illegible] have been to emulate British ways and attain [illegible] their conduct and conversation they have been B[illegible] only in their opposition to the British officialdom in their country. Intellectual and moral slaves of their foreign masters, they have only aspired to social and political equality with them.

This was, really, the predominant type, in any case in Bengal, before the birth of our new Nationalism at the beginning of the present Christian century.

Sir Ashutosh's patriotism has never been of this type. He is not a disappointed placeman. He easily won the only official position to which he ever aspired. In the days of his youth nothing higher than this was really open to Indian ambitions. The regrettable disturbances in Bengal and elsewhere following upon Lord Curzon's indiscretions, forced the need of drastic reforms upon British statesmanship; and a few high executive offices have since been thrown open to qualified Indians. But Sir Ashutosh's administrative record as Vice-Chancellor of the Calcutta University, has unfortunately offered little encouragement to the Government to take him into their inner counsels. I do not really know, even if high executive office were open to Sir Ashutosh, whether he would care to exchange the free air of the High Court Bench for the

1

Introduction

Bipin Chandra Pal a journalist, essayist, orator and thinker was one of the leaders who awakened India to a new sense of inner strength.

According to Prof. Paravate, those who push the pen powerfully are said to be shy of the platform. This is not all axiomatic because numerous examples of those who wielded their tongue and pen with equal power could be easily cited. In the case of Bipin Chandra Pal, perhaps his tongue was more effective and sharper than his pen. But this differentiation could be easily dismissed as that between Tweedledom and Tweedledec. His oratory was not mere command over words.

Bipin Chandra Pal, who has rightly been described by Sri Aurobindo as one of the mightiest prophets of Nationalism, and perhaps the best and most original thinker in the country at that time, and by Professor Benoy Kumar Sarkar as 'the father of revolutionary thought in Bengal' was one of the learned thinkers of modern India.

According to B.C. Roy, Mr. Pal was a born orator and his eloquence in the early part of this century roused the youths of their country. Even the aged and the wise listened to him with respect and he was always prepared to convince them, as he often used to say, "not by magic, but by logic".

As Aurobindo Ghosh said, "he spoke under an inspiration which he himself was unable to resist" Srinivasa Sastri remarked with reference to Bipin Chandra Pal's Madras speeches of 1907, "oratory had never dreamt of such triumphs in India. The power of the spoken word had never been demonstrated on such a large scale".

Profile

Bipin Chandra Pal was born in a village in Sylhet district, now in Bangladesh, on November 7, 1858. His father, Ramchandra Pal, was a man of strong character. In 1875, after passing his Entrance examination, Bipin Chandra Pal joined the Presidency College, Calcutta. His college career was not distinguished by any brilliance. In fact, he was seldom seen in the classrooms. "About a couple of hours every day", he says in his autobiography, "and some days only an hour, I used to be in my class. The rest of the time I played truant".

The period which covered his public life (1882-1932) was also a period of great changes in the religious, social and political life of the people in India. As Lord Ronald Shay said, "His pen played a not inconsiderable part in the social and political ferments that have stirred the waters of Indian life" during the period.

Being sensitive, his mind quickly responded to the influences of the movements of his time. Sir Francis Younghusband, described him as "of fine spiritual disposition as well as of high intellectual attainments".

His journalistic career, which began at the age of 22, continued till his death in 1932. He was on the editorial staff of the Bengal Public Opinion. Calcutta, edited *The Tribune,* Lahore (1887-88) started and edited the English weekly journal New *India* (1901), started and edited the English daily *Vande Mataram* in 1906 (later suppressed by the government), published the English weekly journal *Swaraj in London* during his exile from India (1908-11), founded the English monthly journal *Hindu Review* (1912), edited the daily *Independent, Allahabad* (1919-20). He was also a regular contributor to the *Modern Review, Amrita Bazar Patrika. Statesman,* etc. till his death.

His father made his will on his deathbed and made over all his property to him. To those present he said, "For ten years I did not see Bipin's face. By a previous will I disinherited him absolutely. All those years I would not allow him to come near me. But I am convinced that while he went his own way, out of regard for what he believed to be his *dharma,* he did not by practising one thing and professing another destroy my *dharma.* He is not a *haramzada.* Besides I thought this also; that thought there are people who would like to have what little property I may leave behind me, there is no one except Bipin, whatever may be his religious principles, who would after my death protect with all his life, the honour of my wife and my daughter. This is why I called him back".

What Bipin wrote in *Vande Mataram* of September 8, 1906 would be very typical of what he spoke and wrote in those days. He was quite frank about it as usual. Bipin said, 'the time has come when in the interest of truth and civic advancement and the freedom of the people, our British friends should be distinctly told that while things they have done for us already, the sacrifices they have made to make our lot easy and their yoke light, we cannot any longer suffer ourselves to be guided by them in our attempt at political progress and emancipation. Their point of view is not ceasing in any sense to be essentially British; we desire to make it autonomous, absolutely free of British control'.

He was a nationalist and wanted to see India as a free nation. To achieve this, he emphasised the method of passive resistance. In a speech in Madras in 1907, he declared, "Our programme is that we shall so work in the country, so combine the resources of the people, so organise the forces of the nation, so develop the instinct of freedom in the community, that by these means we will compel the submission to our will of any power that may set itself against us. If you ask me to state in general terms what are the methods and the means, what are the instruments that will further this ideal of Swaraj in this country, my reply shall be that these means and methods are in what is known in political science as the methods of Passive Resistance. It means not resistance that is not active, but non-aggressive resistance. We stand within the limits of the law that we have still in this country. We shall respect that law as long as that law shall respect our primary rights which constitute the authority of every government whether that government be a despotic government or a constitutional government, right which no government can create and which, therefore, no government can destroy. As long as the laws of this government will respect our primary rights of life, person and property and other similar primary rights, so long we purpose ourselves to be within the bonds of law; and passive resistance means resistance offered by a people from within the limits of such law.

Political Ideology

B.C. Pal was a great nationalist. According to B.C. Roy, he made great sacrifices for his love of country, truth and God. It was perhaps the great sacrifice of his life when on account of his strong convictions he lived in splendid isolation from his erstwhile colleagues and friends during the last few years of his life. His greatness lay in the fact that he never yielded to anyone in his devotion to truth and God and to his country, with him. As it was with many other politicians of this country, service of the country was a religion and a service to God.

The Historian's History of the World spoke of him as "the chief purveyor of seditious ideas who promulgated the doctrine of Swaraj or complete political independence".

His political ideas can be broken down as under:

> "On Nationalism, Sri Aurobindo Ghosh referred to him as "one of the mightiest prophets of nationalism". Prof. Benoy Kumar Sarkar regarded him as "the father of revolutionary thought in Bengal".

The nationalist propaganda of Bipin Chandra Pal made, however, the opponents of freedom extremely uneasy. They could not deny that he was "a man of great intellectual force and high character, who had the peculiarity of expressing extreme views in modest language".

To Pal 'Nationalism implied that, collectively, we the composite Indian community are a distinct, and individual social organism and as such, we have a distinct end unto ourselves and a specific law of our own National Being, through which we must seek to reach and realise that end'.

Bipin Chandra's patriotism was free from any hatred of the British. In an article in Vande Mataram in 1906, he said;

> "The time has come when in the interest of truth and civic advancement and the freedom of the people, our British friends should be distinctly told that while we are thankful for all the kind things they have done for us already, the sacrifices they have made to make our lot easy and their yoke light, we cannot any longer suffer ourselves to be guided by them in our attempts at political progress and emancipation. Their point of view is not ours they desire to make the Government of India popular without ceasing in any sense to be essentially British; we desire to make it autonomous, absolutely free of British control".

Bipin Chandra noted an important difference between the old and the new Nationalism.

> "The new Nationalism was intensely realistic, it had a strong grip on the actualities of Indian life and thought as against the imitative character of the older and earlier social and political activities. The older generations drew their inspiration of freedom and progress from European, and specially British history and literature. The old patriotism did not feed upon the actualities of Indian thought and life but upon the idealisties of Europe and America... There was scarcely any sense of political wrong. On the contrary there was the general impression that the British had established peace where there was turmoil, and a settled government where there was anarchy. The old patriotism, therefore, simply represented an awakening of the educated classes to consciousness of their inferior position in the modern world... it was just beginning of a reaction, but not the birth of a new life".

On Swaraj, B.C. Pal said:

> "The idea, of Swaraj is that true freedom does not lie in isolation but fellowship and association with the rest of creation. This is the first idea involved in the conception of Swaraj in our ancient spiritual experience. That is the first implication of the Upanishadic idea on this subject. And the second idea involved in it is that this freedom can never be attained in a state of war or conflict, with other object or persons in the universe.
>
> As long as I have any enemies so long, I cannot be free to regulate my life and activities just as I like. Self-determination is really a meaningless term for any people or nation which stands perpetually in fear of rival, or enemy peoples or nations".

Pal was of the view that Swaraj, it must, therefore, be clearly realised, was not a spiritual condition, not a state of the mind, but an objective system of government and administration. And it must be sought and attained by such methods as have been tested by political science, which means the generalisation of universal political experience and not even the vanity of doing something which nobody has ever done or attempted, should be a permitted to tempt us form the approved and verified generalisation of the experience of the race in matter pertaining to political life and organisation.

The term Swaraj is the compound of the words. *SWA* and *RAJ*. The Swa in Swaraj means the Swa or self to the nation. And a nation is a group of human beings who stand differentiated from other social units by its geographical habits, its cultural history and evolution, as well as by its political history and Constitution. This Swa is not the Universal or the Absolute Self or Swa. This Swa is no doubt a revelation of the Universal Swa or Self of the Absolute, to use a philosophical term but so are all the other national was or Selfs. And these different national Swas stand differentiated from one another by their geographical borders, their state authority and by those numerous other things which constitute what has been described as their respective

'Nationalities'. This nationality has been very aptly defined by Joseph Mazzini as the individuality of a people. And the moment we understand the undeniable character or our own National Swa, we see that Swaraj is not, and cannot be in reality and truth, something that admits of no definition.

Bipin Chandra said that the Swaraj which we desired to secure for India must, in the first place, be the Raj of the people of India and not Raj of any particular individual or community belonging to India, or it must be a Democratic Swaraj. In the next place, this Swaraj must be the government of the country by agents who shall be responsible to and removable by the common authority of every class and section and community of India, exercised through such arrangements and instruments as should secure to every individual Indian irrespective of wealth or rank or culture or creed or caste or sex, his or her right to direct and control the machinery of the administration set over them; provided those classes or communities renounce their allegiance to all outside countries and communities upon any pretence whether it be racial or cultural or religious affinity of association, so far as their political life and obligations were concerned.

In the next place B.C. Pal further said that to ensure to every individual and community the fullest share of the direction and control of the machinery of administration or the common state-life established over them, the unit of this Swaraj Administration must be the village, or groups of adjacent villages having a social solidarity and the members of which live in intimate association with one another and are bound together by old and hereditary associations and a thousand common interests — economic and social and among whom it may, therefore, be possible to establish real self-government. And these village administrations must be joined into a federation to form the district administrations, while these district administrations must be federated to form the Provincial Federations. This was the only conceivable ideal to reasonably ensure a true Swaraj in modern India.

> "Non-violence in our present Swaraj", said, B.C. Pal "must not, therefore, be understood as non-resistance. It must not be confused with mere absence of physical violence. This non-violence here must not be judged

and determined by our inner motives. But that alone must be accepted as non-violence which preserves the continuity of the present law and order in the country while seeking to remove the alien Bureaucracy which has made itself responsible for it now. There must not be violent break in this Law and Order. The authority of the government as the government, must represent this authority now must be replaced by others who's all be responsible to and removable by the governed".

B.C. Pal said, "the attainment of the true Democratic Swaraj in India in the existing condition is only possible, therefore, through friendly settlement with the present foreign power, which holds political authority over us. Friendly settlement means a compromise without any appeal to the arbitrament of physical force. It does not mean anything more in the present context. This compromise must come also through mutual consultation between the Government of India and the British Cabinet and British Parliament on the one side and accredited leaders of the Indian people on the other. The first step towards this compromise is the creation of conditions which will convince the present government of the necessity of coming to terms with the Indian Swarajists for the preservation of their own reasonable interest.

"The realisation of the ideal of this democratic Swaraj, wrote B.C. Pal, "requires the existence of a truly political-minded people. This condition is as yet absent in India. The creation of this political-minded people is the supreme need of the hour here".

"And this education", B.C. Pal said, "will have to be imparted not merely by means of books or lectures but with the help of organisations which will be real nursenes of political self-government among the people. This may be done in two ways, first, by covering the whole with a network of voluntary political associations and secondly, by using the existing legislative constituencies for this purpose. In this way, partly with the help of voluntary organisations aiming to build up what has been aptly described as a state, and partly with that of the existing legislative constituencies, and work up a real political mass-awakening in the country upon which, and upon which alone, can the true and solid foundations of democratic Swaraj be laid".

He declared in a speech in Madras in 1907:

"Our programme is that we shall so work in the country so combine the resources of the people, so organise the forces of the nation, so develop the instinct of freedom in the community, that by these means we shall — shall in the imperative — compel the submission to our will of any power that my set itself against us".

He said:

"If you ask me to state in general terms what are the methods and the means, what are the instruments that will further this ideal of Swaraj in this country, my reply shall be that these means and methods are included under what is known in political science as the method of Passive Resistance. It means not resistance that is not active, but resistance that is not aggressive. Passive Resistance is not non-active but non-aggressive resistance. We stand within the limits of the law that we have still in the country. We shall respect that law as long as that law shall respect our primary rights which constitute the authority of every government whether that government be a despotic government or constitutional government — rights which no government can create and which, therefore, no government can destroy. As long as the taws of this government shall respect our primary rights of life and person or property and other similar primary

> rights, so long we propose ourselves to be within the bounds of law; and passive resistance offered by a people from within in the limits of such law.
>
> "The broad application of this method of passive resistance has brought out two or three special movements in India. One movement is the boycott movement. It is a movement of passive resistance. The other movement is the movement of national education; and the third movement is the movement of organisation of our public life building it up from our village life".

To B.C. Pal freedom meant the supreme right of each individual human soul. It asserted the dignity of the person as a person. But this personal self-realisation was only possible through individual self-realisation of other persons, with whom each individual stood in an organic relation, in the larger social organism of which both were constituent and organic elements.

Therefore, Freedom was not all-sufficient, even for individual self-realisation, which was its logical and aim, but must be allied to fraternity, to a sense of organic kindship with and responsibility for the well-being of brother-man and sister-woman associated with the organic life of their common society or nation.

B.C. Pal said:

> "There is a very wide difference between a race and a nation. In the first place, territorial unity is an essential condition of nationality but not of raciality. A race may spread over different and distant territories, and occupy various parts of the globe; but a nation must be confined to a definite habitat. A race is essentially a homogeneous thing. It has a special physical structure, a special thought structure, and a special social structure. This threefold structural affinity is of the very essence of the race-idea. This structural affinity is observed among the different branches of the so called Aryan family".

To B.C. Pal a nation was, however, a more complex and heterogeneous thing. More than one race could go to the making of a nation. There was a good deal of racial intermixture in all the developed nationalities of the world. The growth of nationalities indicated a higher stage of social evolution and a more developed order of social life than was found in mere racial units. There might, therefore, by primitive race, but hardly and primitive nation.

B.C. Pal said:

> "The Empire idea is essentially larger and broader than the nation idea. It aims at the unification of widely separate territories, of widely divergent interests, of widely different cultures into one organic whole. As families combine into tribes, each family contributing its peculiar characteristics and possessions to the common life of other families, in and through the unity of the tribe-life; as at a subsequent social synthesis, tribes combine to form races, which though divided by space, controlled by different environment evolving under divergent historic epoches, still pursue a common ideal and, are moved mainly by a common regulative-idea, and thus make for a larger union of mankind than had been realised before; and, as at the next synthesis, different racial units combine to form a larger, more complex and yet more intimate unity, namely, that of the nation; so the unification of these national units into an imperial organisation or organism is really a higher and larger social synthesis than even what has been attained through the nation idea. It is impossible to deny, therefore, that the Empire idea is positive: lager, grander, nobler than the nation idea. This is the fundamental truth of the concept of Empire".

Pal said that the Empire-idea, offered a broader ground for the unification of humanity than the nation-idea, even as the nation idea offered a broader basis of human fellowship than the unity of tribal or racial relations. This was the fundamental claim to superiority of the Empire idea. It was the claim, really, of a broader generalisation and a higher synthesis. The family, the tribe, the race, the nation, all these were what might be called, social synthesis; each succeeding synthesis being broader and higher than the preceding ones. The social synthesis offered by the Empire-idea was broader and higher than all others. The first condition, therefore, of the realisation of the true Empire idea was a correct and clear understanding of the nature of this synthesis.

An Empire was a much larger unit than a nation; and the smaller can never hold the larger. Nay more, the family the tribe, the race, the nation, the Empire, all these were distinct social categories; and one could not, therefore, be converted into the other. A family might multiply to a hundred members, still it would be nothing more than a family; a very large family, no doubt, but never a tribe. Similarly, a tribe might contain a hundred thousand or even a million individuals, but it would still be a tribe, as much as the smallest tribe, but never a race. So with races and nations also. A nation might multiply itself to any extent, might expand its territorial possessions to any length, but it would still be a nation and not an Empire. Even the possession of sovereign authority over many nations would not convert a nation into an Empire. When a nation assumed the name of an Empire on these grounds, it only added what might be a terminological usurpation to its already achieved territorial usurpations. This was all.

B.C. Pal believed in Socialism in the highest and trust sense of the term, and not merely what it was understood to mean by the followers of Marx; this socialism and not individualism.... were the rudimentary concepts of our social and political philosophy.

He suggested to immediately demand these three things:

> "(1) High wages for labour, (2) equal hours of work and (3) the appropriation by the state of all excess profits... If it comes to the state we shall have enough money to pay for every thing that we want enough money to improve our sanitation, enough money to educate the people, enough money to grow to the full stature of our manhood through the help of our government. In view of this conflict, writes B.C. Pal,

> of interest between the government and the people of India, the policy of Indian patriotic politics ought to be the old liberal policy of *Laissez faire*, that is to restrict the government to its primary responsibilities only because every beneficent work that a despotic government does, increases the hold of that despotism upon the affections and the allegiance, upon the acquiescence of the people ... Therefore, our policy is a policy of *Laissez-faire* ... by restricting the activities of the government to the primary functions of granding protection to the people of this country, we hope to develop the spirit of self-sacrifice, the spirit of self-reliance, and the spirit of self determination in the people, and by this means we hope to attain the ideal of Swaraj".

Bipin Chandra Pal was a journalist throughout his life. At the age of 22, he started *Sylhet Weekly*, Bengali Journal *Paridarshak;* and the career thus begun in his native town, he retained till the end of his days. Me edited *The Tribune* in 1887 started *New India* in 1901 and the *Vande Mataram* in 1906, published fortnightly journal *Swaraj* in London in 1909, and founded the monthly *Hindu Review* in Calcutta in 1912. He edited the daily *Independent*, and the weekly *Democrat* in 1919-20, and the *Bengalee* in 1924-25; besides he was a regular contributor to the *Modern Review*, the *Amrita Bazar Patrika* and many other journals".

Jiten Sen wrote that Bipin Chandra Pal, architect of the Bengal renaissance, strode the country like a giant in the last quarter of the nineteenth century and first-two decades of the twentieth. Through the written word and the spoken, through a long life of suffering and sacrifice, an unrelenting adherence to the principles he professed, and with a rare clarity of vision, he reawakened his countrymen to a consciousness of inner strength. With Lokmanya Tilak and Lala Lajpat Rai, he played a leading role in the early freedom movement.

Bipin Chandra's oratory was not mere command over words. He spoke, said Aurobindo Ghosh, "under an inspiration which he himself was unable to resist". Commenting on his famous

Madras speech of 1907, Srinivasa dreamed of such triumphs in India, the power of the spoken words had never been demonstrated on such a scale.

In fact, Pal was a born orator and his eloquence in the early part of this century roused the youths of this country. Even the aged and the wise listened to him with respect and he was always prepared to convince them, as he often used to say "not by magic, but by logic".

He made great sacrifices for his love of country, truth and God. It was perhaps the great sacrifice of his life when on account of his strong convictions, he lived in splendid isolation from his erstwhile colleagues and friends during the last few years of his life. But his greatness lay in the fact that he never yielded to any one in his devotion to truth and God and to his country. With him, as it was with many other politicians of this country, service of the country was a religion and a service to God.

Bipin Chandra Pal was a born publicist. His contributions used to appear regularly in practically every important organ of the nationalist opinion of his days. In them he, time and again reverted to his theme that the ultimate interests of Indian Nationalism and British Imperialism were identical.

> "It is in the interests of Indian nationalism to seek to perpetuate the British connection, so it is equally important to the interest of British Imperialism itself to help and foster the spirit of Nationalism, and to coordinate these great forces with those of Great Britain and her Dominions".

He had said.

Social and Religious Ideology

Rigid in Ideology

A man of undaunted spirit, Bipin Chandra Pal made no compromise in the sphere of politics, when it was a question of conviction and conscience. He revolted against the evils and abuses of the Hindu society at a very early stage of his life. He championed the cause of Indian education with special emphasis on female education and advocated the equality of male and female.

Liberal in Religion

Bipin Chandra accompanied Sundari Mohun regularly to the weekly prayer meetings of the Brahmo Samaj. He would sit silently for hours hearing the words of Keshub Chandra Sen. Though, greatly impressed, he did not formally join the Brahmo Samaj. In 1876, he met Shivnath Shastri, a Sanskrit scholar, whose Brahmo ideal seemed to be filled more with the freedom of spirit and individualism. Social and national freedom were a vital part of Shivnath Shastri's beliefs that were tempered by rationalism. Inspired by this, Bipin Chandra and a few friends organised a small society that pledged to fight against social evils.

Shivnath Shastri and a group of young Brahmos established the Sadharan Brahmo Samaj. Bipin Chandra felt closer to Shastri's ideals than to the ardent preaching of Keshub Chandra Sen.

Although, Bipin Chandra did not inform his father about his break with Hindu orthodoxy, his father heard about it. He was called back immediately, in 1877, but he kept postponing his return. His father stopped sending him money. A little later, his father remarried. He sent Bipin Chandra money soon after, but with a letter formally disinheriting him.

On Status of Women

Bipin Chandra believed that, compared to England, the position of women in India was superior. Men in India were taught to regard every woman as 'mother'. Though, in India, a woman took no direct part in politics, she indirectly influenced it. Not educated in the sense an English woman might be said to be, in character, religiosity and culture the Indian woman was superior to her British counterpart.

2

An Illustrious Life

Bipin Chandra Pal valued personal freedom. As a social reformer, he revolted against evils such as untouchability, child marriage and *sati*. He championed the cause of the poor and the downtrodden and fought for the Indian labourer. He was a leader of the Indian renascence movement and his life was a mirror to his contemporaries.

Bipin Chandra Pal a 'beacon of Indian politics', was in the forefront of public life for more than fifty years. He was an eminent nationalist and a social reformer. Sri Aurobindo described him as 'one of the mightiest prophets of nationalism'. Bipin Chandra Pal boldly preached the ideal of *Puma Swaraj* (complete freedom) long before the Congress adopted it as its goal. In his opposition to the partition of Bengal, he advocated passive resistance and boycott of English goods. The nationalism he preached was not a narrow one but a part of his ideal of universal humanity.

Early Life

Born in his ancestral village home at Poil in Sylhet district (now in Bangladesh), Bipin Chandra Pal belonged to a middle class family. Poil had been his family home for twenty-five generations. His father, Ram Chandra, was a *zamindar* and a man of considerable standing in the locality. He had no formal

English education, but was a Persian scholar. A strong-willed man, he was a Vaishnavaite by faith; there was a blend of Hindu ritualism and Islamic thought in his religious views. Bipin Chandra's mother, Narayani Devi, was reserved, self-reliant and a disciplinarian. Bipin Chandra had a sister, Kripa.

> "For five years a son shall be treated with great tenderness. For ten years, he shall be subjected to rigorous discipline. When he attains his sixteenth year, a father shall treat his son as a friend".

Ram Chandra, while moulding his son's life, was guided by this dictum of Chanakya.

Till his sixth year, Bipin Chandra was regarded almost like a young divinity. Each and every whim of his was satisfied. No one was permitted to lift a hand against him. Though, at times, his father himself did not observe this law, he resented a violation of it by any.

Bipin Chandra grew up in an atmosphere steeped in religion. He was neither allowed to disturb his father when he sat down to his puja nor touch the things that were used by him for his daily worship. His mother, too, would not touch either food or water till her puja had been completed. At the age of twelve, Bipin Chandra was allowed to join these pujas.

School Education

Bipin Chandra enjoyed few luxuries during his school days. He was given a pair of trousers and a coat to wear to school and was allowed one pair of shoes every year. The shoes lasted, generally, for five or six months. For a few months, invariably, he had to go without shoes.

With the advent of the Western system of liberal education came the conflict between the old values of the Hindu orthodox families and the emerging new ideas. Bipin Chandra's career in school followed an uneven course. He was withdrawn from school as his father felt that the school encouraged his son to violate certain rules of caste. It was after much persuasion that Ram Chandra permitted his son to rejoin school.

Around that time, new thoughts of change were sweeping across Bengal. Hindu orthodoxy was being questioned. Keshub Chandra Sen's Brahmo Samaj formed an umbrella, under which young, dynamic persons came together to challenge rigid customs and mindless rituals. When Bipin Chandra was in his pre-entrance class, he met Sundari Mohan Das, who was studying in the Presidency College, Calcutta, and had returned home for the summer vacations. Sundari Mohan had embraced the Brahmo faith. Their association resulted in a relationship that lasted throughout their lives. Sundari Mohan encouraged his friend to be familiar with the literary trends of the times. Bipin Chandra wrote poetry, which was published in newspapers.

College Education

Finishing his school, Bipin Chandra passed the entrance examination of the Calcutta University, which qualified him for higher studies. The city appeared to him more like a suffocating 'brick and mortar jungle'.

With a Government scholarship of ten rupees a month, Bipin Chandra got admission into the Presidency College. This was in 1875. His classmates were promising personalities. Bhupendra Nath Basu, his contemporary, became an eminent leader of the Indian National Congress. Heramba Chandra Moitra, a reputed scholar, later became the Principal of the City College.

The Principal, Suteliffe, was a strict disciplinarian and Bipin Chandra always attended his classes. The latter had deep affection for his teacher, Peary Charan Sarkar. His college career was not distinguished by any brilliance. In fact, he was seldom seen in the classroom. "About a couple of hours everyday," he wrote in his autobiography, 'and some days only an hour, I used to be in my class ... I played truant. He found it more profitable to spend his free time reading books in a neighbouring bookshop.

Bipin Chandra went back to Sylhet during the summer holidays. The vacation turned out to be tragic. His younger sister, who was two-and-a-half-years old, died in his arms. Bipin Chandra's mother could not bear this loss and she died within a few days. The *sradh* (rites for the departed) had to be performed.

His father was grief-stricken; Bipin Chandra was sent to Kalighat in Calcutta to perform the last rites.

After six months, in 1876, when his First Arts examinations were to take place, Bipin Chandra had a severe attack of chickenpox. Sundari Mohun, who had by then joined the Calcutta Medical College, nursed him. When he got well, Sundari Mohun fell ill. Bipin Chandra took care of him. By then the examinations were over. Bipin Chandra wanted to stay on in Calcutta for the academic session, but his father wanted him home. So he returned to Sylhet.

In the First Arts examinations which Bipin Chandra took from Cathedral Mission College, he could not clear the mathematics paper. His differences with his father over questions of religious and social beliefs made the latter angry. His father stopped the financial allowance for six months and his son underwent great difficulty.

The years 1875-78, which synchronised with Bipin Chandra's life at the Presidency College, saw the birth of nationalism. The literary influence generated by Madhusudan Dutt and Bankim Chandra Chatterjee, the ideal of social and religious freedom as enunciated by the Brahmo Samaj, the cult of nationalism preached by Surendranath Banerjee contributed to the making of his life and character. Suffused with the spirit of burning nationalism under the influence of his political guru, Surendranath Banerjee, Bipin Chandra began to take interest in politics. His main preoccupation still lay in his missionary work on behalf of the Brahmo Samaj.

At college, Bipin Chandra contributed articles to Bengali journals like *Srihatta* and *Prakash.* At the age of 22, he started a Bengali weekly. *Paridarshak,* from Sylhet. His national consciousness was inspired by Bengali literature especially Bankim Chandra Chatterjee's *Banga Darshan,* a journal which started in 1873-74.

Family and Birth

Bipin Chandra Pal was born on 7 November 1858 in Sylhet in a wealthy Hindu Kayastha family. His father Ramchandra Pal, a village zamindar and a prominent member of the Sylhet Bar was influenced by Hindu rituals and Islamic thought he was a follower of Vaishnavism. The only son of his parents, Bipin Chandra Pal took his early education from a Maulvi in Sylhet town. He had his formal education at Sylhet Government High School from where he passed the Entrance Examination. He then got himself admitted in the Presidency College, but gave up his studies before graduating. His literary competence was, however, remarkable and he studied the *Gita* and the *Upanishads* extensively.

Marriages

B.C. Pal married Nrityakali Devi, a Brahmin widow. After her death, he was married to another Brahmin widow, Birajmohini Devi, a distant relation of Surendranath Banerjee.

Sons and Daughters

He had three sons and five daughters by two marriages.

Early Career

When he was unable to clear the FA examinations and when his father disowned him, Bipin Chandra started his career outside Bengal, as Headmaster of the Cuttack Academy in Orissa. This was in 1878. He did not remain Principal for long, tendering his resignation the same year in November.

Pal had started his career in early 1879 as the Headmaster of a High School and served in this capacity in different schools in and outside Sylhet. For sometime (1890-91), he worked as the Librarian and Secretary of the Calcutta Public Library. While in Calcutta during his student life, he came in close contact with some prominent personalities like Keshab Chandra Sen, Shibnath Shastri and Bijoy Krishna Goswami.

Under the influence of Keshab Chandra Sen he was attracted to the Brahmo movement. Bijoy Krishna Goswami also tremendously influenced his spiritual ideas. His association with Sivanath Sastri made him conscious of the spirit of social revolt and patriotism.

Bipin Chandra was appointed Headmaster of the Arcot Narayanswami Mudaliar School in Bangalore, in 1881.

Founding a School

Back in Calcutta, Bipin Chandra, along with two colleagues, was persuaded by the Sylhet Union to shift to Sylhet and set up a high school, the Sylhet National School. The school, with Bipin Chandra as the founder, started functioning in January 1880, gaining in prestige and strength under his able administration. He was also engaged in missionary work for the Sadharan Brahmo Samaj and in the publication of *Paridarshak.*

Out of Favour from his Father

There were trying times. Bipin Chandra's father was adamant that his son should sever ties with the Brahmo Samaj. He had cut him out of his will. It was after much persuasion that Bipin Chandra was given a monthly allowance of Rs. 100. Bipin Chandra was struck by a pulmonary infection. He left Sylhet for Calcutta, the humid climate not being conducive to good health. It took a year for him to recuperate. Though, Sundari Mohun appealed to his father for financial assistance, it was not forthcoming.

Father Kind Again

At the end of 1883. Bipin Chandra received a message about the ill-health of his father in Calcutta. Without any loss of time, Bipin Chandra decided to return. His father made Bipin Chandra a trustee of all his assets and property. Within a few hours of making his will, he died. Bipin Chandra attempted to look after the property he inherited. But he did not conform to the cannons of *zamindari.* Besides, his wife and children started keeping bad health owing to the moist climate in Poil. So in mid-1886, Bipin Chandra Pal returned to Calcutta.

Sojourn in England

During his sojourn in England (1908-11), Bipin Chandra Pal developed a new political thought which he called the Empire idea. He pleaded for a reconstitution of the British Empire as a federal union in which India. Great Britain and all the British self-governing colonies would co-operate as equal and free partners. His nationalism acquired a distinct international outlook. India itself, he said, should have a federal structure for its future national government, in which the different regions and communities would have complete freedom, consistent with national unity and integrity, to develop themselves.

Back in India

On coming back to India, Bipin Chandra Pal tried to popularise the idea through the monthly journal, *Hindu Review,* but without much success. Bipin Chandra Pal joined the Home Rule Movement of Annie Besant and Bal Gangadhar Tilak.

Journalistic Career

Bipin Chandra Pal encouraged journalism and started the Bangla weekly *Paridarshak* in Sylhet (1886). He worked as Assistant Editor of the *Bengali Public Opinion* (1882) and served the *Lahore Tribune* for a short time (1887). For sometime he was the editor of *The Democrat* and *The Independent.* He published a biography (in Bangla) of Queen Victoria in 1887. Among his other books *Indian Nationalism, Nationality and Empire, Swaraj and the Present Situation, The Basis of Social Reform, The Soul of India, The New Spirit* and *Studies in Hinduism* are prominent.

Last Phase

Much of the last decade of Bipin Chandra Pal's life was filled with misery. Poverty added to the difficulties. It was the story of a mastermind seeing his work scorned by men, who according to *The Statesman,* 'lisped at his knees'. Yet, Bipin Chandra Pal stood and fought for his principles throughout. His last public appearance was in 1928 at the All Parties Conference in Lucknow. His influence had come to nought.

The Demise

On May 20. 1932, at the age of seventy-four, Bipin Chandra Pal died 'unsung' after half a century of public life; during this period he elevated resurgent Bengal to a pedestal and took the country to a new political consciousness.

3

Political Career

In Political Arena

Veteran politician Surendranath Banerjee inspired Bipin Pal to take part in active politics. Soon, however, he became a convert to the extremist ideas of B.G. Tilak, Lajpat Rai and Aurobindo Ghosh, though he could not accept Tilak's concept of Hindu nationalism. He was an exponent of 'composite patriotism' which, he thought, was suitable for a country like India. Bipin Chandra Pal was connected with the progressive force of the Congress since 1885 and attended the second and the third annual sessions of the Congress held in Calcutta and Madras in 1886 and 1887 respectively. He compelled the Congress to take up the cause of the Assam Tea-garden labourers who were cruelly treated by the planters.

Ideal of Swaraj

Bipin Pal went to study comparative theology in England in 1898 but after a year came back to India and started preaching the ideal of *Swaraj* (complete independence) through his weekly journal the *New India*. Imbued with great patriotic zeal, he devoted himself to the freedom movement of India. He presided over the Bombay session of the Indian National Congress in 1904. Following the Partition of Bengal, 1905, Bipin Pal started a daily paper the *Vande Mataram* and became its chief editor. He firmly stood against the partition of Bengal on the ground that it was a calculated move of the government to split the Bengalis and thus to break their growing political influence. With a view to enlisting the mass support behind the anti-partition campaign, Bipin Pal, along with other anti-partitionists, organised propaganda tour in various parts of Bengal, Assam, UP and Madras.

Architect of Swadeshi Movement

Pal was one of the architects of the Swadeshi Movement, which swept over India during the days following the partition of Bengal. He suffered imprisonment for six months in 1907 for his refusal to give evidence against Aurovindo Ghosh in the so-called Vande Mataram Sedition Case. On his release, Pal went to England in 1908 'to lead the life of an enforced exile' and stayed there for three years. After the First World War, he visited England for the third time in 1919 as a member of the Home Rule League deputation led by Tilak. He presided over the Bengal Provincial Conference held at Barisal in 1921. He did not involve in the Non-Cooperation Movement because it was merged with the Khilafat cause and criticised the Bengal Pact of Chitta Ranjan Das. He could not share the views of Maulana Mohammad Ali on the nature of the communal problem in India. From 1925 onwards, he, however, retired from active politics.

Leader of Congress

Bipin Chandra Pal had joined the Indian National Congress in 1886, giving his first speech in Madras the next year, on the demand for repeal of the Arms Act. His speech was received with wild cheers, and delegates wanted him to continue even after the time allotted to him was over. As an orator, few could equal Pal and he was rightly called the 'Burke of India'.

> "Babu Bipin Chandra Pal," recorded V.S. Srinivasa Shastri, "burst into full frame in Madras as a preacher of the new political creed. For several days on the sands of the beach, he spoke words hot with emotion

and subtly logical, which were wafted by the soft evening breeze to tens of thousands of listeners, oratory had never dreamed of such triumphs in India".

In October 1891, on the occasion of the Bengal Provincial Conference, Bipin Chandra Pal spoke forcefully on the resolution on Assam tea labourers. The resolution urged upon the Government to withdraw the labour Supply Contract Acts of 1859 and 1882. He expressed his concern for labourers through the columns of New India during 1901-02.

Bipin Chandra Pal supported the boycott resolution at the Congress session held in Calcutta 1906, presided over by Dadabhai Naoroji. Though, it evoked protest from Gopal Krishna Gokhale, it was highly acclaimed by the Nationalist Party and the delegates present. Pal's ability and courage contributed a good deal to enlivening the proceedings of the session. A strong supporter of the cause of nationalism, he leapt out of his 'oppressive loneliness' (to use his phrase) to the leadership of an organised party.

Leaving Congress

After the Surat split of 1907. Bipin Chandra Pal left the Congress with others. The doctrines of passive resistance, boycott of English goods, severance of all association with the foreign government, and national education were fervently preached by Pal during his tour of Bengal. Assam, Uttar Pradesh and Madras that year.

Back in Congress

In 1916, he returned to the Congress.

In February 1919, two repressive Bills known as Rowlatt Bills were introduced in the Central Legislature. These provided for the arrest of any person and his conviction without trial in a court of law. The mass satyagraha following the Rowlatt Act led to the infamous Jallianwala tragedy in April 1919. As is well known, in protest, the poet. Rabindranath Tagore renounced his knighthood.

The Congress decided to send a deputation to England which included Bal Gangadhar Tilak and Bipin Chandra Pal to place India's case before a Joint Parliamentary Committee. That was

Pal's last visit abroad. In England, Bipin Chandra Pal stressed upon the constitutional reforms based on democratic principles. He returned in December 1919.

Extremists Leader

Along with Lokmanya Bal Gangadhar Tilak and Lala Lajpat Rai, Bipin Chandra Pal led the extremist group in the Congress and successfully challenged the moderates. They dominated the political arena for a number of years and captured the imagination of the young Indians of this period. The period is, therefore, most aptly known as the Lal-Bal-Pal era.

Clash with the Mahatma

Bipin Chandra Pal opposed Gandhiji's non-cooperation movement which was associated with the Khilafat cause and which, he felt, was pervaded by blind reverence for Gandhiji's leadership. He also criticised C.R. Das and got into a controversy with Maulana Muhammad Ali over the nature of the communal problem in India. Though, a life-long exponent of swadeshi, Pal could not countenance the idea of there being any 'sin' in wearing foreign clothes.

Bipin Chandra Pal had proceeded to England on August 20, 1908, on a national propaganda mission, sponsored by Shyamji Krishnavarma, a prominent revolutionary in Europe. Pal earned the displeasure of the Indian revolutionaries in England, led by Veer Savarkar, because he declared that he was an extremist and not a revolutionary. Pal was forced to cut short his visit owing to financial crisis. He returned in November 1911. Arriving in Bombay, he was arrested on board the ship, on charge of sedition for his article in the *Swaraj*, entitled "The Aetiology of the Bomb in Bengal".

Bipin Chandra Pal pleaded guilty, much to the disappointment of his nationalist colleagues. He was sentenced to a month's imprisonment in Bombay jail.

Barisal Session

Bipin Chandra Pal presided over the Barisal session of the Bengal Provincial Conference held from March 25-27, 1921. Attended by nearly 2,000 delegates, including 200 women, it was a major event. Pal placed before his countrymen a detailed programme of nation-building work. In spite of Gandhiji's absence, the Conference became a landmark in the history of the freedom struggle.

Bipin Chandra Pal criticised the programme of the non-cooperation movement in respect of its scope and size, for it touched but 'a small fraction of the nation'. Pal defined Swaraj as a 'democratic' Swaraj. He said no real democracy grew under a unitary system of government. He further argued that such a system of government was against the spirit and tradition of India.

On the next day (March 26), a large meeting was held outside the *pandal* where several delegates criticised Pal for his reservations on the Gandhian programme. Chittaranjan Das declared, "Swaraj was Swaraj and Swaraj did not specify any scheme or any form of government". The critics did not understand its real meaning. It required 'culture' of the soul. C.R. Das pleaded with the audience to accept the non-cooperation programme as conceived, without reservation.

The conflict of views of C.R. Das and Bipin Chandra Pal caused a rift between the two. It widened. It ended in the total withdrawal of Pal from the Gandhian movement and the Congress. Bipin Chandra Pal resigned from the Bengal Provincial Congress Committee as well as from the All India Congress Committee.

Bipin Chandra Pal felt he was misunderstood, and he suffered political and even literary isolation. The media shied away from him. He tried to clarify his stance, "There was nothing personal in this fight, though the Mahatma's followers did not hesitate to attribute personal motives to me". Thus, placed, Bipin Chandra Pal accepted an offer from the British-owned daily, *Englishman*, to write a column, 'What India thinks'. This incensed the public further. Pal separated himself from his dear friend C.R. Das and cut himself adrift altogether.

Apart from political differences, a difficulty had arisen on a personal issue. It was C.R. Das's daughter's marriage which was to be performed according to Hindu rites. A Brahmin was to officiate as priest, and the *saligram sila* — an icon of orthodox Hindu worship — was to be brought in. With his strict adherence to the Brahmo faith. Bipin Chandra Pal personally disagreed with the propitiation of the rite, and the use of the services of a priest. He, therefore, refused to attend that ceremony.

In Legislative Assembly

Bipin Chandra Pal entered the Legislative Assembly from a Calcutta constituency in 1923 as an Independent candidate. For about three years Bipin Chandra Pal represented Calcutta and occupied a prominent seat in the Opposition benches. In the Assembly, Bipin Chandra Pal spoke on 'all the burning topics' affecting the nation. A sworn and lifelong rebel. Pal was the 'left of left-wingers'.

On National Scene

Bipin Chandra Pal had broken away from his family, society, and even religion. Meanwhile important events occurred — the nationwide protests against the Simon Commission, 1928, the cry for *Purna Swaraj* from the banks of the Ravi during the Lahore session of the Congress, 1929, the Salt Satyagraha and the march to Dandi, in March 1930, with mass agitations in many parts of the country, the Round Table Conferences in London, 1930 and 1931.

Tour of South India

Bipin Chandra Pal went on a tour covering most of South India in January 1907. His lectures in Madras in May 1907 were memorable. He went back to Calcutta when he heard of Lala Lajpat Rai's arrest.

On May 26, 1907, Bipin Chandra Pal was summoned as a witness to identify a letter. The Judge wanted him to identify Aurobindo Ghose as the editor of *Vande Mataram*, Pal refused to answer any question.

He was sentenced to six months imprisonment. The British tried to suppress the national movement by filling jails with youth and swadeshi leaders. This resulted in severe press restrictions.

Championing Nationalism in South India

Bepin Chandra Pal was destined to become the harbinger of the movement in the south. The credit for sowing the seeds of militant nationalism in the soil of the Madras Presidency can be given to this Bengali agitator who arrived in Vizagapatam on 11 April 1907, and left Madras for Calcutta on 12 May 1907. During his stay in the Madras Presidency he delivered public lectures on political subjects at Vizagapatam (April 12-14) and Vizianagram (April 15-16), in the Vizagapatam district, at Cocanada (April 17) and Rajahmundry (April 19-23) in the Godavari district; at Bezwada (April 24-25) and Masulipatam (April 26-27) in the Kistna district; and in the Madras city (May 1-9). He was accompanied by four young men. Mutnuri Krishna Rao, the editor of the *Krishna Patrika,* was one of the first in Andhra to come under the influence of the Bengal brand of nationalism. Krishna Rao had left Masulipatam four months before on a political mission and later organised the tour of Pal in the Madras Presidency. Others were Kunjokisher Chander, Siwash Chander Deb, both of them from Bengal, and Desermantu Dowlat Rao from Nagpore. S.C. Deb was Pal's Secretary. Leadership in Vizagapatam, in those days, was in the hands of confirmed moderates like S. Narasimheswara Sarma, and of the Zamindars. No wonder, leading native gentlemen were reluctant to make necessary arrangements for Pal's tour programme in Vizagapatam. When he arrived there on 11 April, the Secretary of the District Association, V. Jagannadham Pantulu, received him at the station, and made all arrangements for Pal's lectures there. A few leading gentlemen of the town protested against giving the Town Hall for such political lectures as Pal's, on the ground that schoolboys were being spoilt. But B. N. Sarma, the Municipal Chairman, allowed its use on payment of Rs. 3/-.

Pal delivered altogether three lectures in Vizagapatam. There were large gatherings at all these three meetings. The major portion of the audience consisted of school boys who welcomed B.C. Pal with shouts of 'Vande Mataram'. On 14 April several school boys formed a procession and led Pal from his residence to the Town Hall. Pal went on foot, with the school boys numbering about 100, walking on either side of the road in rows. Two boys who led the procession held flags bearing the words 'Vande Mataram'. While on the march, and on reaching the Town Hall, the boys who gathered in large numbers cheered the procession, with cries of 'Vande Mataram'.

In response to an invitation from the students of the Maharaja's College, Vizianagram, Bepin Chandra Pal proceeded thither on 16 April. A batch of about 25 or 30 students met him at the Railway Station. They were shouting 'Vande Mataram' and carrying flags bearing these words. In his lecture he said that in Bengal they had held meetings attended by 30 to 50 thousands. When they were belaboured with lathis by the police, they disgraced the authorities by a dignified submission. Subsequently, the authorities were clearly given to understand that if lathis were further used they would exercise the right of self-defence. This frightened the authorities. People were forbidden to shout 'Vande Mataram' in any public place and so the boys used to jump over walls into private grounds and shout 'Vande Mataram' in the face of the police.

In another lecture he advised his listeners to boycott all government institutions, employments, schools, colleges and all English trade. In the course of his address he recalled that as a college student, he had learnt English words without being taught the true meaning of them. He and others were simply mesmerised by an ideal which they worshipped till the scales fell off from their eyes and they found that it was England that they were worshipping. The true meaning of college education dawned on them with the partition. "He advocated boycotting everything English till the government of the people was by the people, for the people and in the people's interest".

At the Cocanada Railway Station there was no public reception for Pal who had reached there on 17 April for a three day tour. On the day of his arrival he delivered a lecture on 'Religion' which was attended mostly by students. On the 18th Pal lectured on Swadeshi, Swaraj and National Education. Cocanada failed to present him with a crowded audience. The students of Piṭṭapur Raja's College did not appear in large numbers to welcome him.

Pal reached Rajahmundry on the morning of 19 April on a five day lecture tour. About 2000 people greeted him at the railway station and led him in triumphal procession along the main road with shouts of 'Vande Mataram'. He began his lectures on Brahmoism the same evening, and lectured daily until his departure on 24 April to Bezwada. On the evening of 23 April, in the Town Hall compound Pal addressed a gathering of about 3000 people on National Education. During this lecture it is said that Rs. 3,000-was subscribed on the spot in addition to several promises of monthly subscriptions. In Bezwada he lectured on Swaraj and on Philosophy. He arrived at Masulipatam on 26 April and delivered a lecture on Swaraj. On 28th he gave a third lecture on boycott and National Education; his appeal for funds for National Education resulted in the collection of Rs. 2,000/-.

While all these were going on between 11 and 29 April, arrangements were being made in various other places in the south like Cuddalore, Tanjore, Kumbakonam, Madurai and Salem to receive Pal. In Salem, 'Vande Mataram' banners, flags, lockets, etc. were made, and songs to be sung on the occasion were composed. In Tanjore, the Desabhimani Sabha resolved to give Pal a fitting welcome and an address on his arrival at the railway station, and to take him in torch light procession along the main streets of Tanjore. Schoolboys of the town of Mayavaram raised subscriptions to the amount of Rs. 100/- to receive B.C. Pal there. Under the leadership of V. Subramania Aiyer students of the colleges in Madras started a fund called "Pal's Reception Fund", and collected a sum of Rs. 250/- to meet the expenses incurred in connection with Pal's arrival and his lectures. Invitation to Pal was sent by K.R. Narayana Aiyar, Secretary of the Student's Mutual Association, Madurai, to speak at that place. But later, K. V. Srinivasa Rao, President of Students Mutual Improvement Society, Madurai, discovered the action of some of its members and doubted the propriety of receiving Pal owing to differences of opinion among the members about the character and lectures of Pal. Students who were not allowed to take any part in the discussion of the elders tried to raise subscriptions among themselves to give Pal a welcome on their own accord. Of all the towns in Tamil Nadu, Madurai and Kumbakonam alone seemed to have cherished doubts regarding the propriety of receiving Pal.

Although, Pal's visit to Madras was fixed for 27 April, he could visit only on the 30th. Unaware of this change in his programme, students numbering 200 or 300 went to the Basin Bridge railway station on the evening of the 27th. When they were refused entry to the railway station, they became restless and noisy. They shouted 'Vande Mataram' and on seeing Tavener, the District Traffic Superintendent of the Railway, on the platform, some of them called him "White Monkey" and later pelted stones towards the platform. Necessary police arrangements had been made at the station on 30 April, but no row occurred.

A printed notice was circulated in the city that day requesting the presence of students at the station to join the procession from there to Royapettah. In pursuance of this circular, about 400 students assembled at the station carrying flags with the inscriptions of 'Vande Mataram' and 'Swaraj-ki-jai'. To accord a reception to B.C. Pal, students had to wait outside the fencing to greet him, as they were not allowed entry to the platform. On his arrival, the students hailed Pal with shouts of 'Vande Mataram'. Pal was received outside the station by G. Subramonia Iyer, Subramonia Bharathi, V. Chakkarai Chetti and a host of students, but no other citizen took any part either in receiving Pal or in the procession. The students insisted on their pulling the carriage in which Pal travelled, but abandoned the idea when Pal disapproved of it. He was taken in procession to his place of stay at Royapettah by a large group of students. When the procession passed the Mint Buildings, the Swadesha Vastu Pracharini Sabha, a society organised by the student followers of G. Subramonia Iyer, greeted him. Pal thanked them for the address which he took as an index of the ardent love and patriotism they felt for their motherland. The students of Madras presented him with another address which hailed the presence of Pal in their midst as "an epoch in the political life of the Carnatic".

The text of the address was a proof of his personal and magnetic impact on the student population. It read, "You come to us as an exponent of the new thought which, we believe, is destined to transform the life of the nation. We have been keenly watching the inspiring attempts made by you to rouse in us the spirit of self-help and self-dependence which has been so conspicuously absent in the political propaganda of the past. We are confident that the spirit will be grown from more to more till we are all strengthened and sanctified by it". At Thambu Chetti Street a greater number of students joined the procession, and, when it reached the destination, their number was estimated about 4000. At this point Pal was welcomed by the students of the Madras Christian College with shouts of 'Vande Mataram'. The major portion of the crowd began to disperse when the procession reached Mount Road. A few students accompanied Pal to Mohan Vilas, Rayapetta, where he resided.

Pal delivered, in all, seven lectures, most of them on the south Beach opposite to Lady Wenlock's Park where about 5000 people, chiefly students, were present. On 10th May he abandoned a lecture he had promised to deliver on Vande Mataram, and subsequently cancelled his lecture tour in the southern districts, as the unexpected news of the deportation of Lajpat Rai came to him as shock. He kept quiet on 11th, and on 12th he drove to the Central Railway station to board the train bound for Calcutta, and was seen off only by students numbering about 100.

Bepin Chandra Pal attempted in his speeches to explain the doctrine of Swaraj or self-government and advocated Swadeshi and boycott to be the arms to fight with. An abstract of Pal's lecture as reported by the police authorities is given below:

> "Swaraj is not a new word in the literature of the world politics or Indian politics ... In the Madras Congress of December 1903 the revered old leader of Indians, Mr. Dadabhai Nowrojee, sent a message to the Congress to the effect that its ideal should be self-government under British Paramountcy. In December 1906 as the President of the Congress, he pleaded for self-government, an autonomous India free from foreign control. That is real Swaraj. Swaraj cannot be tantamount to colonial self-government. Colonial self-government implies self-taxation, making their own budget, self-legislation, right of granting or refusing admittance into their territories of any person to whatever nationality he may belong. ... What the form of Swaraj is to be in India if at all it is to come to pass — it will not be in our time or our great grandson's time, but in the womb of the distant future — is of purely academic interest. What is true of social evolution may also be true of political evolution and it is heredity,

> environment and epoch that regulate evolution. Of course critics naturally ask, 'Is it to be Muhammadan Swaraj or Hindu Swaraj? 'Is it monarchical or republican Swaraj'? It is difficult to say really what the future may disclose it to be ... Whatever shape it may take, this ideal of self-government is the ultimate ideal of this nation, as history shows it to be of every nation in the globe. So it means an ideal not immediately attainable ... The methods for realising Swaraj are swadeshi, boycott and National Education, Swadeshi is an honest attempt at improving the economic condition of the country ... Boycott is a necessary result of Swadeshi enterprise, and a resort to it is certainly not going against the Government... When prayers, protests and petitions do not move the Government, people can have no alternative but to work out their country's good by the use of all legitimate means in their hands. This unfortunately put out some short-sighted servants of Government whose prejudices getting the better of their discretion have created intense mischief in Bengal during the last two years. The harmless use of 'Vande Mataram' which means merely "Hail Motherland" drove them to their wits' end and they promulgated orders and circulars which wrought untold mischief in this country. The regulation sticks of the police were freely made use of over boys and adults who attended constitutionally — held meetings in Barisal ... The Government's action has stirred people to greater activity and closer application to the furtherance of the country's interests'".

V. Bhashyam Iyenger, the Acting Advocate General, has given a summary of the speeches delivered by Bepin Chandra Pal thus:

> "The speech on 'Swaraj' is not only an attack upon the Foreign Government established in India, its existence, its essential characteristics, its motives and feelings towards the Indian people, an attack which is calculated to excite 'hatred' against such

> Government, but it is also a direct appeal to the 300 millions of Indians to work out their political salvation by overthrowing the sovereignty or, as for the matter of that, even the sovereignty or overlordship of the British Government and establishing a 'Swaraj' in their motherland for all Indians without distinction of race, nationality or religion, and if need be by summoning in the near future the present Ameer of Afghanistan as the first Director or Dictator of the Indian Republic. The Babu earnestly endeavours to impress upon his audience that the Indians should not aim at establishing 'Swaraj' by obtaining a gift of it from the British Sovereign or Parliament and he also impress upon them that by all possible means of passive resistance the Indians should thwart the good and beneficial Government of Hindustan by the British, lest by reason of such good beneficent rule they should become attached to that Government and the desire to establish 'Swaraj' by overthrowing British Government in India should be stifled".

The impact that the speeches of Pal produced in the South was so tremendous that the famous liberal leader, Srinivasa Sastri, characterised them in the following words: "Babu Bepin Chandra Pal burst into full flame in Madras as a preacher of the new political creed. For several days on the sands of the beach he spoke words hot with emotion and subtly logical, which were wafted by the soft evening breeze to tens of thousands of listeners, invading their whole souls and setting them aflame with fever of a wild consuming desire. Oratory had never dreamed of such triumphs in India; the power of the spoken word had never been demonstrated on such a scale".

On April 19, the day of Pal's arrival in Rajahmundry, the Principal and the chief lecturers of the Rajahmundry College were away in Madras attending a conference. The Vice-Principal of the Training College wrote to him that "the students were idolising Pal, that they had conducted him through the streets in noisy processions, that a large number of the public of the practising school had absented themselves from work without leave". On his return from Madras on 22 April, the Principal came to know, from the junior members of his staff who had attended Pal's lectures out of curiosity, that Pal "indulged in utterances of an openly treasonable and seditious character", and that students had frequented the house where Pal was staying and had sought his advice. On one such occasion Pal had expressly exhorted them to go on 'strike' taking as pretext the prohibition regarding the wearing of 'Vande Mataram' medal. The Principal who had expected that a mere three days' good conduct on the part of the students would have brought them to the end of the term and "would have entitled them to expect the removal of the last shred of an even imaginary grievance", found himself on the horns of a dilemma.

On 23rd the Principal attended the college as usual. No regular classes were held that day as the half-yearly examination was to commence on the following day. Students who were working in the library were found not wearing the medal. That evening, Pal delivered a lecture on 'National Education'. A member of his staff, deputed by the Principal to be present at the meeting, reported that Pal had declared that all natives serving the government were "treacherous slaves who had betrayed their country, that all advice given by such people was to be distrusted and the college discipline when it clashed with what he styled 'duty to one's country' was nonsense". The Principal considered that to an audience largely composed of students of a Government college, whose entire staff with the exception of himself were Indians, those words were "intended as a direct incitement to defy authority".

The leading members of the Bala Bharat Samithi were found to be prominently involved in the reception of Pal. In this, the role of Gadicherla Harisarvottama Rao, M.A., a student-trainee and a government stipendiary, was conspicuous. He publicly read an address to Pal. The Principal considered this to be an act of violation of the educational rules by which he had executed the bond and owed implicit obedience. On 24th April, the day Pal left Rajahmundry, Rao again presented him with an address. The address which was published in the press contained expressions of adherence to the principle of Swaraj as defined by Pal and approved the methods recommended by him to secure its realisation. Pal defined Swaraj to be complete independence from British control and urged as methods a general boycott intended to wreck the functioning of the government. The influence of Pal's thoughts on students was his great hit. This was very evident from the marked difference in the tone of the public address read to Pal by Harisarvottama Rao on his arrival and departure. The events were soon to assume epic proportions.

After the departure of Pal more than half the students of Rajahmundry attended the college wearing medals or paper tickets bearing the words 'Vande Mataram' printed in large characters both in English and in Telugu. On subsequent enquiry the Principal learnt that the paper tickets were printed overnight in accordance with a resolution passed at a students meeting. 'Ring leaders', posted near the college entrance that morning, "by inducements and threats" had sought to force the tickets on other students who were on their way to the college. Some had apparently escaped their attention, some had taken the tickets and put them in their pockets, but the majority had, willingly or reluctantly, fastened them on their breast pockets. The "aggressive wearing" of the tickets and medals, while the prohibition was still in force, was considered an act of insolent defiance by which the students were deliberately determined to provoke Hunter "to action which should serve as some sort of excuse for secessions".

The Principal, on reaching the Arts College at 11 O'clock that day, came to know about the goings on there from Shankar Rau, the Senior Lecturer, who had judged it best to await his arrival before taking any action. Hunter, on entering the hall where the senior F.A. and B.A. classes were undergoing examination, ordered the badges to be removed; and it was obeyed after some hesitation. J. Ramachandra Rao, who had been suspended previously and later readmitted on solemn promise of good behaviour, was expelled on the spot. He was the only student who dared to wear the medal in question at a time when prohibition against its wearing was first pronounced. The candidates in the next room proved to be recalcitrant. Hunter warned them that they should have to leave the college if they persisted in disobedience, but they chose to leave the college. While he was admonishing them, the cry of 'Vande Mataram' was raised by someone on the verandah, which was taken up immediately from all parts of the college, followed by a sudden rushing out of students from lecture rooms and verandahs. Some of the students coming from the first lecture room were found wearing the badges which they had removed earlier. In a state of exasperation, the Principal caught hold of one of them on whom he had high expectations and handled him rather roughly by the arm — an undignified action, for which he later expressed regret. The students who left the college *en bloc* took an oath not to return to the college until the Principal apologised to them unconditionally.

Hunter strongly felt an "organised plot" behind all that had transpired before and after the cry of 'Vande Mataram', which he considered as a 'pre-arranged signal'. The tickets and medals, he firmly believed, were worn deliberately to provoke him to action which should serve as some sort of excuse for a secession. He believed that the students might have known perfectly well that he could not countenance proceedings which he had already forbidden and that the conduct of the students was an act of insolent defiance of "all authority and discipline which it was impossible to tolerate".

About 25 students were absent on the day of the revolt whereas 24 others took no part in it. While only three or four each of the I & II F.A. classes and 17 of the Junior B. A. class seceded, of the senior B.A. class the secession was total. J. Ramachandra Rao had already been expelled; other secessionists were subsequently suspended. The Principal remarked that the suspension was "obviously rather the declaration of an accomplished fact than the imposition of a punishment, the seceding students having elected to suspend themselves".

The college was closed for the vacation, two days after the revolt. On the days following the revolt, the Principal was busy hearing and reading representations made on behalf either of individual students or of all the punished students collectively, urging him to intercede with the government. "On the one hand, it is urged that the punishment is too severe for the offence, that there was no really organised revolt, that the offence was due to a sudden impulse, that the offenders are young and ignorant, and so or. On the other hand it is said that distinction should be made in individual cases, on the ground that some of the students acted as they did from fear of the others and on compulsion. Then the deliberate offence which is denied in the former pleas is implicitly admitted in the latter".

Of the alleged intimidation several instances were cited. Some students were forcibly prevented from returning to college. Complaints of some parents were that their sons whom they had sent back to college, had been intercepted and that they had not returned home or could not be found. The case of junior student who lived with his mother was referred to the police, when this student asserted that other students had come to his house and frightened his mother with threats of violence. The action of one hostel student, who deliberately shut and barred the door and window of his room against the Hostel Superintendent and the Principal, was also cited as an example of the bad behaviour of the hostel students. It was also noted that until the Hostel Superintendent had intervened, the hostel reading room had been used as a base of operation by seceding students engaged in intimidating waverers.

The Principal found no extenuating circumstance to excuse the very different conduct of the senior B.A. students. They were considered to be the 'chief offenders' who, in most cases, influenced and intimidated the students of the junior classes. Hunter wrote: "No doubt they have been subject to outside influence of a pernicious character, but they are old enough to understand their duty and responsibility. At the best they proved themselves more than willing instruments of mischief and as such merit punishment. Not only have they in the most insolent manner defied my authority, but they have vehemently resisted all attempts made by members of the staff and gentlemen of position in the town to bring them to a sense of duty, and have shown no consideration for the wishes of their parents and guardians. They have forcibly restrained well-disposed students from returning to college; they have sent a telegram to government containing utterly false statements. They have assembled and passed insolent resolutions and forwarded their resolutions to the press. They are apparently under the impression that there is no outrage in which they may not indulge with impunity, that they may continue to defy authority as long as they please, and when they please may return to college, presumably on their terms. It does not seem to occur to them that the game is not altogether in their own hands, and that when it suits them to return they may find the door closed against them".

This sentiment found expression when he made various judgements against the secessionists. While the Principal was willing to readmit all the suspended students who might submit themselves on or before the reopening of the college for the second term, he was unwilling to receive the members of the senior B.A. class into the college at any time or on any terms, and preferred to recommend that they should not be admitted into any other government college. However, he proposed to grant transfer certificates to those who made proper submission before the end of the year to enable them to join non-government colleges in 1908. Those who were found guilty of conduct aggravating the original offence were recommended for summary expulsion. The Principal suggested that the names of those students who were not readmitted but possessed all the term certificates required by the university regulations were to be reported to the Syndicate with the recommendation that they should be debarred from appearing for the successive university examinations. Accordingly, the government resolved:

- That Harisarvottama Rao, M.A., be debarred from employment as a teacher in any government or aided school or college;
- That as to Ramachandra Rao, the Director of Public Instruction be requested to move the Syndicate to debar him altogether from appearing for the B.A. Degree, that mid-term and transfer certificates be-refused, and that he be not readmitted into any government or aided college;
- That as to those students of the fourth year class who possess all the term certificates required by the university for any division of the B.A. degree examination, the Director of Public Instruction be requested to meet the Syndicate to debar them from appearing for any branch of the B.A. degree examination for a period of two years. None of the seceding students belonging to this class will be permitted to continue their studies for any branch of the B.A. Degree either in the Rajahmundry College or in

any other Government or aided college, and to such of them as do not possess term or transfer certificates, these certificates will be refused;

- That the junior students who were under suspension on 20th May, 1907 be expelled, the grant of term and transfer certificates refused to them, and that they be not readmitted into the Rajahmundry College; that as to those of them who are students of the second year class and who possess all the term certificates required by the University for the First-in-Arts Examination, the Director of Public Instruction be requested to move the Syndicate to debar them from appearing for that examination for the period of one year".

It was clarified that the order was aimed to "inflict a more severe penalty upon students who do not already possess the certificates required for admission to the B.A. degree examination and to the First-in-Arts Examination, respectively, than upon the students who do possess the required certificates". It was further clarified that the government had no intention to refuse indefinitely the transfer and term certificates to the students of the two classes. The intention was to debar all the offending students of the third and fourth year classes, whether they possessed term certificates or not, from appearing for the B.A. degree examination before December 1909, and those of the second year B.A. class before December 1908".

Thus, the object of the government was to arrest the progress of the senior students of government and aided colleges for two years, and that of the junior students for one year. It was the term certificate over which the government had power, and the issue of the transfer certificate would follow the granting of the term certificate. The government by itself had no power to take any action on students who possessed term certificates. But the issue of the term or annual certificate was entirely at the discretion of the Principal of the college, who could refuse the same on grounds of unsatisfactory conduct. The loss of certificate involved loss of an entire year, and, if the transfer certificate with the approval of the Syndicate was withheld for another year, the student had to lose two years in all.

Though, the college was closed for the vacation, the Principal, who expected that the junior students would seek readmission during the vacation or at the beginning of the ensuing term, had made arrangements for their readmission. When the Rajahmundry College reopened for the second term on 1 July, the Principal reported with satisfaction that the demeanour of the students was perfectly quiet and respectful. There was no disinclination on their part to submit to discipline. The Principal observed: "The punitive order of Government has had an excellent effect, and that the students here now realise, as they unfortunately have failed to realise hitherto, that they are responsible beings who will not be suffered to offend with impunity". Students who were non-participants in the secession and those who were readmitted recognised that there was every reason to believe that they had escaped, and so they were unlikely to expose themselves to similar risks in the future. But students who were punished, accompanied by their parents and guardians, met the Principal with representations.

To some of the applications which were found to be unexceptional, the Principal replied that he had no power to remit punishments inflicted by government, while he gave favourable endorsements to some other applications. Three students were readmitted into the college as they were absent on 24 April, 1907. Parents and guardians of four students personally sought readmission for them immediately after the disturbance, and the Principal orally promised them readmission on their making submission. Parents and guardians of three students left with the gymnastic director, letters to the Principal seeking readmission; but they were not forwarded to the Principal immediately. Yet Hunter admitted them also. The case of P. Ramiah Pantulu, son of a retired Deputy Collector, was considered to be exceptional. He had stated that he did not wear the locket or even attend Pal's lectures. As he had joined the Rajahmundry College only at the end of March, he was frightened and hence seceded. Prohibition against the boy from appearing for the B.A. examination for two years was hence withdrawn.

It was noted that the punitive order was meant "not only as a first punishment for breach of discipline, but as a permanent warning to other students, the effect of which would be lost if after a while, it could be evaded, on pleas of intimidation, fear of violence, ignorance, etc., excuses which could not be proved". While the government secretaries concerned endorsed the action of Hunter in readmitting the ten students, they hesitated to ask for pardon to any of the other memorialists.

The Syndicate at a meeting held on 1 October resolved permanently to exclude Ramachandra Rao from the B.A. examination, not to exclude K. Janardhana Rao from the B.A. examination in view of the recommendation made in his favour by the Principal, to exclude from the B.A. examination of 1907-08 seven students of the IV year class possessing all the B.A. term certificates, to exclude from the F.A. examination 13 students of the second year class and to exclude B. Ramanayya of the second year class from the F.A. examination of 1907. The details of the Syndicate decision were communicated to the Commissioner for Government Examinations, thus making the prohibition applicable to their sitting for a government examination. Harisarvottama Rao, the Government Training College student, was debarred from employment as a teacher in any government or aided school or college". Certain students who took part in the demonstration on 24 April 1907 were either dismissed or suspended. The Governor-in-Council directed that Harisarvottama Rao and J. Ramachandra Rao were to be permanently debarred from government service and that the other students in the list appended to the government order No. 864, Pub. 16-11-1907 were to be debarred for the periods noted against their names.

The government sanctioned the following alterations proposed by the Senate at its special meeting held on 2 August 1097, in Regulation 96 after clause (iv): "(v) to have cognizance of any misconduct by any student in a college or hostel connected with a college or colleges, or by any candidate for matriculation or for any other university examination, brought to the notice of the Syndicate by a Director of Public Instruction or Chief Educational Officer of a Province or by the responsible authorities of the college or hostel or school concerned or in the case of a state college in a native state by the Chief Educational Officer of the state, or in any case a Fellow or the Registrar of the University, or by a Chairman of a Board of Examiners, or chief superintendent at any centre of examination and to punish such misconduct by exclusion from any university examinations either permanently or for a specified period, or by deprivation of any university scholarship or endowment held by such person or by both".

The memorial submitted by the parents and guardians of the students of the Rajahmundry College gave a new dimension to the issue. Since the parents lived at a distance from the college, notices of suspension of their wards by the Principal dated 26-4-1907 reached them after 20 May, the date before which the seceders were required to tender their apology and submission. While some received them in June, some others did not receive them at all. As such they had no idea when they should tender their apology and submission and were under the impression that the same could be done on the reopening day after the holidays. At the outset, the memorialists observed that the Sastras inculcated proper obedience and respect to the teachers and any rebellion or defiance against the authority of a teacher was abhorrent to the Hindus. They argued that the students while at school had visionary ideas of freedom and liberty, and little sense of right and wrong, and that "their abstract idea are only modified when they come in contact in actual life with the outside world". They did not urge that students guilty of disobedience to any disciplinary orders should be allowed to escape; instead, they should be dealt with, but only as students and not as grown up men.

The orders awarding severe punishments to the students of the Rajahmundry College tended to blight the prospects of the young men. They caused great concern and pain to the memorialists as they fell heavily on parents who had spent much money on their account and had been giving their wards education with great inconvenience and sacrifice, with the fond hope that their children might be of help and support to them and their families.

The memorialists asserted that the students of the Arts College had always been obedient to the Principal and had given him no occasion to feel otherwise. Their wards were never associated as members of the Bala Bharat Samithi. They never wore the 'Vande Mataram' badge and the Principal had no reason to find fault with them on that account. The allegation that the tickets were worn deliberately to provoke the Principal to action which would serve as some sort of excuse for secession from the college, was also refuted. The memorialists ascertained that neither a meeting was held on 24 April nor a resolution passed to print 'Vande Mataram' tickets overnight. In fact these tickets were already found in circulation and were worn by some students and others even before 24 April. The parents denied the allegation that the rebellion was a preconcerted attempt. Most of the wards of the memorialists were in the first room, which Hunter visited, taking the examination along with the senior B.A. class, when they were ordered to remove the tickets. The memorialists submitted that their wards left the college as a "result of the momentary excitement due to extraneous influences", when the wards saw a large body of students leaving the college in accordance with the Principal's order, they too followed them "thoughtlessly in the excitement of the moment".

The memorialists denied the allegation of the Principal that their wards showed continued disregard of his orders and that they took part in an organised scheme for defying the authority of the Principal and the disciplinary orders issued by him as stated in the G.O. The Principal's reference to the connection of their wards with the "telegrams and memorials" which were sent in their name to the government and other authorities was also denied.

The memorialists brought to the notice of the Governor of Madras that the Principal took no explanation from their wards and that they were summarily dealt with *en bloc,* along with others, without an enquiry into the part allegedly played by them.

A memorandum signed by Gadicherla Surianaraina and 158 other students was submitted to the Viceroy on 29-4-1907, in which they upheld their right to wear '*Vande Mataram*' lockets and prayed to His Excellency to grant them permission to wear them and to cancel the orders of the Principal expelling J. Ramachandra Rao and suspending other students. The memorialists pointed out that, in Bengal, silver and gold lockets bearing the impression of '*Vande Mataram*' were permitted. Even though the memorialists submitted to the Principal a written petition on 25-3-1907 praying for permission to wear the lockets, he issued no orders, written or oral, prohibiting them from wearing the lockets.

Certain devotees of Lord Rama used to imprint the word 'Rama' on their bodies in sandal. Lingadharis put on *'Lingam'* pendants. Christians wore crosses, the votaries of the Theosophical Society put on the hexagonal pendants, and the members of the Masonic Lodges wore their badges. *'Vande Mataram'* loclets were worn in a similar sense as an external mark to indicate one's respect for one's mother country. But the wearing of *'Vande Mataram'* medals, as it was associated with the demonstrations in Rajahmundry, appeared to Hunter as incompatible with a proper submission to constituted authority. Hunter believed that agitation was improper on the part of the undergraduate students, and that the excitement involved in such agitation was detrimental to studies and discipline. It was not proper either for the government or for their subordinates to interfere in religious matters.

Hunter had received instructions neither from the Director of Public Instruction nor from the government to remove the badges by force or to punish the wearers. If Hunter could legally check the use of the lockets, he might as well have issued orders declaring that students should not enter the college unless they wore foreign clothes or removed the caste marks (of sandal paste, vermilion, ashes, etc.) on their forehead. In these circumstances students should not be held as offenders for having disobeyed those orders of the Principal which were illegal and ought not to have been issued. Probably the government, on the other hand desired that the students should obey whatever orders the Principal issued, justifiable or unjustifiable, and that they would be considered offenders if they transgressed them.

The national festival of Sree Rama Navami used to be celebrated annually with special grandeur at Rajahmundry between 22nd and 26th of April. Students in their memorial to the Viceroy had remarked that they wore lockets on this occasion, as it was customary, and attended the college wearing them, on the 24th. The wearing of the lockets was considered to be a matter purely of religious sentiment or conscience. That day the Principal came to the several rooms in which the students were taking the half-yearly examination papers and then ordered them to remove the lockets in two minutes. "He then began to count the half minutes and seconds. The students remained silent seeing the angry tone of the Principal and the suddenness of the order directing the removal of the lockets, which they amongst others have always considered to be harmless. Upon this the Principal asked them to leave the college at once, which they did". According to the memorandum, the Principal had abused the students by using words such as "Rascals", "Scoundrels", "Rogues" and "Wretches". The student memorialists argued that the Principal acted without any provocation and justification. The Principal's action of accusing the students of disobedience, without promulgating any order, was not only arbitrary but unjust and uncalled for in the extreme. The Principal held a "strong but mistaken political significance which the students vehemently but respectfully disclaim". The parents in their memorandum to the Governor condemned the action of the Principal on 24th April as nasty and ill-considered. They alleged that "instead of dealing with the situation with tact and foresight, he precipitated matters and without consulting the college council and his colleagues, he had ordered the students either to remove the medals and tickets or to leave the college at once. It is to be deeply deplored that instead of at least issuing a written order then or giving time to them to consider over the matter, or opportunity to their guardians and others interested in them, to remonstrate with them, he gave them 3 minutes' time to decide whether they would remove the tickets or leave the college and counted minutes and seconds to enforce his views peremptorily".

The more the Principal insisted on the students' removing their lockets, the stronger they resisted. The students had no alternative but leave the college when Hunter pronounced that unless they removed the lockets they would not be allowed to remain within the college precincts. If the students went to the college with the tickets which they considered to be perfectly harmless and right, it was explained that "Mr. Hunter would overcome his personal scruples in the matter and raise no objection to their wearing them, and that they never contemplated that the Principal would ask them to leave the college".

The students would have gained the case if they had obeyed the orders of the Principal first and then protested against its illegality, unreasonableness and unjustifiableness. But their youthful zeal and spirit prevailed upon them and, carried away by sentiment and impulsiveness, they resolved to wear the lockets and appear in the college. The Principal had grossly exaggerated the juvenile spirits and aspirations and read into them intents and resolves of deep political significance. He saw it all as an organised revolt and an open defiance of authority as he failed to understand their youthful exuberance or enthusiasm. "The genesis of the whole thing seems to be the giving of undue and exaggerated importance to the wearing of lockets, and there would have been no difficulty if the whole thing were looked upon with supreme indifference and undisguised contempt. But at times strange ideas present themselves to strange men having strange impulses, and they are readily prone to give it a colour as those strange ideas keep haunting them and thus give way to reason and sobriety".

The very fact that the government had not discussed the '*Vande Mataram*' question at all shows that the wearing of the lockets was perfectly legal and justifiable. To obey or not to obey an illegal order was the question. On the issue whether the students were right in disobeying the order of the Principal though it was an illegal one, opinions varied. One group held that every order, whether legal or illegal, good or bad, salutary or injurious, issued by the Principal in the interests of discipline, should be obeyed first. Representations could be made to the proper authorities only later. Students should not take the law into their own hands to decide the validity or correctness of the order, and the question whether it should be obeyed or not.

This group feared that otherwise, the centre of authority would be transferred from the Principal to the students, thus subverting all discipline which was the essential foundation of all scholastic career. The other group believed that the students had not to obey an order which was obviously illegal, unjustifiable and interfering with the freedom and conscience of the students outside the scope of their scholastic discipline. They asked whether students had to obey if the Principal asked them to remove their sacred threads, sectarian marks or some such things, and argued that the Principal had no authority either to issue orders regarding the private life and conduct of the students, or under the pretext of maintaining discipline, to enforce submission to all kinds of illegal orders. Except in the imagination of the Principal who issued the order, the wearing of the BM lockets would not in the least subvert the maintenance and upkeep of discipline in the college. Such an order was unwarranted since the enforcement was in no way conducive to the maintenance of discipline. In the context, usages such as "interest of discipline, maintenance of order" are all catch phrases of the Education Department — high sounding enough and affording a basis for the issue of unjust orders which hamper the freedom and liberty of the student.

Except for the Principal of the Rajahmundry College, authorities of no college in the Madras Presidency had raised any objection to their students' wearing the lockets. Any other Principal in the place of Hunter would have suppressed the whole thing by his personal influence, and the affair would not have attracted the attention of the government. Hunter could have punished the students with suspension or fine or otherwise, and pacified them by tact and personal influence. But, instead, he allowed the whole thing to assume gigantic proportions. The presence of Bepin Chandra Pal had unconsciously added colour to the situation which pave scope for wild imaginings and strange political readings. No wonder, the hope that he would merit the thanks of the government and win more official distinction might have motivated Hunter to report to the government with exaggerated tint, the incipient rebellion of the students as if the whole British Empire were at stake. The issue at hand, with some political significance attached to it by Hunter, created an occasion for the government to inaugurate an array of repressive measures.

The government, on the basis of the Principal's report on the misconduct of the students and the circumstances leading to the crisis, reviewed the affair and published an elaborate order punishing the students in various degrees and commending the Principal for having conducted himself very patiently, skilfully, and boldly. But the government order became a meaningless document as it evaded the main point in question between the Principal and the students regarding the wearing of *'Vande Mataram'* lockets. The government order did not consider "whether the Principal was justified in prohibiting the students from wearing the said lockets, whether the wearing of them was to be construed as improper conduct on their part and whether they transgressed the rules of discipline in ignoring the said prohibitory orders".

It would have been easy to comprehend the attitude and the reasoning of the government if it had pronounced that the wearing of *'Vande Mataram'* lockets was illegal and punishable. But the government had shown "its wisdom and common sense by not propounding such an astounding, absurd and ridiculous theory that the wearing of the Vande Mataram lockets is illegal and penal". The government knew well that, in all conscience, if they had to express any opinion it had only to be in favour of the wearing of lockets, in which case the students could not be punished.

Hence, they deliberately brushed aside the main question and slid over it. "The Government without giving any finding has punished the students. It has come to a conclusion without the premises. It has passed a sentence without a conviction". Thus, it was "more of a vindictive character than partaking of the nature of equity, justice and good conscience in legal phraseology".

The government order rusticating the students of the Rajahmundry College for various terms was quite in keeping with the times and was no a par with the other repressive measures then inaugurated in different parts of India. The view taken by the government on the conduct of the students and the punishment inflicted upon them was in "consonance with other measures calculated to cow down the people and to nip the new spirit among the younger generation in the bud, so that it may not take root and spread forth its blossoms and fruit".

4

Literary and Journalistic Career

A Profound Writer

Bipin Chandra Pal was gifted with a flair for writing. He could write freely without reference to notes or books. His intellect, creative genius and clarity of thought were reflected in his writings.

Sojourn in Journalism

In 1883, Bipin Chandra Pal worked as Assistant Editor of the *Bengal Public Opinion,* an English news weekly from Calcutta. He functioned virtually as its editor, penning many of the articles that appeared.

It was a period of turbulence and conflict between the rationalism advocated by the progressive movements and the Hindu orthodoxy.

Bipin Chandra Pal started a Bengali monthly *Alochana* (1884), synthesising Hindu conservatism and Brahmo ideology. The journal had many eminent and intellectual contributors, such as Shivnath Shastri, Dwijendranath Tagore and Rabindranath Tagore. Pal used the journal fully as an instrument to spread new, rational ideas on political, literary, social, historical subjects. It made quite an impact.

In 1887, Bipin Chandra Pal accepted the post of subeditor of the *Tribune* in Lahore. With the editor, Seetalakanta Chatterjee, on leave, Pal ran the paper practically single-handedly, writing the whole paper himself, leaving only the news columns in charge of my two subeditors'. Pal became well-known amongst the thinking public in Lahore. He did not stay on for very long. He left Lahore in 1888. In 1892, Bipin Chandra Pal started a Bengali monthly, *Asha.* Two years later, in 1894, he started *Kaumudi,* a Bengali fortnightly.

Study Tour to England

In 1898, Bipin Chandra Pal went to England for theological studies on a scholarship granted by the British and Foreign Unitarian Association. He gave up his scholarship after a year and utilised his stay in England to preach Hindu theism and carry on political propaganda. At the invitation of the National Temperance Association of New York, he visited the USA on a lecture tour. In 1900, he returned to India imbued with great patriotic fervour. He plunged into the freedom movement.

Publication of Journals

Bipin Chandra Pal brought out *New India,* an English weekly, on August 12, 1901. His aim was to make the Indian education system rational and to propagate secular culture. The partition of Bengal, in July 1905, convinced him that the moderates approach was 'utterly futile'. The call for boycott of British goods came from a Bengali journalist Krishna Kumar Mitra's *Sanjivanee.*

The moderates, radicals and revolutionary nationalists of Bengal met in Barisal to show their unity in the Bengal Provincial Conference of April 14-15, 1906. The processionists were beaten by the police for shouting *'Vande Mataram'.*

Bipin Chandra Pal started a newspaper, *Vande Mataram,* with Rs. 500 donated by a friend. The first issue of the *Vande Mataram* came out on August 6. 1906. Within a week of its launching, the cry *Vande Mataram* made its impact in India and outside. The paper gained the reputation of being a 'flaming newspaper which struck a ringing new note in Indian journalism ... the most effective voice of what we call nationalist extremism'. Bipin Chandra Pal started the nationalist propaganda sharing the apostolate with Rabindranath Tagore and Aurobindo Ghose.

Bipin Chandra Pal published the English weekly journal, *Swaraj,* in London: founded the English monthly journal, *Hindu Review* (1912); edited the daily, Independent, Allahabad, founded by Motilal Nehru, and the weekly. Democrat, Allahabad (1919-20); and edited the *Bengalee* founded by Surendranath Banerjee (1924-25). He also regularly contributed to the Modern Review, Amrita Bazar Patrika, The Statesman, Englishman and many other papers.

One evening, Bipin Chandra Pal went to the office of the *Amrita Bazar Patrika.* The editor was Babu Motilal Ghosh. He asked Pal if he could think of a new article on a topical subject that had cropped up during the day and write it out. Pal was there just on a friendly visit, but he did not refuse to write. He dictated his article on the 'Topic of the Day'. It took him about forty-five minutes and it was published as an editorial in the paper.

Bipin Chandra Pal continued his vocation as a journalist till the end. Even on the day before he passed away, he dictated an article entitled 'Autonomy and Federation' for a Madras paper. He wrote on the condition that his articles would not be amended.

As a patriotic journalist, Bipin Chandra Pal was intimately associated with Chittaranjan Das's Bengali journal, *Narayan,* and was one of its chief contributors. He was also instrumental in reviving *Banga Darshan* and *Vijaya,* the two noted periodicals of the time.

Bipin Chandra Pal was a freelance contributor of articles to nearly all serious contemporary journals after 1913. Many of his articles published in India, the USA and Europe were marked by a striking note of virile individuality on burning topics of the day, and constituted milestones in the politics of the day. To live by journalism alone, in a country with hardly five per cent literacy, was no mean achievement. Pal did just that.

Success in Journalism

In 1924, Bipin Chandra Pal became editor-in-chief of the daily, *Bengalee,* and contributed articles to other publications as well. He wrote essays on the socio-cultural movement of Bengal after Raja

Ram Mohun Roy's times. His autobiography—*Sattar Batsar* — was serialised in *Pravasee,* a Bengali monthly, from 1926 to 1928. (The first volume of his English autobiography. In the Days of My Youth could, however, be published only posthumously.)

Literary Pursuit

Around 1896, Bipin Chandra Pal wrote *Krishna Charitra,* a well-known work in Bengali literature. Through a careful analysis of traditional records, he established Sri Krishna in *Krishna Charitra* as the Perfect Man. Like Sri Rama in the *Ramayana,* he felt Sri Krishna was worthy of being emulated and adored.

Work on Lord Krishna

Bipin Chandra Pal composed many articles in Bengali under the rubric '*Sri Sri Krishna Tattwa*'. His Sri Krishna is the Ultimate Reality.

Bipin Chandra Pal wrote many articles in Bengali on the different moods of the love of Radha-Krishna based on the Vaishnavaite lyrics, and also on the transcendental character of the eternal process of union and separation in the Radha-Krishna relationship. In 1911, he wrote a book, *Soul of India.*

In later years, Bipin Chandra Pal was often busy in the study of *Chaitanya Charitamrita,* the scripture of the Bengal Vaishnavaites, woven around the life of Sri Chaitanya.

Work on Jesus Christ

Bipin Chandra Pal's articles on the message and mission of Jesus Christ clearly state his mature views on Christianity. To him, the Christ of Christian consciousness was a living force. He shared Raja Ram Mohun Roy's views on the modern world, especially in his notable thesis, *Precepts of Jesus*—The *Guide to Peace and Happiness.* Pal followed Keshub Chandra Sen's lectures on Christian ethics, doctrines, dogmas and rituals, with all the moral fervour of his emotional nature, and particularly the remarkable address of the great Brahmo leader on 'Jesus Christ in Europe and Asia'.

A student of comparative religion, Bipin Chandra Pal could not accept the claim of universalism for Christianity, as asserted by theologians of the West. This universalism, Pal maintained, was attained by Hinduism.

5

Bipin Chandra Pal's Views

Absolute

The things that we know are always conditioned by us as their knower. They are here the subjects, and what we know is our object; and the subject always conditions its object. The Absolute cannot be so conditioned. Consequently the Absolute cannot be known as object but in knowing out object we also know ourselves as the subject. As subject we are not conditioned by our object but only condition it. The Absolute may be known, therefore, not as object but as subject. *(Object of Knowledge)*

Administration

In fact, one of the greatest advantages of the British Parliamentary system is that while the permanent officials are charged to carry on the routine work of the administration, the initiation of policy is left to men who are in touch with the outside world, and who are able to bring to their task a fresh mind and broad outlook. When we have full responsible government, the same thing will happen in our country also. The permanent officials, both Indian and non-Indian, will continue to administer the laws of the country. But those who will make these laws and initiate public policy will be outsiders like the British Parliamentarians.

(Official Publicity, Hindu, Vol. 7, No.2, 23 April 1932, pp. 5-6)

Aurobindo's Political Thought

"The youngest in age among those who stand in the forefront of the Nationalist propaganda in India, but in endowment, education, and character, perhaps superior to them all — Aurobindo seems distinctly marked out by Providence to play in the future of this movement a part not given to any of his colleagues and contemporaries. The other leaders of the movement have left their life behind them, Aurobindo has his before him. Nationalism is their last love, it is Aurobindo's first passion. They are burdened with the cares and responsibilities of large families or complex relations. Aurobindo has a small family and practically no cumulative obligations. His only care is for his country — the Mother, as he always calls her. His only recognised obligations are to her. Nationalism, at the best a concern of the intellect with some, at the lowest a political cry and aspiration with others, is with Aurobindo, the supreme passion of his soul. Few, indeed, have grasped the full force and meaning of the Nationalist ideal as Aurobindo has done.

"Aurobindo has received the best modern education that any man of this country and generation could expect to have. He had for some years been a teacher of youth in Baroda, and had acquired a considerable practical experience in his art. He had clearly realised the spirit and actualities of the life of his nation, and knew how the most advanced principles of modern pedagogy could be successfully worked into a thoroughly national system of education in India. He went to Calcutta as an educationist. He knew that the foundations of national independence and national greatness must be laid in a strong and advanced system of national education. He had a political ideal, no doubt; but politics meant to him much more than is ordinarily understood by the term. It was not a game of expediency but school of human character, and, in its turn, reacting upon it, should develop and strengthen the manhood and womanhood of the nation. Education could be no more divorced from politics than it could be divorced from religion or morals. Any system of education that helps such isolation and division between the various organic relations of life, is medieval, and not modern. It is the education of the cloister — abstract and unreal; not the education of the modern man, eager to realise his fullest manhood in and through every relation of life. Aurobindo is an apostle of modern education. Indeed his ideal of modern education is even higher than what is understood by modern education ordinarily in Europe. It is a supremely spiritual ideal. Its aim is to actualise the highest and deepest of God-consciousness of the human soul, in the outer life and appointments of human society....

The Nationalist School was without a daily English organ. A new paper was started. Aurobindo was invited to join its staff. A joint stock company was shortly floated to run it, and Aurobindo became one of the directors. This paper — "Vande Mataram" — at once secured for itself a recognised position in Indian journalism. The hand of the master was in it from the very beginning. Its bold attitude, its vigorous thinking, its clear ideas, its chaste and powerful diction, its scorching sarcasm and refined witticism were unsurpassed by any journal in the country, either Indian or Anglo-Indian. It at once raised the tone of every Bengalee paper, and compelled the admiration of even hostile Anglo-Indian editors. Morning after morning not only Calcutta, but the educated community almost in every part of the country eagerly awaited its vigorous pronouncements on the stirring questions of the day. It even forced itself upon the notice of the callous and self-centred British press. Long extracts from it commenced to be reproduced week after week, even in the exclusive columns of the "Times" in London. It was a force in the country which none dared to ignore, however much they might fear or hate it, and Aurobindo was the leading spirit, the central figure, in the new journal". (Excerpts from Sri Bipin Chandra Pal's famous article on Sri Aurobindo's life and work written in 1909-1910 and published in B.C. Pal's book *Indian Nationalism: Its Personalities and Principles.)*

Artisans

Our artisans and manufacturers were never exclusively artisans or manufacturers, except in the great cities. All over the country they joined their crafts and arts to their essential agricultural occupations. Expert artists and craftsmen enjoyed freehold land from which they got their subsistence. Consequently, they did not need outside capital to keep their families going, during the time they were engaged in the production of their wares and until those were ready for the market. The economic independence of our artisans and craftsmen was thus, fully secured in the past. Our skilled labourers, who produced all our old manufacturers, were thus, hardly labourers in the European sense of the term. *(Socio Economic Structure)*

Autonomous

The time has come when in the interest of truth and civic advancement and the freedom of the people, our British friends should be distinctly told that while we are thankful for all the kind things they have done for us already, the sacrifices they have made to make our lot easy and their yoke light, we cannot any longer suffer ourselves to be guided by them in our attempts at political progress and emancipation. Their point of view is not ours. They desire to make the Government of India popular without ceasing in any sense to be essentially British: we desire to make it autonomous absolutely free of British control.

(An Article-Vande Mataram-1906)

British Labour

British labour is gradually and increasingly coming to realise that the existence of a dependent Empire, that is large tract of territories with undeveloped or ill-developed natural resources and teeming millions of frugal and abstemious humanity living on a very low standard of comforts, and supplying therefore an almost inexhaustible source of cheap labour constitutes the greatest stronghold of capitalist exploitation, and consequently, a very serious menace to the future of British labour itself. The British labourmen are commencing to foresee that Indian resources and Indian labour exploited by British capital will dump Indian goods upon their home markets and upon the markets of the world to an extent that will be bound to tell upon British industries and thus hurt the interests of the British working men ultimately. And in the recognition of this menace to their vital economic interests that is coming from the capitalist exploitations of the dependent Empire, lies our hope in securing the powerful support of the

British workers, in the fight for India's freedom on constitutional and peaceful lines. *(Wrote - Congress Propaganda in England - Amrita Bazar Patrika - 14 November 1919)*

British Voter

The British voter is master of his government only one day in seven years, when he elects his Member of Parliament. After the polling day, he is as much the slave of his rulers as any oriental subject. The constituencies that elect the members of Parliament cannot compel it to obey their will between one General Election and another. They cannot initiate any legislation. They cannot recall their members during the lifetime of the Parliament to which they are elected. There is no provision in the present British Constitution to compel the Government to refer any question to the vote of the general body of the British electors. The British people have no effective voice in the administration of their State; the fear of losing the next General Election, and of thereby being driven from office is the only thing that restrains the British Executive. It is a very feeble restraint.

(British Constitution - Under Monarchy)

Caste-Distinction

It is true that in Europe, there is no such caste-distinction as we have in our Hindu society; but they have an acute type of class-distinction. It is never my intention to perpetuate the caste either in the name of ancient scriptures or modern science, or by quoting Manu, or by blending Mendel-Weisman and Manu in the same vein. But what I like to say emphatically is that the casteless England does not have a fraction of the social sympathy and social interrelations, which we have in our caste-ridden country. In Europe, an underling can find an entry into the upper strata on the strength of money. But in India a non-Brahmin could not become a Brahmin by money. It would be useful to remember this fundamental difference in discussing the class-distinctions of England and caste-distinctions of India. *(Buddhimaner Karma, Narayana, 3rd Yr. Vol. 3, 1323 B.E., pp.829-830)*

Central Idea

As in portrait-painting every line that the painter draws on the canvas is moved by the idea of the original before him, and as all the lines work together to bring it out, so every step in the evolution of an organism is moved and regulated by the central idea, the arch-type, which it is meant to reveal and develop. The arched-type of the horse is the regulative idea in every colt: that of the dog is the regulative idea in every puppy, that of man is the regulative idea in every human baby. These regulative ideas constitute the inner principle of differentiation even in the earliest cell-formations, which gradually develop into the colt, the puppy, or the human baby. *(Regulation - Evolution of Idea)*

Character

All autocracy is of the same character, and all bureaucrats, whether official or non-official, whether white or black or yellow or brown, are of the same colour, the wide world over.

(Published in Vande Mataram Daily-17 September 1906)

Civic Responsibilities

I want to start schools in every village. I want to train every villager not only in the 3 R's but also in the elements of civic responsibility and political rights because, after all, unless the people are trained in civic responsibilities and educated in the matter of their political rights and duties, responsible government cannot be properly established among them. Consequently, if I have charge of education, I will try to conduct the educational policy as it is conducted in every self-governing country.

(Speech - 12 December 1917 - Calcutta)

Complications

We can make the Government impossible without entirely making it impossible for them to find people to serve them. The administration may be made impossible in a variety of ways. It is not actually that every Deputy Magistrate should say: "I wont serve in it". But if you create this spirit in the country the Government service will gradually imbibe this spirit, and a whole office may go on strike. This does not put an end to the Administration, but it creates endless complications in the work of Administration, and if these complications are created in every part of the country, the Administration will have been brought to a deadlock, and made nonetheless impossible, for the primary thing is the prestige of the government and the boycott strikes at the roof of that prestige. *(Passive Resistance)*

Culture

The question with us, as a nation is — are we to live or are we to die? It is not a question whether, as between our ideals and theirs, which is true and which is false, for neither is absolutely true nor absolutely false. Nor is it a question as to which of these cultures is good and which evil, for neither is absolutely good nor absolutely evil. There is a mixture of truths, half-truths, fancies and falsehood, as much in our thoughts, speculations, philosophies and religions, as in those of Europe. Some institutions are good, some indifferent, some bad here as well as there. The most vital question, therefore is, how to save our own culture and civilization from being swamped by the imported ideals and institutions of this new and forceful civilization that has come to us with the foreign rulers of the country. *(A Specific Character)*

Deadlock

If you have two governments, one popular and the other bureaucratic, there will be deadlock. The popular government will want money, the bureaucratic government will say: "we can't give you". The popular government will want freedom to organise the resources of the people; the bureaucratic government will set the dogs of the police on their heels. There would be deadlock and more than that. *(Speech - 12 December 1917, Calcutta)*

Democratic Ideal

We stand for democratic ideal in every walk and relation of life. This ideal recognises no privilege arising from physical accidents as they are called either of birth or sex or economic or political accidents of wealth or rank. It demands that all human beings shall be given exactly the same social opportunities for the higher possible realisation of their inherent humanity and no man or woman shall be restrained in the freest exercise and enjoyment of their powers both of mind and body as long as they do not, in pursuit of their own freedom, infringe the equal freedom of others to freely pursue their own personal or social ends. Democratic ideals demand a common concern of social or political life. Collective ideals, wishes and interests of all shall prevail over individual ideas and wishes and particularistic or sectional interests, and voice of all shall direct the common business of State or Church.

(Pal, Good Government Vs. Self-Government, Editorial. The Bengalee - 9 May 1925)

Demoralisation

Action and reaction, excitement and exhaustion are recuperative processes. What we call demoralisation is only another name for moral exhaustion. Demoralisation is a confession of failure. Confession of failure implies recognition of facts hitherto ignored or underrated. Demoralisation means the curing of conceit, and the dispelling of illusions. All these are the compensations of demoralisation. We do not regret this demoralisation. We are thankful for it. In evolution, there is no confession of failure, which is not at the same time an assurance of final success. *(The Situation in India, Swaraj, Vol. I, No. I, 1st March 1909, p.7)*

Dharma

As there are constitutional differences between one individual human and another, so the *dharma* of one man cannot truly be the *dharma* of another. It is something essentially specific and personal. The law and course of ethical and spiritual evolution in one person, cannot, therefore, be necessarily the same as that of another. What is good for one may not, therefore, be good for another. There must consequently be great diversities of both faiths and cultures in the community, owing to fundamental constitutional difference between the individuals composing it.

(Different Expression in Different Objectives)

Discipline

No man can afford or ought to avoid, the disciplines that shape and mould him from an individual human unit to an organised social being. But all the same it cannot be denied that these disciplines do lend an air of artificiality to our character and conversation. *(Review of Life of Swami Vivekananda - 1913)*

Disobedience

The good that these movements have done is as undeniable as the evils that have come in their wake. These evils will be bound to manifest themselves more and more after the present conflict is over and Indian leadership comes to its own. Disobedience is easy to instigate, but exceedingly difficult to lay when the need of it is over. What the Indian leaders are sowing today, they will have to reap inevitably when they are charged with the responsibility of law and order themselves.

(Evils of Civil Disobedience Movements and Boycott, The Englishman -26 January 1935)

Education

The present system of education is bad, but the cure for bad education is not no-education, but good education. The fundamental defects of our present system of education are two, namely — (1) that is not a national system and (2) that is not a rational system. *(An Economic Problem)*

Empire

We have got a new view of society, a new philosophy of social life, a new consciousness of sociology and when we approach this question in the light of the highest principles of the social philosophy, we find that as tribes, clans and communities are formed by the combination of individuals, and nations are formed by the combination of clans and tribes and communities, even so the real Empire is formed by the combination of different nations.

(Farming of Empire)

Eternal Principles

Religion merges into politics, politics into ethics; the secular becomes sacred; and the temporal spreads its wings into eternity itself; for all these are based upon eternal principles, all are guided by eternal law are mere evolutions, mere manifestations, under various conditions, of the eternal varieties of human nature, and all are designed by God to help the eternal progress of man.

(Lecture in City College - Calcutta 1889)

Evolution

The aim and objective of evolution, whatever may be its passing and apparent phases, is not to kill but to save, not to destroy but to develop, this principle of Love and Goodness in the world. *(Goodness of Love)*

I was a baby, I became a boy, I went to school, I became a man, I married and had children, I retired upon becoming old these are changes, because they have reference to one and the same individual, whose continuity is maintained unbroken through all these changes. They are all evolutions of one and same person. This "I", this first person singular, this what we call "self persisted through all these changes. If with each one of these various changes, continuity of this personal consciousness the sense that I am, I's were destroyed, then they would not be parts of an evolutionary series. Thus, we find that the fundamental fact in evolution is that it allows and effects almost endless changes in an object organism, without breaking up its continuity or destroying its unity.

(Object continuity unbroken)

The fundamental fact in evolution is that it allows and effects almost endless changes in an object or organism, without breaking up its continuity or destroying its unity. The law of Evolution cancels thus every conflict between change and permanence, between continuity and progress. Change and permanence are contradictions in formal and verbal logic. But Evolution cancels and reconciles these.

(The Positive Value of Nationalism in Nationality and Empire, Calcutta, 1916, p. 69)

Freedom

National freedom is a separate question which should not be confused either with the class division of the industrial society of Europe or with the caste division of the traditional society of India. Europe and America are politically free in spite of class-division. Why India should not be a self-governing state in spite of her traditional social structure? *(Explained to Sister Nivedita - B.C. Pal, Markine Charimas (Bengali) pp.45-49)*

Gift

If God were to appear before me with the gift of absolute but isolated sovereign independence for India in the right-hand, and of an equal partnership with Great Britain and her colonies in present association called the British Empire, in his left hand, I would unhesitatingly say. Father, give us the gift in your left hand. *(Spoke in London to His Friends - 1911 - B.P. Pal, Nationality and Empire, p. 11)*

Head of the Family

The common life of the family, the common power of the family, the common authority of the family, is exercised by the head of the family. He is the keeper of the privy purse of the family. And so long as the head of the family does not identify himself with any particular individual belonging to the family, the family synthesis exists, the family life endures, the unity of the family life is not broken up, and the family authority remains unimpaired. The moment the head of the family identifies himself, either economically or in any other way, with any particular member of the family group, whenever the head of the family identifies himself with his own wife, in his relations with his family life, when he applies the common property of the family to personal ends, — when he gives a present — a pearl necklace to his wife and leaves only a silver bangle for the wife of his brother — when the head of the family does that — the synthesis is broken up — the reconciliation is destroyed, the authority becomes vicious — because that which ought to represent the whole and to seek the interest of the whole is identified with a part and the part becomes the whole, and when, the part usurps the function of the whole, the whole ceases to be whole and the partialities commence to fight with one another. That is what happens in the family. *(Common Power of Family Member)*

Hindu Philosophy

In the Hindu's philosophy there are endless appearances but one reality. In the Hindu's pantheon there are countless gods but only one Supreme Lord or Isvara. In the Hindu's social economy there are numerous castes, but one organic Social Whole of which these castes, the highest as well as the lowest, however mutually exclusive they may be, are mere limbs and organs. And the Hindu's view of other races, other communities, other religions and other cultures is that these, like his own race or community or his own religion or culture, are all parts, moments or manifestations of that one Supreme Unity which fulfils and realises itself through these endless differences and diversities. *(Ultimate Unity)*

Hindu Religion

Hindu religion is not one religion, with one creed, one theology, one scriptural authority one calendar of saints, one set of dogmas and doctrines that must be accepted and pursued by all and each Hindu, a like what we find in Christianity or Islam. But it is composed of many scriptures, many creeds, many disciplines, and many theologies, which are not infrequently in open conflict even with one another. Still it is one religion. And this Unity of the Hindu religion is due to its federal character. Freedom of the parts inside the unity of the whole, this is of the essence of the concept federation. Hinduism is not one religion, like Christianity or Buddhism or Islam, which are all creedal religions.

(An Interpretation)

Hindu Society

The Hindu society is not a homogeneous unit but rather a highly developed organic hole which seeks to realise its essential unity not by denying but openly accepting and harmonising in the totality of its life, the endless diversities of its component organisms. Like the Hindu religion, Hindu society is also not a unit, but a federation of many units. The freedom and integrity of the parts inside the unity of the whole, is the very soul and essence of the federal idea. And in no religion or society that I know of, has this organic federal ideal been sought to be so fully realised as in the Hindu religion and the Hindu society.

(Pal, The Soul of India, pp.6667)

The Hindu Society is really a group of many communities, each practically independent of the others and autonomous within its own sectional or communal or caste life but combined with the others in the pursuit of a common ideal, namely, the revelation of God in Man. *(Federal Character)*

Hindu society is also not one society like for instance the Christian or Muslim communities, but a federation of many communities or castes. Each caste is more or less autonomous within it, but joined to the other castes as limbs and organs of one great society. *(Federal Structure)*

Hindu System of Government

The Hindu system of government, when the Hindus had a government of their own, was not of a military and despotic character in which the will of the sovereign was the law to the people, but was that of an essentially and highly developed constitutional monarchy. The separation of the executive and the legislative functions — the soul of constitutional freedom — had from almost the very beginning, been worked out most successfully among them. The King was, really, the executive head of the State; the council of Brahmins, aided by more popular councils, represented the legislative authority; and he essentially theocratic character of the Hindu polity saved it from those conflicts between the King and the people, through which constitutional freedom has had to build itself up in most Western countries.

(Constitutional Freedom)

Hinduism

Hinduism is not like some of the great historical religions, an individual religion so to say, but it is a community or a family of religions, some in lower and earlier, some in higher and more advanced states of growth. *(Pal, An Introduction to the Study of Hinduism, Pub. Calcutta, 1908, p.4)*

Human Life

What we lack in the actualities of our individual life and experience, the poet, the painter, the musician, — every true artist, secures for us, in the idealities of their divine creations, so that we may through their help, at least imaginatively realise these rarer and deeper notes of the human life and character, and vicariously gain, in some measure, those wider experiences, for which there may not be sufficient opportunity and scope in our limited lives. *(Pal, The Stage and the National Life, New India Vol.11, No.25. 13 February 1904, p.358)*

Human Qualities

Every section of the society, men or women, rich or poor, has a right to that education which helps to develop human qualities. And it is for the successful realisation of these human qualities that women must be conferred with all the rights that a political system offers. *(Pal, Bange Narir Nirvachanad hikar (Women Frenchise in Bengal) - Calcutta - 1921, p. 12)*

Ideal

The ideal of manhood which has always inspired and allured my mind throughout this long life, the core of which is to make way for others, keeping oneself in the background, which is based on the principle of restraints and graciousness — that ideal I did not learn from any book, but imbibed from the character and manners of my parents. *(B.P. Pal, Matri Tarpan - Bengali Monthly - Jaishta. 1335, B.E., p.541)*

Indian

To correctly present India, one must first be himself an Indian, not merely by birth, but in heart and in spirit. But such self-effacement is almost impossible of attainment by the ordinary European; for the European, can never cease to be a European, nay not even in imagination. *(Canon of Hindu Art)*

Indian Nation

The Indian Nation is not a Hindu nation. The Indian nation is not a Mohammedan nation either; nor is the Indian nation composed of Hindus and Mohammedans alone. There are others. And these different cultures, all these different communities constitute the new Indian nation. *(Explained - Character - Young Men's Mohammedan Association - Madras - 1907)*

The future Indian nation will not be a nation that will profess one social code. The future Indian nation will not be a nation that will submit itself to one particular set of spiritual or ethical disciplines. The future Indian nation will be a federated nation.

(Spelt Out Blue-Print of Independent India)

Influences

As a boy of eighteen, I would not sacrifice my conviction to obey my father, as a young man I rose to revolt against Keshub Chandra Sen when he developed pontifical tendencies. I fear these a million-fold more in politics. I cannot lend myself to this new spirit of hero worship in the masses, which kills people's freedom of thought and practically paralyses, by the dead weight of unreasoning reverence, their individual conscience. I am not blind to the possibilities of good in the great hold that Mahatmaji has got on the populace. But there is the other side, and in the earlier stages of democracy these personal influences, particularly when they are due to inspiration of medieval religious sentiments, are simply fatal to its future.

(Pal's Letter to Pt. Moti Lal Nehru - 10 September 1920)

Labour

Labour, manual or mental, is honourable Labour alone should be rewarded. Speculation is a crime against majority; inheritance is theft. To promote one's country's welfare as a step towards altruistic internationalism is a virtue; to make it an end in itself is a crime. The political strike is the most efficient form of strike. It constitutes the peaceful revolution, midway between Evolution and Revolution.

(B.C. Pal, Memories of My Life and Times, Appx. II, p. 657)

All labour is honourable, whether manual or mental. Labour alone should be rewarded, and not lazy leisure. Our work is our highest reward. We labour for love. Wages are mere bye-products.

(Editorial - The Bengalee - 22 October 1924)

Light of God

The object of the social life and social disciplines is to bring out Divine nature in every man and woman. The ignorance of man prevents the revolution of the light of God in him. The degradation of man degrades the Deity who resides in him. The bondage of man hurts the freedom of God. This is our philosophy of life. *(Development of God - in Man)*

Lord Ripon

Lord Ripon's Indian policy has been interpreted in some quarters as prompted more by cunning diplomacy than by honest regard for India's legitimate political freedom in the modern world. It did, no doubt, help to strengthen and prolong the hypnotic spell, which the British had cast over our people. But those who knew Lord Ripon personally could find no support for this suspicion in his mind and character. And history must give to the most popular Viceroy that India had a high place among the makers, politically, of modern India. The immediate result of India's awakening under Lord Ripon was the birth of the Indian National Congress about a year after he retired from the Indian Viceroyalty. *(Reconciliation of Desire for Autonomy)*

Love

There was a time when the Bengalis going over to England used to develop a disregard, if not hatred, towards their own country. Just as a man in love loses his sense and forgets his domestic attraction, similarly, those England-returned fellows, in their love of England, became forgetful of their own country. But as I saw the health, vigour, beauty and prosperity of England and America, my feeling for my native land became more intensive. It was this feeling which made me to plunge into the Swadeshi movement when I came back from the continent.

(Sonar Bangla, New Series - Bengaly Monthly, Cal., 1332

Loyalty

I am loyal to the British Government, because with me loyalty to the British Government is identical with loyalty to my own people and my own country. I am loyal to the British Government because I believe the British Government to be an instrument in the hand of God for the salvation of my people. I am loyal to the British Government because I love self-government, I am loyal to the British Government because I love this Congress. And gentlemen, the love that I have for the British Government compels me to condemn strongly the suicidal policy enunciated in the Arms Act and to call for its repeal. *(Barest Truth)*

Measure

To all truly great men, the real measure of what is good and what is bad, what is right and what is wrong, is in themselves and not in the smiles and frowns of others. It is a common characteristic of all our greatest saints.

(Review of "Life of Swami Vivekananda" 1913)

Motherland

We are born unto this land. It receives us into its bosom even as our human mothers do. It supports our life with its own substance even as the nursing mother supports the growing life of her own baby. This land is literally the mother of our physical existence. It is indeed the physical body of the soul of our land and nation. *(Motherhood of God)*

Motto

Spirituality and Freedom, — the one as the Ideal End, the other as the Essential Way, must be the motto of every nationbuilder in modern India. *(Message of Indian History)*

Nationalism

There is a creed in India today, which calls itself Nationalism. It is not a mere political programme, but a religion, it is a creed in which all who follow it will have to live and suffer. Let no man call, himself a nationalist today with a sort of intellectual conceit.

To be a nationalist in India means to be an instrument of God, and to live in the spirit. For the force that is awakening the nation is not of man, it is divine. We need not be a people who are politically strong; we need not be a people sound in physique; we need not be a people of the highest intellectual standing but we must be a people who believe... Nationalism is a divinely appointed power of the eternal, and must do its God-given work before it returns to the universal energy from where it came.

(System of Control)

Natural Selection

A nation rarely or never weighs and balances the truth or untruth, the good or the evil of any thought or course that presents itself before it, but accepts or rejects it simply according to the law of its own inner affinities or repulsions; that which is in harmony with the sum total of its past and present life and experiences, and that which is most calculated to help it in its struggle for existence, it accepts readily and perhaps even greedily; that which is not of this character, it rejects automatically. This law of natural selection operates equally in social as in biological evolution.

(National Psychology)

New

The new can only be born by destroying the old. The remnants of old crop should be burnt and its ashes mixed with the earth; then only can grow the sapling of the new. For, is it possible that the dry, dead and arid hay of the old crop would stand erect and in its midst would the seedlings of the new grow.

(Nava Jivan, Part I, 1" Issue, B.E. pp. 25-26)

New Spirit

The abdication of the right of England to determine the policy of the Indian Government, the relinquishment of the right of the present foreign despotism to enact whatever law they please to govern the people of the country, the abandonment of their right to tax the people according to their own sweet will and pleasure, and to spend the revenues of the country in any way they like, it is these that will alone meet the requirements of the New Spirit.

(Pal, The New Spirit, p.237 - Article Written on 1 October 1906)

Non Co-operation

What they call non-cooperation is what we call passive resistance. Absolute non-cooperation can never be a constitutional movement. The primary function of every State Government is the preservation of peace and order; therefore, any movement, which strikes at the primary functions of the State, cannot call itself constitutional movement. *(Views - Session Congress - Calcutta - 1920)*

Opposition

The object of the opposition is by every means in their power to create opinion in the constituencies against the Government. Bad measures we shall oppose because they are bad, good measures we shall oppose because they ought to have been better. Legitimate and constitutional obstruction must be our Policy. *(Theory of Parliamentary Opposition - Amrita Bazar Patrika -5 June 1920)*

Organism

The family is an organism; the individual is an organ of that organism. Though, as an individual, he himself is an organism, yet he belongs to the larger organism of the family of which he is a part, a limb, and an organ. Similarly the family though itself an organism has its own specific ends — has its own specific organs — has its own specific needs, and its specific means and instruments for the satisfaction of these ends, the family also though an organism, stands united with, and is subordinate to the clan or the tribe or the community, and in the fulfilment of the collective life of the tribe or the community, the family fulfils and realises its own individual family life also. And from the tribe, the commune — we come to the nation, which is composed of many clans, many tribes, many communities and each of these different communities, these different clans, all these are organic elements in the common and complete life of the nation to which they belong. *(An Organ of Family)*

Physical Base

No nation can be properly built up, except on a sound and strong physical basis. Physical health and physical strength are as much needed for the up building of individual life and character, as for that of national life and destiny. Occasionally there may be found people in whom most powerful intellects are associated with exceedingly poor health, but they form only exceptions that prove, but do not in any way modify, the general rule. The usual experience is, however, that feeble body and shattered health always act on the intellectual and moral life, and lead, inevitably, to the weakness of both. *(Value of Sound Culture)*

Physical Body

This physical body, which evolves from what is called a primary cell in biology, must have for its Regulative Idea a perfect and eternally realised form of the body into which it ultimately develops. This 'form' is not a thing of flesh and blood. Flesh and blood merely organises the idea. Behind our physical body this idea can only be what is called a spiritual idea. Our physical bodies posit, therefore, at the back of their biological evolution an eternally realised idea of spiritual form.

(Bengali Vaishnavism, p. 128)

Physical Life

Reform of our diet and in our habitations, healthier food and healthier habitations, these are two primary requirements of our physical life; as long as these are not secured, all our efforts to introduce any sort of physical training in this country, either through the existing schools and colleges or through the establishment of independent gymnasiums, will necessarily fail.

(Foodstuff and Habitations)

Prohibition

Fear is the rule of life of the lower animal Kingdom that knows no moral law. Fear breeds universally hypocrisy and deceit. Legal prohibition must tempt the individual craving for strong drinks or drugs to a thousand subterfuges, which must inevitably hurt his higher moral nature and cripple his manhood. Though, I have all my life been a teetotaler practically and an ardent advocate of temperance and even total abstinence on moral and spiritual grounds, on the selfsame moral and spiritual ground,

I find it impossible to support the demand for absolute prohibition which can only be tried by penalising the use of strong drinks by any one who may not be able to fight down the hankering for it.

(Pal. The Plea for Prohibition: Morality under Compulsion, The Englishman, 9 June 1927)

Protection

One generation pays more for the articles it uses and which enjoy protection, so that another generation may pay less, even under a state of normal free trade. Wherever protection is adopted with this object, it is fully justified. But at best it must always be a temporary devices, just like the railings with which valuable saplings are protected from harm from animals that love to make their meals out of them. When the saplings grows up into its proper stature and strength and is protected by its own trunk and bark from the depredations of its enemies, there is no need for keeping up the artificial protections. Even so must be the case with infant and weak industries. *(Economic Protection)*

Responsible Government

The government of India is represented by the Viceroy and Governor-General and his Executive Council as well as his Legislative Council. That Government is responsible not to you and to me but it is responsible to the Secretary of State across the seas. The Secretary of the State in his turn is responsible to the Cabinet and the Cabinet is responsible to the British Parliament, and the British Parliament is responsible to the British electors. So far as India is concerned, the Government of India is not responsible, as I have said to any part of the people of India. The Government of India is not responsible to those whom it governs. That is the present condition. But here, we are told for first time, that it is the goal of British Policy in India to make the government of India a responsible government. *(Speech - 18 November 1917)*

If you want to make the Government of India responsible government, you shall have to construct it, you shall have to arrange its functions that the government of India, as represented by the Executive Government headed by the Viceroy and Governor General of India, that Government shall be responsible, not, as now, to the Secretary of State but to the people of India and the members of this Government shall be appointed or elected by the people of India through their chosen representatives, and shall be accountable to the people and removable by the vote or voice of the people of India, which shall find its expression through the vote of the Legislative Assembly. That is what is meant by responsible Government. *(Speech - 22 November 1917)*

Responsible Government in India would mean that the central government, viz., the Imperial Government of India must be responsible to the people of India as well as the Provincial governments. That is the meaning of Responsible Government: - complete full responsible government in India would mean that the Government at Delhi or at Simla should be responsible to the representative of the people of India in the Indian or Viceregal Legislative Council. That would mean complete responsible government. *(Speech 12 December 1917 Calcutta)*

Right

If you cannot let us govern ourselves as you do in your own country for God's sake give us the right to protect ourselves from an evil, which you yourselves are suffering so seriously.

(Appeal to British Government - B.C. Pal, Memories of My Life and Times, p.569)

Self-Government

The whole civil service might be Indian, but the civil servants have to carry out orders — they cannot direct, they cannot dictate the policy — one civilian, 100 or 1,000 civilians in the service of the British government will not make that Government Indian. There are traditions, there are laws, there are policies to which every civilian, be he black or brown or white, must submit, and as long as these principles have not been amended, as long as that policy has not been radically changed, the supplanting of European for Indian agency will not make for self-government in this country.

(Suspicion of Bureaucracy)

The Indian executive will be absolutely subject to the Indian legislatures, as the Indian legislatures will be entirely responsible to and removable by Indian constituencies. The attainment of real democratic self-government or responsible government in India must mean the ultimate transference of the authority of the British Parliament over Indian Administration to Indian Legislatures.

(Racial Problem in India: Need of Clear Understanding - The Englishman - 28 October 1927)

Shree Krishna

Shree Krishna does not stand for Christ, but for the Father of the Christian Trinity. Shree Krishna is the Absolute, but not the Absolute of metaphysical abstraction. He is the Eternally-Self-Differentiated Absolute, realising His personality through this Eternal Self-Differentiation. The father is also the same Absolute, the same person, realising His Personality through the same eternal method of Self-Differentiation. But not with standing all this, the Father of the Christian Trinity is only One of the Three persons of that Trinity, and not the Whole Trinity.

Shree Krishna is Bhagwan, the Absolute Person. He is, what in our modern phraseology would perhaps be called, the Concrete Universal — We seem to miss somewhat this concrete character in the Father of the Christian Trinity. The Concrete Universal in Christian consciousness is not the father but the son, not God but Christ. *(Concrete Universal)*

In presenting Shree Krishna as the Soul of India. I may be accused of sectarian prepossession. But Shree Krishna is presented here not as a sectarian ideal, but as the principle and personality in and through whom, as in the past so also in the present and even in the future, the great Indian Synthesis was, is being, and will be worked. *(Pal, Prefaced His Book - The Soul of India)*

Social Distinctions

With larger experience of life we find that social distinctions cannot be so easily and summarily eliminated from any conceivable social economy. There are these distinctions even in England and America, where there is nothing like our caste system. Here, in India, we have caste-distinctions; there, in Europe and America, they have class-distinctions. Neither here nor there have we any real social equality. The ideal of human brotherhood is as yet an unrealised ideal as much in caste-ridden Hindustan as it is in class-divided Christendom. Yet in both the countries persistent attempts have been made from of old to realise it. The highest spirits both among Hindus and Christians have preached against these social inequalities, and have sought to override these distinctions in their own life and conduct.

In place of the old divisions of caste, we have set up, even in our advanced and reformed community, new divisions of class, after the manner of England and America. Our old caste divisions were based upon birth; these new class-distinctions are based upon money and official or professional rank.

And when one calmly thinks over these actualities and their serious moral and spiritual implications, one cannot gather up enough courage to claim that our present "reformed" condition is intrinsically better than our old state; or that the new social economy and arrangement carry us nearer to the ideal of human brotherhood and human equality than the old and orthodox arrangement did. *(Caste Exclusiveness)*

Socialism

Socialism represents the protest of European Democracy against the existing economic arrangements of European society. It is a demand for a more equitable distribution of economic privileges than what obtains at present. Competition is the basis of the existing economic structure in Europe and individualism is the fundamental philosophy of this competitive economic arrangement. In this sense, and to this extent only, does Socialism represent a reaction against the excessively individualistic philosophy of the French Illumination? But though to a certain extent anti-individualistic. Socialism is in no sense a synonym for Nationalism. Socialism is recognition of the limitations of individualism in one department of life only, namely, the economic. Nationalism recognises these limitations in every department of life. Socialism is a theory in Economics; Nationalism is a fact in Sociology. It is a higher generalisation.

(Nationalism and Nationalist II, Karmayogin, Vol.I, No.23. 2nd Magh, 1316, p.5)

Sociologist

People call me an Extremist, but I call myself a sociologist, and anything I may do in future in a public sense will have sociology as its basis. One noticeable feature about the demonstration made in my honour, today, cannot have escaped the thoughtful observer. The cry of *Vande Mataram* you have heard is no idle shibboleth. It means that the spirit of nationality has become a potent factor and a vital force in the political life of the country.

(The Statesman, 11 March 1908)

Speculations

The difference between, Buddhism and Hinduism lies in the fact that while Buddhism there is, practically, an absence of metaphysical speculations, Hinduism does not eliminate these speculations, but tries, rather on the contrary, to seize and realise them as verified and verifiable facts and factors of the deepest spiritual life and experience. Buddhism is essentially agnostic. Hinduism is predominantly Gnostic. But it is agnosticism, which does not repudiate and deny but fully accepts and transcends the fundamental facts of agnosticism. *(Hinduism - A Culture)*

Standard of Values

With the European, the standard of intellectual, moral and spiritual values is, more physical than mental, more external than internal, more sensuous than spiritual. If a European walks from one place to another, he will measure the distance in the terms of miles and furlongs. If he stands before a mountain he will scan its attitude by the theodolite, and express it in relation to the sea level. If he sees a human being he will psychometrate him, with a view to know his exact proportions.

His intellect cannot be satisfied unless all the details, which means the particularities of an object, are clearly seized and sized and put in their proper place and pose.

The Hindu, however, has quite a different standard of intellectual, moral and spiritual values. If he walks from one place to another, he would often times measure the distance not by chain and compass, but by his own muscles and nerves, and will report it in the terms of his own sensation and emotion.

His standard of value is internal not external, intellectual not physical, emotional and not rational in the usual narrow sense of the term. By temperament he has an instinctive and intense distaste of details. *(Different Standards)*

Statesman

It seems to me that Lord Harding is a man of great imagination, — and no man can be a statesman unless he has the gift of imagination — he is a "statesman who sees coming events long before they come, long before they appear on the horizon and seeing that they are coming he tries to prevent the evil possibilities in them so far as it is possible to do so, and to increase the possibilities of good in them by so shaping his present conduct and policy that it may increase the possibilities of good and minimise the possibilities of evil in that which is coming. This is statesmanship. A statesman is not a petty politician, a statesman does not say "I leave the future on the knees of the gods": that is improvident statesmanship. An improvident householder cannot manage the affairs of his own house, much less can an improvident statesman manage the complex affairs of a large Empire like that of the British Empire at the present time. Lord Harding was a man of vision, he saw the future, he saw what was coming, and he was making the ground ready for that which was coming.

(Meaning - Dispatch of 25 August 1911)

Submission

If the Government were to come and tell me today 'take Swaraj,' I would say thank you for the gift, but I will not have that which I cannot acquire by my own hand. Our programme is that we shall so work in the country, so combine the resources of the people, so organise the forces of the nation, so develop the instincts of freedom in the community, that by this means we shall-shall in the imperative, compel the submission to our will of any power that may set itself against us. *(Key to the Future)*

Swaraj

I have not been able to give what many of you wanted. The honest truth is, I have absolutely failed to give what I think the vast majority of this conference wanted. You wanted enthusiasm and inspiration. I have failed to inspire either in you. You wanted magic. I tried to give you logic. But logic is a bad colour when the popular mind is excited. I have never spoken a half-truth when I have known the truth. I have never tried to lead the people in faith blindfolded; I have never accepted anything on trust from anybody and I have always thought it a great wrong to the fundamental rights of human reason and conscience to wish, much less to demand, that my opinion and ideas should be accepted on trust even by the youngest and most inexperienced of my fellow beings. I knew that all of you would not entirely agree with the view I take about the non-cooperation movement. But I never dreamt that there would be any protest against my presentation of the ideal of Swaraj. This protest, coming from one who is the leader of the present movement in Bengal, has given me the greatest surprise of my life. I have been asked -'why seek to define Swaraj? Why call it democratic or any thing else? Swaraj is Swaraj. Swaraj is to be felt within and not defined by words'. I confess that I am very much perplexed. My only salvation from this confusion lies in accepting one of those various authorities as established on Divine revelation and rejecting the others as human fancies. *(Closing Conf. Words - Congress Platform, as its President - 26 March 1921)*

Symbols

There can be no religion, strictly so called, though there may be any amount of philosophy and theology, without symbolism and rituals. The symbols must be natural, rational and adequate; but there must be some in every true religion.

(Pal. The New Spirit. Calcutta. 1907. p.4)

Synthesis

The family is a social synthesis, from the family the clan, the commune, is a higher social synthesis, from the commune the nation is a still higher synthesis and from the nation the Empire is and must be a higher, indeed, the highest synthesis.

A synthesis is the reconciliation of conflicting and separatist influences and interests. In the family we find a reconciliation of individualistic interests, individual inclinations, tastes and desires, of the different members of the family. *(Social Life)*

Trust

We are loyal because we believed that God himself has led the British to this country to help it in working out its salvation. And so long as Britain remains at heart true and faithful to her sacred trust, her statesman politicians need fear no harm from the upheaval of national life in India.

(Speech - Shivaji Festival - Calcutta - New India, 26 June 1902)

He indeed is not the wisest man who never made himself a fool. The basic principle of democracy is trust in the people, and respect for their opinion. "Our responsible" leaders have yet to cultivate these, and as long as they have not done so, they may ignore the voice of the people, but will never command or control their affections of their movements.

(Published in Vande Mataram Daily - 17 September 1906)

Trustee

A trustee in private life is required to administer the estate of the trust exactly in the same way, with the same regard for the interests of his charge, as the latter might be expected reasonably to do himself. When one nation assumes the government of another nation, really, as a "trust," it is expected to administer the affairs of the latter exactly with the same care and consideration for its interests, as the subject nation, if they had a national government, might be reasonably expected to do under present conditions.

(Loyalty to Trust)

Truth

You wanted magic; I tried to give you logic. But logic is in bad colour when the popular mind is excited. You wanted *Mantram.* I am no *Rishi* and cannot give *Mantram.* I am ordinary mortal who has all his life been beating his music out, sometimes stumbling upon truth, sometimes arriving at it through tedious process of introspections and circumstances, sometimes perhaps groping in half-truth or deceived by falsehood owing to the limitations of say intellect and education. But I have never spoken a half-truth when I have known the truth. I have never tried to lead people in faith blindfolded. I never expected that all of you would agree with everything I said. Such agreement is neither possible nor desirable. But I never dreamt that there would be protest against my presentation of Swaraj. This protest coming from one who is the leader of the present movement in Bengal has given me the greatest surprise in my life. I for one have no option but to part company with them. Conscience demands this practical protest against a tendency, which I believe to be fatal to our future.

(Delivered - President's Closing Address - 27 March 1921)

Understanding Culture

A tree must not only be judged by its fruit but should be interpreted by it. The child should be interpreted by the man, and not the man by the child. The meaning of the individuals belonging to a type must be sought for and found in its prototype. It is, therefore, that if you really desire to correctly understand and truly appreciate our life and culture, you must seek, my child, first and foremost of all to study, to love, and thus to understand the holy men of India. *(Proto-Types of Humanity)*

Union

What the world, not India nor Europe, but the world wants now is the union of the Indian spirit with this European body.

(Pal, Westwar HO, The Indian Miror, 3 November 1898)

Vaishnava

To the truly pious Vaishnava his body is not his own, but that of his Lord Shree Krishna. The service of his body, therefore, is really service of Krishna himself. His care and regard for his own flesh is of the same character as his care for the image of his Krishna, and he seeks to cultivate the same sacred sentiments in relation to the daily service of his own physical body, as those with which he worships his Deity, through his special symbol.

(Spiritual in Man)

Vow

I for one, can take this vow for myself that if the Government were to strike at the root of higher education in the country, and leave no room for independent action or initiative in the matter of the education of our youths, I would choose poverty and penury for my boys, to sending them to any Government institution.

(Observed—New India, Vol. I, No. 49, 7 August 1902, p.795)

Wages

We have earned only the wages of the labour, and these wages have also gone back, to a very large extent to these foreign exploiters themselves, in the shape of the price, for imported commodities that have been thrust upon us. Leaving practically little or no margin of these increased wages either to the wage earner himself or to his people. *(Economic Resources)*

Yogis in our literature, so discipline their sense, their mind, their emotions and their will, that these outward movements, natural to the senses, the intellect, the emotions and the will, are brought absolutely under control and so these Yogis can remain this state of super-consciousness as long as they desire.

(Driving in Consciousness)

6

Significant Writings

Study of Hinduism

What is Hinduism?

Its General Value: What is Hinduism? The question has not, we are afraid, been satisfactorily answered as yet Not to speak of foreigners whose knowledge must necessarily be more or less superficial, even our own scholars have not as yet cared to render an exhaustive and clear answer to it. Hinduism includes so many things, means so much, and at the same time, one might say almost so little, that though the name has become pretty familiar all over the world, the thing is still more or less unknown to and un-understood by most people. It is a religion, but there are people who would not even call it a religion at all. They understand by it a social economy and nothing more, and judged from certain standpoints, their views would be hard to controvert. A religion Hinduism is not. One might as well take Islam and Christianity and Judaism and the religion of Zoroaster, and that of Confucius, and Taoism, with a good deal of what is known as religion oven among primitive peoples, and forming a compendium of all these, call it a religion. In Hinduism you find elements that coincide with the essentials of most other world-religions, from the lowest to the highest, standing in a mysterious and profound unity. Worship of gods and goddesses like those of Smallpox and Cholera, or even of the Plague; incantations to Sylvan deities, offerings to ancestors, all these are found here standing side by side with the mysteries of the Trinity and the Divine Incarnation, both not less mysterious, though perhaps they might appear to some at least, as far more rational than the essential dogmas of Christianity, — the theosophy of the Mystics and the transcendental emotionalism of a Hafeez, an Omarkhayyam or a Madame Guion. The contradictions of tenets, the complexities of disciplines, the varieties of cultures, that go to form what we know as Hinduism today, are absolutely bewildering, and we cannot blame people for having failed to discover the unity that underlies these.

This very complexity, however, offers to the students of the science or, more strictly speaking, the philosophy of religion, a most interesting subject of study and investigation in this great world-religion. It may justly claim to be somewhat of an epitome of all world-religions, and the history of religious evolution may be traced in it almost from beginning to end, so far as that end has been yet reached by man. And the value of it, to the student of religion, lies in the fact that in almost all its phases, Hinduism is still a living thing. What you discover as fossils of bygone ages in some of the other religions, you may find, perhaps, in this curious system as almost a living specimen, by which you can, therefore, better understand and more carefully and correctly interpret the mystic and mysterious records of other times and other systems — dogmas and disciplines that having fallen into disuse, have lost their key altogether.

The late Professor Max Muller was, therefore, essentially right in his attempt to start his Science of Religion, practically, with an examination of the earlier records of the religion of the Hindus. It was due, no doubt, to his oriental and especially his Vedic studies. Largely it was due also, we believe, to his special theory regarding the origin and growth of the so-called religious sentiment which found such ample support from certain aspects of Vedic and Upanishadic Hinduism. Both these had their limitations, and his conception regarding the evolution of religion needs considerable amendment and correction no doubt, but inspite of it all, he was intuitively on the right track when he sought for the key for the elucidation of the mysteries of human religions, in the experiences of the Hindu people. We do not, however, mean to suggest by this that the other races, had not this key themselves, or that the Hindus have, in any supernatural sense, been a chosen people of God as the Hebrews are described in the Christian Scriptures. By no means so. All that we mean is, as already mentioned above, that while the other religions have passed beyond their earlier stages, Hinduism, as known to us, has not done so, though it has reached in some parts, the stages wherein even the most advanced Christian or Muhammadan religious consciousness stands today. We mean that Hinduism is not like some of the great historical religions, an individual religion so to say, but it is a community or a family of religions, some in lower and earlier, some in higher and more advanced stages of growth.

Indeed, it is this peculiarity that distinguishes ethnic types of religion from the credal types. All credal religions grew out of some ethnic religion: Buddhism grew out of Hinduism, Christianity out of Judaism, and Islam out of the old Arab ritualism and idolatry. And Hinduism, Judaism, as well as the ancient religion of Arabia, are all ethnic religions, that owned their peculiarities to the peculiar race characteristics, both mental and social, of the particular ethnic groups with which they stood related, and that took their special lines of evolution under the influence of their special nature surroundings, of their social contacts and conflicts with and accretions from their neighbouring groups of humanity. These ethnic religions are always exclusive, counterminious with the particular ethnic groups related to them, refusing accession to their ranks, by mere religious conversion, from other ethnic groups. Ethnic religions are, therefore, also extremely tolerant of other ethnic religions. Not so, however, the credal religions.

A definite creed makes these somewhat of a non-national religion: men of all climes and all colour, by accepting the creed may enter its fold, and become members of the same Church or religious denomination. This, however, makes all credal religions more or less rigid, exclusive, and intolerant. The uniformity of creed and the necessary uniformity of discipline and worship and ritual, leave no room for vital divergence of thoughts or cultures within a credal system. Wherever and whenever such divergences do appear, as they are bound to, owing to the variety of human, capacity and the diversity of man's experiences and ideas, they are decreed as heresies. Contradictory things cannot, therefore, find place in credal religions.

Where the anti-credal stage is remembered and the ancient and preparatory process of evolution still recognised as sacred and divine, as is done by Christianity, it is preserved as the Old Testament, — an old law, and old ideal, which was good in the olden time, but practically superseded by or subsumed into the new, as childhood is superseded by and subsumed into youth, and youth is done by and into maturity. The old exists as a memory, which may be cultivated for the deepening of love or quickening of gratitude; but for all that it is not the living present, and has not, therefore, a substantiality just now.

Though transcending the limitations of ethnic codes and characters, and therefore assuming a kind of universality, yet credal religions for the new exclusiveness they develop, which is far more rigid in one way, because of its claims to absolutism, than the social but otherwise tolerant exclusivism of ethnic system — cannot find us a key to the elucidation of the infinite variety of human rites and human beliefs; Ethnic systems are somewhat better guides in this matter.

When an ethnic system reaches the universal stage, directly without passing through the mediating credal stage, its value as a key to the solution of the mysteries of the religious experiences of man is simply immeasurable. It stands then as a living museum of human religions, where the diligent student may study the dead with the help of the living, and interpret the past in the light of the present.

The study of Hinduism has, however, apart from this general value to the student of religious Philosophy, a special value to our age. The religious thoughts and ideals of humanity are passing through strange and mighty transformations around us. Not to speak of Europe, even in what has hitherto been regarded as the sleepy and changeless land of the Orient, human culture seems to be running fast into new channels, revolutionising ancient ideals and institutions everywhere. New influences are at work creating new problems; new thoughts and new knowledge are spreading, quickening new doubts, and working up new conflicts that demand everywhere a new synthesis and settlement in Persia. We have not only new political forces pushing themselves up for a democratic Constitution, but new religious movements as well, one of which, that of Babism at least, has already made itself heard outside the Kingdom of the Shah. In Afganistan, the working of the new leaven is seen in the ideals and activities of the young Prince who rules her destinies.

Not to speak of Japan, which openly entered into the larger life of modern humanity, upon her own rights. Even China, the eternally changeless, is throbbing under the pressure of new thoughts and aspirations which, though the details are so far as known to us, could not but create fresh doubts and raise fresh demands for a reinterpretation and readjustment of the old life and religion of the people. In India the religious thought and life of the people are passing through the throes, it seems, of a new birth. Hinduism and Islam have both felt the shock of the new world-thoughts and world-ideas, and have, somewhere consciously and openly and some where secretly and unconsciously, been adapting themselves to the new forces and conditions about them.

The Hindus, bewildered by the sudden influx of alien ideas and ideals, seem as yet to have scarcely had the needful peace and leisure, to take a full and correct measure either of their old ideals or of the new ones; and while some are trying to embrace the new to the prejudice of the old, and others are seeking to cling with the tenacity of unreasoning faith to the old, to the entire exclusion of the new, the religious life and thought of the nation at large seem to be slowly but surely breaking out of their old moorings, without competent knowledge or guidance. It is an age of universal questioning and universal doubt; and restatement of the old varieties of life has become imperative, to settle these at rest, in every part of the civilized world. A study of Hinduism, in the light of the highest culture of the times, is absolutely necessary for the purpose of this restatement, to the Hindus themselves.

Such a study has also, we hold, a special value even to the modern western students and thinkers. There are many problems of modern religious thought and life in Europe and America and even problems affecting the very future of modern Western civilization and humanity upon which Hindu experience and Hindu ideals may possibly throw much helpful light. Hindu theology has, it seems, passed through a good deal of the trials through which Christian theology seems to be passing today.

The conflicts of science and scripture, of reason and revelation, of ritualism and ethicism, of Popery and Protestantism, not to mention the profounder problems concerning the Personality and the Incarnation of God and the religio-ethical problems of Divine. Immanence and Providence and human freedom and responsibility, — problems before which modern Western thought seems so often to sit down almost in utter despair, leading some to abandon reason altogether and seek refuge in unreasoning and unquestioning faith, and others to give themselves up to a so-called rational, but essentially materialistic view of life; — all these or most of them in some shape or other seem to have been faced and more or less satisfactorily solved by the ancient and medieval Hindus. All their solutions may not be acceptable to our age.

It would, indeed, be too much to expect such absolute and unerring illumination from ancient experience anywhere, for the solution of modern problems. Our age is different from theirs. The forms of our thinking are, also, more or less different. Though the character of our present day problems may be the same as that of the problems that faced people a couple of thousand years ago, still their contents are not, and could not in any case be expected to be the same. It is not, therefore, contended that the Christian consciousness of our age will be able to solve its complex problems by bodily accepting the solutions of similar problems that may have satisfied the ancient or medieval Hindus. Yet at the same time we do claim for a careful and reverent study of Hinduism this much, at least, that it is capable of furnishing valuable hints and suggestions, by working up which even modern Western thought might find its way made a bit clearer than before, and might thus, arrive at more satisfactory conclusions, on some points, than what it has hitherto succeeded in doing.

In fact, it would be impossible to deny that the study of non-Christian systems, and more particularly of Brahmanical philosophy and Buddhistic religion, has already had an almost perceptible influence in the broadening and possibly even the deepening of modern Christian thought. The strongest note in current of religious life and thought, on both sides of the Atlantic, is undoubtedly that of Divine Immanence. The speculative philosophy of the last century and the highest generalisations of modern science have both contributed very materially, no doubt, to bring about this result. But the influence of Oriental researches seems to have been almost as effective, in helping this some what novel thought-movement in Latin Christianity especially in its spiritual aspects, — an influence that has received the spiritual ideals that had been contributed by Greek thought and more particularly by the Alexendrian Fathers, to the growth and expansion of Christian-thought and piety in the earlier centuries. And yet the deeper notes of Hinduism have not as yet been sounded by any of these European Orientalists.

The best of them have only presented partial views of this great world system. The interpreters of Hinduism among our own people also have either been too much under the influence of modern Materialism, miscalled rationalism, or too blind and unreasoning adherents of ancient mysticism. And both these, rank Rationalism and blind bigotry, are equally unfitted for the work which they seem to have laid out before them.

Indeed, the need of a critical and intelligent study of Hinduism has been recognised by Western scholars from the days of Sir William Jones, Cole brook, Horace Hayman Wilson, J. Moore and others. And Christian scholars and missionaries have now and again applied themselves to this work during the last hundred years, and more. Even the Hindus are beholden to some, of them for their own revived interest in the study of their own literatures. They owe a special debt of gratitude to Sir William Jones, Colebrook, Wilson and Muir, for their researches into their ancient book's, and the rites and creeds of even their existing sects and denominations, a good deal of which had lain even beyond their own knowledge so long.

But these scholars, though great linguists and painstaking and well-read Oriental students, were not philosophers and they could not therefore properly interpret the meaning and significance of what they so faithfully described or translated. Their successors in the study of Hindu-religion have many of them been Christian Evangelists, and these had no doubt, something of a philosophy of religion with them; but it has been only Christian Philosophy, the generalisation of a different kind of religious thought and experience, allied to a somewhat different type of piety, and their sectarian philosophy has necessarily been able to render them but little help in the interpretation of a foreign system. To most of them what did not run on all fours with Christian dogma or Christian ethics, was necessarily an untruth or an evil and what did seem to do so must have been due to Christian influence. At best, in their estimate the Hindu records referred only to "The unknown God.

Professor Max Muller's was, without doubt, an attempt not merely towards a wider propagation of Hindu lore, but also at a rational and modern, that is scientific and philosophical, explanation of it. His is, so far, the only interpretation of Hinduism that has been attempted for the English speaking peoples at any rate. But the late Professor's interpretation of Hinduism suffers from the limitations of his particular Philosophy of religion, and equally also from the somewhat narrow view that he took of both the comparative and the historic methods upon which, as a matter of course, he had sought to build up that philosophy.

It seems, indeed that Professor Max Muller's theological studies grew out of his philological studies and he therefore sought naturally, to apply the same kind of comparative examination to theology as had rendered such excellent results in establishing an organic kinship, for instance, between Sanskrit and Greek and Latin, in the domain of philology. He followed his German masters and fellow-workers in recognising in one common pre-historic stock, the origin of the Hindu, the Greek, the Roman, the Tueton, and the Saxon and other European races. The linguistic affinity was too marked and unerring to be ignored.

So far he was on the right track. But Professor Max Muller's philology stopped short of the fundamental philosophy which it suggested and which alone could fully explain it. What is the significance of this common linguistic structure? This is a question which does not seem to have troubled Professor Max Muller further than to suggest that people who speak languages that reveal an original structural unity or affinity, must have at one time, lived together and belonged to one and the same race or tribe.

And yet, the close and organic affinity that he seems to have recognised between thought and language should have revealed a much profounder significance in the affinity between Sanskrit and Greek and Latin and other languages of the Indo-European group, than what Professor Max Muller seems to have fully realised, or at least than what he cared to utilise in building up his so-called science of comparative religion. The discovery of this structural affinity among these different languages is a tiling of supreme value to the student of comparative religion. For the structure of a language reveals the original structure of the thought, — the primordial cast of mind — of those who have been using that language from pre-historic times.

Linguistic affinity implied affinity of a deeper kind, — namely, thought affinity. It meant that people to whom this family of languages belonged have, from pre-historic times, been approaching the same world-problems, practically from the same mental standpoint. And the wonderful affinity that the study of the primitive religions of these peoples discovered in the fundamental religious conceptions, could thus, be very easily explained by this thought affinity. And had the learned Professor approached the fundamental problems of his so-called Science of Religion from this viewpoint, his contribution to the study of Comparative Religion would have been far more valuable, and his interpretation of Hinduism also would have been richer by far and more satisfactory than what they are generally found to be.

Max Muller's Presentation of Hinduism

The fundamental problem before Comparative Religion is the origin of the religious consciousness in man. Professor Max Muller sought to solve it by the Infinite first ascribing it to an innate sense of the Infinite in man; and this intuition of the Infinite in man was first quickened by his nature-surroundings. This is the fundamental idea of Professor Max Muller's philosophy of religion. Possessed with this one idea, he sought for its illustrations in the earliest religious experiences of man as recorded in Sanskrit and Greek literature, and starting from this Nature-Religion he sought to trace the evolution of the religious sentiment, up to what he called Theosophy, — culminating in the consciousness of God as the Soul of the Universe and the Self of man, throwing, in the course of this up-building of his Science of Religion, considerable light, now and again, upon the affinities between, not only Vedic and Hellenic religions, — but even between the more advanced forms of Hinduism, Christianity and Islam. But valuable as his history of Hinduism undoubtedly is, it is, after all, more or less partial, and does not cover the whole field, nor advance the solution of the most perplexing problems of this strange and weird system.

Professor Max Muller, more perhaps than any other European Oriental scholar, has himself, however, raised some of these very perplexing problems before the modern student of human, and specially, of Hindu religion. In his studies of the Vedic religion, he has presented the world with a charming picture of the particularistic or naturalistic religion of the primitive Hindus. And one can understand this phase of religious evolution more or less. This sort of Naturalism or Particularism is not peculiar to ancient Hinduism alone. For religion in the earlier stages is always and everywhere of a Particularistic or Naturalistic type. We find these Nature-deities in ancient Greece and Rome. They are common to all Aryan religions. And we find traces though not of a Naturalistic stage, but distinctly of a Particularistic one, even in Semitic records. Even the so-called Monotheism of the ancient Hebrews is pretty generally admitted, by modern scholars, to have been really not Monotheism, which would preclude the very possibility of more than one God, but simply *Monolatry*, which, without denying the existence of other gods, simply adhered absolutely to the worship of one God. Indeed, the existence of these other gods, — "Strange Gods," as they are called, — is never denied absolutely in the old Hebrew records. In the Psalms we have it that—

"In the council of the gods sat God, where the existence of the other gods is not denied, but only the supremacy of God — the Lord Almighty of Israel, over them is declared and assorted. In the earlier records we find Taleveh, in fact, struggling to secure and prove his superiority to these other gods. He is there only one

God among many gods. Other peoples have their own gods, and so long as these peoples do not come into conflict with the people of Israel, the God of Israel does not come into conflict with their gods. The God of Israel does not, in the earlier records, claim authority over other nations.

This, indeed, as we have already pointed out, is the common characteristic of all Ethnic religions. They are all, in the lowest stages, of a particularistic type. And though Vedic or Hellenic particularism differs very materially from early Hebrew particularism, still the former is not absolutely un-understandable by those whose religious traditions have been more decidedly Semitic than Aryan.

Thus European students can generally enter into the spirit of Vedic-naturalism and they more or less enjoy the poetry of the religious imagination of the primitive Hindu. When Professor Max Muller worked up his studies from the Vedas to the Upanishads, and presented to the English-speaking peoples, the profoundly spiritual and ethical ideals and cultures of philosophic Hinduism, — what he termed, Theosophy, — and especially as in doing so he tried to explain and interpret the *Brahma-Jnanam* or Gnosticism of the Hindus, in the terms of Christian gnosticism, seeking to establish some sort of a parallelism between the teachings of the Hindu saints and sages, and those of the Alexandrian Fathers. Oregon, Clement, Tertullion and others, he was able to present something both intelligible and interesting to the European reader. And all this has helped to awaken curiosity, if not to create an interest in Hinduism among a large and increasing class of people on both sides of the Atlantic.

We are thankful for all this pioneering work. Indian culture and civilization owe a debt to Professor Max Muller for all this, which is immense, and must remain always unpaid and unpayable. And it casts no reflection upon the worth of his works to say that some of the most complex problems that these works have raised, have not been satisfactorily solved by them. Every student and scholar, however valuable their works, and whatever finality might be claimed for some of the results of their labours, must raise questions which either elude their grasp, or which they find it impossible to tackle within the short span of life granted them here below. Professor Max Muller has done more than what has been even attempted by any other person so far, to popularise Hindu thoughts and ideals among English-speaking peoples; and if still a good deal remains yet to be done, it does not reflect upon the richness of his intellect or the breadth of his acquisition, but proves only the depth, the complexity and the vastness of the field in which he laboured with such zeal and such success throughout a lifetime.

Professor Max Muller's presentation of Hinduism seems, owing to this reason, to have as much interested as it has perplexed the English and American reader. For, people have failed, so to reconcile the spiritual teachings of Hinduism, which the learned Professor tried to emphasise, with the current ceremonialism and so-called Idolatry of the Hindu people. The problem of this so-called Idolatry is an unsolved problem even to the vast majority of educated Hindus themselves. As, for European and American readers of Professor Max Muller, many of them have even been tempted to regard his interpretations of Hinduism as far-fetched and ingenuous, — the result of a reading of his own advanced views and ideals into the crude utterances of the ancient rhapsodists and mystics of India. And this suspicion has received support from the fact that neither Professor Max Muller, nor, so far as we know, any other European Orientalist has trial to present a consistent and philosophic study of present day Hinduism, though many have written and spoken very highly of its ancient records, while Christian propagandists have almost uniformly painted the former in the darkest colour possible. And all this conflict and confusion of estimates and interpretations have left Hinduism an unsolved and insoluble riddle to the general European mind.

General Observations

Methods of Study

What is needed to remove this confusion is a right method of study. In the first place, it must be always borne in mind that Hinduism does not fully explain itself. Nothing, indeed, in the universe ever does so. For, everything is in an almost endless chain of relations and must, therefore, to be fully understood, be interpreted by and through these varied relations. Isolation is not only death, but it is chaos and unreason, in God's world. The particular never can interpret itself; it must, to be rightly understood, be brought under the light of the general or universal. Hinduism is a particularity, it presents a particular class or classes of group or groups of religious phenomena, or spiritual experiences, the real meaning and purpose of which can never be got at, unless they are brought under some general truths or principles. In other words, the study of any particular religion must be entered upon by the light of some general Philosophy of Religion, — which shall sum up the highest generalisations of the religious experiences of mankind.

And the method of study here must, at once, be scientific and philosophical, — scientific, that is, based upon an exanimation of actual facts and experiences, and its results must be capable, to some extent at least, of verification, and philosophical, that is, have for its background the ultimate generalisation of all human knowledge and experience. This combination of science and philosophy is necessary in a right method of investigation of the religious phenomena, for the very simple reason that religion itself is both a science and a philosophy.

It is a philosophy because dealing with ultimate principles and varieties. It is a science because it aims by various methods and disciplines, — physical and psycho-physical as well as intellectual and moral, — to actualise in life and conduct, the ultimate realities of philosophy.

Indeed, religion and philosophy are one. In India, at least, this truth has never been lost sight of. For religion in its theoretic aspect is philosophy; philosophy in the practical side is religion. The methods of investigating the phenomena of religion cannot, therefore, be purely speculative or *a priori,* nor yet absolutely positive or a *posteriori,* but there must be a combination here of both science and metaphysics. Indeed, almost every attempt to build up a Philosophy of Religion, from the time of Hume up to our own days, has partaken, more or less, of this dual character; and Prof. Max Muller has even called his Philosophy of Religion, openly and defiantly a Science, and the methods that he adopted in his investigations, though they need considerable correction and amendment, — largely justified the name.

The analysis and classification of experience is the universal end of all science. The science of Religion means a systematised knowledge of religious experience. Its end is or ought to be the analysis and classification of the particular class of human experience called religious; and the science of Religion in seeking this end must follow the approved methods by which it is sought in other departments of human experience. But every science takes for granted the ultimate varieties which form the fundamental ground of the particular group of human experience it seeks to investigate. The necessary postulates of Physical science, for instance, are the truth and reality of universal sense, perceptions that testify to the so-called properties of material objects and prove their existence.

It is not the province of this science to examine, analyse, and verify the truth of these perceptions, or discover their real character. The existence of the material world and our relations with that world through our senses, the general trustworthiness of universal sense testimony, these are the assumptions of Physical Science. It starts with these necessary assumptions. The psychological group of the sciences also do, and must, similarly start with and work upon certain truths, which they must accept on trust, and take for granted. It is the function of philosophy, or strictly speaking, of metaphysics, to investigate, discover and establish the fundamental varieties involved in our psychological experiences. And as we ascend in the investigation of our experience from the material to the mental plane, — using this word in its widest sense, to include every department of our inner life, from the mere psychological to the highest spiritual aspects of it, — its dependence upon philosophy or metaphysics increases in a direct ratio.

The physical sciences may not trouble themselves with ultimate varieties; but yet even those cannot move one step without the aid of Mathematics, and Mathematics, though regarded popularly as the most positive of all the sciences, can not divorce itself altogether from philosophy or metaphysics. Time and Space are the two things with which Mathematics deals, and Time and Space are really unintelligible except in the light of the most profound and abstruse metaphysics. Space is extension, time is succession, and both inhere, so to say, as primary properties, not in the matter but in the mind. Mathematics takes for granted the infinity of both time and space, which is made possible really by positing an Infinite Mind behind them; and thus even Mathematics runs dangerously into the bewildering labyrinths of metaphysical speculations. There is, however, a view of the physical sciences, which does avoid philosophy or metaphysics, and for all so-called practical, that is empirical purposes, it may well do so. But the biological group of the sciences cannot as easily do it. For though biology in the lowest stages may possibly avoid psychological investigations, in the higher forms, not mere birth, growth, and decay, with the functions of reproduction, represent the only, and least of all, the highest manifestation of life. In the higher forms, sense-activity is very closely associated with life, and sense-activity cannot be interpreted by biology alone; but we must seek for its real meaning and significance at the hands of psychology, which is again very intimately related to metaphysics and cannot, indeed, move one single step-without it.

And the group of human experiences commonly known as religious cannot by any means, be put on the same level with those that furnish materials for astronomy or physics, or chemistry, or anatomy and physiology, though all these have always had a great influence in shaping man's religious ideals and conceptions. They belong, taking the lowest and least speculative view of them, to the domain of psychology. They are mental or emotional experiences, and are therefore, more directly and intimately allied to philosophy and metaphysics, than any others. Philosophy and metaphysics cannot, consequently, be at all ignored in the investigation of these experiences, and any attempt to reduce them to systematised knowledge, must first of all discover their philosophical or metaphysical foundations. The Science of Religion, in other words, must be, as we have already said, different from the other sciences in as much as its treatment must be partly philosophical or metaphysical and partly scientific.

Method of Science of Religion

In fact, until very recently, theologians and philosophers had almost exclusively followed the a *priori* method in the investigation of religious truths; and any strictly scientific treatment of the subject was all but absolutely inconceivable to our forefathers. David Hume was, perhaps, the first English thinker, who sought to approach the phenomena of human religion from a purely natural, as opposed to a supernatural standpoint. Since then deists and sceptics have occasionally tried, no doubt, to follow in his wake and to trace the origin of the religious consciousness in man to his ordinary physical or psychical experiences, but the standard works on the subject followed still the old a *priori* methods, and the general literature on religion continued, for a long time, to belong to the domain of speculative philosophy.

It was only in the last century that "the discovery of Sanskrit," and of the Comparative Method that directly resulted from it, on the one hand, and the birth of the science of anthropology which sought to investigate and classify the primitive life and experiences of humanity and the critical study of the religious records of the different nations of the world, on the other, commenced for the first time to almost revolutionise the old and familiar methods of investigating religious truths. And yet, a little over thirty years ago, even Professor Max Muller had to plead piteously before an enlightened Oxford audience, in justification of what he called this Science of Comparative Religion.

Every Science has its own proper methods of investigation. What are the special methods of investigation for the Science of Religion, then? The answer to this question has already been partially anticipated by the assertion of the close and organic relation that this science has to Philosophy or Metaphysics. Observation, experiment, verification, these are the common methods of all science, and these must also, more or less, be applicable to the study of the religious phenomena; we say more or less because the methods of experiment here must be psychological and owing to the almost infinite variety, complexity and subtlety of all mental phenomena the verification of results here must, necessarily, be less positive, and must be examined more in the mass than in isolated or individual cases as is necessary in the case of mere physical or even biological phenomena.

But still, any strictly scientific investigation of the religious phenomena cannot altogether ignore these common methods of science. The methods that must, however, be peculiar to the Science of Religion, are the Comparative and the Historic methods, the two worked together, and always under the guidance of the Law of Evolution.

Evolution of Religion, however, must follow the universal lines of mental or emotional evolution, — must follow, in other words, the Dialectics of Reason. This necessity is imposed upon religion by its very nature as both a mental and an emotional phenomenon. As both thought and sentiment move from unity to duality and fulfil themselves in totality, as the movement of reason is from thesis to antithesis and from antithesis to synthesis in which it finally fulfils and realises itself, as all evolution, in the words of Herbert Spencer, is from homogeneity to differentiation and from differentiation to integration, so also the course of religious evolution whether in the individual or in the race, must be from unity or homogeneity or thesis, through duality or differentiation or antithesis, to totality or integration or synthesis. And this course of evolution which speculative philosophy lays down as the only natural course for the growth of human religions, is found upon a careful study of the different world religions to be what has been actually and universally followed by them. It has been the one universal course of evolution of religion whether in India or Judea, China or Greece.

This Dialetic is the contribution of philosophy to the Science of Religion. This is, so to say, its primary assumption and like every postulate of science this Dialectic is fully verified and justified by a critical study of and research into the actualities of religious history. Whatever methods, whether comparative or historic, we may adopt in the investigation of the phenomena of human religion, their results must always be tested, connected and verified by this Dialectic of Reason, this Law of Evolution. For, the application of this law of mental evolution can alone verify the truth of our interpretations or correct the errors of our assumptions and inferences. This is of special value in the working out of the Comparative Method, in religious investigations. To cite a concrete instance, let us take the so-called idolatry of primitive culture, and the worship of stocks and stones by an advanced people like the Hindus, or the Greeks. A Negro walks out of his hut and stumbles upon a piece of rock or flint, and says — "ta ta" — "thou art here, I did not know," and putting it in his bag, proceeds, on his day's errand. Should he succeed in his errand, he attributes the success to the kindly influence of the rock or flint, brings it back home, and sets it up among the other objects of his reverence or worship, and henceforth it becomes a fetish to him. Here is distinctly some kind of idolatry. And there is also the so-called stone-god (the sacred black-stone) worshipped by some Hindus. The one form of worship looks, from the outside, very much like the other; and judging from the outside, comparing the two phenomena with one another, one may easily be led to set Negro fetishism and Hindu idolatry on the same plane.

The application of the mere Comparative Method would be bound to lead to such a conclusion. But the question is, are all comparisons valid? Does not the validity of comparison, as a method of the investigation of truth, depend upon some fundamental unity existing between the objects or phenomena thus brought up for comparison with one another? The same class of objects or phenomena alone allow valid and scientific comparison between them, and not those that have no such community. Can we put Negro fetishism and Hindu idolatry in the same class? This is the primary question here. And the Historic Method can alone render a correct answer to this question. Negro fetishism and Hindu idolatry can both, no doubt, be classed as religious phenomena; there is thus one common basis between these, to justify comparison. But is this sufficient? The history of Negro fetishism and of Hindu idolatry can alone answer this question. Is there any similarity in their history, in the story of their growth? So the historic method must be brought in to verify or correct the comparative.

Nor will this be sufficient The history of these institutions must be read in the light of evolution; and then, and only then, could we arrive at the truth about them. There is worship of stones among the Negroes, and it is also found among the Hindus. But does a fetishistic interpretation of Hindu idolatry, fit in with the other aspects of the Hindu religion? Religion is only one, though undoubtedly the greatest, of the many concerns of lift. It represents only one side of human culture. Do the other sides of Hindu religion, and the other departments of Hindu culture, agree with the religion and the culture of the Negro? If not, how is it that their religion should, even in some part, show such strange similarity? Mere comparison cannot solve the riddle. Isolated similarities or even apparent identities do not justify scientific comparison, and the application of the comparative method to such cases must necessarily produce wrong results.

Take, for instance, again the institution of divorce. Divorce is very common among the primitive races of the Pacific. In India the custom obtains among the hill tribes. Divorce also exists in England and America. Comparing, then, the institution of divorce as existing among the barbarians of the Pacific or the aborigines of India, with that found among Englishmen and Americans, shall we ascribe the same significance to both, and conclude that at least so far as their marriage customs or laws are concerned, the Indian aborigines stand on the same level of higher civilization and culture as the European races, and are, necessarily, superior so far to the Hindus among whom divorce is unknown? Yet the comparative method alone gives no other result; and it only shows up its utter insufficiency and fallibility unless corrected by the Historic Methods and verified by the general Law of Evolution.

In the example under notice, for instance, the application of the Historic Method at once brings out the fact that divorce, among primitive races, is associated with loose marriage bonds, while, among civilized peoples, like those of Europe or America, it exists along with very strict and rigid marriage ties and we at once discover the truth that the meaning of divorce among people whose marriage customs are very loose, and who have not as yet risen, indeed, to a sense of the sanctity of the marital bond, must necessarily be very different from what it signifies among people whose marriage customs have passed through many advanced stages of evolution, and the institution of marriage among whom has reached the state of absolute monogamy. Divorce is common in loose marriage customs, where men and women can unite and be separated almost at their will without any serious let or hindrance from the social authority over them. It is, again, a device, consciously organised to meet an almost dire necessity arising out of the very rigidity of the marital bond and the sancitity of the nuptial relation on strictly monogamous countries. And its meaning, its moral and spiritual significance, differ very widely in the two cases. But this difference is discovered only by those who have studied the history of the institution of marriage and are thoroughly acquainted with the course of its evolution. And it shows that the Comparative Method is a very misleading guide to truth unless associated with the Historic Method, and illumined by the General Law of Evolution of the objects, ideas or institutions to which it is sought to be applied.

There can, therefore, be no valid comparison between Negro-fetishism and the so-called idolatry of the Hindus, because the two do not stand on the same plane of religious history or religious evolution. The one belongs to primitive culture, and fits in well with the general level of intelligence and civilization of the inhabitants of Tropical Africa. It is not, so far as we know, associated with any refined religious philosophy, nor has it any long course of religious evolution behind it. The other is found in a far higher state of intelligence and culture. It is supported by an abstruse philosophy, however casuistic it may scorn to us. It has a course of most wonderful religious evolution behind it. There are indications of a kind of primitive fetishism in the Vedas.

But the ceremonialism of current Hinduism stands on an altogether different plane. It is not even what Taylor would call a survived of Vedic religion. Hindu idolatry, as we find it today, is decidedly post-Vedic. It is positively post-Vedantic as well, developed after the inculcation of the profound gnosticism or *Brahma-jnanam* of the Upanishads. It is an offshoot of Pauranic Hinduism. And the moment we thus trace its history, we find that whatever may be its origin or significance, whatever value may be attached to it as a method of religious or spiritual culture, whatever may have been its moral effect upon the Hindu people, we can by no means class it together with the fetishism of primitive culture. Primitive fetishism, in any case, is not much of a mystery, — Hindu idolatry undoubtedly is. And the mere comparative method will not solve it. It is likely to increase the existing confusion more than ever. What is needed in the study of Hinduism, therefore, as in the study of any other world-religion, is to combine the Comparative with the Historic Method, and work the two together under the guidance of the Law of Religious Evolution.

Theory of Religious Evolution Logical and Chronological

Logical Moments

The evolution of religion means the evolution of man's ideas, sentiments, and activities in relation to God, or whatever may stand to Him, for the time being for that complex concept. It is, therefore, an essentially mental or psychological evolution, and it must consequently follow the dialectic reason. The progress of this evolution must, in other words, be as we have already stated, from Thesis to Antithesis and from Antithesis to Synthesis, or to use Herbert Spencer's phraseology, from Homogeneity to Differentiation and from Differentiation to Integration. This much must be conceded; but some people have, however, mixed up the logical process with the idea of a chronological succession, and have laid three distinct stages of religious evolution. Even no less a person than Prof. Caird, the present Master of Balliol, has lent himself, unwittingly, to this misconception, by dividing the course of religious evolution into three distinct stages, namely, the Objective, the Subjective, and the Universal.

Our first objection here is to the word 'stage' itself, as an exceedingly misleading term to apply to the process of evolution, though for want of a more accurate word, it is often, and loosely, used in the literature of evolution. A stage is associated, in the first place, with the idea of a halt, a temporary cessation of movement, and even where there is no halt, it indicates, at any rate, a definite end to what has gone before.

But does evolution know anywhere such a halt or rest or separation? In biological evolution are not what are called the lower stages reproduced always, in quicker succession or under subtler forms, in the higher organism? Does not every human organism react the whole past of its race, in its growth from the cell to the human foetus and from the foetus to the grown up baby, and from the baby to the full developed man or woman? And is it not the universality of evolution everywhere? If it be said that the word stage means here mere landmarks and is not meant to suggest any actual bait or separation, even then the idea seems to be incompatible with our conception and knowledge of the law of evolution. A land mark is what marks the progress of a moving thing. It must, therefore, necessarily stand outside that tiling. But what are called stages of religious evolution do not surely stand outside the evolving religion, but form parts of itself. But in evolution, religion is perpetually changing and cannot have such landmarks or stages in itself, though these may exist outride as memories and records. And if we take up these records again, we find as we shall see, not three but almost countless stages or landmarks of progress in every one of the great world religions.

The fact, indeed, seems to be that in tracing the evolution of religion, Professor Caird has naturally followed the dialectic of Reason; and his Objective, Subjective, and Universal, are only synonyms for Thesis, Antithesis, and Synthesis or Homogeneity, Differentiation and Integration. As an indication, therefore, of the logical process of the evolution of the religious consciousness this enumeration may well be accepted as unexceptionable. But still, it cannot be dented that it lends itself easily to what may be regarded as a chronological succession, and is, consequently, somewhat misleading.

Indeed, this misconception is likely to arise from the survival among half-educated people of the old pre-Darwinian notion of evolution, as a rectilinear process, which easily admitted of stages that had been reached and left behind. But the modern conception of the evolutionary process is that its movement is not rectilinear but spiral, that it is a progression through what may be called a dual process of evolution and involution that it is marked as moving constantly forward and backward, both these movements in this zig-zag fashion, perpetually leading to a higher point. And this mechanical, and therefore necessarily, very inadequate and imperfect symbol of what is essentially an ideal mental principle, makes the nearest approach to the truth about evolution, on account of its suggesting, if it may not reproduce, the dialectic of Reason. For in the evolution of thought or in the process of reason, Thesis, Antithesis, and Synthesis are not three permanent stages, so that when Thesis is passed and Antithesis is reached, the former is passed for ever, never to recur again, and when through this Antithesis, the third or last stage, that of Synthesis is reached, thought attains its finality and perfection, and further movement of reason comes to an end.

By no means so, thought never attains such absolute perfection. The movement of Reason never reaches finality. Its process has been described of old, as that of eternal generation. And movement is of the very essence of thought — the movement of Reason from Thesis through Antithesis to Synthesis or from Homogeneity through Differentiation to integration, — is the very soul of it. When this movement is stopped, thought or Reason ceases to be. It is the state of what the Buddhists would perhaps call *Nirvana*. It is the state of Undifferentiated Being, what Hegelians call Pure Being, and Pure Being, according to Hegel's dictum, is Pure Nothing. It may be an unconscious, or what some call a super conscious condition. But religion is a concern, very largely, if not absolutely, of our conscious life, and in religious evolution, there can be no such finality as the enumeration of a definite number of its stages of evolution of growth would seem to suggest reason or thought moves perpetually and recurrently from Thesis to Antithesis and from Antithesis to Synthesis.

There is no point in the history of Thought, wherein this process is absent And there is no point in the evolution of any religion which is essentially an evolution of Thought or Reason where also this process or Reason is or can be absent. To say that any religion was Objective at the beginning, became Subjective subsequently in the middle, and finally reached the Universal stage in the end, is to declare that it has fully and absolutely realised itself, that there is nothing further for it to strive after and attain, and that the Religious Idea has reached its finality, its consummation, its Nirvana here. It means that it has ceased to evolve any more. And to say so is, really, to condemn it beyond the pale of all organic movement and growth, declare it, in other words, to be no more a moving living religion, but a dead one.

We do not forget that almost all the so-called historical religions — Buddhism, Christianity, and Islam, owing to their credal character, have claimed some sort of a finality for their revelations. But even here, as history shows, there has been growth, if not of the religious ideal, in any case of the religious consciousness of their votaries, through the centuries that they have held sway over the life and thought of a large portion of humanity. The History of all these religions has a story of almost incessant struggles and conflicts to either understand their message or to actualise their ideals and doctrines in life and experience. Even if the fundamental dogmas of Christianity be held to have remained the same since the days of St. Paul or the Councils of Trent or Nice, yet not even the most rigid Christian orthodoxy would for a moment refuse to admit that there has been all through these centuries a growth in this world of what may be called the Christian consciousness.

No one, indeed, can read the history of the Christian Church without noticing the evolution of Christian thought and life through the last two thousand years. The same process of evolution is also seen in the history of both Buddhism and Islam. Even in our day there are what may be called progressive movements in all these credal systems. There is the New Orthodoxy in Anglican Christianity, there is neo-Buddhism in Siam and Ceylon, and there is Babism, the latest phase of change in Islam, in Persia. Indeed, such changes are inevitable. When men's conceptions regarding Nature and society are passing through transformations on all sides, it would be idle to expect that religion alone would remain unaffected by this influx of new world ideas and ideals.

In fact, the history of every religion bears testimony to the perpetual recurrence of the three moments of the dialectic of Reason in them. Commencing with the earliest or Perceptive and Naturalistic state, man's religion proceeds perpetually onward describing what may be called an endless series of elliptical figures in almost incessant succession. Thus what in the present state of our knowledge we have accepted as the earliest state of religious evolution, may be regarded as the state of Thesis or Homogeneity, — though even this may have been, for aught we know, preceded by still more primitive states of evolution; and what we accept now, somewhat arbitrarily; it will have to be admitted, — as the state of Thesis in the religious evolution of the primitive man, may have possibly been itself the Synthesis of a previous circle or series.

For we know from subsequent history that the Synthesis of a lower and preceding state, becomes always the Thesis of the next higher and succeeding process. And so on the course of evolution proceeds recurrently and perpetually, from Thesis through Antithesis to Synthesis. And this is so, because of the progressive nature of human thought and human culture.

Stage of Conflicts and Progress

The history of religious progress ever so far as we can trace it, is really the story of the recurrent conflicts between ancient tradition and modern experience. Tradition hands down certain dogmas, disciplines, certain ideals, cultures, as true, and binding upon every man to every generation, with the latest interpretations and commendation of these, and they are, at first accepted on trust, and without question. This is the state of thesis. But the new generation also gathers new experiences, either through closer views of its own environments or through foreign contact and influence. And there arises slowly a conflict between new experiences and old traditions, between new truths, and old authorities. This is the state of antithesis. This conflict, however, cannot last for ever. Thought abhors these conflicts and contradictions, and puts forth all its efforts to set these at rest. Victory, however, is never found to belong, in these conflicts, absolutely either to the new or the old.

There is always a compromise. A fair settlement is needed by the very character of the combatants. Because the old as well as the new, whatever exaggerations or untruths might be found in the inferences mixed up with them, are both results of actual experience, and both possess, therefore, the soul of truth. The error or what is condemned as such is in the later interpretations of the old by people who had not the original experience themselves, or in the exaggerated claims and unwarranted inferences of the new. By duly correcting the fanciful and second hand interpretations on the one side and the exaggerated pretensions or unwarranted inferences on the other, a fail-settlement is not difficult to arrive at.

There are other ways by which these conflicts are overcome and fresh synthesis arrived at. We find proofs of these in the canons of scriptural interpretation and in the exegetical literature of the different world-religions. But by whatever methods it is overcome, antithesis is never allowed to exist for long anywhere. For thought or reason cannot exist for any length of time in contradiction to itself. Thought-life cannot bear contradictions, its very soul is harmony. The state of antithesis is always a state of unstable equilibrium. It cannot vest on itself, and is, therefore, necessarily followed by some sort of a synthesis that sets all doubts and conflicts at rest for a while, until fresh questionings arise creating fresh conflicts, demanding a fresh settlement or synthesis. This is the general outline of the history of religious evolution. Faith, doubt, settlement or solution of the difficulty, creating a new faith, and again new doubts, new solutions and so on recurrently this is the universal story of religious progress and evolution, as much in the individual as in the race.

And in the face of this universal story how can we set down the different stages of the evolution of religion, as we may, for instance, that of the butterfly. The caterpillar, the chrysalis, the butterfly: these are the stages in the evolution of the latter creature. Can we similarly lay down three definite stages of the evolution of man's religion? Every generation has its own peculiar faiths, — the result of its peculiar experiences, mental, moral, and spiritual, — its own peculiar doubts which it seeks to solve in its own peculiar way leaving an exceedingly complicated legacy of faiths, doubts, and possible solutions for the next. Even if we skip over the minor changes that are being constantly worked in man's conceptions regarding religious duties by his advancing knowledge of Nature and his changing views of himself, even the larger and broader transformations that are perceptible after comparatively long periods of time, scarcely give us materials for such generalisations as will justify our laying down a definite number of stages of universal religious evolution. For the very simple reason that the character of these transformations is not the same, or even is not similar, in all religions.

In tracing the evolution of Hinduism, for instance, it has been the usual practice with modern students, to take the Vedas, the Upanisads, and the Puranas, as marking its three principal stages of growth. But when we examine the Vedas closely, we find that these cover not one but many stages. Indeed, they indicate a long course of the evolution of Hindu thought and theology. The Vedas are a compilation of mantras or what are called *Sanhita* texts and Brahmans or directions for rituals, interspersed with exegetical interpretations and numerous stories, legends and ancient anecdotes. But even the *Sanhita* texts of the Vedas, which are regarded as the most ancient portion of these Scriptures, do not refer, it is clear, to any one particular period of the primeval history of the Indo-Aryan family, nor to any definite stage of their mental or social evolution. There are verses in the Rig-Veda, for instance, that very distinctly refers to the time when the Vedic Aryans were engaged in jungle-clearing, that is, when they were in the earliest stage of evolution that sociology or Anthropology has been able as yet to trace in the history of the human race.

The view of the jungle-fire as a friend of man, in as much as it "shaves the surface of the earth and clears it of all having growths," like a clever barber, clearly conveys the memory of the times when man was engaged in the arduous work of clearing the earth for his habitation. Side by side with these texts, which are, however, not very numerous — we find others that could have been composed only by a people that had more or less settled down to an agricultural life; while there are other texts again, that give us a vivid picture of a people who had, to a very large extent, attained a civilized state, who lived in cities, built stone structures, possessed horses and elephants, and used them in their wars, who rode and fought on chariots, and adorned their persons with gold and silver ornaments, who had developed laws and institutions of a comparatively advanced type for their social and civic government.

All these records could not belong, surely, to one and the same period of the life of the Vedic Hindus, nor mark, in any way, one single epoch or stage of their social or mental growth. Even there is a marked evolution in their religious ideas as between, for instance, the first and the tenth Mandala of the Rig-Veda, — a gradual growth from a particularistic and naturalistic to a kind of universal and monotheistic idea of the Godhead, — as seen in the well-known text. The one truth, the Brahmins call by various names, such as, Indra, Varuna, Gadutmat, Rudra, etc. It is not at all reasonable, therefore, to treat this varied collection, even of the Sanhita texts, as marking one stage of Hindu evolution. The growth of these texts, — from these that are undoubtedly representative of the earliest known period of Indo-Aryan evolution to those as in the tenth Mandala of the Rig-Veda, for instance, that indicates one advanced synthesis, — could not by any means be accounted by the five hundred years that Professor Max Muller gives as the outside limit for their growth in such an absolutely arbitrary and summary fashion. Professor Balgangadhar Tilak basing his calculations upon astronomical and geological evidence, the truth of which would be more difficult to contest, — would give as many millenniums and something more also, to measure the growth of the existing Vedic texts, as Prof. Max Muller gave centuries. And how can we then take the Vedic Sanhitas, not to mention the other branches of the Vedic literature, as representative of one single stage or moment of Hindu evolution?

And the same remark applies to the Upanishads also. Not to take cognisance of those Upanishads, like the Gopal-Tapini and others, that are of an obviously modern, or what, at any rate, may be boldly called the post-Pauranic period of Hindu history, — even those that have been accepted as canonical by ancient commentators, do not bear proofs of an absolutely single stage of thought and speculation. It is clear that some of these belong to later, like, for instance, the *Svestasvatara* and to a much earlier period. Professor Max Muller gives 200 years as the probable period of the growth of the Upanishads, and here also his conclusion is unsupported by any valid evidence. But even two hundred years may, under certain circumstances, be not a very insignificant period of a nation's life and history, and they may work, as we know from our own times, mighty changes in the thought and life of a people, such as can never be brought together under one single step or stage or moment of their evolution.

How can we class all the Upanishads together then? And there are distinct evidence of violent conflicts of thoughts and strivings after a settlement and solution of these, in the canonical Upanishads themselves, as we shall see in detail when considering their contributions to Hindu evolution. In some, for instance, the earlier ritualism of the Vedas is absolutely condemned, marking a distinct period of Antithesis. In others, which evidently mark what may be called a stage of Synthesis, there is a clear attempt to work out some settlement, some compromise, some *via media* between the way of knowledge or *Brahmajnana* and the way of works and rituals, or *Karma*. Indeed, it is impossible to study the Upanishads without marking in them a long and laborious course of conflicts and settlements, of progress and evolution. And like the Upanishads, the Puranas also are many, and the so-called Pauranic Hinduism, with its exuberance of symbolism and ceremonialism, is not as some people seem to think, a pathological development of Hindu thought and theology, — but mark a distinct advance upon those of the Vedas and Upanishads, and cover not only a long period but many courses of real progress and evolution. And finally, are we to understand that all progress in Hinduism ceased with the last of the canonical eighteen Puranas? Some of the Tantras are of later date.

And what about the successive commentaries of these Puranas by sectarian thinkers and propagandists? What about the comparatively modern movements, and more particularly the Bhakti-movements, or the movements of Love and Faith, both Vaishnavite and Saivite, in Northern as well as Southern India? These are pertinent questions and they tend to show that even modern Hinduism is not a fossil, is not an object-lesson in religious degeneration, — but still a living, growing, changing, expanding, evolving thing. And of a living thing or thought it is impossible to mark, except in a very arbitrary and unscientific way, definite and limited stages of evolution. We can trace the history of a living organism, and this history will necessarily indicate the different moments of its evolution, but there is no warrant whatever, to fix these moments down to any definite number.

Prof. Caird's Stages of Religious Evolution Critically Examined

This characterisation of the earliest phase of human beliefs as known to us, is, in one sense, true; but the term "Object" is essentially a philosophic term implying relation to a Subject, and as suggesting any differentiation in consciousness, between the Self and the not-Self, which this term does seem to imply. Objective would seem to mean surely, a good deal more, when applied to the earliest phase of man's God-idea, than is justified by facts. In the first place, any form whatever of a God-idea, is not phase of human religion known to primitive culture. There are tribes a universal feature of the earnest primitive culture. There are tribes among whom religion appears in the form of a common and social custom alone. Leaving these cases aside, even where religion, as understood by us is discovered as a specific fact or institution, the word Objective would hardly express adequately the central idea of it. Man in the objective stage, according to Professor Caird, looks upon himself "as an object among other objects," and he conceived his God also as such. But is this analysis of the idea of himself of the primitive man strictly accurate? Has he really any concepts? He forms, no doubt, some generalisations. Without some such generalisations there could hardly be any association of ideas and without such association of ideas there could be no memory. But even lower animals have memory, which also must possess some background of generalisations behind even mere animal intelligence.

If these rudimentary generalisations could be called concepts, primitive man may claim to have them, but he has them only in common with the higher orders of the animal kingdom. But the concepts that are generally recognised by us as such, are, however, more advanced and organised forms of thought. They are the fruits of reflection, and the earliest stage of primitive human intelligence can hardly be called reflective. It would hardly be correct, therefore, it seems to us, to say that at that stage man either knows himself as an object, or that he knows any other thing as such. The truth is that in this stage man knows himself really and absolutely as his body — as tall or short, lean or fat, white or black, strong or week, hungry or full, happy or miserable or as moved or calm, as safe or frightened and so on, and this is about all that he knows or feels of himself directly. To this he adds also some indirect knowledge of himself, derived from others, as having been born of such and such parents, and belonging to such and such family or tribe, and having; as such, certain social obligations. This is all that primitive man, in the earliest known state of his mental evolution, really knows of himself.

And this, surely, is not knowing himself as "an object among other objects," unless the expression is taken to mean simply that man at this stage knows himself, just as he knows the things about him — only through his senses — by means of his perceptions and such crude generalisations as are common to all intelligence, animal or human. Our analysis of his experiences, in the light of our own advanced thought and philosophy, which out of the implications of his immature mind, does present him in the shape in which Prof. Caird describes him. We see that all the while primitive man was looking upon himself us an object among other objects, but he did not exactly see himself in this light. He approached himself as much as he approached everything else, simply through the gates of his senses. That seems to us to be the real truth. And whatever distinction he made between himself and others was simply a distinction of me and Not-Me; and not in any sense of Self and not-Self or of knower and known or Subject and Object. And Prof. Caird's terminology seems, therefore, to us to be open to considerable misconception, and we would prefer to call the earliest phase of the evolution of religion as the Perceptive or following Prof. Max Muller, the "Naturalistic" state, using the term naturalistic in the sense of unreflective, in which the words "nature" and "natural" are not infrequently used in common parlance.

But the reading of advanced philosophical ideas and intentions into the history of religious evolution is patent throughout Prof. Caird's study of this subject. As he calls the first stage of religious evolution the objective stage, so he calls the second stage the subjective stage, and the third or last stage he characterises as the universal stage. In some religions there is a phase which may very properly be called subjective, but in some religions only; and even in these, it would not be possible to prove, we are afraid, that this is the second stage in their evolution. But we do not see this strictly subjective phase in all religions, because, owing to difference in race-characteristics, the religious sentiment had not everywhere the same original spiritual sense to work upon, by which alone could a strictly subjective character be developed in any religion. The particular phase of Hinduism represented by some of the ancient Upanishads may well be called subjective, we admit.

For in the religion of these Upanishads there is a distinct and preponderating emphasis on the subjective to the more or less entire neglect or denial of the objective. Here the subject is constantly set up over against the object, and practically while all reality is appropriated by the former, the latter is relegated to the realm almost of dreams and shadows. The subject or the Self is the Truth, the object or the not-self is untruth. The subject is everlasting and eternal, the object everchanging and ephemeral.

The subject is the reality, the object is mere appearance. The subject is absolutely independent of and different from the object. It is pure being. This is the keynote of these Upanishads. No one can read through these Hindu scripture? without being impressed with their intense, their excessive and exclusive subjectivity. And coming to these studies after those of the naturalistic poetry and ceremonialism of Vedic religion, this subjectivism of the Upanishads does seem to mark a fresh phase, if not a new stage, in the evolution of Hindu religion.

The same thing, though in a much less accentuated form, is also marked, to some extent, in the evolution of the ancient religion of Greece, which also bears evidence of a phase of naturalism prior to the philosophic speculations of the later sages and seers. And if all religions were like those of Greece or India, Professor Caird's classification would have some justification. But all religions are not alike, have not had the same original endowments, nor the same historic setting. We do find a subjective phase in Aryan religious evolution, it is true. But do we find it clearly marked in the evolution of the non-Aryan systems? Is there any trace of a truly subjective phase in the history of Judaism? The characteristic of the subjective phase — Prof. Caird's subjective stage — as described by himself is that here God is apprehended as the subject, and as such stands eternally apart from all objects.

But where do we find God apprehended thus in the Old Testament records? When and where? There is an objective, or as we would prefer to call, a perceptive phase in Judaism, as we shall see later on. There is a later phase where: God is apprehended as a Super-sensuous Being, but at no time was he apprehended really as the subject by the ancient Hebrews. The God of Judaism is super-sensuous, but super-sensuousness is not the only, nor an absolutely essential characteristic of what is called the subject in philosophy. He is omniscient but even omniscience does not directly and necessarily cancel all objectivity. Either we must accept the term subjective in a much looser sense than is admitted in philosophical literature, or we must confess that even an Omniscient being is not necessarily the Subject or the Absolute. We are all subjects in relation to our objects: we are also objects in relation to other selfs or subjects. Our being a Subject does not preclude, — except at the final analysis of the concept subject which leads to absolute monism — our being also at the same time objects. God may similarly be omniscient and may have the whole creation for his object, and yet, in as much as he becomes an object of our knowledge, he too becomes to us an object. When, therefore, God, whether He be seen or unseen, finite or infinite, becomes an object of man's knowledge, the religion which apprehends and presents him as such, becomes objective. And mere omniscience or omnipotence or any other attributes ascribed to the Deity in such a religion would not lend to it, what Prof. Caird calls, a subjective phase.

In the entire range of human religions, so far as it is known to us, the religion of the Upanishads alone can claim really to present a truly subjective phase. Because there is absolutely no suspicion of any objectivity in the Upanishadic conception of the Deity. The Upanishads distinctly say that the Supreme knows everything but of Him there is no knower. And thus they cut off the very roots of all objective ideas concerning the Godhead. Is He then absolutely unknown and unknowable? Yes, reply the Upanishads without any doubt or hesitancy.

"The eye does not go there (i.e. to Brahman), the speech does not go there, neither does the mind or the understanding. We do not know it, we know not how to impart instruction about it. It is distinct from what is known, it is beyond what is unknown; this is what we have heard from former teachers who have explained it to us".

But this nescience is not the final teaching of these scriptures. All that it means is that Brahman is unknown and unknowable as an object. But Brahman is known and knowable as subject, known and knowable, that is, — not as the known but as knower. We know Brahman just as we know ourselves. Those who know their own Self know Brahman, for the Self and Brahman are one. This, briefly, is the real subjectivism of the Upanishads. This is the true subjective conception of the Deity. Every other conception of God as an object of our knowledge, is distinctly objective. This Upanishadic phase of Hinduism is the only strictly subjective phase of religious evolution we know of in the entire range of the existing religious records of humanity. Do we find it as the second stage, — if we find it at all, in the evolution of the other world-religions? Are there proofs of this phase in Judaism? Are there traces of it in Islam, except in the teachings and experiences of those who have been condemned as heretics? Had this stage been reached at any time by Latin Christianity? And if there are no proofs of this, the only true subjective phase or stage of religious evolution in so many of the grown-up religions of humanity, how can we follow Professor Caird and accept it as a universal moment in the evolution of man's religion?

The third and last stage of religious evolution is characterised by Prof. Caird as the Universal stage. In this stage, the conflict between the subject and the object that marked the second or the subjective stage, is overcome by the consciousness of an essential unity between the two. The Subject and Object are both here apprehended as moments or phases of the Absolute, which cancels this differentiation between them immediately it is formulated. And thus, Prof. Caird reaches, in this the last and highest phase or stage of religious evolution, the philosophy of Absolute Idealism of which he is one of the ablest exponents in England. Logically his scheme of religious evolution is correct, because it represents, as we have already pointed out, the dialectic of Reason, the universal procession of thought and knowledge.

But the confusion in this presentation arises out of its application to actual religious history. For as we have, no doubt, a truly subjective phase in Hindu evolution, in the religion of the earlier Upanishads, so we do find a truly universal phase also in the later Upanishads, and as we shall see in course of our investigations, in a more developed form, in the religion of the Puranas, especially in the philosophy and religion of the Hindu Schools of Love and Faith, — both Vaishnavite and Saivite. But do we find any traces of this universal phase in any other world-religion? Not to speak of Judaism or Islam, do we find it even in Christianity, except in the life and experiences of solitary saints and sages, — and these generally belong to the Catholic Church, — in whom what may be called, the Christ-consciousness assumed a universal form, cancelling, all conflicts if not all differentiations, and revealing itself through all creation; as well as, in a feeble though extremely pregnant note in the philosophy and culture of the Alexandrian Fathers, and also in that form of philosophical Christianity which has come to be associated with the name of Hegel, the new school of Christian Theology to which Prof. Caird himself belongs?

It seems to us, indeed, that the scheme of the evolution of Religion, presented by Professor Caird is somewhat arbitrary and subjective. He marks three stages of this Evolution. But why three at all? The dialectic of Reason suggests no doubt three logical stages of evolution, but can we apply it chronologically to any particular evolution? History of religious evolution?

Thesis, antithesis, and synthesis, or homogeneity, differentiation, and integration, these do represent the logic of the evolutionary process. But in actual course of evolution do not these follow one another very rapidly, and is not the circle repeated almost endlessly in the history of every form of psychological evolution? In thought or reason, thesis, antithesis and synthesis do not appear, at any time, in what may be characterised as a static or stationary aspect. They form an ever-recurring circle. Thesis, antithesis and synthesis represent, so to say, the dynamics of reason or thought. The whole process is in perpetual motion. Thesis as soon as formulated, commences to create its own antithesis, which also immediately sets in motion its own synthesis. The logical process of evolution is really, as we have said, a process of what Christian theologians call, eternal generation. And in evolution, whether biological or psychological, it is absolutely impossible to say where one stage ends and another begins, and consequently we cannot, as a matter of fact divide these stages at all. All such division must be merely theoretic, abstract, and arbitrary; and at best it can only be logically but never chronologically true.

The Source of Religion

Max Muller's Theory of its Origin

Philosophy of Religion, or what Max Muller preferred to call the Science of Religion, as far as it has been investigated and worked up, traces the origin of the religious phenomena either in nature-worship or in ancestor worship. Hume, and following him, Herbert Spencer, attribute the birth of religion to ancestor worship. Max Muller, on the other hand, has sought to trace the origin of man's religious consciousness to his intuitions of the Infinite within and his contact with and contemplation of the natural forces and phenomena without, which acted as the first stimuli to quicken his inner intuitions of the Infinite. But both Spencer and Max Muller seem to us to present only a half-truth. Prof Max Muller defines religion as the sense of the infinite in man. But what is this infinite? He could not, consistently, claim that his theory of religious evolution was a science, when he presented an abstruse philosophical term as expressing the very essence and substance of the phenomena which he undertook to investigate.

Science goes no further than the indefinite: it knows no infinity. The highest point in mathematics, for instance, though far courtesy's sake called an infinity, is really not infinite but simply indefinite. If it can at all be called an infinity, it is what may be called a spatial infinite, which, every student of metaphysics knows, is no infinity at all, but is only another name for that which the vision of man cannot comprehend, and in thinking of which the mind of man loses itself in immensity.

But true infinity is not realisable by the eye, but by the self, the spirit, which itself is infinite. The Absolute alone is Infinite, and not science but philosophy or metaphysics alone can reveal the Absolute to us.

But though the ultimate meaning and truth of the Infinite or Absolute can only be realised and attained by deep abstraction and great mental and moral excellence, the result of long and laborious training and disciplines, there is, yet, it must be admitted, a general and vague feeling or intuition of it in every man. Man's affinities with, his longing for, his groping after the Absolute does constitute, therefore, the universal background of his religious life and experiences, and this vogue sense of the Unknown, if not reality of the Infinite, is present at every step of the evolution of human religion from the lowest to the highest. And in this sense Prof. Max Mutter's definition is capable of defence. But where it fails is in its interpretations of the Infinite, as actually apprehended by the primitive mind. The sense of the Infinite is intuitional.

But every intuition needs external and objective stimuli to be quickened into activity and consciousness. What is the objective and external stimulus that, acting upon the mind of man, first quickened, however feebly it might be, his intuitions of the Infinite, and thus gave birth to his religion? It is Nature, says Professor Max Muller. The "infinitely large" and the "infinitely small" things and objects about him quickened man's earliest intuitions of the Infinite. The sky, foremost of all; broad expanse of plains, sometimes; lofty mountains; meandering rivers losing themselves in unknown realms and coining also from unprospected regions; — the sea, the forest, the phenomena of light and darkness; — these and similar natural objects and phenomena aroused men's sense of the Infinite.

This is Prof. Max Muller's view. It is partly true also. But only partly, and its lack of fullness is a fatal limitation. A definition must cover, and an explanation must meet, the whole field and every phase of its object. Professor Max Muller's fails in this. The Nature-sense, so to say, had, no doubt, a potent influence in the development of religion among Aryan peoples, but surely not among all peoples. In others the primary emphasis is not on man's contact with his Nature surroundings, but rather on his relations with the social organism to which he belongs. Among the Chinese, for instance, Nature is approached through the prism of the social experience, and interpreted in the terms of the Social life. The head of the social life, the Emperor, is also the head of the life of Nature, and he used to issue edicts deposing the heavenly bodies just as he did in regard to his earthly mandarins.

To trace the origin of the religious sentiment, therefore, to man's sense of Infinity as quickened by contact with his Nature-surroundings, would fail to meet the case of the Chinese, and to some extent, perhaps, even of the Semitic races, with whom also the social sense seems to have dominated over what may be called the Nature-sense. The religion of Israel is called covenantal religion; it owed its origin to a covenant or contract between the God and the people of Israel. In the Old Testament the expression Lord of Hosts means in the earlier stages, simply the Commander of the Army of Israel, — an idea fully supported by the theoretic form of the social and civic government of the early Jews. It is only subsequently that the celestial army of stars and planets came to be included in the "hosts" of the Lord. And this shows very clearly the social emphasis of Judaism, in the entire literature of which the Nature-note is exceedingly feeble and subordinate. Had Professor Max Muller applied his theory of the origin of the religious sense, to the religious history of the Chinese, or even to the history of the Old Testament religion, he would, we are sure, have himself discovered the fatal limitations under which it laboured, and for which his interpretations of the phenomena of human religions have failed to some extent.

The fact, really, is that what Prof. Max Muller calls, in a somewhat loose way, the sense of the Infinite, is only a consciousness of what may be called the "Not-Me". This "Not-Me" is what man comes to feel first of all, surrounding him on all sides, — opposing him sometimes, and, perhaps helping and befriending him at other.

The so-called Infinite of Prof. Max Muller is only this "Not-Me" of the primitive would be absolutely correct to say that man's religion grows always and everywhere out of his contact and conflict with this "Not-Me". What Prof. Caird characterises as "object," is only this "Not-Me". Others have called the earliest phase of religious evolution, as particularistic, instead of objective. But like Prof. Cairds "objects," their "particular" are also found, at the final analysis to be only forms of the "Not-Me," — what in Hindu Philosophy is characterised by the general term *Idam* or this, that is, what is not *Aham* or I or me. But this is speaking in the terms, it may be said, of the unknown, what in mathematics is called X and Y, the "Not-Me" is an unknown quantity, and may mean, therefore, as much or as little, as Prof. Max Muller's "Infinite". No, by no means so. For this "Not-Me" is a very tangible thing to primitive man. It is the Power-not-Himself that constantly curbs and controls him.

In his nature-surroundings the primitive man stands perpetually face to face with a power-not-Himself that curbs and controls his activities. He sees it in the roaring thunder, in the rushing storm-wind, in world-devouring forest fires, in running volumes of water, in cataclysms like earthquakes and tornadoes, as well as, at a later stage, in the movements of the heavenly bodies, and the mysterious play of light and darkness at nights, and at dawn and eventide. All these are his "Not-Me," represent powers and personalities to him that have a hold upon his life and that can make or mar his happiness at their will. This perception of the Not-Me in nature is the origin, really, of all nature-deities whether found in the ancient records of the Hindus or the Greeks or of any other race. All the mere prominent Vedic gods, like most of the earlier Hellenic deities, belong to this class. And it is, evidently, a consideration of these that had led Prof. Max Muller to attribute the earliest quickening of man's intuitions of the Infinite to his contact with and contemplation of the awful mysteries of Nature.

Hume and Spencer's Theory

Nature, however, is not the only aspect in which the "Not-Me" or the "Power-not-Himself" that sought to control man, stood face to face with him, in the earliest state of his existence. As in his Nature-surroundings primitive man saw and felt the presence of a Power-not-Himself that stood in opposition to his desires and activities, so also in his social life, in the authority of his tribe, in the rites and customs enjoined upon him by tribal law and tradition, that had behind them the sanction of his ancestors, primitive man became, at every step, conscious of a controlling and awful outside agency.

While Max Muller saw, from his study, specially, of the primitive records of the Aryan religions this power-not-Himself that quickened man's earliest consciousness of religion, in his nature surroundings, Hume and Herbert Spencer, from their special examination of the records of the life and thought of savage man, as found in books of travels, saw this Power-not-Himself only in the social authority and traditions of primitive man, and the one took nature-worship as the first expression of human religions while the two others took ancestor-worship to represent that earliest phase. The fact, however, is that the earliest phase of religious evolution testifies to the presence of a dual force acting upon the instincts of man, one, what may be called the Nature force, giving rise to the worship of what has been called Nature deities, such as are found in early Hindu and Hellenic religion, the other, social force, which led to the worship of ancestors, as the source, the sanction, and the fountainhead of it. Out of this dual consciousness of a Power-not-Himself, — that manifested in Nature-phenomena and in social authority, — man's earliest religion seems to have grown up.

Man's Earliest Religion Product of Both Elements

Indeed, as Nature formed an essential factor in the life of man, so did also Society, at every stage of its growth. His nature environments have been as constant a factor of his evolution as his social-environments. We know of no time, in the history of man, when he did not live in, and form part of, some social organisation. It is his relation, organic almost, and pre-historic, with other men and women, forming members of one and the same community or tribe, speaking the same dialect, observing the same customs, tracing a common origin, that really differentiate man even in the most primitive state from every other species of animal. We can conceive of no time when man was not a social being, and even pre-historic research furnish no evidence of such a period of human evolution. And this social bond has universally constituted an essential element of his religion. In fact where we had absolutely no idea of a Godhead, no injunctions regarding worship, no records, direct or indirect, of any instinct or sense that might be referred to the Unseen, where, in short, we find no trace of what is usually known to and understood by us as religion, even there we find this obedience to social authority, in the form of observance of social customs, as the only substitute for religion.. But his social environments supplied only one-half of man's religious incentive, the other half was supplied by his natural or physical environments. And these two, Nature and Society, constituted always the two agencies that worked up, everywhere, the religious consciousness of mankind.

But there has been considerable variations in the emphasis that has been laid on these two essential stimuli and vehicles of man's religious ideas. In some people, the emphasis has been on Nature, in others on Society, while in some, again, it has been fairly divided between them two where the emphasis has been stronger on the Social than on the Nature environments, as it seems to have been, for instance among the Chinese, and, in another fashion, among also the Hebrews as well, there, Nature-forces have been viewed and expressed in the terms of the social life and relations, — the conception of a social hierarchy rising, in gradation, from family-authority, represented by the worship of ancestors, to the imperial authority, represented by the Sovereign, the earthly manifestation and instrument of the Royal-dead, is transferred also to the Government and organisation of the physical world, as we see in China; or the conception of an earthly theocracy is transferred to represent a similar rule in Nature, and the hosts of Yahveh represent an earthly army here, and an army of stars and planets above, as we find in the records of the children of Israel.

Among the Aryans, however, this emphasis has been, it seems, very fairly divided from the earliest times, between the Nature-forces and the social-authority, and we find in the Vedas a dual religion, so to say, one consisting of the worship of Nature-deities and the other that of ancestors, and these two lines of religious sacraments and duties run parallel to each other throughout the entire course of the evolution of early Vedic Hinduism. And even in subsequent evolution, as the Nature-deities gradually united and coalesced, so to say, in the conception of Brahman, the One Truth — the *Ekam Sat,* as it is put in the tenth Mandala of the Rig Veda, so the social deities, the ancestral spirits, also united and coalesced in that of Prajapati, Brahman represented the highest synthesis, in the pre-Upanishadic stage, of the Nature-Gods while Prajapati represented that of the social Gods or ancestral spirits; and Brahman and Prajapati, like the Devas and the Pitris, divided Vedic worship equally between them, for a very long period, it seems, of the evolution of primitive Hinduism.

And even when it reached the stage of monotheism, the social-emphasis was not entirely lost, but Prajapati was not entirely lost, but Prajapati was still retained, as we shall see later on, in the conception of Hiranyagarbha, the first born of Brahman, the origin of social life and order, the first teacher of truths, the first promulgator of Law. But Society forms one essential element of man's religion. The other essential element has been supplied by his physical environments. In the earliest stage, his mind was naturally absorbed by terrestrial phenomena. He was then engaged in clearing the earth, and making it fit for human habitation. His mind was, naturally, fixed on the earth. At this stage fire must have played a very important part in his life. Primitive man first stood face to face with fire, in its natural manifestation of jungle-fire, — self-produced, forest-devouring, terrible and overwhelming to both man and beast, yet ultimately turning out to be the greatest friend of man, in as much as it cleared the surface of the earth of both beasts and vegetation, opening it out, thus, for human habitation. Fire, therefore, we find in the Vedas, described as the first-born of the gods.

In the jungle-clearing stage man had; really, no leisure to contemplate the majestic sweep of the heavens. He was then too absorbingly engaged in fighting his terrestrial enemies, and overcoming the obstacles that Mother Earth raised before him, to indulge in pleasant dreams of the Sun and the Moon, or the brilliants of the blue vault above him. Celestial phenomena came later to receive his notice, and of these storm and wind, thunder and lightning, must have received much earlier notice. The heavens as the panorama of light and darkness or as a symbol of all-embracing, all-pervading immensity, which Max Muller calls the symbol of the Infinite, entered much later into man's reflections, to form, thus, an element of his religion or a vehicle of his worship.

But natural objects and phenomena, whether terrestrial or celestial, supplied always, at every stage, and everywhere, one aspect of the great Not-Me, through which man first commenced to feel after his Maker, while his Society formed the other aspect of it And the truth, about the origin of the religious sentiment, does not lie, therefore, either in the theory of Hume or Spencer on the one side, nor in that of Max Muller, on the other, but partly in both; the full truth being found in the combination of the two. For man's religion has always been an attempt on his part to adjust himself to his nature-surroundings on the one side, and to his social-surroundings on the other.

Religion may, therefore, be defined, with the Greeks, as Harmony: the harmony of the individual man with his environments in every aspect and department of his life and activities, as well as, in the higher and more spiritual stages, harmony also with his inner self — his inner ideas, ideals, desires, aspirations, and cravings, and his outer life and activities and the social and civic institutions in and through which that life and those activities find their instrument and fulfilment. And the true History of Religion is only the history of the attempt that man has always made, with varying success, to adjust himself to his physical, his mental, his moral or social, his civic and economic conditions, and, through this progressive adjustment, to develop the highest possibilities of his nature, and realise the loftiest promise of his soul.

This, it seems to us, is the view of religion, in its most general aspect that a comparative study of the religious experiences of humanity most fully supports. It supplies a key by which almost every religion may be unlocked, — from what is called the lowest forms of animism, fetishism, or totemism, to the highest forms of monotheism or theosophy or gnosticism, whether Hindu or Christian or Islamic.

Evolution of Religion

It Evolves with the Evolution of the Views of Self and not-Self

Contact with the "Not-Me" in its dual aspect of Nature-force and Social-Authority, is the originating cause, then, of the religious consciousness in man. It grows and expands, necessarily, with the growth and expansion of this contact, and the consequent advancement in man's knowledge and ideas concerning his natural and his social life and limitations. All differences between one religion and another is explicable by the different estimates that man has formed in different countries and at different times of these two aspects of his Not-Me, as well as by the difference of the emphasis that has been laid, by different peoples, on one or other of these dual factors of their life.

The study of these variations, as well as of the fundamental unity underlying them all, with a view to work out the general laws and principles involved in the origin and growth of human religions, is Science or Philosophy of Religion. And, as we have already said, the object of what may be called the methods of investigation here are the common methods of Science, namely, observation, experiment, comparison, classification and generalisation, to which must be added the two most important methods of investigating living and growing objects and institutions, namely, the comparative and the historic method, corrected, verified, and illumined by the general law of psychological or mental evolution.

Religion being, thus, in its broadest and most universal sense, the attempt of man to adjust himself to his "Not-Me," with a view to the realisation of his own highest end, the evolution of religion must, necessarily, follow the course of relationship in which man enters, in his progress through life, with this Not-Me. And, indeed, we find it always in actual history that man's religion has always changed or advanced in accordance with his progressive or changing views of this Not-Me, as his views of this Not-Me also have, themselves, changed and evolved, in accordance with man's changing and advancing views of himself.

Man's relations with his Not-Me are of three classes. The Not-Me is, in the first place, an object of man's knowledge. All his senses operate on and through this Not-Me. He sees it, he smells it, he hears it, he touches it, he tastes it, — in Nature, and he feels its presence and power in his relations with it, in his social life. By these means he comes to know of the Not-Me. Man here is, though he may not always know it himself, — what we would with our advanced knowledge call, the knower of the Not-Me, the Not-Me is the object of his knowledge he is the subject, the Not-Me is his object. This is one relation. And it is the character of every relation that any changes in one of the factors of it, brings on a change necessarily in the other factor also, so far as the particular relation is concerned.

Consequently man's views of himself have always changed with his altered views concerning his Not-Me, as his changed views in regard to the Not-Me have also changed similarly his own estimates and ideas concerning his own self. Change in man's nature-surroundings owing to his migration to a different and distant region of the earth is a real change in his Not-Me. So also is what contact with an alien social organisation must necessarily work in the other, the social aspect of his Not-Me. And these changes have contributed very largely to very distinct changes in man's religious ideas and ideals where even the original religion seems to have been one. Differences between Judaism and Islam are of this class and character, as well as the differentiations that are observed in the religions of ancient India and ancient Greece. In the one case these were brought about by the dispersion of the Semitic, in the other by that of the Aryan race.

As the Not-Me stands to man in the relation of known to knower, or object to subject, so also it stands to him in that of enjoyer and enjoyed. Man not only knows the Not-Me through his perceptions, but every act of perception calls up sensations of either pleasure or pain, and thus, man, stands perpetually related to the Not-Me through his sensations or feelings. And here also, progressively to man's capacity to feel, as well as to the Not-Me's power or opportunity to make him feel, his relations with it must change, and such changes must necessarily lead to important developments in his religious ideas and ideals.

And, finally, the Not-Me is not only an object of man's knowledge or of his emotions, — is not something that he perceives by his senses, or something that causes him pleasure or pain, fills him with admiration or disgust, or awe or contempt, — something that works upon his emotions, but it is also something that calls forth his energies and impels him to some form or other of activity always. In our present state, there may be things that we perceive about us but which neither draw nor repel us. In these cases perceptions do not evoke emotion, and in the absence of emotion, the will is not moved. But this is largely, if not wholly, due to the comparatively higher stage of mental evolution that we have reached. In this matter, the adult man or woman in civilization differs very much from little children whose perceptions are uniformly associated with sensation and volition.

It is universally observed in babies. Savages, not trained to habits of reflection, are like babies in this respect, and the necessary relation between perception, sensation and will-movement is proved more clearly in their life than in ours. But the Not-Me is to us, as it is to them, equally subject to the operation of the will. Man knows the Not-Me, and stands to it in the relation of subject to object. He feels the Not-Me and stands to it in the relation of feeler and felt, — or as we have in Sanskrit, enjoyer and enjoyed — *Bhogya-Bhaktaram*. He is moved to action by the Not-Me, and stands to it, thus in the relation of agent to the object of his activity.

And the course of evolution in religion is determined by the actualities of this triune-relation in which man stands always to his Not-Me, as represented by his Nature-environment, and his Social organism, the changes in this triune-relation accounting for his changing ideas both of his Deity and his Duty.

Its Psychological Process

The course of religious evolution must, therefore, be studied as an essentially psychological phenomenon. It must be studied, that is, in the light of the evolution of human reason, human emotions, and the human will. The earliest stage in this psychological evolution must mark the earliest stage also of religious evolution, and so on the two courses of evolution must, necessarily, advance along parallel lines.

In the earliest stage of mental evolution we find three tilings, namely, (1) Perception of sense-objects (2) Sensations of pleasure and pain, and (3) Activity to attain the one and avoid the other. This is, in most general terms, child psychology. This is also, more or less, the psychology of primitive man, in the earliest stage. This is what may be called the naturalistic stage of human culture.

Its Naturalistic or Perceptive Stage

Man here is not but little removed from the brute creation. His senses are his main guides in life. Instinct is in possession, here, of his reason. When he reasons at all, as he must necessarily do in taking his experiences of yesterday as a guide for today, he does so instinctively, so to say, and not by any conscious, reasoned, process. His experience is limited. His vision is narrow. His generalisations are few, such as are observed in the play of intelligence even in lower animals. His emotions also are of a very simple character. The complexity observed in the thoughts, emotions, and impulses of civilized man is absolutely unknown here. And his activities are also of the simplest, the most direct and crude nature. This is the inventory of the mental life of primitive man. And his religion also is in perfect consonance with this life of perceptions, sensations, instincts and animal impulses; — perceptions supplying the object of his worship, sensations the motives for it, and instinct and impulse furnishing the methods and appliances, the rites and ceremonies of his worship. This may very properly be called the naturalistic stage or phase of religious evolution.

And, as we have already said, this term naturalistic, or as we would ourselves prefer to call it, perceptive, would seem to be a more accurate characterisation of the first phase of religious evolution. As this fast evolution than Prof. Caird's objective, because they follow more closely, perhaps, the dialectic of reason. In the dialetic of reason, the first or earliest stage is that of unity, — undifferentiated and homogenous unity. But the term objective presupposes differentiation, breaking up, that is, of this homogeneity; for there can be no consciousness, strictly speaking, of an object without that of a subject, which stands over against it. Where the subject is unconscious, there is really and truly no object either.

Indeed, the first movement of knowledge is an undifferentiated perception, and mere perception, though it does generate knowledge by differentiating it from other perceptions and putting them on a line, (integrating) with it, does not imply differentiation of subject and object. Indeed, what may be called, in some sense, a pure state of nature, is decidedly a state of homogeneity. In our mental life it is the stage where no distinctions have yet arisen between the knower and known, between subject and object, except that of me and Not-Me. All knowing in this earliest stage is almost entirely perceiving, an operation of the senses without much analysis, reflection, or generalisation. It is therefore that we prefer to call the first stage of religious evolution, as the Naturalistic or the Perceptive stage.

The Earliest Stage Essentially Perceptive

And the actual history of human religions supports this nomenclature. In the earliest stage the senses play a dominant part in the development of the religious sentiment. The Deity here is not really an invisible, supersensuous Being, but are all visible and "sensible" gods and goddesses, only though visible, there is always something "uncanny" and mysterious about them, something that suggests hidden powers for good or evil and undiscovered possibilities. And this element of mystery is essential to raise an object or phenomenon, however close and clear it may, otherwise, lie within the range of man's senses, to the position of a thing to be feared, and, therefore, to be worshipped, that is, either conquered or propitiated. But this element of mystery notwithstanding, man's earliest religion, like the earliest phase of his mental life, is essentially one of perceptions. We should like, therefore, to characterise the first and earliest phase of human religion as Perceptive, instead of Objective.

Religion originates, as we have seen, in man's attempt to adjust himself to his Not-Me. This Not-Me presents itself to primitive man always and everywhere in the dual aspect of Nature-Force and Social Authority. And, in the earliest stage, both Nature and Society are viewed by man absolutely through the senses, unassociated with any reflection, except what is essential to the exercise of memory, and what is, consequently, common to all animal intelligence. Even in this stage fundamental differences are observed in the religious ideas and acts of different races. Among some the emphasis as we have said, is more on their social life than on their Nature-environments; among others it is more on the Nature-environments, perhaps, than on their social life; while among certain races, from the very beginning, so far as we can see from their most ancient records, this emphasis seems to have been pretty fairly divided between the natural and the social aspects of their Not-Me.

But whatever differences might, thus, be observed even in the earliest phase of their evolution, between different religions, the fact of their being based essentially upon sense-perceptions is common to all. The earliest Vedic deities, *Agni*, *Varuna*, the *Maruts*, *Rudra*, *Indra*, the twins Aswini Kumars, are all visible objects. So also are all the oldest, Hellenic gods. So also is the earliest God-perception of the Hebrews, inspite of all their claims to a superior and supernatural revelation of divine truths. El-Elohim, translated as Lord Almighty in the English version of the Old Testament, walks the earth, and is visible to his first creatures. Adam and Eve see him, and he sees them, and that this seeing is literal and not metaphorical is proved by their hiding themselves from their creator, and by the creator calling out for them, showing that he could not see them in their hiding, and their answering him from their secret shelter. The entire story is clearly the record of a very human, that is, sensuous drama. Scholars are of opinion, no doubt, that the story of the Fall is not original to the Hebrews, but that they borrowed it from others. But whatever may be its source, the fact is absolutely undeniable that this story in the Book of Genesis represents the perceptive phase of religion, and even the Jews must have had such a phase, as otherwise it would not have been possible for them to adapt it to their traditions. All these are remnants of very old records, no doubt, as all ancient cosmogonies everywhere are, more or less, and there is absolutely no justification for interpreting these passages in the light of our larger experience, in a figurative sense. The Negro who, in obedience to ancient custom, still offers in our own time, food to the tree or the bush that has been worshipped from time immemorial by his ancient forbears may say that the invisible spirit of the tree eats the invisible essence of the offerings, and it is, therefore, that though eaten, the food, apparently remains the same, but still, it is a fact that his primitive ancestors made no distinction, like him, between the tree or bush, as they saw it, and its invisible spirit.

Such a consciousness would presuppose the cognition of the self as distinguished from the not-self, a consciousness of the soul or spirit of man as not only differentiated from, but absolutely independent of the body. Yet nowhere, nay not even among people who have had, it seems, an original endowment of a spiritual sense, is this consciousness seen so fully developed in primitive culture. The earliest conception — if we may at all apply the term to what was only a perception — of the Godhead was nowhere that of an invisible, supersensuous being or thing, but that of something which, though cognisable by the senses, was still shrouded in some profound or awful mystery, either owing to its very nature, or owing to some memories associated, by tradition, with it.

Indeed, not only in the Book of Genesis, but even in Exodus, where we come across the records of a somewhat advanced phase of Judaic religion, we find mention of a "sensible" Godhead. Elohim walked the earth at Eden; and was seen and heard with their mortal eye and ear, by Adam and Eve, in the Book of Genesis. Yahveh or Jehovah, the new name in which the God of Israel presents himself to Moses, in Exodus, is also seen by him, though somewhat mediately, in, or through, or as, a burning bush. Yahveh talks to Moses even as Elohim had done to Adam. He too is almost a visible, and undoubtedly an audible God. Gradually, however, he passes out of both man's sight and hearing. But even long afterwards the tradition is kept up; and the Ark of Shilo becomes the symbol or mnemonic of the old vision and a whole party of Israelites are punished with immediate death, in verification of the old saying of Yahveb, — "no man shall see God and live" for foolishly, and possibly in a sceptical spirit, prying into the sacred mystery.

The Perceptive Charactor of the God-Experience in Early Hebrew Records

In fact, the sensuous or perceptive character of the God-experience of the early Hebrew records cannot be denied. In Genesis 3, 8-10 we read. — "And they heard the voice of the Lord God walking in the garden in the cool of the day; and Adam and his wife had themselves from the presence of the Lord God amongst the trees of the garden". "And the Lord God called unto Adam and said unto him, Where art thou?"

"And he said, I heard thy voice in the garden, and I was afraid because I was naked and I hid myself".

And next follows what sounds like an enquiry into the facts of their disobedience: God asks Adam; he refers to Eve; he next asks Eve, who refers to the serpent, and they are all punished.

The same perceptive God-experience is recorded also in Genesis 4, for here also God appears before Abel and Cain, and has a long converse with the latter, and being punished for killing his brother, Cain "went out from the presence of the Lord and dwelt in the land of Nod, on the east of Eden". (verse 16).

In the next place, God repents his creation — (Genesis 6. 6 and 7), and sends the flood, but appears before Noah and directs him to make the Ark and go and take shelter in it. After the Deluge, Noah builds an alter unto the Lord, and offers burnt offerings on it. "And the Lord swelled a sweet savour; and the Lord said in his heart, I will not again curse the ground any more for man's sake; &c—(8. 21-22)

The Lord appears before Abraham, however, subsequently, "in a vision" (15. 1.); but he talks to him as he did to Adam and Noah— But the visible sign does not yet pass away. For, when the Lord made a covenant with Abraham, just after the manner of the ancient Hebrews, (15-9-10) though the terms of it were revealed to him in "deep sleep" (15-12-10&c) the actual ratification was made, as was the custom, by the Lord passing between the pieces of meat, as "a smoking furnace and a lamp of fire" (15. 17).

Subsequently, however, the covenant is reaffirmed by God who "talked with" Abraham (17.3.)

The Lord, next, comes "down" to Sodom and Gomorrah to "see whether they have done altogether according to the cry of it, which is come into him, "and if not," (he says) "I will know". (Genesis 18, 21).

Next we find the same, perceptive God-experience, distinctly, repeated in the case of Jacob:

"And Jacob was left alone; and there wrestled a man with him until the breaking of the day. And when he saw he prevailed not against him (Jacob) — he said — Let me go, for the day breaketh. And he (Jacob) said, I will not let thee go, except thou bless me. And he (the wrestler) said unto him (Jacob) what is thy name? And he said Jacob. And he said, thy name shall be called no more Jacob, but Israel: for as a Prince thou hast power with God, and with men, and hast prevailed. And Jacob asked him and said. Tell me, I pray thee, thy name. Wherefore is it that thou dost ask after my name? And he blessed him there. And Jacob called the name of the place Peniel (i.e. the Face of God): for I have seen God face to face, and my life is preserved. (Genesis 32. 24-30 &c).

In Genesis 35, 9–15, is recorded another "appearance" of God to Jacob, and his converse with him, and also how God pointed out the spot where Jacob had first talked to him, so that he might build a pillar there, in memory of the event; — "And God went up from him (Jacob) in the place where he talked with him. And Jacob set up a pillar in the place — and called the name of the place where God spoke with him, — Bethel" (verses 10–15).

It would also be impossible to deny that the God-experience recorded of Moses in the Old Testament is also of a distinctly perceptive kind.

In Exod 3-2 where is recorded the first vision of Moses, we read — the Angel of the Lord appeared unto him in a flame of fire out of the midst of a bush, and he looked, and behold ! the bush burned with fire, and the bush was not consumed. And Moses said, I will now turn aside, and see this great sight, why the bush is not burnt? And when the Lord saw that he turned aside to see, God called unto him out of the midst of the bush, find said, Moses, Moses. And he said, Here am I, etc. (verses 2-4)

A reference to Isaiah, 63, 9, tells us what the Angel of the Lord means, — it means not a messenger of the Lord, but his presence. "In all their affliction he was afflicted, and the angel of his presence saved them, etc. (Is. 63-9)

Subsequently, we read of the Lord going before the Israelites, in their journey through the wilderness, — "in a pillar of a cloud" by day and "in a pillar of fire" by night. (Ex. 13. 21.)

And all these bear ample, and it seems to us absolutely convincing evidence of the perceptive, the "sensible" or sensuous character of the earliest God-experience of the Hebrews.

In Islam

Muhammed (Pbuh), the most iconoclastic, and in some sense, the most rationalistic of the founders of religion, though he did not see God, yet heard his voice in mount Horeb. If it be said it was not audition, but cognition, not a sensuous but a soul-experience, expressed in the terms of the sensuous only, still the actuality of the visions of his disciples — visions of him and Hazrat Ali and others, could not be so explained away. Nor should we forget the comparatively advanced state of Arab consciousness and culture when Muhammed (Pbuh) was born. Islam belongs, really, not to the perceptive but to the reflective state of religious evolution.

It Cannot be Entirely Subjective

All these, however, disappear from the later Jewish records. It is no longer God himself who appears directly to man, but his angels, — bene-Elohim, — the sons of God as they are called, become messengers between God and man. Gradually even these pass out of the stage of Judaic religious thought and imagination, and not God, nor even his angels, but most frequently the "Voice of God," comes to the Prophets to communicate to them, and through them to the people of Israel, the wishes and admonitions of Yahveh, until we find in the New Testament that neither the visible presence of God, nor that of his angels, nor even his "voice" comes to man, but it is the Spirit of God that descends, — and here also in a visible form, though evidently symbolic — upon Jesus immediately after his baptism to declare that this is his Son in whom he is well-pleased. And the gradual dropping out, in these records, of the previous visions and auditions of God is extremely significant, as indicative of the fact that in the earliest stage, even according to Jewish tradition, man did hold intercourse with visible and audible gods, and this vision, in any case, was not entirely subjective.

Its end Sensuous

The earliest phase of religion appears to have been either nature-worship, ancestor-worship or a combination of both. And, in every case, the object of man's earliest religion was cognisable, either directly or indirectly, by his senses. The nature-deities were all visible and audible objects, and the ancestors were also, in a way, such. They were human beings, having all the powers and functions and forms of visible men and women, though removed, by death, from the field of their earthly labours. These ancestors appeared, often times, to their children in dreams and thus testified to their existence, and not infrequently even indicated their wishes, their pleasure or their wrath, through the same psychological phenomena. And it is well-known that to the primitive man, his dream-life, though mysterious and awful, was not a bit less real than his waking-life, and that his dreams supplied much ampler materials for his crude but absolutely natural and unsophisticated religion, than even the experiences and activities of his waking hours. So, from whatever point of view we examine the earliest recorded or even the earliest conceivable, state of human religion, we find that it was almost entirely a product of man's sense-activities and his sense-life, the only life, that is, that he may be said to have had then.

His deity was always something that he perceived by his senses. The end that he sought through his religion was the furtherance of his earthly, his animal, his sensuous life — he knew then of no other — the attainment of pleasure, and the avoidance of pain, both being almost entirely sensuous; and his mode of worship was also sensuous. Where religion appeared in the form of submission to custom or tradition alone, as we find it in some savage peoples, there also the motive was the safety and pleasure of the individual or of those who were dear and near to him.

It is Unavoidable

Nor, indeed, is there any warrant whatever, even in the experiences of the most developed forms of human religions, for looking down upon these primitive efforts of the human mind to reach itself out to the Absolute or Infinite, as belonging not only to a lower, but essentially and generically, an altogether different plane. For, can it be held that even Christianity or Islam, the two most iconoclastic religions of the Christen world, has been able completely to get beyond every form of sensuousness in their religious ideals and cultures. What, for instance, are the deepest experiences of Islam? Do not these all gather around the relations that are realised by the faithful with the Prophet? And how are these cultivated? Is it not through the contemplation of the earthly life and even the fleshly form of the Hazrat, or of His immediate disciples, Hazrat Ali or Hazrat Abubakar and others? The lives of the Muhammadan saints all bear testimony to the fact that some, at least, of their profoundest spiritual experiences gathered around the vision of Muhammad (Pbuh) and his personal friends and disciples.

And every devout Muhammadan would, we think, unhesitatingly admit, that in the profoundest beatitudes known to Islam, the figure or the person of Muhammad (Pbuh) is always or almost always present in the consciousness of the devotee. And the same remark applies to Christianity as well. The profoundest experiences of the Christian-consciousness have gathered around not only the character of Christ, in a vague or formless fashion, but around the figure of Jesus, especially of his figure on the cross. The vision of Christ on the cross is universally regarded as a very superior spiritual attainment in every form of Christian meditation, and St. Francis of Assisi, who so deeply realised this vision as to reproduce in his own body, the passion of Christ, has been almost universally accepted as the ideal Christian devotee. The figure of Christ, and that of the Madonna, are accepted institutions for spiritual discipline and culture in both the Catholic and the Greek Churches. They are not absolutely discarded by Protestantism either. They are found in the Anglican Church, for instance; and though some Protestant denominations have banished these figures from their Church, have they been able to put the vision of Christ on the cross altogether from their consciousness, or even from their religious exercises? On the contrary, do they not enthusiastically preach this vision as a vehicle of Christian worship and Christian culture? And those that have entirely-banished it: have they gained or have they suffered in their religious and spiritual life by it?

It is Universal

The fact really is that man's sense-perceptions forming an organic element of his life, constitute always an organic element also of his religion.

Even the most modern of our religions, those that pretend to have known God as Spirit, and that try, therefore, to worship him, in spirit and in truth, have not, really, reached that super-sensuous state which they preach. Their God is found, at the final analysis, to be either a mere abstract idea, and if so, it is no doubt super-sensuous, — or a mere word, an empty sound, — an acoustic symbol, so to say, around which whatever religion they have sought to grow, — or it is some sensuous imagery, a poesy or a phantasy and nothing more. The meanings of sense-perceptions may and do vary as between a primitive and a civilized man, but the fact that these contribute the most vital elements to human religion seems to us to be Universal.

It is a Question of Fact not of Reality

In any case we have it almost on the universal testimony of both ancient records and modern researches into the psychology of primitive life that in the earliest state of the evolution of religion, the object of human worship was always either visible objects or phenomena, or some visible social authority. Man does, in primitive culture, see and hear his God. This much is undeniable. And in studying the phenomena of religious evolution, we are not concerned here with the truth or falsehood of these visions and auditions, — truth that is, in the sense of their objective reality. It would be difficult to establish the objective reality of the experiences of even our more philosophical religions. But this question stands, however, outside the range of our investigation. We are considering here a mental or psychological phenomenon, namely the original ideas of man regarding the deity, and how they took their birth.

The truth of the ideas, as a matter of actual experience, and the way in which they have grown up, tills is what we are trying to understand; and this truth is absolutely independent of the objectivity or reality of those ideas and ideals. A man may, for instance, jump off in a fright at the movement of a black creeper dangling before his face from the branch of a tree in a tropical jungle, taking it for a deadly viper, and the fact that what he got so frightened at was not a viper but a creeper, will not disprove the truth of his fears or the fact of his running away from it. Similarly the question here is not whether what primitive man saw and heard was in reality God as we have come to understand that concept, but whether his God-idea did or did not reveal itself through these visions and auditions; and whether the feelings and activities that resulted from these visions and auditions were not what must be regarded as truly religious. And when we find that it was so, we can safely assert that the earliest known and conceivable phase of religious evolution is what may well be called naturalistic or perceptive.

Forms and Characters of its Deities

Nor is it altogether impossible to trace even the form and diameter of the deities or gods of this perceptive phase of human religions. The Vedic deities are indicated by their very names. Agni is fire, and no one who reads the texts of the Vedas dedicated to this god, can mistake his actual form or character. It is not possible, without doing great violence to the texts, to interpret the Vedic Agni in any but a purely natural sense. Agni, for instance, is described as having two, mothers, *dvimatrika,* which clearly refers to the production of fire, in that primitive age, by the help of the fire-drill, that is, by rubbing two pieces of sticks against each other. We are next told that it is a strange character of this

God-Agni, that he eats up his parents immediately he is born. Like Agni, Varuna also is unmistakably this visible firmament, and so are Maruts, — the winds; and the heavenly twins, — the Aswini Kumars are without doubt the morning and evening twilight. Soma is the juice of the plant of that name which served as a beverage, possibly fermented and intoxicating, to the Vedic Aryans.

Indra is sometimes the Sun, sometimes the clouds, — the holder of the thunderbolt, and sometimes, in later records, he seems to represent the entire hierarchy of the shining spheres overhead. Saraswati is distinctly a river, and we shall see while studying what Professor Max Muller calls the biography of these Vedic deities, how by an exceedingly natural and simple process, this Saraswati came to develop into the presiding Deity of all human arts and sciences, and even the inspirer of divine wisdom, and its personification. Vedic deities are of two classes, *devas and pitris.* The devas, as their name implies, represented nature forces and phenomena, especially those manifested in the heavens; the pitris — the fathers, represented the ancestors of the Vedic Aryans, And both these conveyed to their worshippers forms and characters easily apprehended by the senses and what may be called the lower intellect of man.

We have already referred to the oldest Hebrew records that have come down to us, where we find distinct traces of what we have called, the perceptive or naturalistic phase of primitive religion. It is difficult, however, to ascertain from these records, what was the actual form of these earliest perceptions of the Deity among the Semitic peoples. Both Elohim and Yahveh are, to us, mere names. We can find out from the Vedas what Agni, or Varuna, or the Maruts, and other Vedic deities meant in real, sensuous life. But what Elohim or Yahveh really meant similarly, is more than what we can say in the present state of our knowledge of Hebrew religion and Hebrew language. All that we know of Yahveh is that it was a mere sign among devout Hebrews, who expressed it by bringing together five characters of their Alphabet — Yodh, Aleph, Vow, Aleph and He — without any *nookta* or vowel sounds being joined to them, and the combination, therefore, stood as a mystery which could not even be pronounced. A similar mysterious combination also appears in the Scriptures of Islam, namely, *aleph, lam and meem,* but without any vowel sounds and which also is, consequently, an unpronounceable word. But *aleph and lam,* in the form of *El,* is a term common to both Arabic and Hebrew and seems to be the oldest word for God in the Semitic languages. We find it in the Arabic Allah, as well as in the Hebrew Elohim. This is all, that we know of Elohim also. But what was the original meaning of El or Elohim, — what of Yahveh? Do these terms refer to something that the primitive Hebrew or Arab, or the common ancestors of both saw or heard or felt in his nature-environment, or were they suggested by his experiences of or relations with social authority to which he was subject? These are vital questions.

El-Elohim is rendered into English by God Almighty. Here is evidently the idea of might, strength, power, But whence derived? What was it that suggested this term to the early Semitic man, as a word for invincible might or power? Did the perception of might that gave Elohim as a name for the Godhead, originally grow through man's contact with some nature-force, or with his social authority? These are pertinent questions here, and a satisfactory answer to these questions can alone reveal the actual object, the anginal experience which evoked this god-sense in the primitive peoples from whose records the present Old Testament books were clearly compiled.

But if Elohim suggests its origin in the perception of power or might, whether in Nature or Society we cannot say, Yahveh seemes to our mind to suggest its origin somewhat more definitely in social experience alone. For Yahveh is, undoubtedly, the real God of the covenant in the He brow Scriptures, though what was the original form through which the percept first commenced to grow is more than what we can say or is ever likely to discover from existing records. But Elohim, clearly, belonged to an earlier period of the evolution of Judaic religion than Yahveh. In the Old Testament, though Yahveh refers to his Covenant with Abraham he presents himself in this new name for the first time to Moses. It is not unlikely, therefore, that Yahveh came in at a later and more developed stage, when Judaism was passing gradually out of the early perceptive and naturalistic phases, and consequently when the old vision of God had commenced to grow dim and the process of generalisation and abstraction had already started in Hebrew thought to a more or less extent.

The Reflection Stage

But though religion takes its birth, naturally, in the sense-life and the sense-experiences of man, it soon commences to transcend these. For, our senses themselves gradually reveal their own inadequacy even to explain their own workings. They cannot permanently confine the thoughts, the ideas, the emotions and the activities of man, with the narrow limits of what may be called a mere perceptive life. With the expansion of experience, primitive man, like the child in civilization which necessarily reproduces in itself every phase and process of both the physiological and the pychological evolution of the race, — commences gradually to compare one thing with another, and thereby to think, to reason, to reflect, and thus slowly but surely to transcend the apparent evidence and suggestion of the senses, and rise, step by step, to a consciousness of the super-sensuous.

We see this process of slow evolution very clearly in the development of early Vedic religion, where almost all the gods, Agni, Varuna, Rudra, Indra, Saraswati, that clearly took their birth in the sense experience of the primitive Indo-Aryans, are gradually vested with super-sensuous and ethical properties. Agni which took its birth from the fire-drill comes to be conceived as existing, in a latent form — in the shape, as it is subsequently put, of an unmanifested cause — in the two pieces of wood constituting the drill, and though unseen its substance or form is, thus, never destroyed, and this all-pervasiveness is transferred to inner experiences of man; and Agni, finally, becomes even an all knowing God.

Similerly Varuna too, first apprehended as this visible firmament covering and overlooking every living and moving, as well as every inanimate and fixed thing, comes gradually to be vested with the idea of over-lordship and omnipresence and slowly, with that of omniscience also, until the Vedic worshipper is able to cry out, almost like the Hebrew psalmist, that Varuna knows his uprising and down-sitting, and can find him out from the most secret place of the earth. In studying the biography of these Vedic gods, we shall see how gradually these super-sensuous concepts gathered, by a very easy and natural psychological process, around the original sensuous and sensible ideas of the Godhead of the early Vedic texts until in the Upanishads we find a phase of religion that has grown absolutely beyond all tinge or suspicion of sensuousness. But even these books themselves, with all their super-sensuous and subjective emphasis do bear occasional testimony to the original sensuousness of Vedic religion and to their growth out of it. *The Kenopanishad* of the *Sama Veda,* distinctly states how its questionings about the super-sensuous, arose out of its contemplation and examination of sensuous experience. It starts with the question:

> "By whom directed, does the mind move to its own objects? Under whose guidance, does the vital power, the first of the internal organs, perform its functions? Under whose leading are these words uttered ! Who is that God who leads the eyes and the ears to their own objects?"

And it shows that the Vedic Hindu had, already, commenced long before the time this Upanishad was taught, to reflect upon and analyse his sense-experiences, and had found out the utter inadequacy of the senses to explain and interpret themselves. And when the insufficiency of the senses themselves was thus realised by him, it could not, possibly, take long, after this, for the Vedic Hindu to discover the inability of the old naturalistic and perceptive deities to justify their place and character as objects of human worship, and we, therefore, find them dismissed almost with scant courtesy, by the devotees of the Upanishads.

There (in Brahman) the sun does not shine, neither the moon, nor the stars, nor do these lightnings shine there: how then shall this fire (illumine it)? All these shine after Him, the Shining (One). By His light are all these illumined.

The Emotional and Volitional Phases of Religion

Religion always concerns the whole life of man; and it has, therefore, three departments, so to say, corresponding to the three aspects of the human life, namely, those of (1) intellection, (2) emotion, and (3) volition. The first concerns man's ideas regarding his deity, the second concerns his feelings towards his deity and third his activities in relation to his deity. And the character of the second and third aspect of man's religion is always determined by the first. His emotions towards his God are the direct fruits of his knowledge of, or his ideas concerning that God, and his religious activities or acts of worship are always determined by these emotions. In the earliest, or what we have called, the perceptive phase of human religion, as the Deity is an object of man's senses, so his religious emotions are also, really, sensations and have reference more to his physi-dominant feeling in all primitive religion, fear arising out of the apprehension of some physical pain or loss.

And from the records of very primitive peoples, like the cannibals of the Pacific or of Central Africa, it seems that the deities in this phase of early religion, are almost always regarded as malevolent, and consequently magic, incantation, sorcery, — these constitute the chief elements of worship here, if worship at all it may be called; and sorcerers and medicine-men are their priests. Possession is a very common religious experience in this stage, and magic, sorcery, and the other concomitants of cannibal religion, seem to grow-out of these curious nervous and psychological phenomena.

The object of worship here is not propitiation, really, but subjugation or expulsion of the deity which clearly is engaged in doing evil to the children of man. And the most common forms of these magics, incantations, and exorcisms, are the infliction of distinctly visible torments on the subject. Consequently, even primitive magic does not work through absolutely unseen agencies. In the later phases, hypnotism and other allied psychological phenomena came to be closely associated with magic and sorcery; and the agencies became consequently more or less unseen and mysterious; but in the earliest stages, these were clearly visible, and worked through purely physical or physiological means.

We do not find this phase, however, very markedly, if we find it at all, in the Vedic records. There is, no doubt, a good deal of exorcism, and magic, and incantations, in the Vedas. Indeed, the best part, perhaps of the *Atharva Veda* may be said to consist of these. They are, possibly, the contribution of the non-Aryan and aboriginal tribes of India, to the Vedic culture and religion, which first opposed and subsequently, with the wonderful adaptability of all ethnic systems, quietly absorbed these aboriginal ideas and ideals into themselves. But whatever their origin, these exorcisms and incantations generally refer, not to the real Vedic gods, but to the evil spirits, the Asuras and the Rakshases, as well as to one's enemies, the unknown and known causes of the ills that befall man. Even if magic, sorcery, incantations, and exorcists and medicine-men, be accepted as representing the earliest forms of human religion, we find but scant records and recollections of those in the scriptures and traditions of the great world-religions.

The records of the past history and evolution of which seem to refer, clearly, to a later and higher phase of these religions; and though fear is still found to be the dominant motive of religious works and worship, the method adopted is propitiation, and no longer subjugation or expulsion of the deity by the infliction of counter-punishment or counter-injury on it.

And the form in which the god or gods are sought to be propitiated corresponds, very naturally, to their sensuous or sensible character, in the earlier phases of religious evolutions. In Vedic ritualism, hom or offering of clarified butter and sacred and scented herbs to fire, constitutes, possibly, the earliest form, and it was a distinct and visible mode of feeding the fire, and Fire was, as we are told, the first-born of the gods, in the Vedas. When the other gods came to appear upon the Vedic altar, the Vedic devotee must have been perplexed somewhat as to the means of making offerings to them. Varuna could not, possibly, be so directly worshipped as Fire. Neither could the Maruts, nor the Aswini Kumars, nor Rudra; indeed, none others of the Vedic gods could be so directly tended and so visibly worshipped as Fire. How to make offerings to them, must have, therefore, been a perplexing problem to the simple-minded Vedic Hindu; and with characteristic aptitude he seemed, subsequently, to have solved it, by setting up Agni or Fire as the messenger of the gods, — he who, not only accepted these himself, but also carried the offerings of the children of man to their heavenly lords and gods. Here is suspicion of a somewhat advanced state of culture, no doubt; but we cannot say exactly when these other gods also were born in the consciousness of the primitive Indo-Aryans. One thing, however, is clear, and it is this, namely, that Agni as jungle-fire must have received the attention of his worshippers much earlier than any of the heavenly gods. Agni was, in this particular form, distinctly a terrestrial phenomenon; and terrestrial phenomena received necessarily much earlier attention from primitive man than the celestial phenomena, specially those associated with light and darkness. Even the Upanishads, belonging admittedly to a much later and higher phase of ancient Indo-Aryan evolution, record the perceptive character of the ancient worship of Fire by the Vedic devotees, though condemning it as incapable of producing any lasting spiritual good.

"When, on the fire being kindled, the flame moves about, the worshipper should pour libation with reverence, etc. Kali, Karali, Munojava, Sulohita, Sudhumravarna, Sphulingini, and the bright Bishvaruchi, these are the seven moving tongues (of the sacrificial fire). When one performs sacrifices at the time those flames are kindled, offering libations in proper time, — attains to the region of the Supreme God".

Ritualistic and External Method of Worship in the Perceptive Stage

In the earliest phase of religious evolution, so far as we can discover it either in ancient records or in the life and institutions of primitive races still existing, as the god-idea is universally what we have characterised as perceptive, or what Max Mullar calls naturalistic or what is described by Old Testament scholars as particularistic, — so the method of worship is also universally ritualistic and external. But the character of this externality is, however, not the same everywhere, because the nature of the original religious emotions or relations is not the same among all races. In considering the earliest phases of religious worship as found, for instance, in the Vedas and the Old Testament, we observe a very wide difference in the character. In the Vedic religion and ritualism we find what may be called a most pronounced note of fellowship between the devotees and their deities. There is a distinct note of friendship, mixed with that of awe and tear, of course, in vedic chants and mantras, which we miss very much in the earliest phase of Judaic religion. The relations between Agni or Indra or the other Vedic deities and their worshippers, are touched always with love and affection, and these gods are very often, if not uniformly, addressed and approached in the terms of the family and social relations. But it is very different in the case of Yahveh and his people.

There we find the relation to be almost rigidly legalistic and commercial. Indeed, it must necessarily have been, owing to the contractual or covenantal character of the Yahveistic religion itself. Yahveh enters into a covenant with the ancestors of the Israelite people, by which he agrees to be their God and Lord, and give to them and to their seed, the inheritance of the earth, and they, on their part, agree to serve him to the absolute exclusion of other gods, and follow his laws and his injunctions. There is little or no room for the play of any real affection or love, in such a purely legal and commercial transaction; and we find no trace of these softer human sentiments in the religion of Israel until we come to the times of Jeremiah. Indeed, the word love as expressing a religious sentiment first occurs in the Book of Deuteronomy.

In all the previous records the motives for the observance of the Yahveistic law is presented as mere earthly rewards, as its violation is threatened to be met likewise with earthly punishments. The whole scheme is external. In fact, the covenant or contract between Yahveh and the people of Israel having been made collectively with the whole race, and not with individual members of it, there was little room for the play of any human emotions, as there was absolutely no sense of individual responsibility also, in the earlier religion of the Hebrews.

It took a long time indeed, for any kind of real inwardness even of an ethical type, to grow in Judaism and a distinct ethical note we find for the first time, in the Prophets Amos and Hosea. In the pre-prophetic period, Judaism seems, thus to have been, in its own way as much external, objective, and perceptive, in spite of its somewhat supersensuous ideas of the Godhead; both in its forms of worship and in its general religious life as the ritualism of the Vedas.

In fact, animal sacrifices are common to both the early Hindu and the early Hebrew religion. Attempts have been made to impart a superior ethical significance to the sacrificial religion of Israel, and to interpret these interpret ethically as a cruder symbol of the great ethical and spiritual truth revealed through the passion of Christ, — the greatest sacrifice ever made on earth — that of the "only Begotten Son of God," — for the salvation of the world. But there is nothing absolutely in the idea of sacrifice as found in Judaism, specially in its earlier perceptive or particularistic state, to justify the reading of any ethical significance into it. The only thing common to both the Judaic and the Christian idea of sacrifice is its legality, and absolutely, nothing else.

The sacrifice of Christ propitiates the offended majesty or outraged Divine Law, and the sin-offerings and peace-offerings of the Jews had the same idea in them. Beyond this pure legalistic idea there is nothing really common between the Jewish conception of sacrifice as found in the earlier books, and the Christian conception, in which a new element that of Infinite love and tenderness, entered to raise it from the discharge of a contractual and legalistic obligation, to the spontaneous outpouring of Eternal Love and Infinite Sympathy. Indeed, both the Vedic and the Talmudic conception of sacrifice have in them the common idea of propitiating the deity by making acceptable offerings to it.

Both are external acts, and have no inner significance in them. The difference between the two being this, namely, that while the Vedic sacrifices were made in the spirit, more or less, of friendly offerings, in the expectation, though, of favours to come, and were, thus, partly of a spontaneous character, the Talmudic sacrifices were made distinctly in the discharge of a clear contractual obligation, in the spirit of rigid legalism, and were not, therefore, allied to any necessary sentiment of love or affection or gratitude.

These sentiments did grow, no doubt, in Judaism in its later developments, and they abound in the Psalms, and also are found in some of the Prophets, but that was long after Judaism had passed beyond the primitive period we are here considering, when, indeed, even the old contractual, conception of religious duty, as well as that of the God of Israel as a mere party to a rigid civil contract or covenant, had been largely modified partly as the result of the inner evolution of Judaic life and thought, and partly as that of foreign contact and influence.

Transition to the Reflective Stage

And, as we have already said, such transformations were bound to result from the expansion of human experience and the growth of reflection. And the course of religious evolution may, therefore, be said to proceed, from the earliest or perceptive phase to the reflective phase. If, thus, the earliest phase be called Perceptive, the subsequent phases, for a long time, may well be characterised as merely Reflective; because these phases distinctly grow out of man's thoughts and reflections on his primitive sense life and sense experiences. And as we have named the first or earliest known or conceivable phase of religious evolution, Perceptive, in preference to Prof. Caird's Objective, to avoid the possible suspicion of the presence and operation of any sort of reflection or reasoned process in early religious growth, so we prefer to call the subsequent phases of religious evolution Reflective in preference to Prof. Caird's Subjective, because, as we have already truly subjective phase in all religions, we do find these reflective phases not only in the records of all the great world-religions, but in their earlier forms, we find them even in the history of primitive culture.

The term Subjective indicates the birth of real philosophical or metaphysical speculations, but reflective raises no such anticipation. We find evidence of these speculations in the Upanishads, which may, indeed, claim to be the only speculative books accepted as Scriptural authority in the entire range of the religious, literature of mankind. But there are parts even of the Rig Veda, characterised by Max Muller as the oldest existing records of the great Aryan family, that distinctly show that the Vedic Hindu had already commenced to think, to reason, to reflect, upon the primitive religious ideas and practices of his race long before the birth of the Upanishads. And we find the same process of reflection — though nothing that might be classified with the philosophical speculation of the Upanishads — in the Old Testament records, as well as in the records of ancient Egypt and Chaldoea.

Indeed, we can hardly characterise even the most advanced teachings of the Prophets of Israel, which represent surely a very developed state of Judaic culture and religion, as really speculative, in the sense in which we apply this term to the Upanishads. In the evolution of Judaism, there was, no-doubt, a speculative, though not a truly subjective phase.

Perhaps we find evidences of these speculations in what are called the Maccabbean Psalms, and in a more marked degree in the Cabillistic interpretations of the Jewish Law and the Prophets. But these are, practically absent from the Old Testament records, represent in its higher phases, simply what may be called reflective Judaism, as it indicates, in its primitive forms, the perceptive phases of Hebrew evolution. Buddhism, Christianity, and Islam, representing the credal phase of Hinduism, Judaism, and the ancient religion of the Arab people, respectively, came into being in the reflective state of these older religions, and all these, in their way, did, naturally, develop various speculative systems, representing higher and more complex phases of religious evolution.

But both Christianity and Islam can hardly claim to have been at all speculative at their birth. Speculative Christianity took its birth really through Greek influence, in the interpretations put upon the life, death, and teachings of Jesus, by St. Paul and the author of the Johanine Gospel, and specially by the Alexandrian Fathers, Origen, Clement, Tertullion and others; while we find the growth of a speculative theology out of the teachings of the Prophet and the Koran, most distinctly in the writings of the Matazalas and the Suphis. But both Christianity and Islam, in their original forms, do not represent a speculative, but simply a reflective phase of religious evolution.

While the word subjective indicates, really, an antithetical state of religious evolution, this term Reflective covers both this and the synthetical states of it, and is applicable, therefore, to a much longer course of evolution than Prof. Caird's Subjective. And, as a matter of actual history, every religion has been passing almost continually, through repeated processes of thesis, antithesis and synthesis in the course of its growth. It is present even in what we have characterised as the Perceptive or Naturalistic state, as it is in the later Reflective state. What differentiates this state, from the earlier perceptive state is not its subjectivity, but its super-sensuousness. A growing sense of the Unseen is the principal characteristic of this phase of religious evolution, though the actual conception of this Unseen varies very widely in different religions.

In some religions, as in that of the Upanishads, the Unseen is apprehended as the Absolute, as it is understood in the highest philosophical or metaphysical speculations, as the Universal and the Infinite. In others, as in Judaism, the Unseen is represented practically, as, what Mathew Am-old called, a Non-Natural and Magnified Man. The Upanishads, however, do not represent the earliest phase of what may be called Reflective Hinduism.

That phase is found in the Vodas themselves, and more markedly, as we shall see when studying Vedic Hinduism, in the exegesis and apologetics of Vedic Naturalism, which sought to harmonise the primitive, perceptive religion of the Vedas with the earliest doubts and questionings of the Hindu mind. These doubts and questionings really represent the first movement of reflection in Vedic religion. The Upanishads came long after these; and there are traces of an anthropomorphic phase, even in Hinduism, prior to the speculative phase, seen in the Upanishads or the Vedantas.

The Imaginative or Idealistic Stage

In the growth of these anthropomorphic conceptions concerning the Godhead, imagination, naturally, plays a very important part. And the evolution of religion commenses, thus, to branch out into two lines in this Reflective state, one of which develops religious speculation, creates theologies, seeks to discover a rational ground and justification for religious beliefs and practices, and the other develops religious poetry, cultivates the religious imagination, and creates those profound mysteries of the spiritual life that subsequently become the very soul and essence of every higher religion.

'As imagination bodies forth,

The forms of things unknown, the poet's pen Turns them into shapes, and gives to airy nothing.

A local habitation and a name'.

So does the fancy or frenzy or the imagination of the devotee in religious history everywhere. This process is never absent, indeed, from religious history at any stage, or phase of it. But in the earliest or perceptive or naturalistic state, sense and sentiment work simultaneously, and religious perceptions and religious imagination exist together in an undifferentiated form. This is natural and necessary in the state of homogeneity, the earliest stage or phase of every evolutionary process. In the later state, what we have characterised as the Reflective state, — which is essentially a state of differentiation, though repeatedly followed by higher and higher integrations, the old homogeneity between sense and sentiment is more or less disturbed. Reflection takes up, so to say, the sense-perceptions, and puts off the immediate play of sentiment around them, at least for a time. And sentiment thus put off are really sentiments killed, and it is the function of Imagination always to revive and resuscitate delayed or dead sentiments. Religious Imagination, thus, properly, so-called, takes its birth only in the Reflective and not in the unreflective, naturalistic or perceptive phases of religious evolution.

Thus, we find in actual religious history that after the earliest or perceptive state or phases of religious evolution, there are, everywhere, — what may well be called these Reflective phases, and following these, there are the Imaginative phases, the highest, indeed, that have so far been evolved in the religious history of the human race. Whether in Hinduism, or Buddhism, or Christianity or Islam, these Imaginative phases stand still as the high-water mark of religious culture or spiritual life. What Prof Caird calls the Universal stage of religious evolution, is really, characterised by a very high note of idealism. In the earliest stage, according even to Prof. Caird, god-idea is objective, that is particularistic. In his second or subjective stage, god-idea is subjective; that is here, evidently, the consciousness of the Deity or the ultimate reality takes the form of what is called the Abstract Universal. And, in his third and last or Universal stage, it takes the shape of what is called the Concrete Universal.

But though Philosophy establishes the truth of the Concrete Universal, in its own way, following its own methods of study and research, Religion, when it seeks to realise it, as an actual spiritual experience, has, of" necessity, to accept the guidance of what is called Religious Imagination. All idealisation demands an exercise of the Imagination; and the supreme idealisation which reveals matter, so to say, as the thought of God concretised, and man as the Spirit of God incarnated, can only be possible through the exercise of the most superior kind of this faculty.

Indeed, though some people, in our age, may try to deduce some kind of a, religion out of their own special philosophy of life, historically, that is, in the general experience of mankind, religions have not grown out of philosophies but philosophies have, almost always, grown out of religion. In other words, as in the development of every science, actual experience has preceded the investigation and discovery of general laws and principles, so also here, the actual religious experiences of man have universally preceded the development of his religious philosophy or theology. These latter have grown, almost everywhere, out of man's attempt to discover a rational basis and justification of his actual religious or spiritual experiences. Thus, Hindu philosophy has grown out of the inner mental and spiritual experiences of the Hindu; Buddhist philosophy, similarly, out of the ethical and spiritual experience of the Buddhist; Christian and Islamic philosophies, similarly, have grown out of the actual moral and emotional experience, of the Christian and the Moslem saints and devotees. Religious imagination takes precedence, therefore, of philosophical or metaphysical speculations in the history of religious evolution everywhere.

Nor can we summarily dismiss these imaginative experiences as mere figments of the fancy. Language in drawing a distinction between fancy and imagination has corroborated the evidence of human experience, regarding the truth and reliability of the latter. Indeed, most, if not all, of our positive scientific truths, principles, or laws are the products, absolutely, of the Imaginative Faculty. All our generalisations are, really, the children of the Imagination. Scientific laws are not apprehended by the senses, nor are they capable of any "sensible" or sensuous verification. The senses apprehend only particulars of our experience, it is the function of the imaginative faculty to peer beyond these particulars and discover the general or universal truths or principles underlying them. Scientific Imagination discovers the highest truths of science. Similarly Religious Imagination reveals the profoundest truths of the spiritual life. The one is as much a witness unto truth as the other. The Imaginative Faculty exercises, thus, the highest function in our mental and spiritual life. Its function is everywhere, whether in science or in art or in religion, — to transcend the limitations of the real and carry the reason, the emotions, and the spirit of man on its heavenly wings, on to the realms of the Ideal.

And, idealisation is an essential feature of the third, or the highest stage of religious evolution, as discussed by Prof. Caird. His Universal stage is essentially, the Idealistic stage. The highest or the universal stage of Christian evolution is that wherein Christ stands universalised in humanity, and thus the love and service of humanity become identified with the love and service of God or Christ. But how is this to be realised in actual inner experience, except through the help of the imaginative faculty? The Philosophy of the Absolute may have revealed to Prof. Caird and others of his School, the rational ground and justification of the Universal Christianity; but a Universal Christ-consciousness had been realised by Christian Saints and devotees, through the exercise of their Religious Imagination, long before Hegel sought to discover its philosophical or rational meaning and significance.

In tracing the historical growth of the religious phenomena, therefore, we may very safely state that in the earliest phase, religion is everywhere perceptive and sensuous, gradually, however, it becomes reflective and supersensuous, and finally it becomes, essentially, idealistic or imaginative. And if we have to divide, for the convenience of the students of the religious experiences of man, the history or course of religious evolution into definite phases or stages at all, we must call the first phase Perceptive, the second Reflective, and the third Imaginative, from the fact that though perception, reflection and imagination are all present at every state or stage of the religious phenomena, in the earliest states perception dominates reflection and imagination both; subsequently reflection dominates both perception and imagination, and ultimately imagination idealisation dominates both perception and reflection. This, it seemes to us, is, in most general terms, the history of Religious Evolution. The Evolution of particular religions must, therefore, be studied in the light of this general or universal process or principle or law.

Evolution does not Explain Original Differences among Religions

But this general or universal process or principle or law of religious evolution, will not be able to explain and interpret all the endless varieties and complexities of the religious phenomena. By following it, we may be able to arrange and classify the mixed up records of the ancient world-religions, and by the application of this logical test, we may, thus, fix an approximate chronological succession among these records, and build up a more or less connected and intelligible story of that past evolution of these religions. But it will not help us to trace the causes of the wide divergences that exist, both in the character and history between these world-religions. We have already indicated one of the causes of this divergence, namely the difference in the emphasis that different religions have laid from almost pre-historic times, on the one or the other of the two aspects of the Not-Me, out of man's contact and conflict with which his religion seems to have grown everywhere. But this difference in the emphasis on either the Natural or the Social aspect of the Not-Me, of the different religions, does not explain their divergences fully. And a philosophy or science of Religion that fails to do so, to explain their interpreter of the religious phenomena in general. In any case it cannot pretend to have discovered the laws or principles of religious evolution.

For, all evolution is change in permanence. Every form of change or differentiation does not belong to the evolusionary process; but only such as preserve the continuity of the original class or kind or species, which is always discoverable under every change of form or even of functions, and where not apparent, this continuity may still be traced historically. Biological evolution, thus, always works upon two essential factors, namely, hem-dity and environment, the one representing the element of permanence and the other explaining the causes of change or variation, resulting from the operation of the law of natural selection. In working out the law of evolution in the growth of the religious phenomena, therefore, we have, first of all, to discover the element of permanence in religion in general In defining religion as the attempt of man to adjust himself to his Not-Me, we have already indicated this element. Both man and his Not-Me, in its dual aspect of nature and society, constitute thus, the permanent factor in all religious evolution; and changes in the religious experiences of man, may be well traced, generally, to his changed notion of himself or his altered estimates of his Not-Me. It is these changes that, really, account for the evolution of religion from the Perceptive to the Reflective and from the Reflective to the Imaginative states or phases of its growth. Rut this is the general scheme of religious evolution, and though these phases are observed in all religions, at one point or other of their history, the differences that are noticed between one religion and another are not adequately, if they are at all, explained by a reference to these different phases of religious evolution.

For these differences are not merely those of stages, like those observed, for instance, between a tadpole and a frog, or between a baby, a boy, and a young and an old man. They are observed in religions that distinctly occupy the same plane of historic evolution, Judaism, for instance, even in its earliest or perceptive stage appears as essentially different from perceptive Hinduism or Hellenism. And in all its phases Semitic religious evolution presents a peculiarity not observed in Hindu religious history. It seems, therefore, clear that as there is an element of permanence in religion in general, so there is a similar element in almost each one of the great world-religions, — an element that is peculiar to them, and that has been evolving itself through the progressive changes and the past history of these different religions.

A scheme of the evolution of religion in general, — such as we have been considering up to now, — as well a study of the special elements, organic and original that differentiate one religion from another, and elements that have been persistently present in their past history, and that will persist, so far as can be seen, for ever, perhaps, in their future growth and evolution, with more or less emphasis, these are essential for the study of any religion. For it is only in the light of these that we may hope to understand both the general character and the particular and differentiating features of any religion that we may undertake to study and interpret. Heredity, environment, and epoch, — these, says have always played a very important part in the development of the literatures of different nations of the world. These same elements have played an equally and important part in the development of man's religion also; and they have left their mark upon the religious doctrines, dogmas, sacraments, rituals, mysteries; and the religio-ethical codes of the different races of mankind. There are very fundamental differences, for instance, between the religion of the Hindu and that of the Hebrew, as there are also between ancient Hellenism and ancient Hinduism.

In the former case, as we shall presently see, these differences are due to what may almost be called organic cause, — to organic and original elements in the thought and social life of the two peoples, — they are due to what may very well be called differences in heredity, what we prefer, however, to describe as differences in race-consciousness or race-characteristics. In the other case, as between Hellenism and Hinduism, these differences are due more to environment and epoch than to any original and organic difference in the mental or social life of these two peoples.

This element of what M. Taine calls heredity, but what is better understood, perhaps, by the terra race-consciousness, in the case of the collective life of nations, constitutes the element of permanence in the evolution of the different religions, as well as that which differentiates them, permanently, from other religions, while the elements of change are contributed to the evolution of these religions by alterations in their nature-environment, through either natural or physical geographical changes, or their migration to different and distant parts of the earth, having different nature-surroundings or in their social-life brought about either through the natural expansion of it, or through contact and intercourse, whether commercial or political or both, or even religious also, with other groups of men having a different type of social-structure or civic or economic organisation or cultivating different type of piety.

What is this Race-consciousness? It is, what may well be called, the indivi-mankind. As there are evident but inexplicable peculiarities in different men, that differentiate them from other men, peculiarities both physical and mental, which constitute, really, their individuality, so there are also evident and inexplicable peculiarities even in the different races of mankind that may be said to constitute their essential raciality or nationality or what we have called their race-consciousness or racial characteristics. That there are such racial peculiarities cannot be denied.

When and how the human race came to be so fundamentally divided and differentiated, is a question which it would be futile, if not foolish to raise, because it is absolutely impossible to answer it Whether the different races originated with one human pair or there were different such pairs, is what none can say, all that we see, are these differences in social character, differences that seem to be original and organic, and that are absolutely pre-historic. And viewing these differences modern Anthropology starts with not one but quite a number of original human stocks out of which the present humanity has grown. This is the furthest point that induction leads us to in this matter; to go beyond this would be vain and unverified and unverifiable speculation, in which science, at least, sternly refuses to indulge.

But whether the original stock was one or many, that there are fundamental differences between the different races of men, must be universally admitted. These differences are partly physical, differences in physiological and anatomical structure, which modern psychometry has been investigating with such marvellous accuracy, and such remarkable results, both ethically and ethnologically. There are differences in the structure of the cranium and the face, in the pigment of the skin or the character of the hair. These differences are plainly visible as between an Aryan, a Mongolian, and a Negro. No one knows, or can even surmise, the origin of these structural physiological differences. They are there — this is all that can be said. They are pre-historic, this is all that is known of them. And here all speculation is stopped.

But these differences of physical structure are not, however, the only ones that differentiate the different races of mankind. There are equally fundamental differences among them, in regard to what may be called their thought-structure, that is the cast and Constitution, so to say, of their mind and the social structure, or the original type and character of their social organisation and economy.

Anthropology is still an infant science, and we do not as yet know what the possible implication of the differences in the physiological structures of the different races of men actually are, though some people do seem to think that they are an index of racial superiority and inferiority. Criminal anthropology has, no doubt, proved to a very large extent, the close and almost organic connection, that exists between the structure of the cranium and the mental and moral qualities of men and women, in certain typical cases; and whatever truth there may possibly exist in the theory of cerebral localisation and phrenology, that the structure of our skulls, as an indication of brain capacity, has a vital influence upon our mental and moral capabilities can hardly be denied. But though idiots and what are called instinctive criminals, are marked out almost in every civilized race, by the peculiarities of their physiological structure, and especially by the formation of their cranium, the question what mental or moral significance can be attributed to the differences in the angle of the nose, the character of the facial and labial formations, the colour of the skin, or the peculiarities of the hair, — such as are observed between the Aryan, the Mongolian, or the Negro, has not yet been answered. It seems doubtful whether it will ever be answered at all.

But though we cannot as yet say what the differences in the physiological structures of the different races of men indicate, we can say, to a very large extent, what the structures of the thought or of their social life mean. The physiological structure of a man is visible to the eye. We see these structural differences as between an idiot or an instinctive criminal on the one side, and a thoughtful, virtuous, self-controlled and respect-compelling man on the other- We see these differences also as between a typical Aryan and a typical Mongal or a typical Negro. But how do we, and where, observe their thought-structures — the original cast and character of their mental capacities? In their language, Is it not? A man's style, if it be really his own, and not a mere imitation of some body else's — is a sure index to the character of his thought Loose style, whether in conversation or in writing, is an almost unerring proof of loose ways of thinking. A vigorous style, similarly, indicates a vigorous mind, strong and broad mental grasp. Even in individual men and women their language is often an index to their thought-power and thought-life. So it is, very markedly, with races; the structure of their language or their dialect, betrays their manner of expressing their thought, and indicates the character of that thought. And it is in the grammar of these languages and dialects that we must look for the peculiar structure of the thought, of these different races. As Anthropology discovers the peculiarities in the physical and physiological structures of different races of men, so Philology reveals their real thought-structures. Here Comparative Philology must be our guide, for Comparative Philology reveals the structural differences of different languages, as Comparative physiology and Comparative Anatomy reveal differences in physical structures of different animals, indicative of fundamental differences in their physical life and functions.

Without entering into a discussion of the abstruse question whether thought is or is not possible without language, language, it may be safely asserted, never exists without thought. Its essence is the expression of thought, and therefore the structure of different languages must necessarily indicate the character of the thought of those who have been using them. For, these linguistic structures are not arbitrary formations, uncontrolled by any law or principle. The law of natural selection operates as much in the development of language, which may be said to be the organ of thought, as in that of the physiological or anatomical structures and organs of animals. And the essential character of the thought that seeks to express itself through a language constitutes the Regulative Idea in what may be called as Philological evolution. The structure of their language indicates therefore the character of the mental life of a people, even as that of its body indicates the character of the physical or physiological life and functions of an animal. In other words, the grammatical structure of a language speaks always of the peculiarity of the mind which it has always sought to give expression to.

Language An Index to the Mental Life

"All thought consists, whether explicitly or implicitly, of three essential parts, — a subject, an object, and a predicate. This is, however, not merely an analysis of thought, but of language as well. For, in every completed sentence there are these three parts. And the structural differences of different language is mainly due to the different degree of emphasis that is laid in them, on one or other of these elements of a completed thought or on one or other of these three parts of what we understand and know by a completed sentence.

The character of the mind or thought of a race is indicated, that is, by the position that is assigned by the genius and structure of their language, to these different elements of thought. In different languages, for instance, the common fact of a man striking another is expressed differently. In some the construction of the sentences would be — A struck B; where there is a very clear indication of (1) the agent, (2) the act, and (3) the object It shows a clear perception of the different characters of these three elements of thought The emphasis is here on all three elements of the sentence. There are other languages which do not allow a similar construction, and in expressing this common fact of a man's striking another man, it would simply say — B struck. And it shows that in the thought of this people the object dominates the subject There are other languages where this emphasis would neither be on the subject, nor on the object, but on the predicate.

Among some primitive peoples, for instance, we find that they have a different word for drinking different kinds of soup, one for drinking meat-soup, another for drinking fish-soup, a third for drinking vegetable soup and so on; and it shows that the emphasis, in the thought or mental life of this people, is neither on the subject or agent nor on the action or predicate, but on objects only, and, consequently, the same act of drinking, by the same individual, is viewed very differently by them according to the tilings that constitute these drinks. And these differences in the emphasis laid by the languages used by different races of men, on one or other of the different parts of a sentence, on one or other, that is, of the different elements of every completed thought, indicate the different ways in which these races have, from pre-historic times, viewed themselves and their relations with the objects and activities about them. In-other words, the grammatical structures of different languages reveal the original world-idea, so to say, of the peoples to whom these languages originally belong.

Take, for instance, any of the languages belonging to what is called the Indo-Aryan group, Sanskrit, or Latin, or Greek, or any of the languages directly or indirectly derived from these, and certain peculiarities are observed in their structure which are not found in any other family of languages. The construction, "I *am,*" "*Aham asmi*" meaning simple existence or being, absolutely without any reference to any action or object, is impossible in any other known group of languages.

In the other languages this idea of being or existence is expressed by some such sentence as — "I stand" or "I sit", etc. In the same way it is only in languages belonging to the Indo-Aryan family that we find what is known as an appositional case, which allows such constructions as, "This is A," or "He is B," or "This man is great;" in which the idea of identity of being is expressed by a mere copula. In the Chinese language this construction is unknown, like the construction *"I am"* or *"Aham asmi"*. "Jin Ter" in the Chinese means, thus, both what is expressed by the English "Great man" as well as by "the man is great" And all these indicate the different ways in which different peoples have, from pre-historic times, approached and sought to solve the great world-problems. These different thought-structures are indices to their different "world-ideas".

In the structure of a people's language, as revealed by their grammar, we thus discover the original bent and emphasis of their thought. It is here, in the construction of their language, that we are able to read the story of their pre-historic thought, even just, as in the construction of the earth's surface, in the geological structure of the different continents, we are able to study the course of their pre-historic growth and evolution. It is in the original structure of their language that we see how, originally before the birth of history, the earliest ancestors of the different races of mankind, standing, perhaps, "alone to the alone"—fare to face with the overwhelming mysteries of the play of life and force about them, sought to understand their meaning and purpose; and thus developed or discovered the original bent or emphasis of their thought. And this original bent or emphasis of the thought of the different races of man constitutes one element of what we have called their race-consciousness.

Thus, for instance, in the structure of the various languages belonging to the Indo-European group, we at once recognise the speciality of Aryan thought Among this people, we find, that the spiritual and the universal has always dominated the consciousness of the material and the particular, that the emphasis of their thought has, from pre-historic times, been more on the noumenon than on the phenomenal. The consciousness of absolute being, the recognition of the self as existence, by itself, that have been the result of long generations of speculative effort among other races, seem to have been an original instinct with the Hindu or the Greek. This is a very curious fact.

But it is as undeniable as it is inexplicable. There is no conceivable period in the lifestory of the Indo-European languages whether Sanskrit, or Greek, or Latin, when they did not allow, for instance, the very significant construction A struck B, or when they had not in use the cons-traction, I am or its equivalent meaning pure existence, or A is A, meaning identity of being. Nor is there any trace of such a construction or of anything approaching it, by which mere being is sought to be indicated in any of the non-Aryan languages that we know of. In the thought structure of some races we thus find that there is an original instinct or consciousness of the self or the subject, in that of others the not-self or the object has been the dominating element, while, in that of a few so-called aboriginal races, the emphasis is neither on the subject, nor on the object but on the predicate. And these original bents of mind or thought have imparted peculiar characteristics to the entire thought life and thought-history of these peoples, and their literature, their art, their philosophy and their religion have all borne, ever and always, despite all varieties of environments and changes of epochs, the marks of these original casts of their mind and thought.

Social and Economic Arrangements as Elements of Race-consciousness

As different races of men, thus, have their own peculiar way of looking at the world-problem, their peculiar cast of mind and thought, what we have called their peculiar thought structure, which differentiates their mental life, and their view both of themselves and of the outside world, from those of other races; — so different races of men have also their peculiar social organisation and economy, which also are as much an original and organic element of their life as are their thought-structures, and which also, constitute, therefore, elements of racial differentiation. In their thought-structures we see the way in which these different races have, from pre-historic times, sought to approach the world-problems, and to interpret their outer experiences to themselves. In their social-structures we see, similarly, the way in which, from pre-historic times, the different races of men have been seeking to realise their relations with other members of their society or community or tribe individually, and with that society or community or tribe as a whole. In their thought-structure we find how the different races have, from the commencement, so to say, of their life, approached the nature aspect of their Not-Me; in their social structure we see how they have sought to approach the other, social aspect, of that same Not-Me.

The Constitution of some societies has, for instance, been despotic, while in others it has been constitutional, from pre-historic times. What relations the thought-structures of different races have with their social structures, or whether there is any necessary connection between the two, is more than what we can, in the present state of our knowledge of pre-historic and primitive man, say. But we do find that among the Aryan peoples, as their thought-structure is of a decidedly philosophical or metaphysical type, so their social structure also is universally of a constitutional type, while the Semitic races have always had quite a different, that is a despotic type of social and civic Government and organisation. The King among the Semitic peoples has always been a military chief, whose word and will have been the law to his subjects. Among the Aryans, however, whether in Europe or in India, the King has been a constitutional Governor, deriving his authority from the suffrages of his peers.

The tribal chiefs among Aryans have always been, peers among their peers, — the chosen heads of other heads of families, and never an arbitrary and autocratic ruler; and their functions though hereditary had never been of an irresponsible or despotic character. And this ideal of peer-hood or equality in some shape or other, whether latent or patent, unorganised, or organised, has been a universal feature of all Aryan societies. These peculiarities of social organisation and civic ideal are what we have sought to express by the term social-structure, which constitutes an important element of race-consciousness, and gives rise, along with the pecularities of the thought-structures of different races, to all original and organic racial differentiations, presenting a special Regulative Idea, the historic evolution of the different branches of the great human family.

Race-Consciousness the Permanent Element in Evolution

This race-consciousness supplies, thus, the element of permanence in the mental and spiritual evolution of the different races of men. What heredity is in biological evolution, that this race-consciousness is in national and racial evolutions. Both environment and epoch help to bring out and modify this original Constitution, so to say, of the different races, but do not create it. This race-consciousness forms also the base of all religious evolutions.

This, and this alone, can explain the fundamental difference between one religion and another. It is this race-consciousness which offers a reasonable explanation as to why the Hindu or the Hellenic conception of the Deity has been, from even pre-historic times, so different from that of the Hebrew or the Arabs. This element of race-consciousness persists through every change that a people may be subjected to, as a result of foreign contact or outside influence or authority. It is not even obliterated by community of creeds and cries, as is proved by the fact that a common Christian creed and cry, developed different types of Christian philosophy and Christian piety among Eastern and Western peoples.

Of essentially Hebrew or Semitic origin, how it became almost fundamentally transformed and transfigured as soon as it entered into the Greek consciousness; as Roman or Latin Christianity, again, owing to racial differences, became something almost radically different from the Christianity of the Alexandrian schools. The same thing is observed also in the history of Islam, which assumed a distinctly philosophic and idealistic type in Persia, very different from the original Arab type. Buddhism also, the other credal religion, assumed two widely different forms, under the same creed and cry, in its Northern and Southern schools. And all these divergences even in these credal religions are traceable only to differences in racial or national Constitutions and characteristics, — to what we have called, race-consciousness.

Indeed, such divergences are inevitable. For, religion being essentially a matter concerning man's thoughts and sentiments on the one side, and the ideal of his relations with and behaviour towards other men on the other, — it being, in other words, a thing that relates him on the one side to what may be called the Super-Natural, and that seeks, on the other, to regulate his associations with and obligations to other members of his tribe, his community, his society, or his Church, can never divest itself altogether, either of the original conceptions of the Super-Natural or of the original ideals of social life and duty, that he inherits from his race or nation. Even among men and women belonging to the same society and inheriting the same culture and civilization, ideas of religion are almost always found to vary more or less widely, owing to variations of intellectual endowment or attainments and moral culture.

Even in the same family, the religion of little children must, necessarily, be different from that of adult peoples, and though all may use the same terms or receive the same sacraments, or adopt the same symbols, these have, almost universally, special meaning and significance to different persons, according to their culture, their character and the general experiences of their inner and outer life. And the story of the boy who being told that God was his father, at once shuddered at the idea, and said if that was so, he must hate God, because he would be sure to come and beat his mother, — reveals a universal truth. We thus find that among primitive races, God is very rarely addressed as mother, which is due to the degraded and helpless condition of women among them. God as mother is also unknown among even more advanced peoples, who had, somehow, come to cherish a very low and beastly idea concerning the functions of generation, and consequently also of maternity.

In the Old Testament, for instance, we find the Deity repeatedly addressed as the Lord, the King, the Saviour, and as in the Book of Solomon, even perhaps as Lover, but never once as mother. This is common to all Semitic records. Islam would not address God as either Father or Mother, and in the most devout and ecstatic experiences of Islam, God is addressed only as Friend, but never in the terms of the filial or the nuptial relation. And all these go to show that whatever ideas and ideals concerning religion may be presented to man, there is always, what may well be called a law of natural selection operative in his acceptance of them, and he accepts these ideas and ideals, whenever he accepts them at all, only in his own way, according to his own light, — that is in the way that will fit them in with his general notions of things and his ideas and experiences of his special social or domestic relations, — and he always puts his own meaning and interpretation upon whatever may be presented to him as even universal truths.

Peculiarities of race-consciousness have, thus, a very potent and powerful influence, not only in the development of all ethnic religions, but they largely modify even the meaning and message of credal religions when these are presented to and accepted by alien races, — whose original ethnic systems particular credal systems may have at first grown in the natural course of its evolution. And a truly scientific study of the religious phenomena must start, therefore, with the study of these racial characteristics. For it is this study alone that can accurately fix the meaning and significance of the religious terminology, the religious symbolism, and the religious rites and ceremonials of different races. Any other course is bound to lead to gross misconceptions and outrageous misinterpretations and misunderstandings.

Take, for instance, that much discussed passage in the Old Testament, I am that I am. When deputing Moses to the children of Israel then living in the bondage of Pharaoh, this is the name, in which Yahveh or Jehovah said he should be indicated to his people. "I am that I am" hath sent me to you — this was how Moses was asked to go and appear before his people.

Now, what is the meaning of this new name which Yahveh assumes here? What does *I am that I am* signify? It is clear that Yahveh, the name in which God appears to lites. He says, indeed, as much. In the earlier books, the usual name for God is Elohim or El Elohim, rendered by the English translators into the Lord or the Lord Almighty. In fact, scholars are now almost unanimously agreed that in the existing Old Testament there is a clear collation of three different sets of ancient Hebrew records; — one set being called. *Elohistic, i.e.,* which invariably describes the Deity in the terras of *El* or *Elohim,* a second set being called *Yahveistic,* wherein the Deity is named Yahveh or Jehovah, and a third set which contains directions for ritual and conduct, — the laws of Israel, and called, therefore, *Priestly Code.* The Book of Genesis is entirely based upon the first and the third of these original records. It is in Exodus that we clearly come, for the first time, upon the Yahveistic records. Yahveh, whence so ever it may have been derived, is professedly a new name among the Israelites, first introduced, evidently, under Mosaic Dispensation, — new, that is as compared to the older and more familiar, El or Elohim. El, indeed, is the common term for the Deity in all Semitic languages. We recognise it in Arabic Allah, as much as in the Hebrew Elohim. Yahveh, however, seems to be peculiar to Israel, introduced into Hebrew tradition along with that of the Mosaic Dispensation.

We know, however, as yet absolutely nothing as to what Yahveh meant We cannot, as yet, refer it to any actual experience, as its source, just as we can the Sanskrit Deva or the Greek Deos or Teus. For we have the secret in the Sanskrit root *div* to give light. Deva means, thus, the bright one, the shining one, and its origin, clearly, was in the phenomena of light and darkness as observed in the heavens. Similarly we can trace the genesis of the word for the Supreme Being in Hinduism, namely, Brahman. It is from the root *Brrinha* which means large. The original idea of Brahman was thus, immensity, the all-comprehensive, the all-covering, the all-pervading, thing; and thus step by step, it came to mean that which not only covers and contains, but also explains, interprets, illumines all — the Supreme Self, the Over-Soul, Ultimate Principle in the universe.

We can trace the biography, so to say, of all or almost all these concepts. But we cannot, in the present state of our knowledge, trace the biography, in the same way, of Yahveh. But whatever may have been the origin of Yahveh, it is absolutely certain that we cannot interpret this *I am that I am* in any profoundly spiritual or philosophical sense; because such an interpretation has, absolutely, no support or justification in the thought and experiences of the Hebrew people. *I am that I am* does seem, on the face of it, to refer to Pure Being, or the Absolute, in its highest and deepest philosophical cognition; but such a supreme philosophic or spiritual instinct as could account for the growth of so abstract a concept at such an early period of their evolution, was never known to be possessed by the Hebrews. Either the new name was borrowed from some other people more philosophically endowed than the ancient Israelites, or it meant something very different from what we understand by a phrase like I am *that I am.* Conception of the Deity as pure being could only grow among people who had a profound spiritual consciousness, and who recognised their own soul-life.

Such a conception could not, possibly grow among a race that for long centuries of its thought-life had, absolutely, no notion of a future state or of any existence whatever, possible for man, apart from and independent of the body and its diverse organs and functions. And it is well-known that the Hebrews had no idea of a life after death before the Babylonian captivity, and even afterwards their conception of a future existence was always associated with the resurrection of the human body. In the older records there is, no doubt, frequent reference to what is called the Judgement Day; but this Judgement Day refers, as a critical and careful examination of these texts distinctly proves, to this, and not, as in the New Testament, to the next life. In fact, even Jesus's teachings concerning the life of the spirit was woefully misunderstood and misinterpreted by the general body of his own people, and some scholars have even attributed his crucifixion to the ill-feeling produced by the disappointment of his earlier admirers caused by this misunderstanding.

For the Messianic Prophecy which Jeans sought to interpret, did not, as understood by the Hebrews, refer at all to a Kingdom of God in the spirit of men, but to a Kingdom of God, visible and manifest, among his old and chosen people in Israel, — a kingdom that, once more reviving the old theocracy, would put an immediate end " to the sovereign, earthly, authority of Rome over the Hebrew nation. Jesus's preachings of the Kingdom of Heaven, evidently appealed to the patriotism of the Jews, offered them an almost immediate release from the Roman Yoke; and this was, some say, the main cause both of his early popularity among his own people, and of his subsequent downfall; and it would be impossible to deny at least the plausibility of this view. Be that as it may, however, the fact that the Israelites had never any great spiritual or metaphysical instincts can hardly be gainsaid, and how the revelation of the concept of Pure Being, such as a philosophic or spiritual interpretation of *I am that I am* would indicate, came to be made at such an early period of Judaic history and evolution, seems absolutely inexplicable and inconceivable. Judging from the general thought-structure and religious life of the Hebrew people, such an interpretation would appear to be as reasonable and legitimate, as a highly refined and sensitive chromatic or acoustic interpretation of an utterance of Hebu Keller, the gifted deaf and blind young German lady, would be. And such misinterpretations are entirely due to the study of the religious records and experiences of one people with the help of the generalisations of those of another.

In fact attempts towards a scientific study of the religious experiences of mankind have hitherto failed to so large an extent, and have so frequently led to erroneous interpretations and unwarranted generalisations, mainly owing to the ignorance or neglect of theologians, and philosophical writers, of the vital relations existing between the religious ideas and sentiments of a people and their special race-consciousness or race-character. The Right Rev. Dr. Boyd Carpenter in his Bampton Lectures, divides the great world-religions, for instance, into two broad classes — (i) Religion of Law or Legalistic Religion, and (ii) Religion of Fellowship. Under the first head he puts in Judaism, Christianity. Islam, and Buddhism, and under the second, Hinduism or Brahmanism. Apparently the division would seem to be perfectly reasonable and justifiable, but only apparently. For though there is a kind of legalism, no doubt in Buddhism, it is essentially different from that of Judaism, Christianity, or Islam; and the difference is brought out only by an examination of the race-characteristic or race-consciousness of the Hebrew or the Arab on the one side and of the Hindu on the other. Both the Hebrew and the Arab belong to the same stock, their languages have the same origin, the same structure, the selfsame alphabet even. That is, they have a common thought structure. The social structure of the two peoples is also the same, of the military and despotic type, inspite of the fact that among the Hebrews it assumed a theocratic character. And the race-consciousness of the two peoples being thus the same, it is not at all surprising that there should be an essential similarity in their religions also, however widely the forms of these might differ from one another. Judaic and Islamic legalism can thus, very fairly, be classed together. As for Christianity owing to its origin, its legalism also does bear some similarity to that of Judaism, or Islam, though on account of the profound influence that Greek thought and culture had in the development of Christian doctrine and Christian piety, Christian legalism, in some of its deeper aspects, is yet slightly different also from either the Judaic or the Islamic legalism.

But can we, in any away, place Buddhistic legalism in the same class? There is a kind of legalism in Buddhism, no doubt, but is it of the same character as the legalism of Judaism or Islam or even of Christianity, with which it bears in other respects, some strange similarity? In one sense, Buddhistic legalism is much more rigid than Judaic, Islamic, or Christian legalism. In Buddhism, there is absolutely no getting out of the law, except through the law itself. Here, especially in the Southern School, there is no room for grace to suspend or annul the law. The Buddhistic law is absolute and in exorable. Yet this rigid and unbending legalism is fundamentally different from the Hebrew, Christian, or the Muhammadan legalism, with which Bishop Carpenter seeks to classify it. And this difference is due to the difference in their origin, — the difference in the race-consciousness of the peoples among whom these different religions took the birth.

Law in Judaism is essentially the imposition of an outside will and authority. It is, really, an outside law. Indeed, for long centuries, Judaic law never sought the sanction or support even of the inner consciousness of the children of Israel. Its conceptions is that of a contract Its obligations are what may be called covenantal or contractual. The Lord promised certain things to the children of Israel on their doing certain things to him: this is essence of the Hebrew Law. Hebrew legalism' is contractual, covenantal, associated with rewards and punishments, that are essential elements of it. This is the rudimental idea equally of Christian and Muhammadan legalism also. But the character of Buddhistic legalism is very different, indeed, from this. Here there is absolutely no conception of an outside authority which imposed the law, no idea of a personal will enforcing itself upon another. The Buddhistic law is impersonal, absolute, eternal. Its progression is like that of" the tree from the seed, and the seed, again, from the tree. Law, in Buddhism, is conceived as a wheel. A wheel is a circle, and a circle is the only figure that suggests infinity — endlessness and beginning lessness. Every point in the circumference of a circle is its beginning, and that selfsame point, again, is its end also. So also with the Wheel of Law, every point is its beginning, and every point its end. Law is associated, here, in Buddhism to really neither rewards nor punishments.

There are antecedents and consequents: there is causation. There are causes and effects. But every effect is like every other effect, a source of bondage, becomes in its turn a cause producing other effects, to become fresh causes, again. And so on the wheel moves endlessly. What Judaism or Christianity or Islam would call good or what they would call evil, are both equally spokes in this Eternal Wheel, both create *Karma* and bind man to this inexorable and endless chain. In Judaism, or Christianity or Islam fulfilment of the law is the ultimate end. In Buddhism, not fulfilment, for the fulfilment of the end is in the generation of the tree which fulfils itself again in the production of new seeds, for producing fresh trees, — but the annulment, the destruction, the absolute cessation of the law is the goal.

This is salvation. This *is Nirvana.* And when we thus carefully analyse the conception of Law in Buddhism, we find how essentially different it is from Judaistic, Islamic or even Christian legalism. Taking the ordinary classification of our mind into the Reason, the Will and the Emotions, it may well be said that while Judaic or Arabic legalism belongs to the domain of the Will, that of Buddhism belongs to the realm of Reason. The one is almost external, the other is positively internal. The one is distinctly empirical, the other is essentially philosophic The two stand on altogether different planes and can never be placed in the same class. And the difference between them is due to the different character of the Hebrew or Semitic and the Hindu or Aryan race-consciousness.

For Buddhistic legalism is not entirely Buddhistic either. It is, in some sense, common to both Hinduism and Buddhism. For though as Bishop Carpenter says truly, Hinduism is pre-eminently a religion of fellowship, it is equally also a religion of law or Karma. And the doctrine of *Karma* is common to both Hinduism and Buddhism, and Karma is absolutely inexorable in both. Karma is also self-caused in both the systems. And is destroyed only through illumination or *Buddhatwa* The Hindu conception of salvation or *Moksha* is in this respect the same as the Buddhistic conception of *Nirvana.* The beginning less and endless chain of cause and effect must be broken up, in both the cultures, before salvation is attained.

So Buddhistic legalism is not really un-Hindu, nor is Hindu fellowship absolutely foreign to Buddhist thought, for *Nirvana* is in some sense, the same really as *Laya* or *Kaibalya,* or the losing of the individual soul in the Universal soul. And in both Hinduism and Buddhism there is the dominating Aryan instinct of the Spiritual and the Universal, clearly manifest This sense of the spiritual or the Universal transcending the material and the particular, the common element of Aryan race consciousness, has imparted its distinctive features to the Buddhistic conception of law, making it so essentially different from the Judaic, the Islamic or the Christian conception. And the confusion into which Bishop Carpenter fell, in taking Buddhistic legalism as belonging to the same class as Judaic, Christian or Islamic legalism, is entirely due to the wrong method of investigation generally followed by the European students of comparative religion.

> A true application of the psychological and Histrio-Comparative methods discovers that religion is man's attempt at adjustment to the Not-Me.

The generalisation that will discover the permanent elements of the religious phenomena presented by the history of the human race, must be based upon a much wider range of religious experience than is covered by what are known as the great world-religions. It must explore every form of religion from the mast crude to the most refined and subtle. Starting with primitive culture it must trace the evolution of the religious sentiment up to the highest point as yet reached within our knowledge. It must study the history of the different religions in the light of the general laws of psychological evolution. And it must apply the comparative method in conjunction with the Historic method, in its researches into the law of religious growth. And by this means it will discover that as there are permanent elements in the general religious experiences of the race, which establish the essential unity of the religious phenomena, so there are permanent elements in every religion also, that may be characterised as the Regulative Ideas in their respective history and evolution, and that constitute, thus, what may be called the individuality of these religions and differentiate them from the others.

We have briefly considered both these elements in the foregoing pages. We have seen that the highest and broadest generalisation that can be arrived at, by an examination of the religious phenomena in general, is that religion is man's attempt to adjust himself to his Not-Me, with a view to realise the highest end of his existence. This definition covers, we claim, the entire field of the religious experiences of humanity. In primitive religion, call it fetishism, totemism, animism, ancestor-worship — by any name you please, — it is man's attempt to adjust himself to his Not-Me, that is to his Nature or his Social environments, that we always discover its birth, growth and evolution. There have been primitive peoples, it is said, who possess absolutely no idea of a Deity, however crude or gross.

Eighteenth and Early Nineteenth century Deism, miscalled Theism, tried hard to prove the universality of the religious intuitions of a Supreme Being to every man and race, for upon such a universality it sought to build up its so-called philosophy of Natural Religion, which would preserve the truth of religion while discarding the authority of supernatural revelations. The attempt was not, we are afraid, uniformly successful, for every now and then travellers turned up who testified to the utter absence of any form of religion in some one or other of the primitive races whom they had met and studied. But the battle raged, on either side around what we now recognise as absolutely mistaken issues. The old student, whether orthodox or heterodox started with a wrong definition of the Deity, some intuitions regarding whom they were seeking in primitive-consciousness. God-idea as we have in civilization could never be found in naked and cannibal-barbarism. For though impious philosophers have sought to turn pious opinion into ridicule by it, it is still none the less true that: if God made man in his own image, man also has always made, and is still making his God, everywhere-after himself; and anthropomorphism by which orthodox theology especially in Christendom, wanted to scare away people from what is called Natural Religion, conceals a great truth which neither party seemed for a long time to be aware of. Indeed, those who admit that man is made in the image of his Maker, actuality make over the whole case to anthropomorphism. If God made man after himself, where then shall man seek and find him except in his own humanity? The study of religion in our age has, however, justified all anthropomorphic conceptions of the Godhead, as the only ones that man could have of the Supreme Being. For in every age, in every country, in every place of its evolution, his religion has always been built up by man according to the actual character and the pressing needs of his physical and his social life.

In fact, religion in primitive culture is a much more vital thing than we seem to be conscious of in civilization. With us, religion in the usual acceptation of the term is often-times a mere matter of speculation more or less, or of mere habit with the civilized We can live without it, and even die who has already without much thought of it. It is because the problems of life are not so acutely presented to us as they were to primitive man. To a large extent we seem to have adjusted our physical life to our nature-environments more or less, and our conceptions of what is called the Reign of Law in Nature have well-nigh killed our perceptions of the Supernatural in it. The Supernatural plays an almost infinitesimally smaller part in our everyday life than it did in that of our primitive ancestors. Every physical evil was to them due to some supernatural agency.

Every illness was to them the working of an unseen agent that had either to be fought and conquered or worshipped and propitiated. Every natural cataclysm, a thunderstorm, a flood, an earthquake, a tornado, an eclipse, jungle-fires, draughts, flights of locusts, or irruptions of wild animals, — whatever, indeed, disturbed the even tenor of their troublous life, were regarded by them as due to some active malevolent, though invisible agency, very much like themselves. As in his relations and dealings with his human enemies, primitive man had sometimes to fight them, and sometimes to sue for their favour and forbearance by offering acceptable presents to them, with a view to be able to pursue his ends in life without any molestation from them; so also he did with regard to the unseen agencies in Nature. He sometimes tried magic, exorcism, incantations, to beat these evil agencies away, and sometimes he sought to win their favour and appease their wrath by prayers, praises, and offerings. And all this was part of his rude scheme of life to adjust himself to his surroundings, and overcome the conflicts in which he found himself placed. All this was his religion. Religion was, thus, a most vital concern with him in the most acute and literal sense of the word.

It is not so vital a concern in our life, because we can live without what is usually called religion. We have separated our physical, our intellectual, our aesthetic, and even our ethical life from our religious life.

Not so however was it with the primitive man. To him everything was religion, and religion was everything. He was feeling' his way in the dark, haunted by the fears of the Unknown at every step. We too are, perhaps, doing the same; and inspite of all our conceit of knowledge and Our boasted mastery over our destinies, we too are, really, as helpless and as much at the mercy of unknown forces, so far, at least, as the ultimate issues of that life are concerned. But we are not, like the primitive man, so constantly haunted by the consciousness and the fear of the unseen. We have, at least, greater assurance than he. Our life is not homogenous, un-differentiated, like his.

It has been cut up, so to say, into different compartments, of which religion occupies only one; and though we may not have the fullest freedom of that compartment, we seem to feel, at least, that we have the run of the others, and are practically absolute masters there. Loss of health or of wealth rarely drives us to religion now. We seek the aid of the physician or the financier. An earthquake, even like that of Lisbon, or more recently of the West Indies, sends us not to our gods, but to the seismograph. Religion stands, practically, divorced from our nature-environments, with which it is related still only on its aesthetic and poetic side. It stands divorced also, very largely, from even our social-environments. Our social relations are controlled and shaped now by social science, of which politics, economics, and ethics form the three chief elements, and psychology the interpreting principle. Religion is, thus, simply a matter of what may be called our private, our personal, our inner life.

But oven in this narrowed sphere, it means, still, the same thing, namely, our attempt to adjust ourselves to our own ideas and ideals, with a view to attain our highest end in life. But this narrowed aspect of religion among us, is, after all, a mere passing phase. We are just now passing through a differentiating phase, — a most pregnant antithetical moment, in the evolution of our culture and civilization. Primitive religion stood in a state of homogeneity. Modern religion, especially in Europe, and generally all over the civilized world, is passing through a state of differentiation. This is, however, in its very nature, a passing state. Integration follows quick in its steps. Modern European thought even is rapidly moving towards a higher synthesis. The seers and philosophers of the last century and this, Kant and Ilegel, Carlyle and Emerson, Goethe and Schalling, Tennyson and Browning, Ibsen and Tolstoi, Diderat and Whitman — are the pioneers of this new synthesis.

It has commenced visibly to affect is even the Churches. Both Catholicism and Protestantism are passing clearly through the throes of a new birth; and a New Orthodoxy is rising on both sides of the Atlantic, strong after a newer and loftier view of religion that will put an end to the present conflicts, between reason and revelation, science and scripture, independence and authority, and the natural and the supernatural. And it all shows that religion, even in this comparatively very high stage, means the attempt of man to adjust himself to his environments, the difference between this and primitive religion consisting only in the nature of these environments.

In the earliest stage these were wholly external; at present they are mostly internal, consisting in the presentations to his own Reason of the external relation of his life, on the one side, and the interrelations between his intellectual, his esthetic and emotional, and his moral and spiritual experiences and needs on the other. And in this state of conflict, even these inner and subjective phenomena, necessarily, present themselves as the Not-Me.

This, then, — this attempt of man to adjust himself to his Not-Me with a view to reach his highest end in life, — is the broadest and most universal and as it seems to us, the most rational and scientific, generalisation of the religious phenomena. It expresses the fact of religion in the terms of universal experience. It seems to present the one common factor nut only in all religions, but in every phase of its evolution, in every religion as well.

In taking up the study of any particular religion, in a truly scientific spirit, and in seeking to trace its history and evolution with a view to get at the actual truth of the experiences it reveals, we must start with this generalisation of the religious phenomena. We must view it as the attempt of man to adjust himself to his Not-Me, to realise his highest end in life. And this means that our study must divide itself into two parts, namely, first, the study of the man himself, with a view to discover the particular prism through which, from pre-historic times, he viewed this Not-Me; and second, the study of this Not-Me in itself, in its dual aspect of Nature and Society, — as furnishing the materials upon which the instincts, the thoughts, the sentiments, and the energy of this man have always worked. The study of the man will reveal what we have called his special race-consciousness, the peculiarity of this thought life, which furnishes the Regulative Idea in the evolution of his religion. The study of his Not-Me, his nature-environments and social surroundings, will not only show us the farms that this Idea took, but will also give us a clue to the origin and history of those modifications that may have been worked into his original intuitions by his environments, at different periods of his history.

To understand Hinduism, we must, therefore, first of all study the Hindu, from the earliest period of his life, to discover the Regulative Idea in the evolution of his special history and culture, and next we must study the forms that this Idea has taken, and the way in which it has been accentuated or modified from time to time by what M. Taine would call, the surroundings of his race and the epochs of his history.

Hindu History

Its Bearing on Hinduism

Religion is not an isolated phenomenon in man's life, standing, so to say, apart from its other departments. In the earliest state of social evolution the state of homogeneity-religion, as we find in the records of every race, is everything, and everything is religion. As in the human foetus, the liver performs not only its own proper and specific functions but also those of the other organs as well except the heart, so in the earliest state of social life, religion performs the functions of every department of that life. Science and art, politics and economics, commerce and trade, —everything is then a part of man's religion, and the supernatural, the specific element of the religious consciousness, plays a very prominent part in all these departments of the life of primitive man. Subsequently, in the gradual differentiation of the different departments of the social life, the religion or the sacred separates itself from the secular and the profane.

This differentiation has been well-nigh completed in Europe and America. But even in this state of differentiation religion, specifically so-called, can not be altogether abstracted from the other departments of human activities. Religion when standing in this antithetical state, concerns itself with God and man's relations with and duties to his Maker, primarily, and, in a secondary way, somewhat mediately, with his relations with and duties to other members of his society, and his race. But man's conceptions of his Maker are always coloured by, if they are not even directly derived from, his experiences of and relations with his physical and social surroundings.

His physical life, the character of his Nature-environments, his social relations, the Constitution of his society and his State, the general course of his historic evolution, the influences that are brought to bear upon the general development of his intellectual and ethical faculties, all these have a vital relation to the evolution of his religion, specifically so-called. The religious experiences of any race or nation must; therefore, be studied, in the light of the general evolution of its history and culture. The general course of the historic evolution of the Hindu people, must, therefore, be a preliminary study to any truly scientific investigation of their religious records and their religious life. Hindu religion must be studied in the light, that is of real Hindu history.

A right conception of Hindu history is essential to a right understanding of Hindu religion. But where are we to find a Hindu history? One of the most convenient myths of European origin, in regard to India is that previous to the Mohamedan invasion, this country had never any reliable history of its own. The Hindus not only had no history, but never possessed the historical faculty even. Accuracy of observation and faithfulness in recordings actual experiences just as they are, constitute the essential elements of this faculty; and the Hindus have been absolutely deficient in these, as a race. Every suspicion of historical verity is dispelled by the exaggerations of their imagination from even their legendary poems and stories, that supply valuable materials for the primitive history of other peoples.

Unlike, for instance, the Greek epics, the Illiad and the Odyssey, the Hindu epics, the Ramayana and the Mahabharata, furnish no reliable basis for working up even the semblance of a Hindu history of these early and legendary epochs. The descriptions of men and events in these books are often-times, too grossly exaggerated to be acceptable to the historian as even a flimsy basis for any historic construction. Whatever may be the real meaning and explanation of these so-called exaggerations, we shall not stop to discuss here. We simply admit that history, as an accurate chronicle of dates and events, is absent from the existing records of the ancient Hindu people. But this may not, we contend, imply the absolute absence of the historic faculty in this branch of the great Aryan race. In view of the notorious vandalism of some of the foreign invaders of Hindustan, it may not be wholly improbable that whatever annals of this kind may have existed in the royal archives or the sacred temples of the country were destroyed during these alien irruptions.

Indeed, it seems rather incredible that a people, who, judged by the existing remnants of their literature, attained a very high degree of culture and made marvellous progress in almost all the arts and crafts of civilized life, never kept a record of the doings of their Kings or the exploits of their warriors. On the contrary, we do know this much at least, that the court-chronicler was a recognised functionary among ancient Hindus, and Hindu archaeology also furnishes, here and there, strange glimpses into the methods by which memory of important events or personages was sought to be preserved and perpetrated in ancient India. Apart from all this, which create, at any rate, a strong presumption against the validity of the popular European view regarding the utter lack of the historic faculty in the Hindu race, — do a catalogue of the names and dates of Kings and warriors, and a record of their outer deeds and achievements, constitute the real basis, and the most valuable materials of true history? The value of these chronicles is not denied: but are they sufficient, of themselves, to fully elucidate and correctly interpret the real life of any people? Chronicles of dates and events furnish the signposts, so to say, of historic evolution; but these give us but little clue to the regulative idea or ideas that underlie it, and form, really, its very life and soul; nor do these truly and sufficiently explain those subtle intellectual and moral forces that really contribute everywhere and always to the making of important historic epochs.

Not in so-called annals and chronicles, hitherto very frequently misread as constituting true history, but in the records of the thought-life of a people, in their general literature, in the pictures of their domestic and social ideals and activities, in the descriptions of their sacraments rites, and institutions, — do we find the most valuable materials for their real history.What would we know of Greek history without the help of Greek poetry, Greek sculpture, Greek mythology, and Greek philosophy? What would it avail the student of the historic evolution of the English people, if he had an accurate diary of the public events of the Elizabethan or the Victorian era, but not a scrap of the Elizabethan or Victorian literature? A record of the great Rebellion would mean but little to us, as British history, if we had not the writings of the Puritan Divines, and the products of the immortal genius of Milton, to illumine and interpret that tumultuous page of the history of England.

The story of the French Revolution would simply impress upon our minds the hideous excesses of it, — if we had not the works, of Voltaire and Rosseau and the general thought-record of the French Illumination, to find us the real key to that great world cataclysm, to which humanity will be eternally grateful for some of its most precious heritage in the culture and civilization of modern Europe. The thought-life of a people is their real life. The history of their thought is their true history. Annals and chronicles are helpful in the elucidation of otherwise inexplicable points in this thought-history. These are needed for the verification of the facts and generalisations gleaned from, and based upon, a general study of a People's thought-life. But the sciences of comparative history, and sociology, as well as the general philosophy of history, have, to a large extent, made the students of social and civic evolution, which is or ought to be the chief theme of history, independent of these dry catalogues and descriptions of outward events.

The psychological group of the sciences have been revealing to us certain universal truths and principles, regarding the course of human development in general, in the light of which we may now build up a more correct history of any people than what has been constructed hitherto as such, out of the annals of their Kings and the journals of their warriors. From this modern standpoint, regarding the character and function of history, as a science or philosophy, the literature of a nation, — their poetry, their painting, their sculpture, their music, their law, their philosophies, their scriptures and their general religious works, — furnish a far true and more valuable record of their growth and evolution, than what the so-called historical records have ever been able to supply.

And, so far as the thought-life of the Hindu people is concerned, we think there exist ample materials for the construction of a real history of it The Vedas the Sutras, that contain the laws and rituals of the early Hindus, the rich exegetical literature that seems to have grown around the Vedas, and traces of which are found in the works of the Niruktakars or Vedic lexicographers; the Upanishads, so rich not only in their profound metaphysical speculations, but also in anecdotes and stories that throw a lurid light upon the social and civic life of the Hindus of that great speculative period; the philosophical or metaphysical speculations that subsequently grew around these Upanishads; the Puranas, representing not only the highest, the fullest, the most universal, and spiritual phase of what may well be called Imaginative or Idealístic Hinduism, but also giving a vivid picture of the social life and civic government of medieval Hindus; classical dramas; the later philosophical speculations like those of Madhavacharya, (the auther of Sarvadarshana samgraha), and Bijnana-bhikshu; of Sankara and Ramanuja; and finally, the varied Vernacular literatures that developed, in every part of India, under the Moslem rule, — the latest works of Tantrikism and Vaishnavism in Bengal, of Saivaism and Vaishnavism in Southern India, the literature of the religious movements of Kavira and Ramananda in Nothern India, that of Guru Nanak and his successors in the Punjab, the Abhangs of Tukaram in the Mahratta country; — all these, not to mention the revelations of Hindu or Hindu-cum-Dravidian architectures of Southern India, Bombay, or Orissa, furnish the richest possible materials for a true history of the Hindu race.

A good portion of ancient Hindu records and a good deal of the ancient monuments of this people, have no doubt been lost during the first period of Mohamedan invasion and conquest. We have, for instance, no records of Hindu painting, though it seems clear, from occasional references to it in some of our classical books, that even the art of painting had attained a fairly high-degree of perfection among the medieval Hindus. There are similar indications of the astronomical, the physiological, the physical and the chemical investigations of this people; and as we already have through the labours of Dr. P. C. Ray, a history of Hindu Chemistry, so before long we may also have a history of Hindu physics, Hindu Physiology, and real Hindu Astronomy treated apart from Astrology. But apart from these sidelights that a patient study, in a Scientific and critical spirit, of the ancient literature of the Hind us might throw on their general culture and attainments, even the books that are already accessible to us, furnish fairly ample material for building up a real history of this people from the earliest times.

Thus it will be seen, that even if we may not work up a connected account of the outer events of the life of the ancient or medieval Hindus, we may well build up, with the help of existing materials, a very fairly accurate and detailed story of the evolution of their thought and culture. The Vedas, the Sutras, exegetical literature that grew the Upanishads, the Puranas, the exegetical literature that grew around these Scriptures, the Sanskrit classics, and the vernacular literatures, furnish ample and varied materials, if only these could be properly collated, arranged, and interpreted, for a Hindu history, that would by no means be less accurate than what modern Hebrew scholars, like. Keunen, Ewald, Robertson Smith and others, have been seeking to build up, out of the records of the Old Testament, concerning the life and thought of the ancient Hebrews.

Recent researches into Assyrian, Babylonian and Egyptian archaeology, and the discovery of the *cunieform* Inscriptions, have, no doubt, contributed very materially to the working out of ancient Hebrew history, verifying or correcting the theories of old historians, and clearing up many an otherwise obscure print and passage of the old records, and by this means external and objective testimony has been made largely available for lending strength and support to internal evidence and a *priori* inferences. All this is true, and the absence of similar sources of corroboration in the case of the history of ancient or Medieval India, makes the work before the Hindu historians more difficult, demanding much greater care, circumspection, and patient research, but this difficulty does not prove the utter absence of historical materials in the records of the Hindu race.

Indeed, the absence of external testimony simply proves that the Hindus had from time immemorial, been practically a self-centred people. They had but little dealings with the outside world, and barring the Greek invasion and the subsequent relations with the Scythians, the Bactrians and other remnants of the Greeko — Asiatic nations, that came and entered India from the North west, the ancient and medieval Hindus had no foreign contact worth notice. Their method of expansion and colonisation, — strictly confined within the Indian Peninsula, — except the later occupation by them of Ceylon and some of the Islands of the Indian Archipelego — their ways of absorbing alien tribes and cultures, their peculiar social economy and missionary propaganda — if the term could be applied to a religion that has been almost universally described as absolutely non-missionary — all these have helped to practically obliterate all traces of foreign contact or conflict from their literature. One must dive much below the surface to discover these. For, though these traces are lost, the fact that there had been such contacts and conflicts can scarcely be denied, in view, for instance, of the undoubted Hinduisation of the whole of the Dravidian people of Southern India. The story of conversion and absorption of this people into Hinduism, if only it could be discovered, would present this great world-religion in an altogether new aspect, and throw considerable light upon some of the most interesting but obscure passages of its history. It would not only discover some of the most interesting and instructive features of Hindu culture and civilization, but would present a unique phase of religious propagandism such as the world has perhaps, never witnessed anywhere else.

But the process of Hindu expansion was a quiet, a statesmanly, a thoroughly evolutionary process, that has, naturally, left no monuments or inscriptions to glorify it. It is, therefore, useless to search for any corroboration of Hindu history in foreign annals. The neighbours of the Hindus, unlike those of the Hebrews, were almost infinitely inferior to them in civilization and culture, and who even where they did claim a high standard -of culture, as the Dravidians undoubtedly did, were quietly absorbed by their stronger neighbours, almost body and soul, so to say, all but entirely losing, therefore, all traces of their previous, independent, existence.

Indeed, the modern sciences of Comparative History, Anthropology, and Sociology, which reveal the general principles of historic evolution, have, to a very large extent made the student of social and civil evolution independent, of those catalogues of dates and events which had previously usurped the name and dignity of history. The sociological and Psychological group of the sciences, have been revealing to us certain universal truths and principles regarding the general course of human progress, in the light of which, we may now build up a more correct account of their real life than what had before been furnished by the annals of their courts or the journals of their warriors. History is no longer a mere record of outer events and dates, but the story of an evolution. Its aim is to trace the origin and development of particular types of culture and civilization, represented by particular nationalities or races, and discover, enunciate, and explain the laws and principles of social evolution. It views society not as a mere mechanical collection of men and women, thrown together by chance and living together by the needs of mere animal or physical life and that have no deeper bond of union than the occupation of a common geographical situation, or the possession of a common dialect, both, again, the result of mere chance, the work of "a fortuitous concurrence" of historical events, — but, essentially, as an organism, — having a distinct life of its own, with an organic and pre-historic end, regulating and shaping that life to its own essential needs.

Mere geographical situations do not create national life, though they do modify and regulate more or less, the outer expressions of that life. Neither do historical contacts, whether militant or peaceful, create it, though these also have a mighty influence in shaping its course. A nation, like an animal, is subject to the laws of natural selection, and may, therefore, sometimes develop-new organs and sometimes, in degeneration, even lose old organs, under pressure of external conditions, whether geographical or historical, but it never, except in the case of a total extinction, loses its original type. A nation is not a mere mechanical collection of individuals, nor is it of the nature of a voluntary association, like, for instance, a Temperance Society or a universal Democratic Federation, any more than a mechanical toy is a living creature.

Every organism has an end unto itself, a regulative idea which guides and controls all its activities and the manifold processes of its evolution. Every evolution, indeed, is the evolution of an Idea. Biology has neither been able, as yet, to establish the theory of abiogenesis, or the production of life from non-life, nor has it been able to discover any differentiating element in the protoplasmic cells that gradually develop into different kinds of animal organisms. So far as our present knowledge of these cells go, there is absolutely nothing to distinguish a human cell from what is developed into a puppy or a baboon, These differentiations set in later, and the same kind of cell grows into a human baby on the one side, and into a puppy, a colt, a calf, or a monkey on the other. These differentiations could not be uncaused or arbitrary. And the causes of these differentiations must have been present, though undiscovered, in the original cells themselves. It is this which, in evolution, we call the Regulative Idea. As in the development of a portrait, the idea formal in the mind of the painter of the features of his subject, directs every movement of his pencil or his brush, so in the evolution of an organism, the Idea of it as it is to be finally perfected, regulates every step of its growth. It is this Idea, inherent in the very life and Constitution of every organism, which distinguishes these from one another, the puppy from the pony, and the baboon from the human baby. The organic conception of social evolution, the conception that societies or nations or races have, like animal organisms, definite and specific ends unto themselves, — ends that shape and control their evolution, that constitute the regulative ideas in their evolution, and that therefore, constantly, consciously or unconsciously, — and more frequently unconsciously than consciously, work themselves out more or less successfully, in the life and institutions of different nationalities and races, ever since their appearances, on the arena of human history.

This is the view in which History is regarded by modern thought This new aspect of History is seen, in a somewhat crude form, in the story of the Hebrews as presented in the Old Testament. That story starts with the idea of a covenant or contract between Yahveh on the one side and Abraham, the father of the this contract Yahveh takes the Israelites unto him for a people and becomes to them "a God," in a special sense. They become his chosen people, and he their chosen God. And the whole of the history of the Hebrew race is presented in the Old Testament as the working out of this ancient covenant.

This special relation between them, as a people and Yahveh, is what may be called the one permanent and persistent feature of the Old Testament records, — the one regulative idea in the evolution of Hebrew history, as painted in these. What is presented in this pious interpretation of Hebrew history, as an instance of special providence, and interpreted, therefore, in a supernatural sense, in the Old Testament records, is really regarded as a general principle and a quite natural phenomena of historic evolution, by the modern Philosophy or Science of History. Stripped of its supernaturalism the Old Testament view of Hebrew history means that the Hebrews as a race had a peculiar genius, a special type of mental and social structure, a special end unto themselves, as a social organism, the fullest development and realisation of which was the universal end, the Regulative Idea of their history. What modern Philosophy of History has done is simply to rationalise and universalise this supernatural and particularistic historic perspective.

Our modern Historical science or Philosophy of History starts, therefore, with the ultimate truth of modern Anthropology, the truth, namely, of the existence of certain original, pre-historic inexplicable yet undeniable peculiarities of mental and social structures, that constitute the special characteristic and genius of different races and nations, and that furnish the element of permanence, as well as the regulative end and idea to all historic evolutions.

The study of the historic evolution of a people must start, therefore, with an examination of their peculiar race-characteristics or race-consciousness as we have called it, which alone can furnish the right key to the solution of the complex problems of its inner life and outer activities, and indicate the universal trend of its past, and the possibilities of its future career. The elements of this race-consciousness as we have already seen, are two, namely thought-structure and Social-structure.

The study of the history of every people must commence with ail enquiry into these two vital and constituent elements of their nationality or raciality In their thought-structure we discover their world-idea, the special viewpoint from which almost instinctively, they have always approached the great world-problems that faced them from time to time. It is hero that we find a key to their particular philosophy of life, from its earliest and crudest to its most refined, and even-transcendental stage. It is here that we find how they have viewed themselves and the world about them, from pre-historic times. It is in this thought-structure that we see the real character of the mental and moral life of the people. Like their thought-structures, different races have had from pre-historic times, types of social organisation and social economy peculiar to them. This is what we have called their social structure. As in the thought-structure of a race we find their original and peculiar world-idea, the foundation of all their subsequent philosophies and speculations — the cast and character of their peculiar intellectual life, so in their social structure we discover their original and peculiar social ideal and economy. And it is in these, — in the thought and social structures of a people, that we stand face to face, so to say, with the Regulative Idea of their historic evolution, and discover those secret forces that have shaped and controlled the destiny of different nations and traces, — forces, which though sometimes vanguished by foreign ideas and ideals, have never anywhere been completely crushed out, but that have always striven, — as long as the nation or race has not been all but totally extinct, — sometimes openly and consciously, but oftener, perhaps, insidiously and unconsciously, — to reach out, anyhow, to their original ideal and end.

The first question therefore, in the study of real Hindu History is, what is the speciality of the race-consciousness of the Hindu people? What is the Regulative Idea, the element of permanence in their historic evolution? What is that which has perpetually differentiated this strange people, whom more than a millennium of foreign dominations and foreign repressions have failed to destroy, — from the other nations of the world?

What is their peculiar thought-structure, and what their special social structure?

And, as we have already pointed out, the thought-structure of a people must be studied in their linguistic structure. "We know certain forms of language," says Max Muller, "which correspond to certain forms of thought, and the relations of the subject to the objects and of the elements of perception are viewed, and consequently expressed, differently in different languages. Accustomed to Aryan modes of thought, it appears self-evident to us that a language, in order to be a language, must be able to distinguish the subject from the object, — the nominative and the accusative. But as a matter of fact, there are few languages beyond the Aryan group which have distinct forms for these two categories of thought, and where the forms are wanting there must necessarily also be the spirit absent There, among peoples outside the Aryan group, we find that the consciousness of the subject as subject, dominating the object, has been from the very beginning very feeble, so-feeble indeed that it found no place in their linguistic structure".

The thought-structure of the Hindus must then be studied in the structure of their original language, Sanskrit; and Sanskrit, belongs to a large and influential family of languages, of which Greek, Latin, German, and many others, designated by the name Aryan, are members. The thought-structure of the Hindus is, therefore, generically the same as that of these other branches of the Indo-Aryan family. And the distinguishing features of this common, Aryan, world-idea is its perception of the Universal and the Absolute. The peculiar linguistic structure of the Aryans, which reveals "the consciousness of the subject as subject, dominating the object," is, in other words of a pre-eminently metaphysical cast A hankering after the spiritual, a sense of the whole have always dominated Aryan thought, whether among the Greeks or the Romans the Saxons or the Teutons, the Slavs or the Hindus.

The consciousness of the self standing perpetually not only over against, but essentially independent of the not-self, has, in some shape or other, been an original consciousness with these peoples: and though its expression has been sometimes crude and sometimes clear, and been different among different branches of the Aryan family, it has never been altogether absent from their thought-life throughout the countless centuries of their past evolution. There have been variations in the common world-idea, among the Aryans themselves, and different branches of the Aryan family have sought to realise this common world-idea in different ways, creating wide divergences in the genius of the different nationalities of this Indo-Aryan group, but nowhere has it been ever absent, and it is owing to the persistence of this world-idea in them, that we find so strange a family resemblance in the highest thoughts and speculations of such widely different peoples as the ancient Greeks, the modern Germans, and the medieval Hindus.

This original world idea, the conception of the metaphysical whole, the common heritage of the Aryan race, found, thus, somehow, an expression among the Hindus, very different from what it has had among the other branches of this family. The sense of the spiritual and the universal took, thus, a peculiar character in Greece, very different from what it had among the Hindus, differentiating, thereby the Greek from the Hindu culture.

The Greeks, for instance, viewed the Universal and the Absolute from the standpoint of the particular and the relative, the whole through the parts; while the Hindus took, evidently, a directly opposite standpoint, and looked on the particular and the relative from the plane, so to say, of the Universal and the Absolute. The Greeks sought to realise the parts in the whole. The characteristic element in the Greek civilization was, thus, the consciousness of "Form". In Greece the nature elements and the social elements of the National life were all regulated by this supreme sense of" "Form" — the sense, that is, of the proper relation between parts, in reference to the Whole.

And the resulting achievements of the Greeks were, — special development of Logic, having reference to the essential forms of thinking, the categories of the understanding through which the relations in nature are apprehended and understood; the perfection of Art, having reference to the right relations between limb and limb and part and part, in the perfected and harmonious whole; the growth of a very superior kind of political structure, having reference to the just relations of individuals to individuals as organs of a self-governing State; the evolution of Ethics, which regulate the relation between individual and individual and individual and the social whole. Through this innate sense of "form," Greece was able also to enter into a close kinship with all the relations of Nature in the physical world, and thereby, through close observation, to develop the ground-principles of Science.

But, for every good there is always a counterpoise of evil, and while the special emphasis that the original spiritual and philosophic instincts of the Greek people laid on what we would call the Concrete Universal, helped to develop all these peculiar excellences *of the Greek* thought and culture, it also, at the same time, to a very large extent, weakened their hold on the Transcendental. And, the result of it was that the Greek conception of the Godhead, even in its highest philosophic stage of speculations, was more immanental than transcendental. In Art, similarly, Greece represents the classical stage, where there is absolute harmony between the form and the spirit of beauty it seeks to reproduce; but after the classical there is a higher phase of aesthetic evolution, wherein the spirit transcends the forms, — the phase, namely, of the romantic, which had hardly been reached by Greecian Art In society, again, Greece recognised simply the dependence on and subordination of the individual to the Social Whole, of which they were limbs and parts, but had no consciousness of the fact that the individual too had an end unto himself or herself, an end which is only furthered, but not destroyed or even actually overruled by his subordination to the Social Whole; — an end that the latter cannot safely or justly ignore or usurp.

In other words the Greeks; had not a strong grasp of what may be called the transcendental aspects of the human personality. Whoever did not contribute to the general well-being of society, as that well-being was apprehended and understood by them, was regarded by the Greeks as having little or no claims to existence, just as an effete or paralysed limb has no right to burden the body. That absolute sanctity of human life as human life, that majesty and inviolability of the human personality as a human personality, to which Europe owes so much of her later progress and civilization, almost in every department of life, are the special contributions of Roman law and Christian ethics, and Greece lacked these conceptions almost entirely. All these are the limitations of Greek culture, due to the peculiar form that its original sense of the Spiritual and the Universal, the common characteristic of the Aryan race-consciousness, took — due to the fact that Greece apprehended the Whole, only through the relations of life and nature, and not as existing in itself, apart from and transcending all relations.

Among the Hindus, on the other hand, the same spiritual or metaphysical consciousness, the original feature of this race-consciousness, found a different expression. The Greeks conceived the parts in the whole, the particular in the Universal.

The Hindus saw the Whole in the parts, the Universal in the particulars; to see a single man was to realise the presence of Humanity, because Humanity is to the Hindus in truth and reality, in all its fullness, in every human unit, however unmanifested it may be to our uncontemplative and uninstructed vision. For, is not the whole in every part of it, as its regulative idea, its end, as well as beginning? God, says Emerson, is as perfect in the atom as in the Universe; and here the Sage of Concord reproduces the highest God-consciousness of the Hindu. Every atom contained, in his vision, the Universe. Every creature had in essence the fullness and perfection of the Creator.

Where is Brahman? — asks the disciple of the teacher, in the Upanishads. The teacher directs him to bring some salt and a pot of water; and the salt is put in the water and the pot set in its place.

With this the disciple is dismissed for the day. He comes for a reply to his question the next day. The teacher wants him to bring the pot of water where he had put the salt overnight. Where is the salt? he ask. It is in this water, replies the disciple. Where, find it out, — is the next direction. The disciple says, how was he to find it out, it was in every drop of that water. It is like this — says the teacher. Such is Brahman, in every part and particle of the Universe.

This is the burden of Hindu Theology almost all through. The Upanishads, representing what may be called the reflective and speculative phase of ancient Hindu thought, give clear expression to the idea, but it is present as an original and organic element in every phase and form of Hindu thought. Its lispings are heard in the Vedas — in the hymns and rituals of that period, — and it is fairly recognised in the attempts even of the primitive Hindus to read some sort of a spiritual and universal meaning even in their perceptive deities, — their sensible God-experiences. It is, indeed, strange how this people, even in that early and primitive state, rushed from the particularities about them, to an apprehension of the General, if not of the Universal.

Thus, for instance, Agni or Fire, the first born of the gods, as he is described in the Rig-Veda, and whose identity with the physical fire is absolutely unmistakable, is soon found to have established a most significant kingship with the sun, that huge ball of fire up in the heavens, and with the lighting-god, and all these are spoken of as forms of the one and the same god. This consciousness of the Spiritual and the Universal is heard as a most distinct and articulate note in the Upanishads. It controls also every system of later thought and speculation; including, strange as it may seem, even those that may be called materialistic or even atheistic. And it colours every form of the religious sacraments, rituals, and mysteries of the Hindu people, including even what appears to be outwardly most gross and sensuous.

Thus, for instance, the temple sculptures of Orissa and other places, that naturally give such a shock to the refined tastes and morals of Europeans and even of the English-educated Hindus themselves, were meant to serve a spiritual and ethical purpose, in Medieval Hinduism, by creating a disgust in the mind of the devotees for sensuous and sensual enjoyments, and the contemplation of these uglinesses formed part of the spiritual discipline of monks and others, for weaning their affections away from all flesh. The Ethiopean cannot change his skin, nor the leopard his spots, nor can the Hindu get rid of this overpowering spiritual instinct, and for the selfsame reason. Because the Ethiopean's colour, the leopard's spots and the Hindu's spirituality are all special, generic, and organic characteristics of their respective kind or species.

The other branches of the Aryan race also have this common element of the Aryan race-consciousness, it is true. But as we have seen in the case of the Greeks it took a different form among them, contributing those precious elements to Greek thought and culture, that constitute at once the peculiarity and the pride of modern Western thought and civilization which owe their origin to Greece and Rome. While the Hindus saw the Whole in the parts, the Greeks saw the parts in the whole, as we have already said, and what a wide and radical difference between the two-views this simple juxtaposition makes? To see the whole in the parts is an essentially subjective process.

It involves the negation of the particularities of the particulars, the denial of all distinctions and differentiations in the vision or idea of an undifferentiated totality. But when parts are sought for and seen as parts of the whole, they are seen as related to one another and to the whole of which they are parts. So do the particulars exist, in a series of relations, in the Universal. To approach the whole through the parts, these must be put in their right relations. Not the denial but the fullest acceptance of the reality and validity of these relations; not situation and development of these relations, — this is the only way here. And Greek culture and Greeko-Roman civilization, the common mother of modern western civilization, is a most glorious example of what this phase of the spiritual consciousness naturally results in. The Hindu civilization is an example of the opposite process. It leads, — the search of the whole in the parts, — to pantheism in theology, determinism in ethics, and to a fatal fatalism in the general philosophy of life.

At its highest point, on the one side, it leads to absolute quietism as the goal, and monkish monasticism as the way. It is the high road to all sorts of antisocial ideals and other wordly dogmas and disciplines. It is this peculiar view of the Spiritual and the Universal that helped to weaken the sense of personality in certain directions and obstructed the due development of what is understood as the true ethical consciousness, in Europe, and of the higher forms of civic life, among this people. On the other side, if sets up the individual, as representing the whole, above all relations, makes him a law unto himself, and leads to the apotheosis of the human personality, even in its most degraded form, — as really and essentially divine, and through this to the ideal of what may be called a universal divine incarnation.

Hindu history must be studied, therefore, in the light of this peculiarly spiritual genius of that people, and the moment we do so, we find many things that had at first eluded our analysis and our understanding, revealing their reason and meaning to us, as if by a touch of magic.

This sense of the Spiritual and the Universal, which forms an organic element of the Hindu race-consciousness, viewed as what is called the Abstract Universal, explains the meaning of Hindu culture and civilization, finds out the secret of their social economy, and their civic laws and institution, as well as of their philosophies and their religion. It is this which also easily explains and accounts for those limitations and deficiencies in their life and thought that have not infrequently led superficial students of Hindu civilization to relegate it to a lower and comparatively primitive stage of human progress. To properly understand the meaning and significance of the historic evolution of the Hindu people, we must examine, in some detail, the results of their innate sense of the Spiritual and the Universal, in their relation with Nature, Society and God, — results that have lent a special tone and character to their physical, to their social, their intellectual, their aesthetic and their religious life.

This sense of the Spiritual and Universal is the Regulative Idea in the historic evolution of the Hindu people. This is the prism through which the Hindu has always viewed himself, his social and his physical or nature environments. And consequently a sense of the absolute supremacy of the Spiritual over all external and objective forces, whether social or physical, has always dominated al' his relations with both society and nature. Superficially viewed, social authority seems to be absolutely crushing to the individual in India. There is, apparently, but little room for the exercise of what is called personal or individual freedom in either domestic or social relations among the Hindus.

Society, through its caste-codes and its religious sacraments and ceremonials absolutely dominates the life and activities of the individual to its minutest details to the extent even of his choice of food and drink even on different days, of the week or the month. The authority of Society over the individual seems, thus to be as rigid and as absolute here as it ever was among the Greeks. But this is, however, only a superficial view of the Hindu social economy. Society does control the individual here as it did in Greece, but the end was not the same in Greece as it has always been in India. In Greece the individual was considered as a limb of the body politic, and the control of the limb was regulated by considerations of the well-being of the organism, the State. In India among the Hindus, the authority of society over the individual was imposed for a different purpose.

Here the well-being of the organism was not the only, at any rate it was never the supreme end in the regulation of the individual. The individual, the Self itself was that end, Society was only a school for the training of the individual, — for the development and perfection of the real life of the individual, that is, his spiritual life. Social bondage was not an end unto itself, but was only a means to a higher end, and strange to say, that end was the very freedom of the individual whom society sought so rigidly to rule. Through bondage to freedom, that was the process. Subordination to social disciplines was meant to cure the conceit of self, to bridle unruly passions, to regulate the appetites by giving legitimate but restricted opportunities for their satisfaction.

As in his social life, so also in his relations with his nature-surroundings, this innate sense of the Spiritual; and the Universal always asserted itself. Nature is terrible, in its wild aspects, in India. Its majesty stands almost unrivalled, in the snowcapped mountains, the rushing rivers, the endless expanse of arid plains or wild vegetation, — almost all over Hindustan. But awful as his nature Nature-environments, both terrestial and celestial, have always been, the Hindu never allowed these to overawe or overwhelm him, except only as expressions or symbols of the Spiritual and the Universal. Viewed from the standpoint of the Absolute and the Spiritual, Nature appears in one of two ways.

It is either an expression, a radiance, a sign and symbol, of the Absolute, — the outer-body, so to say, of the Over-Soul, the form which the World-Spirit or the Cosmic Soul has thought fit to assume for its own self-revelation, or self-realisation or it is an illusion, a false covering, a hideous nightmare that hinders and distorts the vision of the True and the Real, Nature stands, thus, either as a medium of communication or communion between God and man, or as a veil that shuts his God out of the sight of man. In the one case, Nature will be sought to be idealised and spiritualised, quickening and feeding the faculty of Religious Imagination, to a very high pitch, and giving birth to a most marvellous apotheosis of the cosmic forces and phenomena, both in their totality, as well as, in their varied, differentiated, and fragmentary aspects. In the other case, it will be shunned, ignored, deliberately denied and negated.

But in neither case will there be any attempt or even any desire to enter into any serious conflict with Nature, with a view to its ultimate conquest and submission, And this has been the genera! character of the Hindu's relations with his Nature-environments, all through his past history. In the earliest stages of his life, as indicated in the hymns of the Rig-Veda, for instance, the Hindu too had his conflicts with his Nature-surroundings. Such conflicts are universal in what is called the jungle-clearing stage, when man's first concern is how to clear the earth, both of beasts and vegetation, to make it a safe habitation for himself and his kind. There are just a few Suktas in the Rig-Veda which preserve for us the memory: of this period of primitive Indo-Aryan history. But the generality of the Vedic hymns belong to a later period, when the Aryan settlers in India, had practically 'settled down to a fairly advanced agricultural life, which implied a certain amount of progress in the arts and crafts of, civilization.

The dominant note, therefore, in the Vedic hymns in regard to the view that the Vedic Hindus took of their nature-surroundings, is one of fellowship. The Vedic hymns are very largely addressed to what are called Nature-deities, representing the spirit, so to say, of natural objects and phenomena. Fire, in its dual aspect of terrestrial fire, and celestial light and heat, — is one of the most prominent of the Vedic Gods. The sun, the firmament, the clouds, sending rains and hurling down the thunderbolt, the storm winds, the morning and evening twilight, the rivers that flowed through their settlements, fertilizing their fields, carrying their primitive merchandise, and spreading their culture and their dominions, — all these and others like these, natural: objects or phenomena with which the Vedic Hindu was familiar and which influenced for good or evil his earthly life and happiness, — are the most 'prominent of the Vedic deities, and the hymns addressed to these bear ample evidence to the spirit of friendliness and fellowship, in which the Vedic poets and seers, usually viewed the Nature-forces about them.

This spirit of friendliness and fellowship with Nature-forces and natural phenomena, could not possibly grow without the very closest observation of these forces and phenomena. And an examination of the ritualism of the Vedas shows how careful had been the Vedic Hindus in their crude observation of their nature-surroundings, and more particularly of the phenomena of light and darkness, and the rains and the seasons. Astronomy — *Vedanga Jyotish* — is one of the six recognised branches of Vedic knowledge, without which the study of the Vedas could not be regarded as completed. The minutest observation, as far as it was possible with the naked eye, — of the movements of the sun, the moon, the planets and the stars, was needed for the determination of the right moment for the performance of Vedic sacraments and sacrifices. Astronomical observation became, thus, a religious necessity with the Vedic worshippers. The same need led them to the study, in their primitive way, of animal anatomy and physiology, for with the growth of ritualism, there grew up a very complicated system of animal sacrifices, which demanded a very minute and careful division of the sacrificed animal body, not only for the various offerings made to the gods, but also for its division among the different orders of priests and chanters who took part in these sacrifices. Minute directions for the construction of sacrificial alters and the preparation of the sacrificial grounds led to the discovery of the elements of Geometry and Mensuration by the Vedic Hindus.

And all these indicate some sort of rudimentary scientific observation and research, though conducted not exactly in the spirit of science or after strictly scientific methods, but simply prompted by religious or sacrificial and ritualistic requirements. Besides these, the very needs of ordinary human existence impelled the Hindus, as they did other human groups, to investigate the properties and character of the natural forces and objects about them. A knowledge of the seasons was necessary for agricultural purposes; that of herbs and minerals was needed for manufacturing as well as medical purposes; some knowledge of mechanics was essential to a people who built stone-structures, used cotton and woollen clothing, rode in chariots driven by horses and oxen. And all these imply some knowledge of nature, some conquest of and supremacy over natural forces and phenomena. Indeed, no people could possibly attain the standard of civilization that the Vedic Hindus seem clearly to have done, without the establishment of some sort of a mastery over-nature and without wresting some of her elemental secrets from her hands.

But still the spirit in which the ancient Hindu approached Nature was not in any sense, what would be called a scientific spirit in our age. The Hindu approached his nature surroundings, in the spirit of the poet and the seer, — like a painter or a philosopher. He did not botanise his plants and herbs but he simply sought to idealise and spiritualise the vegetable kingdom about him. He did not bring the sun down from the heavens and press him under the spectrum, nor did he catch up the death-dealing, thunder-discharging, and yet beneficent, because rain producing lightning from the sky, to make it run on his errands of peace or war over measureless miles of vacant space. He did not gauge the rains by inches, nor span the heavenly heights of his snowcapped mountains by the theodolite. He saw, he heard, he felt, and by his own inner sensations and emotions, he sought to take his own soul-satisfying measure of the outer world.

Consequently whatever records we have of the ancient Hindus nature experience, have almost universally, which may be called a soul-reference in them, either direct or indirect, Nature was to him not a thing apart, not a thing that had a real existence outside or absolutely independent of him, but he found it, at the final analysis, when he attained the reflective phases of his evolution, to be a part, really, of the self; and by the experiences of that self, by its sensations, impressions, and emotions, he always measured Nature, and interpreted it, and to the highest ends of that self, throughout his whole history, he tried to turn it. So there is poetry even in his science; which means that he always clothed the real with the ideal, the material was always symbolised by, if not universally transfigured into, the spiritual. And thus the genius of this race asserted itself even in its experiences of and relations with their physical surroundings.

This curious admixture of science and poetry, common to all primitive culture, has, however, a peculiar meaning and significance in the case of the ancient Hindu. It is not the product of wild and untrained imagination. In fact, this is found in records that must have grown side by side, almost with some of the profoundest speculations of the Hindu mind, speculations that reveal the wonderful analytical powers of this race; and when, the Hindu intellect could hardly be called, therefore, very wild or untrained. Nor is it the product of what has been termed, with ill-concealed contempt, as "oriental imagination" — which is an euphemism, plainly, for deliberate falsehood or lying exaggerations. But it is the product, really, of the innate sense of the spiritual and the universal, of this people. What unimaginative.

European critics condemn as "oriental imagination," is really the result of idealisation and spiritualisation, even though it should seek to express itself in the terms of the material and the sensuous. And it would not, we contend, be very easy to determine whether the highest truth is to be found more in what people usually characterise as real than in what the unimaginative and the unspiritual necessarily dismiss as mere ideal. Usually we declare our sense-testimony only as real. For purposes of strictly scientific investigations this definition of the real is correct tentatively, and absolutely needed.

But people who take the testimony of the senses, what is called scientific evidence, as absolutely real and true, forget the tentative character of it, as well as ignore the narrow limits within which the sciences have necessarily to work. For are our senses the only, or the highest witness of reality? What, indeed, is sense-testimony itself, except the impression produced upon a sentient being by the contact of sense-objects with his senses? And these impressions are measured really not by the senses, — the senses only communicate impressions but do not record them — but by the mind, their universal reader.

What happens, really, in so-called strictly accurate or scientific statement or record of our sense-impressions is that the mind works here within certain arbitrary limitations, and reproduces not the whole but simply a part of the impressions of sense-objects communicated to it by the senses. Generally speaking, science, by its quantitative and qualitative analysis, limits the mental records of sense-impressions to their relations in space and time, ignoring for the time being, that both extension and succession, implying relations, are apprehended, not by the senses, but by the mind alone. Thus, in what are called strictly accurate records of outer objects and events, the mind divides itself, so to say, from itself, and gives out, not the whole of its impressions, but only a part, and really, a very contemptible part of them.

In fact, mere sense-impressions do not constitute knowledge at all; nor is such knowing, if knowing it may, at all, be called, in any sense, an evidence of the truth even of external objects. Perception, emotion, and volition these are the three essential constituents of knowledge, and truth or right knowledge is established only when perception is followed by its own proper emotion or feeling, and finally, when this emotion or feeling is followed by volition or activity, and when this activity is justified by the actuality of the thing perceived, it is then only that the real truth of a thing may be said to be thoroughly established. This is the test of truth as recognised, at least by Hindu Logic. And this canon is equally supported by the highest methods even of modern science. How, then, can we abstract the feelings that particular sense impressions produce from our real knowledge of sense-objects? What is called ordinarily accurate statements is only, thus, a partial record of our impressions of objects and events. It is an outside measurement of them. The sensorium or the *Manas* measures things from the outside, the heart measures them from the inside.

The one refers them to things conceived as standing outside the seer or the knower: the other refers them to the seer or knower himself. And why should the one measurement be declared as true and accurate, and the other as false, exaggerated, and fanciful?

The one, really, is the result, of the materialisation of the mind, so to say; the other the result of the spiritualisation of matter. This is the difference between Western truth and Oriental imagination. And this fact must be borne in mind in studying Hindu records, whether they refer to scientific, historic, literary, or religious subjects.

The fact, really, is that what is contemptuously characterised as "oriental exaggeration" is only the preponderating soul-reference or subjectivity of these records, indicating the overwhelming sense of the Absolute and the Universal that possessed the Hindu mind almost from pre-historic times. In the earlier stages of their historic development, the vehicles of their thought were, naturally, not only crude, but also exceedingly limited; and the expression of their sense of the Universal and the Spiritual, by means of such crude and chaotic materials as were supplied by their natural or social environments, naturally became somewhat chaotic, crude, and exaggerated.. Hegel's characterisation of the first stage of the evolution of art, as oriental, in the sense which he uses the term, is, therefore, hardly applicable to Hindu art, be it poetry, or painting, or sculpture or architecture. Oriental art, according to Hegel, is that wherein the form overwhelms the spirit. But in the consciousness of the Hindu, the form never, actually, overwhelmed the spirit, but it is rather the spirit that overwhelmed the form.. Philosophy of Art characterises it, rather as the third, — according to Hegel the highest, — stage of the development of Art. In saying, however, that even in the earliest stage of Hindu art, the spirit overwhelmed the form, we do not mean to claim for it, really, a place in what is called, Romantic-art. In Romanticism the spirit overwhelms the form of art, in a way very different from that in which it is found, actually, in ancient Hindu art.

Romanticism is preceded by classicism, — the stage of art-development, wherein there is an equipolence of form and spirit — "a balance, a harmony, a reposeful interpenetration of form and matter". In romanticism, we have a distinct "transcendence of the matter by the form" of the symbol by the soul. In the earliest Hindu art, we do not find this transcendence, which is characteristic of real romanticism, but simply an overwhelming of the form by the spirit: an attempt to overcome the symbol by the soul.

In fact, since the entrance of Japanese culture and Japanese ideals into the common room of European culture and ideals, even European art-students are being compelled, gradually to re-examine their old estimates and canons of art-criticism; and the dominant or impressionist school of Japanese art, has already claimed a distinct place and position for itself. There is, no doubt, a very wide difference between modern Japanese and ancient Hindu art, and the two cannot by any means be classed together.

But the spiritual note, the sense of the whole, almost independent of that of the relations of the parts to one another, through which it exists and reveals and actually realises itself, — is common to both. For impressionism has necessarily a soul-reference always. It realises or seeks to realise a form of beauty, not, really, as it stands in itself, in its varied relations to its own parts and its own environments, — but as the whole, including the relations and environments, impresses the mind or the soul with itself. The ancient Hindu records belong to this class. They are records not of objects or events in themselves, but of the impressions they produced upon the mind of the recorder. And our mental impressions can merely be indicated but can never be actually photographed. Much less are our spiritual impressions, that are almost infinitely more complex and subtle than our ordinary mental experiences — capable of even an approximately exact reproduction whether by words, by colours, or by hewing and carving. They can never be reproduced with any pretension to exactitude, especially, in the earlier periods of human evolutions, when the vehicles of human thought are, necessarily crude, tentative and limited, owing to the crude and chaotic and limited character of man's experience in that primitive state.

Hindu records must, therefore, be studied and interpreted not as representing the nature or social surroundings of the Hindu, as they existed, actually, in themselves, but as seeking to indicate how they affected his inner, his mental, his emotional, his spiritual life. Viewed in this light, it will be seen that despite the apparent crudities and what appear as wild and hysteric exaggerations to the modern mind, — of the ancient Hindu books, the experiences they record are subjectively real, and as such, absolutely true.

On account of this peculiarly spiritual prism through which the Hindu viewed everything, nature never presented itself to him as merely natural, nor man, either, as merely human. Natural objects and phenomena had always to him a soul-reference. Fire, water, ether, sky, the sun, the moon, the stars, the twilight, the clouds, the winds, the rivers, — all his nature environments, whether terrestrial or celestial, were always soulful, so to say, in his eye. We have some of the finest realistic descriptions of these elementals in the Rig-veda, to be found, perhaps, anywhere, in any human literature, ancient or modern. But this realism is not materialism in any sense of the term.

The pictures have always a halo of genuine spirituality about them, The poetry of the Rig-veda, indeed, defies Hegel's classification. It is not, really, oriental, in the sense that the form overwhelms the spirit, the expression the ideal, the symbol the soul. It is Paganistic either, as having a clear conception and firm control of the relations of things, out of which grows that equipolence between form and spirit, which is the characteristic of Classicism. Nor can it he called, in any sense, romantic, either; for there is really no "*transcendence*" of the form by the spirit here. The poetry of the Rig-Veda stands, thus, by itself, as a distinct class or type, which reproduces nature through the lens of the mind, the spirit, the soul,— neither overwhelmed by its chaotic mass (which would make it oriental in the sense of Hegel); nor standing fairly balanced with it (which would make it classical); nor even exactly transcending it (which would make it romantic); — but simply interpreting it, even as it exactly stands outside, as a spiritual factor, however crude may be the conception of this "spiritual" itself.

This quasi spirituality of the Rig-veda developed into what may be called a pure, though perhaps a preponderatingly abstract, spirituality, in the Upanishads. In the Vedas Nature is, so to say, simply vitalised, on being transmuted as mental experiences, in the consciousness of the ancient Hindu. It stands here simply humanised. The view is not exactly animistic, which would raise a suspicion of the identification of life with the body, — but anthropomorphic. There is, indeed, no suspicion of the identification, in consciousness, of the body with the life principle, of form with spirit, — in the most crude or most primitive of these records. The sense of the spiritual and the universal, — the sense, that is, of the Absolute, being an original, an organic, and pre-historic endowment of the Hindu race-consciousness, such identification of the body with the soul could never vitiate Hindu thought, even in its earliest stage.

It is, therefore, that we find Tylor's animistic theory of the origin of religion, inapplicable to, and unsupported by the records of the Aryan, and especially of the Hindu people. The Vedic view of nature, we therefore prefer to characterise as humanistic or anthropomorphic. In the Upanishads it is distinctly spiritualistic or idealistic, and monistic. Nature has no existence here apart from Brahman or the Absolute. It is his covering, his manifestation, created out of himself by him, existing in him, and in death or decay, going back to and losing itself in him. Brahman terial Cause of the Universe. The Universe sun, the moon, the stars, the immensities above, and the myriads of forms and appearances below, — are all sparks of him, the Eternal, the Absolute, the Infinite Being, These are reflections of his thought, endless ripples rising on the surface of his infinite energy, creations of his absolute will. He throws them out, at his pleasure, and draws them in again at his will.

But while there is a very distinct note of divine immanence in the Upanishads, the growth, really, of the earlier nature spiritualism, so to say, of the Vedic thought, it became gradually lost in what may be called the Abstract Universalism or the subjective idealism of the later Upanishadic speculations. The dominant note here is not of an idealisation, — what, in fact, may even be termed a distinct apotheosis of the cosmic forces and phenomena, united in and conceived as the Virata-Purusha or the Viswarupa, — of Natures, but, practically, that of the denial of all truth and reality to it. With the growth of this Mayic conception of the phenomenal world, — wherein Maya is conceived not, as in the earlier as well as in some of the later speculations, as the creative energy of the Divine, differentiated from himself in the process of his self-revelation or self-realisation, and, therefore, as a *real* and *substantive* moment of the Divine Being, — but as mere illusion, — there grew up a distinct divorce and separation between the natural and the spiritual life. And in consequence of it, after a certain stage, when nature was too strong to be ignored and man too week to meet even the essential requirements of his physical life, and of the state of civilization that he had already attained, — all progress of the natural sciences came, practically, to a standstill.

Sir Ashutosh Mookherjea: a Character Study

(Born, Calcutta, June 29, 1864; Father Dr. Gangaprasad Mookherjea, an eminent medical practitioner of Calcutta. Education — Vernacular School, 1869-'72; home education under father 1872-'75; Matriculation (second in the list) 1879; Presidency College, Calcutta, 1880; B.A. 1884 (topping the list); M.A. (Mathematics) 1885; (Physical Science) 1886; Premchand Roychand Student 1886; Fellow Royal Society, Edinburgh, 1886; B.L. 1888; Enrolled Vakil, Calcutta High Court, 1888; Fellow, Calcutta University, 1889; Doctor in Law 1894; University Representative, Bengal Legislative

Council, 1899; re-elected, 1901: Bengal Representative (co-opted) Indian Universities' Commission, 1902; Calcutta Corporation Representative, Bengal Legislative Council, 1903; Representative of Non-Official Members of the Bengal Legislative Council in the Imperial Legislative Council, 1903; Judge, Calcutta High Court, from 1904; Vice-Chancellor, Calcutta University. 1906-'14; President, Asiatic Society, Bengal, 1907-'09; President, Indian Museum, 1909; Twice President, Bengal Literary Conference, 1916 and 1919; Member, Calcutta University Commission, 1917-'19).

Complex Character

Sir Ashutosh Mookherjea's is about the most complex public character that I have seen. And it has been my privilege to see, at more or less close quarters, most of the men who have made the religious, social or political history of India during the last half a century. This complexity is, I think, responsible for the widely divergent estimates that diverse people have formed of him. He has enthusiastic admirers, whose admiration often-times verges on fulsome adulation. He has persistent detractors, whose detractions seem sometimes to take the colour of malice. But there is one matter in which both his admirers and detractors seem generally to agree, and it is that he is by far the most powerful public character of his generation.

Men attain power over their fellow-men sometimes through their intellect. Others acquire it through the force of their will. Some gain power through their gift of the tongue, their capacity to rouse and control popular passions. Others gain great influence over their fellow-men through their capacity to please, to instruct and to inspire; all the greatest artists, poets, painters, sculptors, musicians and actors belong to this class. Some gain power through their great wealth or high rank or exalted position. Sir Ashutosh does not fall into any of these classes.

Physical Impression

Indeed, it seems very doubtful if Sir Ashutosh's personality has ever exercised much influence over his fellow-men. That mysterious quality called personal magnetism is apparently not the greatest asset of his life. This magnetism is, in most cases, a physical quality. And one has only to look at Sir Ashutosh to discover the absence of any suspicion of this physical quality in him. His build is more massive than fine-cut; and though it betokens considerable strength both of body and mind, it is not the subtle strength that draws men near to it, and by look or gesture, captivates and controls them.

He has, no doubt, a pair of large flashing eyes, overhung with bushy eyebrows; and one feels a little uncomfortable when they play upon one's face, as if one's mind and soul were passing through the prism of a spectrum; — but it is very difficult to say whether this feeling is due entirely, if at all, to the gaze of the man or to one's preconceived notions about him as a shrewd judge of human character. A perfect stranger to Sir Ashutosh's public character and reputation can alone answer this question correctly.

In his physical appearance, Sir Ashutosh apparently represents the type, peculiar to the higher classes of Calcutta Hindus — fat, flabby, and delicate. But though fat and flabby, Sir Ashutosh's is by no means a delicate Constitution. His extraordinary mental vigour and the enormous amount of work which he has had to put in day after day, as a student, as University Senator and Syndic, as lawyer and legislator, as a judge and the executive head of a large and growing University, and as President of more than one learned Society, — prove extraordinary powers of physical endurance, which have been the almost universal foundations of all successful men of affairs. A collection of his Addresses, Literary and Academic — delivered between the years 1907 to 1915, lying before me, covers more than 650 pages of print.

A similar collection of his speeches in the Bengal and Imperial Councils would fill as big if not a bigger volume. These addresses and speeches are not mere orations, full of platitudes, padded with commonplace facts, copybook maxims, and cheap rhetoric, with which we are so sickeningly familiar in the Bengal school of oratory, but are fruits of close study, careful observation, and intimate acquaintance with men and affairs. All this would have been impossible unless Sir Ashutosh had been endowed, despite his apparently fat and flabby physique, with very great powers of physical endurance.

Intellectual Type

It is by no means easy to say how much of Sir Ashutosh's exceptional intellectual powers are part of his original endowment and how much of these is the result of the careful training which he had from his father in the early formative period of his life. That he had considerable native intelligence, the powers of quick perception and incisive analysis, must be admitted; because a plodding intellect could never have helped him to his fairly high position in original mathematical studies and researches, "the substance of which now appears under his name in leading Cambridge textbooks".

But these high intellectual powers do not constitute the secret of his unique position in our public life. Indeed, his intellect is not exactly of the type that draws and controls fellow-men. Quickness of perception, keenness of analysis, combined with a powerful imagination and persuasive eloquence, constitute the special character of that dominant type. And even the most uncritical of Sir Ashutosh's admirers would not claim for him that powerful imagination or persuasive eloquence which always go to the making of great intellectual leaders. Sir Ashutosh's intellect is of a pre-eminently practical type, that which is quick to seize the relations of men and things, not so much perhaps, in their ideal as in their practical aspects, and which can, almost intuitively, discover the ways and means by which these relations may be moved or worked to some desired practical end. Sir Ashutosh's intellect is of the type that is common to all great political leaders and successful administrators.

Administrator and Politician

And here we have, I think, what may very well be called the master-key to his complex character. He has been a brilliant student, a successful lawyer and judge, and an eminent educationist. But in all these walks of life, he has only been one among many. In all these, he has had many equals and even some superiors. It is only as Vice-Chancellor of the Calcutta University, — the executive and administrative head of a great and growing institution, that Sir Ashutosh has attained his unique position in our public life. And here, we see in him, above everything else, the capable administrator and politician.

Some people may, however, feel considerable hesitancy in applying the term politician to Sir Ashutosh. In the first place, he is a high official; and no Indian official can be called a politician without offence. Sir Ashutosh has never meddled also in our politics. There have been High Court Judges who stepped to the High Court Bench from the Presidential Chair of the Indian National Congress. Sir Ashutosh is not one of them.

There are other reasons also why one may hesitate to characterise a man of Sir Ashutosh's character and position, as a politician. The word has got a bad odour about it in India. This is largely due to our unfortunate political position. The true politician is more or less out of place in India. There is no room here for the cultivation of those intellectual and moral qualities that make successful politicians in the self-governing countries of the world. Without any pretensions to the democratic ideals, or the high standards of government claimed by the British, even the administration of the Moguls gave us much larger scope for the development of these qualities than what we now have.

On the other hand, the British Bureaucrat in India has always been jealous of the position and influence of the independent Indian politician, and has systematically sought to treat him with ill-concealed contempt. The politicians themselves also have been equally responsible for the "degeneration" of this word among us. Few of them have given proofs of any real insight into the actualities of the Indian situation or of any grasp of the larger generalisations of modern-world-politics. Almost all of them have built their political philosophy upon ideas and ideals uncritically borrowed from British history and English literature, and have been trying, all these years, to apply these to their own country, ignoring her different condition and the stage of political evolution which she just now occupies.

This is seen, for instance, in the avidity with which our active politicians seek to secure the help of the State in the promotion of their economic or educational interests, entirely ignoring the obvious fact that state-socialism, in any shape or form, is absolutely unsuited, and positively fatal to countries that have not developed a powerful democracy, where representatives of the people in the national legislature do not exercise complete control over the acts and policies of the executive, and where the interests of the people, as they understand these, have not become the supreme and only concern to their government. Nationalisation of the means of production which must go hand in hand with the nationalisation of the instruments of popular education, cannot *precede*, but must always *follow*, the complete nationalisation or democratisation of the machinery of the government. It has been so in all the great democracies of the West. Until this process of democratisation was fairly complete, the policy of the progressives in all these countries, had been not state socialism, but *laissez faire*. But the copybook politics of our English-educated classes have no appreciation of these vital political principles; and all this superficiality and imitativeness are very largely responsible for lowering both the standards of political thinking and the character of active politicians among us.

Indeed, the most successful of our politicians have only been very capable debaters. And even here the type has been British. Some quickness of intelligence, some skill in handling or mishandling facts or figures, and a good deal of ready eloquence and effective retort, these are the usual stock-in-trade of the successful Parliamentary debater. We have had one or two of this type among us, whose ability and sweet reasonableness received open recognition from the highest rulers of the land, a recognition that inevitably helped to make their high reputation in the intellectual slave-mart known as respectable opinion in India.

Broadly speaking, however, Indian politicians fall under two classes, the demagogue and the place-hunter; and our political stage is often marked by the exhibition of quick-change artists who change from extremism to moderatism, from violent critics and opponents of the Government to their ardent friend and supporter, with an eye to the ultimate chance of becoming their respected and respectable colleague. In view of all these things, one feels considerable hesitancy in calling Sir Ashutosh a politician. For, he is not a demagogue, and has never been a political place-hunter. At the same time, I know of no other word that can so faithfully sum up his real public character; and I think both friends and foes will agree to accept him as the most clever politician and capable administrator of our generation.

One might, indeed, go further and say that Sir Ashutosh has perhaps been the only politician and administrator that the modern educated Bengalee community has produced. And, considering his achievements in relation to his environments, it may perhaps even be claimed, — not, by any means, in any spirit of petty provincial rivalry, but in perfect truth and justice, — that Sir Ashutosh is the most capable politician and administrator that British India has yet produced.

In claiming this, I do not forget or underrate the high achievements of men like Sir T. Madhava Rao, or Mr. Rangacharlu or Sir Salar Jung and many others who have made the history of the most progressive of our Native States. But we must not forget the more favourable conditions under which they worked and the comparatively freehand, which the administrative independence of the States they served, gave them.

Administrator and Statesman

There is, however, a view of administrative efficiency which measures success only by immediate results. But administrators, who strive only after quick returns, generally make improvident statesmen, who ultimately lead to the political bankruptcy of the State they labour to serve. The vision of far-off ideals, the historic imagination that recognises future possibilities both of good and evil, long before they commence to materialise, and the grasp of the inner psychology of existing actualities, that enable the true statesman to direct present policy with a view to shape the course of future evolution, providing, so far as may be, for the prevention of possible evil and the advancement of possible good, — these are rarely found in the ordinary successful administrator.

On the other hand, the grasp of immediate actualities, the sensing of immediate evils, however passing they may be, and the mastery of practical details, that characterise the efficient administrator, are not generally found in combination with far-sighted statesmanship. In practical life, the happiest arrangement, therefore, is to leave the initiation of public policy to people endowed with superior statesmanlike qualities, while the carrying out of this policy may be entrusted to practical men of affairs who have complete mastery of actual details, and are able to work for immediate ends.

It is difficult to say how far, if at all, Sir Ashutosh represents that rare combination of superior statesmanship and high administrative efficiency which have occasionally been found in the great administrators of free countries. His field of work has, so far, been much too limited, his opportunities too few, and even these in a subordinate sphere of public life, to give full play to any high statesmanlike qualities that he may possibly have. This is the universal tragedy of our present public life. One thing, however, is absolutely undeniable. Even the most careless student of Sir Ashutosh's career cannot deny that all appearances and outer impressions to the contrary notwithstanding, he has his visions, like the rest of his educated countrymen and his inner soul is as sensitive to our existing actualities, as the most vocal, or — may I say it without offence — even the most extremist of our patriots and politicians; and that his one aim and intention, in all his public labours, has been, as he himself once declared, to:

Draw new furrows beneath the healthy morn

And plant the great Here-After in the Now.

People's Spokesman

Sir Ashutosh is not the "tribune" of his people, has never aspired to that honour. But, as a member, first of the Bengal Legislative Council, then of the Indian, he has been as loyal and courageous a defender of popular rights as the most aggressive of our patriots and politicians. Of course, his style is his own. He never indulged in strong language, and has never appeared on any of our political platforms that offer so much temptation to it. But neither has he trained himself in the courtier's art of saying pleasant things only. His public utterances have always been measured and therefore moderate, in the true sense of the term, but always without any suspicion of falsehood or flattery in them. Sir Ashutosh's speeches both in the Bengal and the Imperial Council would fully bear this out. Discussing certain charges preferred by the Government of India in a letter to the Government of Bengal in connection with the Calcutta Municipal Bill (1899) then before the Council, he said that "Assuming, as indeed it is assumed, in the 13th paragraph of the letter from the Government of India, that the allegation is well-founded, that the existing Corporation has devoted itself to speech rather than to action assuming further, that in order to check the abuses and anomalies complained of, it is necessary to reduce the numerical strength of the Corporation," — assuming all this, — Sir Ashutosh declared,

"It does not necessarily follow that the proposed reduction should be confined to the body of elected Commissioners alone. Indeed, if these positions are granted, and I shall assume for my present purpose that they are granted, it would follow that the reduction should not be confined to the body of elected Commissioners alone, but should be extended to the body of nominated Commissioners as well, unless indeed, the Government is further prepared to affirm that the vice of speech without action is monopolised by the elected Commissioners and the abuses complained of are traceable to them exclusively". Sir Ashutosh's speech on the motion that the Calcutta Municipal Bill as amended be passed, may be quoted as a very fair example of the style and spirit of his public utterances upon vital questions."

"I have no desire, Sir, to review at this stage the history and fortune of this legislation. I will not stop, even for a moment, to enquire whether it was wise, whether it was statesmanlike, for any Government to introduce into the Council chamber a measure of such magnitude intended to mutilate, if not to destroy, the form of municipal government which has prevailed in the capital of the Indian Empire for well-nigh quarter of a century, till the facts had been ascertained by an independent commission of enquiry in whose decision the public might repose implicit confidence. I will not pause for a moment to enquire whether it was wise, whether it was politic, for any Government to undertake a measure of this character upon an alleged and unproved ground of corruption, which was first publicly formulated in a State document more than twelve months after the Bill had been introduced into the Council. These may not be appropriate subjects of discussion now. But I take it, it perfectly legitimate to consider whether the Bill as amended, which in a few moment will become the law of the land does or does not make adequate provision for the removal of the evils to remedy which the Bill was avowedly introduced. One of these so-called evils has been described to be the complete failure of the elective system to secure adequate representation even of the different interests existing in the native city; or, to put it in a more practical and more intelligible form, one of the avowed objects of the Bill was to destroy the dominance of the educated Hindu in the Calcutta Corporation. That object, Sir, I mournfully confess, has been adequately secured by the provisions of this Bill; and I say, with all the emphasis I can command, that the Bill, in so far as it has attained this object, has my unqualified disapproval: in this respect it has not and it cannot have, the smallest measure of my sympathy. But, Sir, it is instructive to enquire, what have you substituted for the dominance of the educated Hindu? You have not satisfied yourself with replacing it by the dominance of the mercantile European or the progressive Muhammadan; but you have replaced it by the irresponsible executive".

"But these, Sir, are not the only objection-features of the Bill. I venture to remind the Council that one of the alleged flagrant abuses to remedy which the promoters of the Bill are so anxious was the growth of party spirit and the appearance among the elected Commissioners of a class of professional and, in some cases, corrupt politicians. I ask, Sir, is there are any provisions in this Bill intended or calculated to remedy these evils, if they really exist. I confess, Sir, I cannot recall to mind any single provision in this direction. On the other hand, I can recall to mind at least one provision which will have the effort of alluring the needy to the Municipal board and of keeping away the honourable who will naturally shrink from a contest which may be construed as a contest for personal gain. I affirm that nothing has been done to remove or to prevent the recurrence of the alleged corruption. You declare that you have discovered a hidden gangrenous sore in a limb of the commonwealth, you refuse to open and examine it, you replace it by a new one, but you provide no guarantee that the sore will not reappear".

"Before I resume my seat, Sir, I desire to take the opportunity of referring to the startling theory propounded this morning by the Hon'ble Member-in-charge of this Bill. I have met with some surprises in the course of this prolonged debate, but I did not know that the greatest of these surprises had been reserved for the very last moment. The Hon'ble Member-in-charge of the Bill has seriously defined the function of this Council to be to carry out the mandate of the Government of the day when the principle of any proposed measure of legislation has been approved by that Government. I would not have been surprised, Sir, if this had been authoritatively laid down to be the duty of the official members of the Council. Thus qualified, I might have left the proposition alone and unchallenged. But I repudiate, in the clearest possible terms, this extraordinary theory when it is applied to non-official members. In spite of the doctrine expounded by the Hon'ble Member-in-charge, I retain, Sir, the right to think and judge for myself. I have made none the custodian of my conscience, and so long as I have the honour of a seat in this Council, it will be my duty to advise the Council to the best of my ability and judgement, regardless of what this or that party may approve or disapprove".

The same style and spirit are equally manifest in Sir Ashutosh's speeches in the Viceroy's Council in 1904 when the Indian Universities Bill was before it. That measure had aroused almost universal antagonism among the politically-minded classes all over India. This antagonism was the bitterest in Bengal, because the conflict between the leaders of the people and the representatives of the Bureaucracy over University affairs was the keenest in Calcutta. Indian politicians judged Lord Curzon's education policy, not by itself, but in the light of his general Indian policy which showed undisguised hostility towards the English-educated classes in the country. Sir Ashutosh's detachment from active politics on the one hand, and his intimate acquaintance with the state of things in the University on the other, helped him to take a more dispassionate view of the Indian Universities Bill than was possible for the general body of his educated countrymen. He was able, therefore, to recognise the good points in that measure. But at the same time he did not hesitate to fight inch by inch the numerous retrograde and reactionary provisions of the Bill and lend his valuable support to the great protagonist of the non-official Indian opposition to these, in the Committee stage, or to record his strong condemnation of these, when the final motion to pass the Bill as amended was brought before the Council.

While dissociating himself "completely from those who maintain that our Universities are ideal institutions and do not stand in need of any reform," he said: "I cannot agree with those unfriendly-critics who maintain that the Universities have failed in the objects which they have in view, namely, in the words of the great Despatch of 1854 — " the diffusion of the improvements, science, philosophy and literature of Europe, in short, of European knowledge," — and I cannot but point out that in some quarters at least, the Universities are disliked and cried down, because there is really a dislike of the culture which educated Indians have attained". But though the Universities are not at the present day all that they might or ought to be; the question remains, are the provisions of the present Bill calculated to meet the requirements of the situation?

The provisions of the Bill, broadly speaking, fell into three divisions, — (i) dealing with the relation between the Universities and the affiliated Colleges; (ii) dealing with the Constitution of the Universities; and (iii) dealing with the functions of the Universities. With regard to the first of these Sir Ashutosh gave his general support to them, with the reasonable reservation that "there should not be any undue interference with the internal management of the Colleges or with the administration of their finances so long as proper efficiency is maintained". With regard to the second division of the Bill which deals with the Constitution of the Universities, he said:

> "My Lord, I wish I could conscientiously say that the constitutional provisions of the Bill are satisfactory and are furnished with the necessary safeguards. Every effort that we have made for securing a statutory recognition of the non-official and of the Indian element on the Senate has been strenuously opposed on behalf of the Government and has consequently failed. I am not one of those who contend that high education must be left entirely to the control of the people. On the other hand, I willingly concede that high education is one of the paramount duties of the State and that it must be nurtured and developed under the fostering care of a beneficent Government. But I deny most emphatically that it is necessary or desirable to have provisions in the law which may

convert the Universities into men-departments of the State. It is quite possible to stunt the growth of a beautiful tree by constant pruning and too affectionate care. I acknowledge with feelings of the sincerest gratitude that the Bill recognises, though to a limited extent, the principle of election, and I hope that at no distant date Government may find it possible to accord it a wider recognition, by throwing open to election a large number of fellowships and conferring the franchise upon professors in our affiliated colleges. But, my Lord, what has caused me the utmost disappointment is the refusal of the Government to define the character of the Senate and to prescribe any statutory rules for the guidance of successive Chancellors; when I add to this the provisions of the Bill which make fellowships terminable after five years, which secure for teachers a position of advantage on the Syndicate by means of artificial rules, which make affiliation and disaffiliation direct acts of the Government and which make it possible, in theory at any rate, for the Government to impose any regulations even on the reconstituted Universities — when I take these together, I feel bound to express my deepest regret that what might otherwise have been a beneficent measure should be disfigured by blemishes of a startling character.

"My Lord, as to one of these particular points of difference I was told that the five years rule was in perfect harmony with the principle which obtains in this country in regard to some of the highest appointments under the State. I was assured, my Lord, that the five years rule works admirably where it prevails. But those who gave me the assurance must have forgotten for the moment a celebrated minute by the late Marquis of Salisbury, dated the 26th of April, 1875, in which the five years rule is condemned in unqualified terms, and it is pointed out that the actions of the Government found a long series of inconsistencies, that it had been found impossible to give permanent force to a new policy and all this was attributed to the fact that "the Indian Government" — my Lord, I will quote the language of the great statesman —"the Indian Government is, by the law of its existence, a government of incessant changes, it is the despotism of a line of Kings whose reigns are limited by climatic causes to five years". My Lord, I have quoted the language of one of the greatest British statesman of the nineteenth century and I hope I may be pardoned if I tenaciously adhere to error in such company".

"My Lord, it may be asked why absolute reliance should not be placed upon the capacity of the Government to administer the universities in a perfectly satisfactory manner. Before I answer this question, may I be permitted to point out that education can never be forced upon a people, and that if you want to educate a race you must carry the nation with you. So far at any rate as high education in India is concerned, the policy of the State in recent years has not been quite of the character one would wish. If, however, we examine the history of high education for the last quarter of a century, we shall feel convinced that the condition of things is far from satisfactory. My Lord, the truth of the matter is that we have reached the ebb tide of high education not because the Senates are inefficient, but because the Government has starved its colleges and has weakened its Education Department.

"My Lord, there was a time, not very many years ago, when the Government maintained well-equipped colleges under the management of professors who would be an honour to any University. I am not asking your Excellency to give us illustrious educators of the type of Arnold and Jowett, Kelvin and Ramsay; such personalities are rare even in England and cannot be imported or transported. If, however, Government will give us professors of the type of Professor Cowell, Professor Tawney, Professor Gough, Professor Clarke and Sir John Elliot — I name only a few who are no longer amongst us, — we should have nothing to complain. Each of them was a tower of strength to my University and commanded universal respect and admiration. But, my Lord, we are fallen upon evil times, when safe mediocrity is the order of the day. We are quite familiar with gentlemen who obtain second class or even third class honours at Oxford or at some other English University and are fortunate enough to secure appointments as Professors in Government Colleges in this country. If, upon their arrival, they pose as eminent educational experts and show no unmistakable contempt for their Indian fellow-subjects, who, with all their shortcomings, may have devoted years of patient toil to the examination and solution of difficult educational problems, are the latter to be blamed if they show their impatience of these self-constituted experts? My Lord, the real danger in connection with this Bill is that in spite of the best intentions and purest motives of the Government, the actual administration of its provisions may fall into the hands of fifth-rate and unsympathetic teachers, of whom recent events have shown there are not a few in this country, who are uncharitable enough to imagine that the interest in the University which the best among the Indians feel is an interest otherwise than educational. My Lord, I yield to none in my appreciation of the words of the poet:

"And not by Eastern windows only When day light comes, comes in the light In front the Sun climes slow, how slowly, But westward look, the land is bright".

The Patriot

Relentless criticism of the Government has been the popular standard of sturdy patriotism among us. It would, however, be hardly fair to measure Sir Ashutosh's love for his country and his people only by his measured, but therefore, nonetheless straight and fearless criticism of official acts and policies. Indeed, opportunities for this criticism were closed to him by his appointment as a judge of the Calcutta High Court, almost immediately he had taken his seat in the Imperial Legislative Council. But the whole outlook is radically wrong. Opposition to the Government may proceed from various motives of different or indifferent moral values. The disappointed placeman is an opponent of Government all the world over.

In India, social disappointments of Europe returned gentlemen who wanted to, but could not get admission into Anglo-Indian society, have occasionally ended in suicide; but, more frequently, these have landed the disappointed individual on our political platforms. There have been others, a much more numerous class, whose patriotism has been inspired by alien social and political ideas and whose aim and intention in all their patriotic enterprises have been to emulate British ways and attain British character. In their conduct and conversation they have been British, and Indians only in their opposition to the British officialdom in their country. Intellectual and moral slaves of their foreign masters, they have only aspired to social and political equality with them.

This was, really, the predominant type, in any case in Bengal, before the birth of our new Nationalism at the beginning of the present Christian century.

Sir Ashutosh's patriotism has never been of this type. He is not a disappointed placeman. He easily won the only official position to which he ever aspired. In the days of his youth nothing higher than this was really open to Indian ambitions. The regrettable disturbances in Bengal and elsewhere following upon Lord Curzon's indiscretions, forced the need of drastic reforms upon British statesmanship; and a few high executive offices have since been thrown open to qualified Indians. But Sir Ashutosh's administrative record as Vice-Chancellor of the Calcutta University, has unfortunately offered little encouragement to the Government to take him into their inner counsels. I do not really know, even if high executive office were open to Sir Ashutosh, whether he would care to exchange the free air of the High Court Bench for the close and, to an Indian conscious of his powers and proud of his own colour and culture, such as Sir Ashutosh undoubtedly is,—painfully stifling atmosphere of the Viceregal Cabinet. If the Government could take courage in both hands and offer him a seat in the Imperial Executive Council, Sir Ashutosh might possibly accept it, not, I believe, from any petty personal consideration, but only to measure strength both of the intellect and will, with the greatest of Anglo-Indian administrators, and prove it to the world, that given adequate opportunities, the Hindu is quite able to hold his own with the cleverest of his political masters, and even to use them as soft clay in the potter's hand. But it is an useless speculation. For, Sir Ashutosh, all his cleverness and diplomacy notwithstanding, has shown his hands too openly in the management of the Calcutta University, to encourage the Government to make any further experiments with him.

Nationalism or Orthodoxy?

To superficial observers, Sir Ashutosh appears as an orthodox Hindu Brahmin whose social and religious ideas and practices cannot be fully reconciled with his intellectual acquirements and the broad outlook that results from modern culture. As a mathematician and scientist, Sir Ashutosh's intellect could not possibly accept the faiths and practices of medieval Hinduism as rational. As a diligent student of the psychological group of the sciences, he must know the value of social reform as contributing the necessary dynamic element to social evolution, and cannot possibly be unacquainted with the essentially progressive character of Hindu Society and Hindu civilization. And, in view of all these things, his unbending-orthodoxy would seem to most people as unreal and hypocritical.

I can well understand that Sir Ashutosh would appear so to the Non-conformist, both Christian and Brahmo. But fortunately or unfortunately, Sir Ashutosh does not possess the queer thing known as the Non-conformist Conscience in English life and literature. I do not know what Sir Ashutosh's private religious opinions are, or indeed, if he has any reasoned religious faith at all. But we all know that the usual Hindu *pujahs* are celebrated in his house; and there is no reason to believe that he has no personal participation in these worships. But it is no new thing in India. There is many a *Naiyaika* and *Vedantin*, who does not believe in the faiths and practices of the populace, but who acquiesces in these as instruments and agencies of religious and ethical culture in; the lower stages of intellectual or spiritual evolution. But, apart from these medieval apologetics and present practices, even modern thought may well accept these rituals, not as idolatry, as they are interpreted by ignorant or unimaginative critics, but as *ideolatry*, which is the only correct and rational meaning that the history of human faiths and the science of comparative religion, correctly studied and understood, must give to these symbolisms of popular Hinduism.

Besides, these Hindu *pujahs* have a variety of aspects through which they appeal to men in various stages of intellectual and moral evolution. To some they appeal through their innate sense of the supernatural which is the universal root and origin of man's religious consciousness. To others these appeal through their artistic sense; while to men with powerful social instincts, these *pujahs* appeal through their social life, — as Christmas-celebrations do to most Christians, though, strictly speaking the Christmas, specially among English Protestants, is more of a limited family than a wide social reunion.

To the modern-educated Hindu with an inborn religious, a large social, and a cultivated artistic sense, and of wide modern culture, these *pujahs* may well appeal through all these various aspects. And, though not entirely ignorant or forgetful of the evil consequence of too much supernaturalism and symbolism to the human mind and spirit, and their enervating effects upon human character, even the modern educated Hindu may reasonably accept the popular ceremonialism of his people without any outrage on his reason or his conscience, as the only available symbols and instruments of their present social life and unity.

Apart, however, from these generalisations, that after all may or may not wholly apply to Sir Ashutosh's personal religious beliefs, of which I frankly confess complete ignorance, — it is difficult to resist the conclusion that Sir Ashutosh's so-called rigid orthodoxy is a part of his strong nationalism. I use the adjective "so-called" advisedly; because Sir Ashutosh's mental and moral outlook are by no means "orthodox". True it is that he thankfully declined the invitation of Lord Curzon to the Coronation of his late Majesty King Edward VII in London; but his reasons for doing so are not known to the public. They may have been personal, regard for the sentiments of his family, particularly of his old mother for whom he had the deepest love and veneration; they may even possibly have been social, his hesitancy to court social excommunication. But, I have no doubt, that these, even if they did influence him, must have been only contributory causes of his decision in this matter, the main reason was his strong nationalist instinct. As regards social excommunication, Sir Ashutosh has braved these things since by the remarriage of his widowed daughter, which is a much more serious social offence, in the eye of Hindu orthodoxy than "crossing the black waters".

Judging, however, from the general tenor of his life, one may reasonably attribute his refusal to go to England for the late King-Emperor's Coronation, to his determination never to break the social barrier between his people and their present political masters. Sir Ashutosh knows it that once a Hindu is tempted to cross this barrier, — "the protecting line," as the spiritualist calls it, in the relations between the living and the dead, — he loses his claim to real social equality with his political masters, and practically concedes to alien ideals and customs the right to sit in judgement upon national ideals and institutions. There have been orthodox Hindu judges in the Calcutta High Court before and besides Sir Ashutosh. But none of them have so tenaciously held to their national ways, in their relations with the foreign rulers of their country, as Sir Ashutosh seems to have always done.

He is rarely seen, outside the precincts of the High Court, in his official dress. Even so orthodox a Hindu as the late Sir Gooroodas Banerjee rarely appeared in public, particularly in public meetings where he had to associate with Europeans, in his national dress. But Sir Ashutosh has done so with the utmost unconcern. Even as a member of the Sadler Commission, he never made any change in this matter. Except where official dress was required by long-established official usage, Sir Ashutosh has never, unless for obvious reasons of practical convenience, affected it. At home he sits and works in his "native nakedness" — which is so sensible a thing to do in our climate, — and has not been known to "change" even when European visitors are announced. These are, apparently, inconsequential little things, possibly due to the necessity imposed upon him by his "flesh" and his climatic environment. But these little things do lend support to the supposition that they may have a deeper origin and meaning, and they may be the outer expression of a profoundly nationalist spirit that resents, and tries to resist, so far as may be, what Mr. Hardayal described as "the social conquest" of India.

Not a Hide-Bound Conservative

But, whatever may be the real motive or meaning of Sir Ashutosh's so-called orthodoxy, it cannot be said that his social outlook is narrow, or that his sturdy nationalism has helped him to any hidebound conservatism, as is so frequently found in many of our "orthodox" nationalists. In a remarkable address, delivered before the first Convocation of the University of Mysore, in October, 1918, he declared that while fully admitting that " Indian History, Indian Antiquities, Indian literature, Indian Philosophy, Indian Religion, Indian Mathematics, Indian Astronomy, Indian Medicine, Indian Sociology, Indian Economics, Indian Administration, Indian Art, indeed, all monuments of Indian culture, imperatively demand critical and comparative study in an Indian University," he could "imagine no step more unwise for an Indian University than to give exclusive prominence to studies peculiarly Indian," and entered an emphatic protest against "all suicidal policy of isolation and stagnation".

> "Let me ask, what course shall we choose, while the world all round us, is making such gigantic strides on the path of progress, ever seeking to gain mastery over the forces of Nature? We cannot disentangle ourselves, even if we wish, from irresistible world-currents and sit on the lovely snowcapped peaks of the Himalayas absorbed in contemplation of our glorious past. It is most emphatically true that the community, the people, the nation, the race, which like the Greek philosopher, will live in its own tub and ask the conquering powers around it to move

> away from its sunshine, will soon be enveloped in eternal darkness, the object of derision for its helplessness and of contempt for its folly. We cannot afford to stand still; we must move or be overwhelmed; we cannot waste precious time and strength in defence of theories and systems which, however valuable in their days, have been swept away by the irresistible avalanche of worldwide changes. We can live neither in nor by the defeated past; and if we would live in the conquering future, we must dedicate our whole strength to shape its course, and our will to discharge its duties. The most pressing question of the hour for the people of every race is, not what they have been hitherto, but what they shall determine to be heretofore; not what their fathers were, but what their children shall be. The past is of value, only in so far as it illuminates the present, the present is of value only in so far as it guides us to shape the future. Let us then raise an emphatic protest against all suicidal policy of isolation and stagnation".

The full significance of this utterance can only be seized when we bear in mind that this was made not before the Calcutta University, with a long past of social revolt and progressive reforms, led by its *alumini;* but before a new University, in a Hindu State, which, all its progressive movements notwithstanding, is still a far more rigid stronghold of Hindu conservatism than any province in British India. Such a declaration, to such an audience, could only proceed from deep conviction.

Broad and Liberal Outlook

Sir Ashutosh's broad and liberal mental and social outlook is still more pronounced in his Bengalee addresses. These addresses, three in number, were delivered during the last three years, as President of Literary Conferences, and therefore deal mainly with literary topics. But he has always used the word literature in the broadest sense, instead of in the narrow sense of *belles-lettres,* in which it is used in Sanskrit and Bengalee; and has discussed the problem of our vernacular literature from the standpoint of our entire social life. The standpoint is essentially modern. To the modern thinker, literature, like every other department of human effort and achievement, is the expression of life. A high literature is only possible in a vigorous social life. Our present social life lacks the vigour and virility of the life of the more progressive societies of our time; and high literary achievements will be impossible unless our society becomes virile and progressive. But literature is also a most powerful instrument of social uplift. And, in the discharge of this essential function, modern Indian literatures must draw their votaries from men who have thoroughly mastered the "improvements, the sciences, the histories and literatures" of the advanced nations of the West.

> "If the masses of our people are to be led along the right path — if they are to be helped to attain the full stature of their manhood — if the Bengalee race is to be organised into a great nation, then, means must be found to progressively increase their mental equipments. To do this we must devise means by which the common people, though ignorant of European languages, may yet learn all that is good, pure, and of universal import and application, in the life and literatures of the Western countries, so that they may apply these to the benefit of their own lives and the good of their own society. Whatever is faultless in Western culture, and at the same time is calculated to do us real good, — qualities which, if we are able to acquire them, will be able to add to the existing beauties of our social life and deepen and strengthen our national self-consciousness, must be preached and taught in our own mother tongue to our masses. We are gradually approaching a great crisis in the history of the world, and if we are to hold our own in the fearful competitions of that critical time, we must be fully armed not only with our own familiar native weapons, but must equip ourselves with all the weapons in the improved and rich armoury of the Western nations of our time". (*Free rendering — Address before the North-Bengal Literary Conference,* 1916.)

But, while nothing must be rejected on the one and all sufficient ground that they are foreign, nor should every thing be preserved simply because they are indigenous to our soil and society.

> "I do not say that whatever is foreign is good, and, therefore, must be acceptable to us. I dare not say that whatever is foreign is evil and must, therefore, be summarily rejected as unholy and untouchable by us. "When a thing is good, I do not care to enquire if it is *swadeshi* or foreign. Whatever is good must be welcomed, whichever land may claim its origin and growth. Whatever is not free from evil must be renounced, regardless of all considerations as to whether it is mine or any body else's. This is the only simple canon of judgement.
>
> "No other canons can be conducive to the good either of our literature or of our society. There may be customs and institutions which, though more or less favourable to social progress in Europe, are entirely unsuited to us, and are likely to work evil in our society. Any attempt to introduce these among us must not only be abortive, but is likely to contribute to the disruption of our well-organised social body".
> — *(Address before the North-Bengal Literary Conference — free rendering.)*

The groundwork of this liberalism or cosmopolitanism, in the truest sense of the term, is a thorough and critical study of national history, national literature and national ideas of society and civilization.

> "Those who do not know what they have, what they had, it is they alone who go a begging to strangers. Acquaint your own countrymen with the acquisitions of your past, analyse those acquisitions and make them realise their value. Quicken the sense of national self-respect in their mind. Then only will it be possible to build up your national life. And the foundations of that life must be laid deep and wide, on a vigorous and expansive national literature".

> "Reasonable and discriminating adaptation of the achievements of foreign nations must also contribute to the work of nation-building. Koine built her wonderful life and civilization by a healthy and helpful assimilation of Greek culture. But Rome had not her own house full of invaluable treasures. Her house was comparatively empty and bare. So, she could greedily take in whatever she found attractive or useful in the life and civilization of the Greecian people. Our position is, however, entirely different. Our ancient treasures are inexhaustible. Great care and discrimination are, therefore, needed here. We must never take anything from outside which is at all likely to depreciate the value or lower the dignity of our sacred inheritance from the past. At the same time, there are things which we lack, but which foreigners have in abundance; we should never hesitate to take these in, provided always that these do not hurt or prejudice our national life. Our house is not empty and bare, like that of Rome, so that we may any how fill it up. Our house is full. Whatever is calculated to add to the beauty and grandeur of our well-furnished house, whatever is in harmony with the furniture and ornaments of this house, if we find these among others, we must cheerfully acquire and accept them. But that which is not favourable to our national life and evolution — we must never touch". — *(Address before the North-Bengal Literary Conference, free rendering.)*

Dreamer of Dreams

Few people would, perhaps, suspect Sir Ashutosh to be obsessed with any exuberant fancies. Indeed, his mathematical and scientific studies, as well his legal profession where he has to deal with solid facts of life, do not give much encouragement to idle fancies. But Sir Ashutosh, like the majority of his educated countrymen, is also a dreamer of dreams. What political dreams he dreams in the solitude of his studies, or in confidential conversations with his intimate friends, the outside public has no means of knowing. As an official of Government, all politics is taboo to him. Even before his "elevation" to the High Court bench, Sir Ashutosh did not throw himself into the mid-currents of our political activities. But there is a very genuine ring of patriotism even in his academic utterances before the Convocations of his University. Addressing the convocation of the Calcutta University in 1913, he declared — "the conviction is deep-rooted in my mind, that India with her great intellectual traditions, India which in olden times was one of the chosen seats of wisdom and learning, is expected, nay, is bound to come to the front rank again and take her place among those nations which are justly regarded as the leaders in the evolution of Humanity in the modern times".

But it is in his Bengalee addresses, again, that we recognise the dreamer, the patriot and the idealist in Sir Ashutosh Mukherjea. His vision of the future of Bengalee literature is exalting and inspiring. He believes that "some day Bengalee literature, in the widest sense of the term, will take its place among the most advanced of modern literatures; and, as students of higher Mathematics have now, for instance, to study Russian to get acquainted at first hand, with the works of eminent Russian mathematicians, even so, a time will come when advanced students, whatever their race or country, will have to study the language and literature of Bengal to acquire at first hand correct knowledge of the contributions of Bengalee savants to the common stock of human knowledge and speculations and universal human culture".

But all literature is only the expression of life. Sir Ashutosh's dreams of the future of the Bengalee literature, were therefore, inevitably bound up with his deep-rooted conviction that the Bengalee people will also some day claim and secure their rightful place among the most advanced and progressive peoples of the modern world, as an honoured and honourable member of the Federation of Universal Humanity, which is the ideal-end of all human history.

But, Sir Ashutosh's dreams are not mere idle fancies in which so many of our sensitive patriots seek refuge from the cruel actualities of their social and political environments. In fact, his sturdy practical sense would never tolerate any idle fancies. Sir Ashutosh's dreams are really visions of his social ideals; and like the ideals of all trained intelligence, these are rational inductions of what must follow from what is. He sees the seeds of the present in the evolution of the past, and foresees the possibilities of the future in the hidden trends and tendencies of the present. His ideals are, therefore, not wild fancies, but the necessary logic of existing potentialities. Sir Ashutosh has been able to pursue these, progressively, through the instruments and agencies that are within our reach and control. And it is this union of lofty idealism with a strong practical sense that raises Sir Ashutosh from the level of the opportunist practical politician to that of the true statesman.

Constructive Reformer

Sir Ashutosh's claims to constructive statesmanship of a very high order seem, to my mind, to be fairly established by what he has done in the Calcutta University to secure a recognised position for the Bengalee language and literature in its curriculum.

"It is now nearly twenty-three years ago," (he said addressing the Convocation of his University, held on December 13, 1913, to confer honorary degrees upon Rabindranath and others) — "that a young and inexperienced Member of the Senate earnestly pleaded that a competent knowledge of the vernaculars should be a prerequisite for admission to a Degree in the Faculty of Arts in this University. The Senators complimented the novice on his eloquence and admired his boldness, but doubted his wisdom, and, by an overwhelming majority, rejected his proposal on what now seems the truly astonishing ground that the Indian vernaculars did not deserve serious study by Indian students who had entered an Indian University.

Fifteen years later, the young Senator, then grown maturer, repeated his efforts with equally disastrous results. In the year following, he was, however, more fortunate and persuaded the Government of Lord Minto to hold that every student in this University should, while still an undergraduate, acquire a competent knowledge of his vernacular and that his proficiency in this respect should be tested precisely in the same manner as in the case of any other branch of knowledge and should be treated as an essential factor of success in his academic career. After a struggle of a quarter of a century, the elementary truth was thus recognised that if the Indian Universities are ever to be indissolubly assimilated with our national life, they must ungrudgingly accord due recognition to the Indian vernaculars. The far-reaching effect of the doctrine thus formulated and accepted, has already begun to manifest itself; but time alone can prove conclusively the beneficent results of this vital and fundamental change".

I cannot say if Sir Ashutosh had in his mind, among the future results of this vital and fundamental change, the institution of a special M. A. Degree in the Faculty of Arts of the Calcutta University in the vernacular literatures of India. It is possible the idea has gradually developed in his mind. And whether it is the result of his statesmanlike foresight and was at the back of the idea with which he introduced the first reform in this direction, in 1906, or whether he has gradually grown into, or even simply stumbled upon it, no one, perhaps, except Sir Ashutosh himself can definitely say. But the far-reaching import of this reform in our university cannot possibly be ignored. And here one is forced to recognise the constructive statesmanship of the man who has initiated it.

Problem of Nation-Building in India

To understand the full import and significance of this new Degree in our University, one must clearly realise the nature of the vital and complex problem of nation-building in modern India. India is not a country but a continent. The Indians are not one people, but are a conglomeration of many communities. They speak many tongues, profess many religions, have diverse usages and customs, own different histories and traditions. All the characteristics of nationhood as known in Europe, are absent here. Judged, therefore, by the common European standard, Indians cannot reasonably lay any claim to it.

India had no unity, political, social, linguistic or religious before the establishment of British rule. It has now one Government, and the educated and politically-minded people have found in English a common language for mutual intercourse. The growth of British institutions and the advancement of English or European culture and civilization will, possibly, on some distant day, work out some sort of an order out of this chaos of many languages, many religions, many social economies, and many customs and traditions of this heterogenous mass of Indian humanity. This is the popular British and bureaucratic view. I am not sure that a good many of our own "sensible and saner" politicians of the type, for instance, of Baron Satyendra Prasanna Sinha, do not largely share this view. If the assumptions at the back of it be true, then we must start cultivating the patience of Job, with a view to the peaceful evolution of modern national life and democratic institutions among us.

A correct study and appreciation of Indian history, however, encourage an altogether different view. The definition of nationhood in Europe is the generalisation of European experience, of European history and evolution only. These generalisations are absolutely inapplicable to India with a different history and evolution. Hinduism is not one religion, like Christianity or Islam, or even Buddhism, all of which are classed as credal, but a federation of many doctrines, dogmas, cults and disciplines, many authorities, scriptural and personal (the authority of the *Guru* for instance), — and many theological and philosophical systems and speculations.

Hindu society is also a federation of many castes and communities, each autonomous within itself, but joined to others in common subjection to a general, but not uniform, social law and order. In view of all this, the particular type of nationhood developed in India has been fundamentally different, both in ideal and structure, from the European type. National unity in India was not secured, as in Europe, by the more or less complete elimination of all vital differences between one community or society and another, but by working out a federation between diverse communities and cultures, standing in different stages of evolution. The fundamental unity of the Indian peoples was not political, as that of the nations of Europe, but cultural.

The emphasis of the ancient Greeco-Roman culture in Europe, out of which the modern European culture has evolved, was on their state-life. The State was the sign and symbol of their Social Whole. Consequently, every other department of life, — religious, moral, aesthetic, — was subordinate to and subsumed in the life of the State. Even the gods formed a part of it, and their worship was enforced by the authority of the State. Christianity spread in Europe only after it was identified with the State, through the conversion of Constantine; and latterly the Rome of the Popes became the centre of European life and culture, by its secret alliances with, and assumption of authority over, the heads of political society in Christendom. Even to this day, European life and society are dominated by political ideals and controlled by political authority. Nationhood in Europe is, therefore, an essentially political fact.

But India followed a different course of evolution. Indian unity was never political, but cultural. The Hindu bound together the diverse races and peoples of India into one communion or community, neither through their conversion to a common credal religion, nor through their subjection to a common State or political authority, but through the inculcation of a common culture among them. The ancient Hindu nation-builder recognised the freedom of other cultures, respected the sanctity of other faiths, and tolerated all diversities and differences; all that he did was to give these diversities and differences a place in a general social scheme, usually known as *Varnasrama Dharma* or the law of caste-and-order; and to accommodate diverse gods and cults inside a wide socio-religious federation.

He respected and gave room for the completest freedom of the units inside the unity of a great organic whole. From of old India developed, thus, a new type of nationhood, entirely different from, and absolutely unknown to, European history and experience. This fundamental peculiarity of Indian history and culture must never be overlooked by the modern nation-builder in India. The problem of Indian unity can hope for a rational solution, consistent with Indian tradition and Indian character, and without destroying the regulative idea that has hitherto controlled Indian social evolution, only from those who will not ignore this fundamental peculiarity of Indian history.

I cannot say if there is any clear enunciation of this problem in any of Sir Ashutosh's writings and speeches. I have not seen it as yet anywhere. But I cannot refuse to admit that though others have put forward this peculiarity of Indian culture and history as evidence of the development of a special type of nationhood in

India, not only different from, but in view of its more complex and organic character, even superior to, the European type, none of them, so far as I know, has indicated the practical method of its preservation and advancement under modern conditions, as Sir Ashutosh has undoubtedly done.

In ancient and medieval times, federation of the different races and peoples of India was worked upon a socio-religious basis; because, the emphasis of the life and thought of those times was distinctly religious and social. It would be obviously foolish, and even positively suicidal, to attempt any reconstruction of Indian unity upon the old socio-religious bases. The old social authority is dead. The old social order is decadent. The old religious faiths have lost their reality. Neither the *Vedas*, nor the *Varnasrama* can build up the unity of India in our time. We have to deal not with Hindus only, but with Muhammadans and Christians, who have their own scriptures and their own socio-religious institutions. We cannot take them in, in any scheme of reinterpretation, re-explanation, restatement and readjustment" of Hindu faiths, practices, and institutions, that may be made to meet the requirements of modern life and thought.

We cannot leave the non-Hindu out of any scheme of national reconstruction in modern India. Raja Ram Mohan foresaw all this; and, therefore, sought to solve this problem, through the institution of a liberal school of religious thought and a common House of Prayer, which came to be known as the Brahmo Samaj. But even in the Raja's scheme, the emphasis is clearly on religion, though he did add works of public utility — of what he called *loka-shreya*, to it. But since then much water has flown along the Hooghly; and no one would think of reviving the form of the Raja's solution of this problem in our time. I use the word "form" advisedly; because the spirit of the solution tried by Raja Ram Mohan seems to be fully present in that of Sir Ashutosh.

The evolution of federal nationality was in its early unconscious stage in ancient and medieval India. We have long passed that unconscious stage. The peculiar environments of Indian society, and the particular historic epoch through which it was passing in those times, forced this line of evolution upon the ancients. But our environments are not the same. Our epoch is different. We can either lifelessly and thoughtlessly drift along the new currents, and resign our future to chance; or we can raise ourselves to the plane of an ever-wakeful national consciousness, and help to shape the course of our future with our wisdom and our foresight, and our unbending determination to ride on, and not fall under, the wheel of modern civilization which, like the Car of Jagannath has commenced already to move among us. And in the institution of the new M.A. degree in the Indian vernaculars, Sir Ashutosh has indicated the line, along which we can move immediately towards the solution of the vital problem of Indian unity and federation in our time. While some of us had long recognised the federal and cultural type of ancient Indian nationhood, it is Sir Ashutosh who has, for the first time, so far as I know, indicated the line along which alone can this peculiarly Indian type of nationality be practically preserved and developed in modern India.

Lord Hardinge had indicated the political ideal of British India, as a federation of provincial autonomies, controlled by a Central Government, the Government of India. But there are possible dangers to national unity in India in the fullest and freest development of these provincial autonomies. The provinces are large in area and population, and command sufficient natural resources, to be tempted to bid for sovereign independence. Bengal, Bombay, Madras and Sindh have extensive sea-boards which will justify the building of provincial navies. Lord Hardinge evidently realised these possibilities, and, therefore, he would not weaken the authority, or alter the character of the Imperial or Central Government, even though His Excellency threw out the ideal of a United States of India. Mr. Lionel Curtis, on the other hand, from sensing the same possibilities, has been for the cutting up of our larger provinces into a number of smaller ones. These are the only devices that the mere politician could think of, to provide against the possible disruption of Indian unity in consequence of any real development of provincial autonomy in the country.

But these cannot appeal to any Indian Nationalist. He cannot consent to any scheme which will perpetuate the autocratic character of the present Central Government of India. No scheme of constitutional reforms can be satisfactory and acceptable to Indian Nationalism which will not give a truly federal character to the Government of India and make it responsible to the representatives of the different states or provinces in the Indian Union. Nor is it possible to destroy the unity and individuality of the different provinces; because this unity and individuality is the growth of countless centuries and has at its back immemorial traditions, long-established usages, special social economies, religious institutions, ancient history and literature. Bengal, Madras, Bombay, Sindh and the Punjab are different from one another as are the existing States of the European Continent. No more can we dismember Bengal, or Maharastra, or the Tamil and the Telugu countries for the sake of Indian unity, than we can dismember the Anglo-Saxon, or the Slavonic or the Latin or Teutonic States of Europe for the promotion of European unity.

The provinces must be preserved intact, full autonomy must be secured for every province, the autocracy and irresponsibility of Central Government of India must be removed, and, at the same time, the foundations of Indian unity, which is based at present upon subjection to a common political authority, autocratic in its character and therefore able to impose its will upon all; and invincible in its strength, and therefore able to check and crush all tendencies to break out in revolt; — must be maintained. This is the real problem before us. And in laying the foundations of an All-India Literature, Sir Ashutosh has indicated, at least, one of the ways along which we must seek its solution.

This ideal of an All-India Literature is the theme of his latest address (1919) as President of the last Bengal Literary Conference. This All-India Literature will not speak in any particular tongue, all the vernaculars of India will be its vehicle. "It will not secure unity of language," but certainly the more vital. " unity of thought and culture". For, though speaking in diverse tongues, it will express the same thoughts and breathe the same aspirations, formulate the same ideas and ideals, and thus once more re-establish that fundamental cultural unity of India which expressed itself in ancient and medieval times, through religious formulas and social moulds. The recent regulation of the Calcutta University, instituting the M.A. Degree in the Vernacular Languages of India, in the Faculty of Arts, has opened the way to the building up of this All-India Literature.

The popular view that Sir Ashutosh has instituted a new degree in Bengalee is entirely wrong. Those who appear for the M.A. Degree in English have to study English language and literature only. But those who will seek the M.A. Degree in Bengalee will have to read up at least one other modern Indian language and literature, whether it be Hindi or Mahrati, or Gujrati, or Telugu, or Tamil or Urdu. Those who take this new Degree in our University will, at least some of them, be able to work as medium of communication between the higher thought of Bengal and the other Indian provinces.

At present we have, no doubt, in the English language, a medium of interprovincial thought-communication. But the masses do not and cannot, partake of the benefit of this intellectual exchange-mart. "Yet it is they who form the Real India". They are innocent of English. Indian unity can only mean the unity of the Indian masses, and not the unity of a mere handful of English educated Indians. If we are to work up a real cultural unity in India, we must help the masses to understand, to appreciate, to enjoy and assimilate this great Indian Culture. And the first step in this direction has been taken by the Calcutta University in the institution of this new Degree, which raises Sir Ashutosh's claim from that of a clever and successful administrator to that of a constructive statesman, with as clear a vision of the future as he has a strong grasp of the present.

Achievements in the "New University"

I have already overstepped the limits of this study, and cannot deal here in detail, with Sir Ashutosh's work and achievement in the Calcutta University. The story of Lord Curzon's University reform in India has not as yet been clearly told. English educationists cannot, therefore, really understand why the endeavours in this direction of the one man who has done so much for the reform of his own University at Oxford and has proved his exceptional abilities there, should have roused so much opposition from the educated classes in India. This question can only be answered by a clear exposition of the different aim and intention, that differently actuated the reformed in the two cases. In Oxford, Lord Curzon was purely an educationist, working with single-minded devotion for purely intellectual and cultural ends.

In India, Lord Curzon was not merely an educationist, but also a ruler responsible for the protection of the political and economic interests of the British people and the preservation of British suzerainty. Here his educational aims were necessarily subordinate to his political aims. Education was not here an end unto itself. In any case, rightly or wrongly, people believed that Lord Curzon's education reforms in India had for their objective the creation of an Indian mentality that would acquiesce in the present political subjection of the people, and accept it even as a godsend. In a word, not the development of a virile manhood, but the manufacture of "loyal citizens" was generally believed to be the main object of these reforms.

This view found expression even in the Imperial Legislative Council when the Indian Universities' Bill was before it and Hon'ble Members frankly said that its practical result would be to convert the Universities into Departments of the Executive Government. That view has been partly justified by the action and attitude of the Government of India in more than one instance, in their dealings with the Calcutta University. But on the whole, however, that object has practically failed; and the credit of this failure, so far as the Calcutta University is concerned, is entirely due to the very high administrative qualities and diplomatic management of Sir Ashutosh, as the first Vice-Chancellor, on whom devoted the carrying out of the provisions of the New University Act. But a detailed consideration of Sir Ashutosh's work and achievements in the University must be left for the future when the organisations now in progress are completed and the whole scheme of his University reforms has had time to mature and justify itself. I will content myself, for the present, by simply quoting his own pronouncement upon the work that he and others associated with him had done during the eight years, 1906-1914, that Sir Ashutosh was Vice-Chancellor of our University. In his last Convocation Address as Vice-Chancellor (March 28, 1914), he said:

> "The joy and pride to which I confess are not, however, all unmixed. I too vividly remember, I too intensely feel the aftereffects of all the struggles we had to pass through before the accomplishment of our aims, not to feel at times seriously anxious as to the future of

> what I may call the New University. Though much has been done, more remains to be done, and who knows what the future may bring. I at times truly feel like the careworn toiler of the soil, when on fields first brought under the plough by him, he at last sees the earliest tender green shoots issue from the ground. He dwells in remembrance on the long series of hard labours he had to undergo in order to carry things so far — the felling of trees, the digging out of stubborn roots and stones, the draining of marshy soil, the clearing of obstructive weeds, and then finally the toils of ploughing and sowing. Now, at last, the first fruits of all this labour begin to show themselves, refreshing his eyes and gladdening his heart. But yet, how much may not intervene before full fruition is obtained, before, from the delicate emerald shoots there have risen the serried ranks of ripe ears, each of them proudly balancing at the top its little treasury of golden grains, and, again, how much may not happen before all those precious grains have been safely gathered and stored in barns, ready to supply wholesome food to the cultivator, for his family, for his tribe. Untimely drought may wither the young stalks, storms and rain may beat down the ears, fierce hail may lacerate them, noxious insects may destroy the ripening grain. The cultivator has done his best; he now stands helpless; nothing is left to him, but to hope, to pray and to trust. I repeat, I at times feel like that toiler of the fields.

I too, or let me rather say, we too — I and my helpers — have worked in the sweat of our brows; have spent laborious days and anxious nights; we too have hoped for a glorious harvest, a harvest not palpable, but not the less real on that account, a harvest in the fields of the spirit and the intellect, supplying nourishment which a great people needs, no less than wholesome material bread, pure water, pure atmosphere. We have prepared the ground and now see the first fruit of our labour. But here also how much may not happen to prevent the full ripening of the harvest. I must admit when I recall to memory all the difficulties it gave us such heavy trouble to overcome, and when I picture to myself in my imagination all the difficulties that may beset the future path of the University, I have moments of deep anxiety. The steady opposition which we had to face is not yet crushed, and it is all the more dangerous when it chooses to move in the dark. Sympathy has failed in quarters where we had a right to demand it, and where we confidently reckoned on it.

But more even then well-defined opposition and clearly declared want of sympathy, I dread want of fortitude and energy on the part of those who at the bottom view our efforts with approbation. I dread pusillanimity which shrinks at the first rough collision with determined hostility, that cowardly spirit of compromise which often induces a weak man to accept a fraction of the reward for which he has hitherto contended, while one resolute step in advance, one bold thrust of the arm, might have secured for him the whole glorious prize. All these dangers are vividly realised, and hence my feelings are sometimes not unlike those of the husbandman when he sees dark clouds massing on the horizon and hears the muffled sound of distant thunder. To me also, nothing is left but to hope, to pray, to trust.

But, far be it from me to close this address of mine with a note of fear and despondency. The spectres of doubt and apprehension which crowd round the bravest even, vanish into nothingness when faced with resolution. When all is said and done, there is alive in the depths of my soul the unshakable conviction that I and my helpers have, during these last years, fought a good fight; that the light, which has kept beckoning us onward on our rough and dark path, was not the fitful gleam of a will-o'-the-wisp, but the steady radiance of a pure and holy flame for ever burning in a glorious temple, however far remote, — a shrine dedicated to the True and the Ideal.

Let us, therefore, advance, the banner of progress in hand, with bold but not unwary steps, drawing confidence and inspiration from the consciousness that so many of the best and truest men of our people are in full sympathy with us, that the rising generation has availed itself with eagerness, nay enthusiasm, of the new opportunities we have created for higher studies; that the spark of the new inextinguishable fire kindled in our midst have already leapt to all parts of India, and that the Sister Universities are eager to imitate and emulate what we have boldly initiated. I feel that a mighty new spirit has been aroused, a spirit that will not be quenched; and this conviction, indeed, is a deep comfort to me at the moment when I take leave from work dear to me for so many weighty reasons. The workers pass away; the solid results of their work remain and fructify. I thus bid farewell to office and fellow-workers, not without anxiety for the future of my University, but yet with a great measure of inward contentment: and — let this be my last word — from the depths of my soul, there arises a fervent prayer for the perennial welfare of our Alma Mater — for whom it was given to me to do much work and suffer to some extent — and of that greater parental Divinity to whom even our great University is a mere handmaiden as it were — my beloved Motherland".

Light and Shade. Sir Ashutosh like all men, has the faults of his exceptional intellectual and moral qualities. The greatest of these, his detractors constantly remind us, is his weakness for doing all things himself and giving little room for the growth of initiative and independence in those with whom he has to work, and the autocracy and one-man-rule, which it in evitably leads to. That there is a great deal of truth in this indictment, if indictment it at all be, cannot perhaps be denied. But no one except his most intimate personal friends can say, how far or how much of this autocracy is temperamental and how much of it is the result of the peculiar conditions under which he has had to work.

It is absolutely clear that Sir Ashutosh accepted the Vice-Chancellorship of the Calcutta University at a time when it was really threatened with the prospect of being converted into a department of the Government of India. The forces ranged against those who were anxious to preserve the legitimate freedom of the University were almost overwhelming. They were, practically, the forces of the Government Education Department and their allies in the non-Indian colleges within the University. In the active members of the earlier Senates with whom Sir Ashutosh had to work, there was an overwhelming majority of officials and European non-officials; and to organise the forces of progress out of such a body was no easy task. And the necessity of fighting his battles with a numerically weaker army, necessarily called for considerable discipline, which inevitably developed autocratic tendency in the leader. As a clever general uses and applies all the well-known methods of discipline and strategy, to keep his forces together and weaken those of the enemy, even so Sir Ashutosh has had to do. He was forced by the necessity of the situation to strengthen support and weaken opposition by judicious distribution of patronage. All these things cannot be done without laying one's self open to charges of favouritism and partiality.

As an administrator, called upon to make bricks almost without straw, Sir Ashutosh could not afford the luxury of what is called the Non-conformist conscience, which repels all compromises as sinful. All this must be taken into account while passing judgement upon his policy and acts. But why should not even his friends admit his weaknesses either. Those who have large patronage at their disposal may sometimes be tempted to misuse it. If Sir Ashutosh has occasionally succumbed to this temptation, it only proves that, however great he may be, indeed undeniably is, as an administrator and statesman, he has the common failings of common men, which in no way take away from his universally-admitted endowments and acquisitions, or weaken his claim to be counted among the most capable administrators and statesmen that British India has as yet produced.

The Future

In four or five years time, Sir Ashutosh will gain his freedom from office. A man of his temperament and habit will not find it possible to live the rest of his days in peaceful retirement. Indeed, to judge from his recent public activities, one is encouraged to think that Sir Ashutosh will, on his release from office, join the advanced Indian political platform. Then will. I fear, come the real trial of his life. For, here he will have to work out the apparently hopeless problem of organising as an effective fighting force the growing democracy of educated India, and of reconciling the discipline of constitutional political agitation, with the freedom of thought, speech, and action, of an assembly like the Indian National Congress. Perhaps, he will succeed Perhaps, he will fail. It is not yet possible to foresee that future. Let us wait, perhaps with mixed feelings of hope and fear, and see.

7

Significant Speeches

Speech Delivered in Madras

[The first of the series of speeches delivered in Madras by Babu Bepin Chandra Pal was on the "New Movement". Mr. G. Subramania Iyer, B.A. Editor of the Swadesa-Mithran, was voted to the chair.]

New Movement

Mr. Subramania Aiyar, friends and fellow-countrymen. When at the close of the last Session of the Indian National Congress in Calcutta, I was asked to go over here on a short lecturing tour, and when in response to that kind invitation I agreed to do so, I did not expect the demonstration that I witnessed last evening while progressing along with you in a procession. I refuse to accept it as a procession organised in my honour and, therefore, I say I was not prepared for the demonstration that I saw last evening. It was not in honour of any particular individual, but of the ideals of *Swadeshi* and *Swaraj* (Cries of Vande Mataram), to which reference has already been made by my friend in the chair. Nor did I expect such a large gathering as I see before me. I was fortunate enough to address very large audiences in Madras on previous occasions, but this audience, I am called upon to face this evening, is absolutely out of all proportion to what experience I had even in your enthusiastic city, 4 or 5 years ago. This is a proof, Sir, I take it not merely of the idle curiosity of the people of this great city, (cries of 'certainly not'), but I take it — and I am glad of that assurance — that it is a proof at least of the interest that has been awakened among my countrymen here in the New Movement, that has already commenced to bring about mighty transformations in the thoughts and ideals of our countrymen all over this great Indian continent (Hear, hear).

What is this New Movement? You read in the newspapers the outer manifestations of this movement. You have come to identify this movement with *Swadesi;* you have come to identify this movement with something more than Lord Minto's honest '*Swadesi*'; you have come to identify it with *Swadesi* that is organically related to boycott (Hear, hear); you have to identify this movement with the new ideal of *swaraj;* you have come to identify this movement also, as your chairman told you, with the Partition of Bengal (Hear, hear). You see ripples of this movement in the outbreak of lawlessness in the Eastern Provinces, first in the outbreak of lawlessness by those who are paid by the people of this country (Hear, hear and cries of shame) to help in the preservation of law and order (cries of shame).

You saw the ripple of this new movement in the kind of lawlessness last year about this time in Barisal (cries of shame). You, I believe, recognised also the outer ripples of this movement in the present outburst of lawlessness in another shape, *viz.* in the outburst of Muhammadan Vandalism in parts of East Bengal. You have come to identify this movement with the incarceration of our young men and old men also, with the arrests of popular leaders (cries of shame) in different parts of Bengal. You have come to identify it with the regulation sticks of the Police and the *Vande Mataram* sticks of the people. I know all this; and you also know all these things. But I do not care just now to speak of these outer ripples. They are merely the manifestations of a force that is flowing through the very heart of the nation.

They are the outermost fringe; as it were, the outermost course of the mighty currents that have commenced to stir to their very depths the still waters of Indian national life. Sometime ago, an English gentleman, a retired Anglo-Indian official, wrote to a friend of mine in Calcutta, wanting to know the inwardness of the New Movement in Bengal. I desire to speak a few words to you this evening on this inwardness of the New Movement.

What is this movement due to? What are the forces of its strength and inspiration? What are the forces that lie hidden at the root of this movement? What is it that this movement desires to achieve and how does it propose to achieve that end? Reference, gentlemen, has been made to the Partition of Bengal. Allow me to tell you that the significance of that measure has been considerably exaggerated outside Bengal. It has been, I confess, exaggerated also to some extent even by a section of the Bengali Press.

The Partition was an evil measure, the Partition was a hateful measure. The Bengalis hated to be divided from their own people, the Eastern Provinces from the Western Provinces. We have been living together for how many centuries past nobody knows; we have developed a peculiar culture of our own, through a common language and a common literature. Belonging though, no doubt, to the wide life of Indian Hindus and Indian Moslems, yet Bengal Hinduism has its own peculiarity, as the Moslem ideals and cultures of Bengal have also their own peculiarity. Bengal has been for many centuries past a nation speaking one language, belonging to one civilization, practically trying to develop one culture, and this original unity based upon the unity of language, religion, civilization and culture, developed and grew — thank God — under the community of civic and political interests. Ever since the establishment of British rule in India, we had been governed practically by one and the same laws, ruled by the same administration; and our political life has, all these years, been controlled by one single policy. Suddenly, however, the Province, united in language, united in past historic association, united in civilization and culture, united in a common law and administration, this Province was proposed to be cut into two, which gave offence to us.

It pained us. We cried, we prayed, we petitioned, we protested, but all to no purpose (cries of shame) and the administrative will — I will not call it administrative necessity, because we do not recognise the necessity — the administrative will had its way. And on the 16th October 1905 two Provinces were made out of the Province of Bengal. The measure was earned out with almost indecent haste, and the reason of the haste was this — judging from the past experience of Indian political life and agitation, the Government of Lord Curzon evidently believed (cries of shame) that as long as the measure was not carried out, so long only would this agitation continue. But once it became a "Settled fact," the agitation also would quietly, like all previous agitations, more or less settle down. That was the prognosis which the acute Viceroy made of the situation.

For once, superior wisdom was blinded, superior intelligence failed to see through the outer garb and gathering of popular agitation and popular excitement (cries of shame and cheers); and the agitation against Partition instead of subsiding, as previous agitations had done, when it was found that they would do no good, continued; it increased, it expanded, it attacked and covered new grounds. It developed new forces and it applied these new forces to the solution of the problem before itself. (Hear, hear) Whence came this new inspiration, this new force? Truth to any, we soon recognised that it is not in the power of any Government, much loss is it in the power of an alien Government, to divide a people whom gods united (Hear, hear). They might with their pen, dipped in red ink, pass a line on the administrative map of the Province (Hear,) add fresh labours to the draftsmen in the Survey Department of the Government. But the stroke of the pen, cannot cut the nation into two.

The stroke of the pen though it wounds, wounds in other ways than by cutting things into twos and threes twenties and thirties. If it were possible for a stroke of the pen to cut up anything, why, we have been applying this stroke, my friend in the chair and I, a humble follower of his (cheers). We have been cutting administrations not into two, but into two hundreds almost every day by the stroke of our pens; but the administration remain all the same. When Lord Curzon passed his gubernatorial pen, cut the Province of Bengal in twins, Bengal remained one, and all that this attempt did was to create a deathless determination in the people to continue to be one to the end of their life (Hear, hear). So, really, the Partition measure failed, and the failure of it was confirmed by the proceedings of the public meeting that we held in Calcutta, on the 7th August 1905. I was addressing an overflowing meeting on that memorable evening from the steps of the Calcutta Town Hall. The audience was as large as this, and when I saw that audience, the idea struck to me that it would be a very good thing if the Viceroy's astral body could descend from Simla and take its position on the top of the banyan tree, that we have near our Town Hall, and if it could see from the top of that tree the crowds that gathered and declared their determination to undo the measures of the Partition. If he could have seen it, he might have known and understood from ocular evidence how Bengal was being partitioned by him.

No gentlemen, "the partition has failed. Mr. Morley says, it is a settled fact. (cries of shame). History declares that it is a bottled failure (cheers), and I think settled failure is as good an expression as "settled fact" (Hear, hear). Now, the Partition has failed, and we do not care whether the Partition goes or whether it remains. Why, because in our eagerness to undo this partition, in the agony of our heart, as our protests, our prayers, our petitions failed to move the obdurate heart of those who are placed over us to govern us and to rule us, in the agony of despair we looked about and found nothing on which we could lean. All was dark, our faith in all the professions had already commenced to wane long before the Partition measure was broached. Our faith in the generosity and the justice of the British policy had commenced to wane before the Partition measure commenced.

Lord Curzon — God bless him — (cheers and laughter). I say it sincerely. God bless him (renewed laughter), because, to my mind, Sir, India has not had a more 'beneficent' Viceroy than Lord Curzon (Hear, hear) Lord Ripon was kind. Lord Ripon (cheers) was considerate. Lord Ripon was good. He was tenderhearted, but Lord Ripon's rule was not so beneficent to India as Lord Curzon's has been. Lord Ripon was like a kind mother, and there are circumstances in the life of a child when a good mother becomes a bad mother, when a kind mother works more mischief than a hating stepmother might have done. Lord Ripon was a kind Viceroy, but Lord Curzon was a beneficent Viceroy. But whether he wished or not, that is another question. That is not a question that need trouble you. Let the English people judge it.

Let them consider in the light of their own interests the Viceroyalty of Lord Curzon; but applying our standard of judgement to his Viceroyalty; I do not hesitate to say that it has been one of the most beneficent, if not decidedly the most beneficent, Viceroyalty that India ever had (cries of no, no.)

We had been brought up, Sir, for too long a period, upon political lollipops. We had been given for too long a period the beautiful and charming baby-comforter to keep ourselves quiet.

Lord Ripon had done it. Others would do it again. But, God be thanked, Lord Curzon threw the baby-comforter away, and by throwing it away he made us feel the hunger that is in us, the hunger for *Swaraj* (Hear, hear), the hunger for political autonomy, the hunger for occupying our definitely appointed place in the council of nations (Hear, hear), the hunger for entering upon our own rights in the universal life of humanity, with a view to deepen, to broaden, to quicken that life by the provisions of our special culture, civilization and ideals (Hear, hear). This is the work that God has done and He chose, in the mysteriousness of his Providence. Lord Curzon as the main instrument for doing this work. Let us thank God for Lord Curzon's Viceroyalty, and let us hope and trust that Lord Curzon will live long and enjoy health, and be the Premier of England when India will place before him the ultimatum. (Shouts of *Vande Mataram*). That will be the fitting end of the drama of which the first act only has been played by that capable Viceroy.

Gentlemen, Lord Curzon did this good. He awakened the dormant consciousness of the nation, but he did not create it.

The consciousness was there. It lay latent, it flowed as an undercurrent, and recent movements only helped to bring the latent forces in the nation to the surface. What was the preparation for this New Movement? When we call anything new, we do not mean to say that it has no relation to things that can be described as old. New and old are only comparative terms.

What was new in 1887 becomes old in 1907. That is all the difference and you must recognise that difference, when talking and thinking about the New Movement, the new thought, ideal or the new methods. There is an evolution, there has been an evolution in the history of Indian Politics also. I remember the first time that I appeared upon a public platform in your city was in 1867, when you had the first Congress here. I miss now some kindly faces whom I first came to know in 1887, and when I appeared for the first time on the platform of the Congress in 1867, in the course of what may be called, so far as Congress platforms are concerned, my maiden speech, I declared that I was a democrat, a democrat of democrats, a radical of radicals; yet I said that neither my democracy nor my radicalism took away in the least measure from my loyalty to the British Government (Hear, hear.)

That was in 1887 and I said it in all sincerity and earnestness. I do not believe that diplomacy is needed or suited to a subject nation friend. Mr. Choudry, had declared sometime ago that a subject nation has no politics. By politics I can only mean one thing and that thing is not diplomacy. Diplomacy is concealment of ideas and purpose, concealment of sentiments and opinions, that is necessary in negotiations between one powerful State and another. It is not necessary between a subject people and its Government, unless that subject people are viciously inclined and desire to bring about a rebellion before the time is ripe for it. In that case, diplomacy may be held good; but, I do not believe, I say, in diplomacy in subject peoples. A subject people must have its politics, but a subject people cannot have any diplomacy and when I said that my democracy and my imperialism combined together to make me immensely loyal to the British Government, I said what I believed to be true then and I said what numbers of my educated countrymen belonging to that generation absolutely believed to be true.

In those days, we had faith in the British nation. We had been brought up with the idea that our salvation and even our political salvation would come from England. We believed, those days that England's mission in India was a conscientiously divine mission. I believe it is a divine mission, but I would qualify that old statement by deleting the word 'conscientiously' from it now. But in 1887 we all believed that England was conscientiously and deliberately working for the political emancipation of India. We believed that she would take us up by the hand and gradually set us in our own proper place among the nations of the world.

We believed that by the gradual expansion of the principles and Organisation of self-Government that had been introduced by Lord Ripon, by the reform and expansion of Legislative Councils, by the introduction of a large number of people of this country into our Public Service, by opening to us the gates of the military services, by granting us the charter of free citizenship and investing us with the right of organising national militia. We hoped, we believed in 1887, that by these means England would gradually train us to become a free nation and take up our place among the free states of the world; and we believed what Lord Macaulay had said many years ago, that if such a day came when the people of India, trained and educated by England in the arts, the sciences, the philosophies and the ideals of the West, would demand the right to govern themselves, would desire to have the same free institutions, if such a day came, England would regard it as a most glorious day in its history.

For, having found an ancient nation in the very depths of degradation, it took that nation up, gave out to that nation its own wisdom, its own inspiration, its own experience and its own strength, and set that ancient nation once more upon the pedestal of free citizenship. That had been declared by Macaulay and the declaration in one form or other had been repeated by successive British statesmen here in this country and across the seas. We looked into these declarations. We accepted them as gospel truth and we believed that if really we depended on England for our political emancipation, followed her guidance, accepted her disciplines, placed ourselves in her hands for our training, then the day would come when under her guidance, with her help, we would be able to realise our highest, noblest and deepest political aspirations and be a free nation among the free nations of the world. (Cheers).

That was the faith that lived in us in the eighties; that was the faith that quickened the activities of the Indian National Congress; that was the faith which governed all our political agitations in the past. I put it to you; have you that faith today? (cries of no, no). You need not be afraid of saying that you have no faith. It is clear for the simple reason that Lord Curzon has distinctly stated that there is no ground for entertaining such a faith any more. That declaration, which gave us a greater charter than the Queen's Proclamation itself, is this. (cheers). I will just refresh your memory. Speaking on the Budget, it was, I believe, in his Lordship's last but one Budget speech, he said that we had misread and misunderstood the Queen's Proclamation. We had been preserving it as our Magna Charta. It was a foolish fancy. Sir, Magna Charta has a peculiar history of its own. Magna Charta was signed under peculiarly complex circumstances, and in the absence of those circumstances, in the absence of these active political forces that begot the Magna Charta, (Hear, hear) in the absence of King John, in the absence of Runnymeade, in the absence of the armed barons, in the absence of the pitiable condition of the English King, there could be no Magna Charta.

It should be some other Charta, but it would not be Magna Charta. But still, we had looked upon it as our Magna Charta — it was the custom in those days to think of every thing Indian in the terms of English life. If there was a great man among us, say Kalidasa, etc., whoever he might be, he must be either a Shakespeare or Milton or Byron or Shelley. If there be a philanthropist, he must be a Howard. He counts for nothing unless he is a Howard. That was the mental attitude of the Indian people then and, on account of this peculiar mental attitude we looked about for our political documents and found this precious document in the Queen's Proclamation. We called it the Magna Charta; that is the psychological explanation, not that our leaders did not know that the forces that created the Magna Charta were not present in India at the time of the Queen's Proclamation.

Whatever that might be, we regarded it as our Magna Charta, and we based all our appeals to the Government upon that great Charter, and Lord Curzon thought that it was time to kill this foolish fancy and from his place in the Viceregal Council, he said that we did not read the Charter, read the Queen's Proclamation as carefully as we should have done. We would repeat it by heart (laughter) with all punctuation from beginning to end. Why, there is nothing in it that we have forgotten, nothing in it that we have omitted. What is the meaning, then, of this Viceregal declaration that we did not read the Magna Charta, we did not read the Queen's Proclamation? Lord Curzon did not keep us long in suspense, because in the very next sentence, he declared that we did not properly attend to the simple qualifying phrase "so far as it may be". We had known of this qualifying phrase, of this conditional clause, but we had interpreted it in our own way, we had thought that this conditional clause had reference to our fitness, to our education, to our character and not to anything else. (Hear, hear) Lord Curzon said, "no — it has reference not to your education, fitness or character,.but to the permanence of British overlordship in India" (cries of shame).

"So far as it may be" means so far as is consistent with the preservation of the supreme authority of the British in this country. You may be qualified by education and character to manage your own affairs, you may be better qualified than those who are brought out, from across the seas to manage or mismanage the British administration, but so long as the administration in India continued to be British, so long the direction of its affairs must necessarily rest with the British. Therefore, you would be given every opportunity of carrying out orders, but not to make one single order. You would be given every opportunity of working out the details, but no right to initiate reforms. What Lord Curzon said has been repeated by Lord Minto only two months back. In his Budget speech, what does Lord Minto say? He says that it is absolutely necessary that whatever reforms are introduced by the Government of India must be initiated by the Government itself; and it would be a mischievous thing for the British Government in India, if the idea got aboard that the Government of India had no conviction of their own, that they initiated reforms under pressure of public opinion here or under instructions from the people and the Government in England.

That is what Lord Minto says, the same thing as Lord Carzon said. It means that the control of affairs, the direction of the administration, the right of initiative shall always be taken by the British people and their representatives here and not by any one else. It means, Sir, an open declaration by the present Viceroy that they are not amenable and they will never be amenable to Indian opinion in those matters (cries of shame). What right have you to expect the British Government to do anything more than what they are doing? Would you do it, I ask you, if you were in their position (no, no)? Then do not cry shame. You regarded them at one time as more than human and little less, if less at all, than God. It was your folly if the disillusionment has come. Do not in the name of truth and justice think them to be more than human. They are men, they have not come here on an altruistic purpose, they have come here for the expansion of their trade, for the spread of their own Empire, for the exploitation of the resources of the country and even the intellect of the land for the improvement of their wealth and intellect (cries of shame).

Look facts in the face. Crying shame is a good sentiment, but it has a very bad reason. Now, Sir, Lord Minto has made this distinct declaration, that public opinion in India will not have any influence with the Government of this country so far as administration is concerned for, reform must proceed from him. Any other source cannot but be a mischievous thing. Why mischievous, Sir? Why, because, if once you and I got the idea into our head that we can force the hands of the British Government in India, then after that what would you find but deluge? Then you will clamour for more, more, more, and more, until you have got the whole thing out of their hands. Therefore, Lord Minto warns you. They will do nothing simply because you want them to do it. They will do nothing under pressure of Indian opinion, and yet we have all these 25 years and more been dreaming of this one thing, namely, that, by the application of popular opinion to the problems of administration, by the creation of enlightened public opinion in India and by applying the force of that opinion upon the Government of this country and the British nation at home, we would be able to obtain every kind of political reform that we might demand.

That has been our belief. That has been the one absolutely settled plan in the programme of the Congress. We have always believed in this, that the Government of India is amenable to Indian public opinion; if it has not been guided by Indian public opinion it is due to the fact that we have not been able to create a sufficiently strong public opinion. That has been our idea, Sir, but Lord Minto knocks that idea on the head at once and he says, "No, we shall not budge a fifth, a tenth, a hundredth or a millionth part of an inch. No pressure of Indian public opinion can influence

Government". So Lord Minto paraphrases Lord Curzon's declarations and Lord Minto has the support of 'honest John' in this matter; because if Lord Minto's declaration is a paraphrase on the one hand of Lord Curzon's ancient dicta, then on the other hand the commentary is John Morley's statement, that "so far as my imagination reaches, so long the Government in India must be a personal and absolute Government." An absolute Government is that which refuses to be amenable to public opinion. An absolute Government is a new euphemism for despotic Government, an absolute Government is a despotic Government.

A despotic government is that which is not amenable to public opinion. An absolute government is that which does not agree to be guided and controlled by the opinions, ideals and sentiments of those whom it governs. It is a despotic government, and what Lord Curzon had said some three or four years back, what Mr. John Morley declared last autumn, that is what Lord Minto has represented in other words and in another context in his last Budget speech; and yet this was not what we had been taught and trained to believe of the British Government in India. We had been trained to believe for the last 25 years, we have lived upon this one faith, that the British Government in India is a constitutional Government. Is it, Sir, a constitutional Government? My moderate friends still claim that it is a constitutional Government. They say that the British Government in India is a constitutional Government.

There is some little confusion of thought in regard to this claim. Every Government must have a Constitution of its own. There can be no Government without a Constitution, because, if a Government had no Constitution, there would be no continuity of purpose and policy. If a Government had no Constitution, there would be nothing to regulate the parts to parts and the parts to the whole. A government, if it has nothing more, has at least an administrative machinery, and a machinery must have a Constitution; though it be a mechanical Constitution it must have a Constitution of its own. Therefore, every Government has a Constitution of its own, but every Government is not called in political science and in political history as a constitutional Government. Is it so? The Government of the Czar has also a

Constitution of its own. Even the autocrat of all the Russians is bound by certain laws, certain precedents, certain customs, certain ideas and ideals, and therefore, there is a Constitution in Russia. But whoever called the Government of the Czar a constitutional Government? Persia, Sir, had a Constitution five years ago. If it had no Constitution, Government would have been impossible in Persia, but still you say that the people of Persia got a Constitution only a few years back! What then do you mean? You mean this.

The word 'constitution' is used in a technical, in a special sense, in political history and political science. What is that sense? It is this; constitutional government is that which organises the State machinery, in which there are recognised organs, through which the opinions of the people may apply themselves on the world of the Government. That is what is understood by constitutional Government. Constitutional governments are governments that allow, by their very Constitution, every right to the people to assert their opinions and ideas effectively upon those who govern. That is a constitutional government. And I put it to you, my dear friends, have we any such rights? (cries of no). And if we have not these rights, if we have not the organs by and through which the unanimous opinion of the people of India could apply itself to the work of the Government of India, if we have no such right and no such organ in a State organisation, how then can we say that the Government of India is a constitutional government? Take Lord Minto's statement.

He distinctly declares that nothing will be done by the Government under pressure of Indian public opinion. Is that the declaration of the constitutional character of the Government of India. I ask? 'shame'. My friends, understand before you cry 'shame'. And if the Government of India is not a constitutional Government, what becomes of the plea of constitutional agitation? The word, in fact, has been used in a very loose way. The words, 'constitution' and 'constitutional' have been used in a technical sense by lawyers and Indian politicians. They understood by 'constitution' and 'constitutional', simply that which is regulated by law, that which is within the bounds of law. It does not matter who made the law, or who makes them. Constitutional means legal, lawful and absolutely nothing more in India. Constitutional agitation means an agitation which is consistent with the safety of the agitator. Constitutional agitation thus means an agitation that will not conjure up the dreaded Section of 124 A, of the Penal Code. Constitutional agitation means an agitation within the limits of the Penal Code. If that be the meaning of constitutional agitation the New Movement has not as yet made any declaration against it. We do not as yet proclaim anything which transgresses the existing laws of the Government of India, and we do not, so far as we see, now believe that it will be necessary for us in the near future to transgress those limits. We respect the laws and we shall respect the laws of the present Government as long as those laws respect the primary rights of citizenship.

There are certain rights which governments do not create but rights which created governments themselves. Those are not constitutional rights. They are not created rights. They are natural rights, as my friend in the chair suggests. They are primary rights, rights that inhere to every individual human being, rights the charter of which is received from no man but from Him who stands on High, who endowed every man with his life, with big limbs, who endowed every man with his human instincts, who endowed every man with his intellect and every spiritual and ethical endowment. The charter of these primary rights comes not from any crowned head, but it comes from the King of Kings, from the throne of God himself. And so long as the British Government in India will respect those natural, those primary, those uncreated rights of persons and property of individual Indian citizens, so long we shall respect their laws and our agitation shall be conducted along such lines.

In this sense we may claim to be as constitutional as are those who refuse to accept the constitutional character of our programme and propaganda. This word, 'constitutional' has been used, I repeat, in Indian political literature in a very loose way, to mean not what is always meant in political science and political history, but simply law-abiding, legal, lawful. Now Sir, Lord Minto, before him Mr. Morley, before him Lord Curzon, and before Lord Curzon successive administrators in India, had worked together to kill the faith that was in this nation, faith in the British people, faith in the British Government faith in England's altruistic mission in

India. This faith had been killed in the course of the last twenty years, and the New Movement has risen up, for it is a new faith out of the ashes of the old faith. In proportion as our faith in the foreign government has been decaying, in proportion as our dependence on the foreign people and the foreign government increased and, the realisation of our national destiny grew weaker and weaker, in that proportion things have appeared in Indian politics. On one side there is an overwhelming sense of helplessness.

If the Government won't do anything how are we to achieve our end? If the Government will not listen to our prayers, how can we realise what we want to realise ourselves? It is an attitude of despair on one side. The loss of faith in the foreign nation, in the foreign Government and in the foreign people has grown keen, not bitter, — I was going to say keen and bitter — I mean a general sense of despair which leads a lot of people to seek for their own regeneration. 'Since improvement is impossible why follow the chimera? Go and improve yourself. Make your pice and enter into friendly relations with the Government. The people won't be the better or the worse for your association year after year, in the participation of this Government. So, why when all are doomed, should you say, I will not have more than all? I will have as 15-9 pices and you keep the three pies in the rupee'. That is one attitude that had grown of late in the public life of this country.

There is another attitude, that with the decadence of the faith in the foreign people and in the foreign Government, with the decadence of our faith in the foreign administration which has come to us. We have learnt to look nearer home. Our eyes have been turned away from the Government House, away from the Houses of Parliament, from Simla and Calcutta and our faces have turned now to the starving, the naked, the patient and long suffering 300 millions of Indian people, and in it we see a new potency, because we view them now with an eye of love which we never had felt before, and in the teeming, toiling, starving and naked population of India, we find possibilities, potentialities, germs that have given rise to this New Movement. That is the cornerstone of this movement, namely, Faith in the people, Faith in the genius of the nation, Faith in God who has been guiding the genius of this nation for the ages by historical evolution, Faith in the eternal destiny of the Indian people. With the decadence of our faith in the foreign Government and in the foreign nation, has grown up this higher, this dearer, this deeper, this more vital and more divine faith in Indian humanity (cheers). And to understand the New Movement properly you must look upon it through the prism of this new faith into the Indian people. To understand this New Movement you must look upon it through the prism of the Indian historic evolution of your race. To understand this New Movement aright, you must look into it through the prism of the highest ideals of your nation, and highest teaching of your scriptures and the highest possibilities of your social, economic, industrial and even your political life. It is not an idle dream. This is the message of Indian history, and this is the highest generalisation, I beg to submit, to a political scientist. Because, after all, what's this Indian problem? Is it a problem of politics? Is it a problem of economics? Is it a problem of administration? I refuse to accept it as such. It is not a political problem, not an economic problem. What is it then? It is a simple, psychological problem.

You do not seem to follow me. How many are the people of this country? Three hundred millions and more. How many are there who govern these people? Less than three lakhs, taking merchants and non-officials together. Now, how can you explain this Government of three-hundred millions of people, not concentrated upon a tiny bit of space like the great island, which is the home of our rulers, but spread over a continent, many times the size of England, the size of Great Britain? You ought to be able to find it for yourself, now, this problem, this strong problem, the government of 300 millions and more of aliens by less than three lakhs of persons over a vast continent. England rules India not by force of arms. It would be an impossibility, utter impossibility. The *Times* might show us this.

The *Pioneer* might remind us of the tiger claws of the Anglo-Saxon, who, I believe, loses his canine character by association with Bengal climate. They might declare that India shall be governed by the sword and by the sword it will have be kept. It was not won by the sword. British bayonets did not win India. If it was won by the sword, it was the sword of the Indian sepoy that won India for the British nation, and it is not kept by the sword either. How many swords have you got in a district? How many have you got in your Talukas? Have you one single bayonet in a village or can you keep one military man with a bayonet in every village in India. It is utterly impossible. There is no army in all the world possessed by any Power, nay, not even by Germany or Russia, who could place one soldier and for his protection another too, in every village in India (laughter).

The sword never won India. When I hear, Sir, ah ! England won the Empire of India by the sword, when I am threatened with the sword of the *'Times'*, I am reminded of the story in the *Upanishads*. In the *Taitreya Upanishads* you know that story that Brahman made the gods conquer the enemies, but the gods forgot all about him. They thought 'it if, our glory, if our conquest'. When the gods were sitting just as they did in the Delhi durbar and Indira was congratulating himself upon the prowess of his thunderbolt by which he had subdued the Asuras and when Agni was also congratulating himself upon his prowess by which he had conquered and Varuna had been doing the same, there appeared a strange figure near the council of the gods. They looked at it but could not recognise it.

Who is that unknown figure? The gods sent Agni, the messenger. 'Go thou and ask who he is'. Agni went and asked, Who art thou?' This strange figure asked Agni, 'Who art thou?' *Agni* replied 'I am Agni, I am fire'. 'What canst thou do' asked this strange figure. Agni said, 'I can burn the earth and the heavens'. That strange figure took up a dry piece of grass and held it before Agni, the god of fire, and said, 'Burn thou this'. Agni applied all his force to burn it and failed. Varuna went, He said, 'I can drown everything'. This strange figure said, 'Drown thou this tiny little weed'. Varuna applied all his forces, but the weed could not be drowned. Then Vayu went and said, ' I can blow away everything'. This strange figure said, 'Blow thou this tiny little weed'.

But he could not do. They all came and said, 'We do not know who he is'. Then Indira was asked to go. As soon as he went, this strange figure disappeared. In its place appeared the symbol of Divine knowledge and she told Indira that this strange person was He by whose power they had conquered the Asuras, but whom they had forgotten. If, Mr. Chairman, the 300 millions of Indian people could once concentrate, not their strength, but merely their determination and not that determination up in the neighbourhood of the Delhi Durbar, if they ask who this strange thing is, then they would know that the power that won India was the power of thin yaksha. The power that governs India is the power of that yaksha. In their pride, in their ignorance and in their folly they see not. They are like the scriptural image that has eyes but see not, that has ears but heareth not, that has intelligence, but the intelligence is not applied to the actualities of the situation about them. Who governs India, Sir? It is we who govern India. (How, how?) Go to any district. How many Englishmen are there in a district? Sometimes two, sometimes three, sometimes four, but never more than half-a-dozen.

To whose tune do the Magistrates, the Police Superintendents and the Judge play? The Police Superintendent answers to the tune of the Inspector and the Inspector is your man. The Magistrate answers to the tone of the Huzur Sheristadar and the Huzur Sheristadar is your man. It is the Judge who adjudicates. He adjudicates properly more often by the light of the native officials and the native lawyers than by his own imported light. Let me ask, who keeps the peace of the country. It is my Constable, my Chowkidar, my Head Constable and my Sub-Inspector. They are Hindus, Muhammadans or Christians. They are all either brown or black, never white. These sit on the top, receive the fattest pay, but we do the most troublesome, the most arduous, the most difficult, complex and complicated work.

The administrative machinery would come to a stand still if we draw ourselves away from it (cries of surely). Then, my dear friends, if it is so, what is the secret of this. Is it hypnotism? Is it magic? Is it incantation? What is it then? (cry of poverty). That is quite a different matter. Now, it is hypnotism. It is Maya, Maya, and Maya, and in the recognition of the magic character of the British power in India lies the strength of the New Movement. What we want is this: — to remove this Maya, to dispel this illusion, to kill and destroy this hypnotism. We have been hypnotised into the belief that though three hundred millions we might be, yet we are weak. The thing has been dinned into our ears, for how many years you all know. For the last 50 years this thing has been dinned into our ears. For the last one hundred years it has been dinned into our ears that we are weak. They set up one Indian against another, and then call it their conquest. That is how they write our history. They are going to celebrate the festival of Plassey, the festival of Clive, but who fought and conquered, and who was defeated at the battle of Plassey? Mir Jaffar stood away.

The treacherous Mir Jaffar stood away. My Muhammadan friends would take note of it, that when the last Muhammadan Nawab was deprived of his Sultanath in Bengal, the only man who fought and tried to die for him was a Hindu gentleman. His Muhammadan General stood aside. Had Mir Jaffar not played the part of a traitor, had Mir Jaffar fought as valiantly and as faithfully as Mohan Lal did, had not that Jagat Sett, that treacherous banker, had not another treacherous member of the Banking aristocracy, had not certain other men, the leaders of the political life of Bengal in those days, conspired in secret against the Nawab, if they had not played themselves into the hands of the tiny little clerk in Fort William, Clive, a record of heroism would never have come into existence. This is how the British Empire is being administered by them, but we know it not. The Sheristadar knows not his own power. The Inspector knows not the measure of his own brains. The Deputy Magistrate knows not the important functions that he discharges in the administration of the country.

He looks to his pay and looks up to the men who can increase or decrease his pay. He has no time to look into himself, nor about himself and, therefore, this hypnotism continues. My dear friends, a moment's consideration will show that if we are weak today this weakness is not real, but illusory. If we are disorganised, this disorganisation is also caused by this hypnotism. If we are disorganised, we must organise ourselves when any vital interest is involved in any matter, and for the safety of that interest, organisation is absolutely necessary. But what vital interest have we in this country outside our personal, private family interest? What interest have we in the Government of this country? You say we cannot govern ourselves because we are divided. You say that we cannot administer our own affairs because there is caste divided from caste, there is religion dividing denominations from denominations. There are the Hindus standing apart from the Mussulmans and the Mussalmans standing apart from the Christians. You say there are so many religions, so many languages, so many castes and so many differences, how will you organise yourselves? Were there not at one time differences of religion, differences, of classes, conflict of interests, of class against class in England? Were there not provincial differences and jealousies in Germany before the master-hand of Bismarck, helped by the late Emperor William, welded together these heterogenious Germans in one great German nation? Common interests, common life, and the same vital community of interest we have that has made other people forget these differences in the pursuit of that vital thing. Have not we lessons in regard to this in our own past? India knows of only two instances within the memory of history of nation-building. One was in the Punjab, the history of the Sikhs, and the other was in the Deccan, the history of the Maharattas. And what was peculiar in the Punjab? What was peculiar in the Maharashtra? Leave the Punjab alone, because that was the problem that was sought to be worked in a very limited field. Take the history of the Maharattas.

What do you find there? Sivaji combined not only the Hindus but he combined the Hindus and the Muhammadans both. He united the interests of the two great communities in his own ideal of a Maharashtra. What did Pratap Aditya do in Bengal. You talk of disunion between the English and the Muhammadans. But, at the time of Pratap, the Muhammadan Satrap, Princes in Bengal fought side by side with the Hindus against the common Moghul Emperor, against Mansingh, Akbar's General, when he came to conquer Pratap. There was Isaph, one of the great 12 landlords of Bengal, who were really the ruling chiefs. Isaph joined Pratap and fought with the Moghuls.

So, if you can create community of interests, if you can present something that can be regarded by all people as one common ideal, if you can present an ideal that can appeal to every community in India, not to their individuality, not to their peculiar culture and character, but the fulfilment according to his own lines of the highest aspirations that quicken in them, if you can present such an ideal, then all these differences will disappear.

We have been told we are disunited and we have believed in it. We have been told that we are weak and we have believed in it. We have been told we are ignorant and we cannot understand politico and we have believed in it, and this belief has been the cause of all our weakness and it has a hypnotic cause. It is induced by magic, by *Maya* and it is upon a recognition of this *Mayaic* character of the present sovereignty in India that the new movement bases itself, and it proclaims, therefore, that the salvation of India must come first and foremost of all through right knowledge *Maya* can be dispelled by original knowledge whether it be Vedantic or politic. It is therefore that we proclaim the strength of the people to them.

It is, therefore, that we proclaim from the housetops our ideal. It is, therefore, that we make no secret of our propaganda, because the thing that has to be cleared is this, the sense of helplessness in the people. The thing that has to be fought against is this despair, killing despair in the nation. What you and I want now is the message of strength. What you and I want now is the declaration of some such ideal that will quicken our intellect and culture and our emotions as well, that will take possession of our wills. Such an ideal will lead us to make one united determination to cut asurder this *Maya* and make us prepare ourselves for those sacrifices which this determination will naturally demand in the future. This determination, this sacrifice, this knowledge, this ideal, it is these that would solve the Indian problem, and which the new Movement tries to place before you tonight.

But one lecture, though extending over a couple of hours, is not sufficient to explain to you all the aspects, all the principles, much less the great sublime philosophy that stands behind this new movement. It is not a merely political movement, though politics has come to receive, perhaps, the largest amount of its attention just now. This movement is not a mere economic movement, though it is applied to the solution of the great problem of Indian poverty. This movement is essentially a spiritual movement. It has its application in social, in economic, in political life of the sublime theosophy of the *Vedanta*. It means the desire to carry the message of freedom. It is the supreme message of the *Vedanta* to carry out that message, to realise that ideal in the social, economic and the political life. What is the message of the *Vedanta*? The message of the *Vedanta* is this: that every man has within himself, his own soul, as the very root and realisation of his own being, the spirit of God; and as God is eternally free, self-realised, so is every man eternally free and self-realised. Freedom is man's birthright. It is his birthright in God. It is inherent in the very making of man. Man is made not out of the image, not in the image, but out of the substance of the maker, and as God is eternally free, so are you, Prince or peasant. Brahman or Pariah, man or woman, Hindu or Muhammadan, Buddhist or Christian, rich or poor, ignorant or learned, free and eternal.

You realise it not, because you are enveloped in ignorance. You realise it not, because freedom has not organised itself as yet in your social life. You realise it not, because this spirit of freedom has not been able to organise itself as yet in your economic life. You realise it not because this freedom, this ideal of freedom has not as yet actualised itself in your political life. They are in the freedom of the free citizen comprising a free state. There and there alone can you recognise, can you actualise, can you objectify, can you bring it before yourself, your own natural freedom. In the citizenship of a free state you regulate yourself, you control yourself, you rule yourself, you restrain yourself; and freedom, my dear friends, is not want of restraint but self-restraint; freedom is not want of regulation but self-regulation, freedom is not want of determination, but self-determination and it only consists, as members of a free state, as free citizens of a free state, in the administration of your own affairs, in your submitting yourself to the laws that you helped to make and in submitting yourself to the regulations that you helped to impose upon yourselves and upon the community at large (cheers).

That gives the clue to this political life. It is the life of a free citizen in a free state, if you realise the freedom of God which is self-restraint, self-regulation and self-determination for the purpose of self-realisation. (cheers). Therefore, I say this New Movement is not a mere political movement. It is essentially a spiritual movement. They do not understand its meaning. They cannot understand its strength. They have no faith in this movement unless they recognised as a supremely spiritual movement and because we recognise it so, we believe that the spirit of our race will fulfil and realise itself in and through this movement and shall realise the divinely appointed destiny of our nation. Our faith is first in God, faith in the history in and through which God reveals himself. Our faith is in the history of our own people, and in the genius of our own nation. It is the manifestation within the limits of the spirit of God and God Himself, and because we have this faith, we believe that. We are disorganised today, but we shall become organised tomorrow. We are weak today but we can become strong in our own native strength tomorrow. We believe we are incapable of self-sacrificing today but we shall attain the strength for making the self-sacrifice tomorrow, and by this means, by determination, by self-sacrifice and by combination we shall be able sooner or later to realise the end that this New Movement has set up, namely that of *Swaraj (continued cheers and cries of Vande Mataram).*

Gospel of Swaraj

[*Mr. Pal, who was received with enthusiastic cheering, addressed the meeting for two hours as follows.*]

Mr. Chairman, friends and fellow-countrymen, the word *Swaraj*, on which I have been asked to speak to you to night, is a new word in the literature of modern Indian politics. This word was given to us during the last session of the Indian National Congress by its honoured President, Mr. Dadabhai Naoroj (shouts of Vande Mataram). Mr. Dadabhai standing on the platform of the Indian National Congress as the representative, the accredited, — I was almost going to say, the elected, — representative of all India declared that *Swaraj*, i.e., self-government, was the goal of his people. This declaration is peculiarly significant. If Mr. Dadabhai stopped after saying 'self-government was our goal,' it would have meant nothing or anything. Self-government is an old word in Indian politics, and it had been applied by different persons, officials and non-officials, in quite a number of ways; but Mr. Dadabhai Naoroji did not stop by merely declaring that our ideal was self-government. His definition was extremely significant. It was significant because of certain things that had happened a few months before the meeting of the Congress. This definition that

Mr. Dadhabai gave of self Government was also significant in view of an earlier definition of his own. The definition that he had given to self-Government, the declaration of the ideal of the National Congress, that he had made on the eve of the session of the Congress in Madras in 1903, addressing the Congressmen in this country in a series of letters from different Congress leaders in England — all these were published in the pages of the *Hindustan Review,* Allahabad — was that the ideal of the Congress was self-government under British paramountcy.

Self-Government Under British Paramountcy

This ideal was not very clearly understood by some of us. We did not exactly understand what the character of this self-government would be, what would be its limits and what would be the conditions that British paramountcy would impose upon our self-government. These are questions that arise in our minds when we read this declaration from the oldest leader of Indian political life. (Hear, hear). Would our self-government mean what it means in other self-governing countries? Would it mean the right of self-taxation? Would it mean the right of self-legislation? Would it mean the right of the people of India to grant admission or to refuse it to whomsoever they like, seeking entrance into their territories from outside? Would it mean, this self-government under British paramountey, these and other essential rights and privileges of other self-governing communities? If it meant all this, where would the paramountcy come in? (Laughter.)

The paramountcy might come in the matter of our foreign relations; but foreign relations can only be controlled by the help of a national army. The ultimate argument in diplomacy among the nations of the world is not an argument of reason, but an argument of force, not applied, but possible of being applied at any moment when the Constitution might demand it and when diplomacy might fail. Without a background of military power, foreign relations have never been known to be controlled any where, in barbarity or civilization (Hear, hear).

England, therefore, if she controlled our foreign relations, would naturally and every reasonably also demand the control of our army and if she had to control our army she would be forced by the necessity of the duty that the controlling of the army would impose upon her, to demand the control of the parse of the nation. And if this is so, where would the right of self-taxation and the right of self-administration go? It would be, I dare say, an exceedingly convenient thing for us if England would mind guarding our frontiers, at her own expense (Hear, hear and cheers) with her own people and allowed as the supremo and precious privilege of taxing ourselves, governing ourselves and doing everything that a self-governing people does. It would be very comfortable for us, but it would be exceedingly uncomfortable for England (cheers) and England would not undertake this great and glorious duty unless we agree to pay her for it.

But, you might say — why England does it in regard to the Colonies, she does it in regard to Australia, she does it in regard to Canada. Why should she not do it in regard to India? The one answer to it is this. England is white. Australia is white. Canada is white laughter. We are black and brown (laughter and cheers,) That is one answer. England would do a great deal for a white people, even for the Boers who had put her to such endless troubles seven years back. But she would not do it for a non-white people. Professor Bryce, I think, it would be admitted, knows something of the mind of his own people. It will be admitted, there are few men in English public life who have had larger experience of modern politics in England and even in Greater Britain than the distinguished author of the Holy Roman Empire and the American Common Wealth. Therefore, his authority most be respected in this matter. And what did he say just about 3 or 4 years back? At an address delivered in the Sheldonian Theatre in Oxford, Professor Bryce said; "The colour sense of the Anglo-Saxon is one of his strongest senses. The Asiatics may overcome their sense of colour, but the European cannot, and least of all, can it be expected of the Anglo-Saxon European".

Again, the relation between England and her Colonies can never possibly be the relation between India and England. England sends out her surplus population to the Colonies and the Colonies receive with open arms the immigrants from the mother country, because they help the Colonies to develop their own resources. They help the Colonies to exterminate the native race. They help the Colonies to strengthen the white power in distant parts of the globe. Therefore England is interested in the upkeep of the Colonies. Can you expect that the same thing would happen with regard to India? Can you expect on your own side, to receive the surplus population of the British Isles into your midst? (no, no) But the Colonies receive them. You would not, but you receive them now, because you cannot help it (yes, exactly so), and therefore the moment you have *Swaraj, the* moment you have self-government, the moment you have the right to exclude whomsoever you like from getting inside your territories, — that moment you will pass a law, as Australia has done, against all undesirable aliens and Australia has passed this law against even the residents, the inhabitant?, the subjects of the British Empire. You and I, unless we know to read and write at least one European language, cannot go into Australia.

It is not in human nature that when you and I have the same right as the Australians have to granting admission to, or refusing this admission to any foreigner, we shall not exercise this right for excluding undesirable aliens. England cannot expect the same help from India as she can naturally expect from Australia, from Canada, and from the other Colonies. India cannot expect the same accession to its national life and strength by the influx of white emigration as the Australians and Canadians expect it. Therefore what England is doing in regard to Australia or Canada, undertaking the expenses for the protection of her Colonies, she will not do, she will not undertake in regard to a self governing India.

The Declaration

Therefore, it seems to me Sir, that this ideal of self-government under British paramountcy is an impossible ideal it might be a theoretically perfect ideal (laughter), making for the universal brotherhood of man but the millennium has not yet arrived, and it is not in any case a practically attainable ideal — that is, the ideal of self-government, under British paramountcy; for either British paramountcy would mean nothing or self-government would mean nothing. We do not understand this ideal of self-government under British paramountcy; we do not make any secret of our opinions and estimates regarding it, and a few months before the Session of the last Congress, some of us were driven by the kindness — I will call it — of the newspaper *India* and its partiality for the Liberal administration in England, — we were driven by certain remarks that were made in regard to Mr. Morely's last budget speech by the newspaper *India* — to make a very simple declaration. That declaration was this. It was made first through the columns of the 'notorious' newspaper called *Vande Mataram:*

> "The time has come when in the interest of truth and the civic advancement and the freedom of the people, our British friends should be distinctly told that while we are thankful to them for all the kind things they have laid all these years for us and the ready sacrifice they have made to make our lot easy and their yoke light, we cannot any longer suffer to be guided by them in our attempts for political progress and emancipation. Their weapon is not ours; they desire to make the Government in India popular. They desire to make the Government in India popular without ceasing in any essence to be essentially British. We desire to make it autonomous, absolutely free of the British Parliament". (Loud cheers and shouts of *Vande Mataram).*

This declaration, a very natural thing even in a subject people — an honest expression of the common human instincts of freedom — this took our Anglo-Indian friends by surprise.

They never thought that such a thing might be said or could possibly be said by any Indian journalist. They held up their hands in *harakiri* and thought that we were going very close to the deluge. The *Englishman* in Calcutta ran into hysterics (cries of shame), the *Pioneer* did the same and threatened us with a series of evil consequences. The *Times of India* did the same. The London *Times* also quoted the paragraph in full, and for a number of days it tried to prove that this was the declaration of a small band of irresponsible persons, who deserved to be put down. That was what the *Times* practically said and the *Times of India* coaxed, bogged, beseeched the moderate politicians, — the model moderates — to make a declaration from the Congress that whatever else might happen, the Congress does not subscribe and will never subscribe till the end of the world, to such a declaration as this. The *Times of India* and even the London's *Times* did something more. They held out temptations to the Moderate leaders in the matter. They said: "If only you expel the extremist, and make an open declaration of policy from the Congress platform that you desire the perpetuation of the British overlordship, then your cause will be strengthened. The Muhammadans who are holding aloof will join it at once and there is a very strong and sensible body of non-official Anglo Indian opinion which would also throw in its strength with you and join the National Congress and by this means the Congress would be a power in the land and the Government would be bound to treat with respect and consideration the representations of such a body".

The *Times of India* asked Mr. Dadabhai Naoroji, in a sudden outburst of love for the old man whom it had abused outright and the London *Times* also said that whatever Mr. Dadabhai Naoroji's views on economics might be, he wan at heart a loyal man and would of course make some declaration that would put an end to all this nonsense. And the declaration than Mr. Dadabhai Naoroji actually made became extremely significant on account of this little previous history. The *Times of India* wanted Mr. Dadabhai, the London *Times* wanted the National Congress to declare it officially and openly, that they would not go in for autonomous India, that their ideal was self-government under British paramountcy.

This had been declared to be the ideal of the Congress, as 'I said, by Mr. Dadabhai some years back. Mr. Dadhabhai, however, standing on the platform of the Congress last year refused to report the old declaration (Hear, hear). He refused to condemn this new ideal. On the contrary, he declared an ideal which practically accepted the declaration of policy made by that notorious paper *Vande Mataram.* What did Mr. Naoroji say? He said self-government is our ideal. What kind of self-government? "Self-Government as in the United Kingdom or in the Colonies". That is *Swaraj.* Those are the words so far as I remember of Mr. Dadabhai Naoroji. "Self-Government as in the United Kingdom," what does it mean but the right of self taxation? What does it mean but the right of self Legislation? What does it mean but the right of self-administration and what does it mean but the supreme control of the nation over its political affairs, home affairs and foreign affairs, civil affairs and military affairs. That is what is meant by self-Government as in the United Kingdom. Mr. Naoroji added also, self-Government as in the United Kingdom or the Colonies. It means that in the opinion of Mr. Dadabhai Naoroji, the self-government that obtains in the Colonies is essentially and practically the same as that which obtains in the United Kingdom, because the Colonies also have the right of self-taxation, have the right of self-legislation, have the right of self-administration, and if the mother country controls the political relations and the foreign relations of the Colonies, it is simply owing to the fact that the mother country undertakes to pay for this control in Military expenditure and when once Great Britain wanted a contribution immediately after the close of the Boer war from Australia towards the expenses of the squadrons of the British fleet stationed on the Pacific, Australia point blank refused to pay even a farthing towards those expenses and therefore practically speaking self-government in the Colonies is the same as self-government in the United Kingdom.

I would draw your attention to the construction of the sentence in which Mr. Dadabhai Naoroji made this declaration. Dadabhai did not say that the ideal was Colonial self-government. He said our ideal was self-government as in the Colonies, and I think, Sir, as a lawyer, you will understand there is a difference between 'Colonial self-government' and 'self-government as in the Colonies' (cheers and laughter). Colonial self-government means the perpetuation of the relation of the existing British Colonies with the mother country; self-government as in the Colonies means self-government similar to that obtaining in the Colonies, not identical with it. Colonial Self-government would declare identity of our ideal with the kind of self-government obtaining in the colonies. Self-government as in the Colonies does not declare that identity. It simply points as a sample and when you copy a pattern, you necessarily copy it with more or less certain slight differenced, differences due to personal equation and here the differences would be due to national equation.

This declaration then from Dadabhai Naoroji is a significant declaration. This is really the same ideal that had been proclaimed by us. This declaration meant an open repudiation by Dadabhai

Naoroji of the claims that had been put forward by the *Times of India* and the London's *Times.* And, gentlemen, Dadabhai Naoroji made this declaration first of all in his presidential address; but towards the close of the session, in his closing speech he emphasised this declaration still further. He declared that as the result of the labours of the last 50 years, this generation had been able to discover this great national ideal of *Swaraj.* He said: "The generation that is passing away gives you, young men, this ideal. It devolves on you to work it out in practice". These are the last words of Dadabhai Naoroji, uttered from the chair of the Indian National Congress last December and they are significant words. After the declaration of Dadabhai Naoroji it is no longer possible, Sir, for Moderates or Extremists to say that they are not Swarajists. They are compelled now to accept with good grace or with bad grace, but they are compelled to accept — this ideal as the national ideal.

Gokhale's Ideal and the Extremist Ideal

Mr. Gokhale went to Allahabad in February and be proclaimed the same ideal at Allahabad. He said that he would not put any limitation, any limits to the aspirations of his countrymen. He said that he wanted his people to live in their country as other peoples live in their own countries. And by other peoples he necessarily meant not the Hottentot, not the Zulu, not the Fiji Inlander, but he meant the free peoples of the world. And he said that be wanted his own people in India believe just as the other peoples of the world, lived in their own countries. That was a paraphrase of the ideal of *Swaraj.* Mr. Gokhale with the emphasis on the ethical side of every question that is so predominant both in his life and conversation, declared farther that he wanted that his people should attain the highest that is in them in their intellectual, in their industrial, in their moral, and in their spiritual life.

What does mean, Sir, unless it means a declaration of the ideal of *Swaraj.* He did not use the world *Swaraj,* it is true; but we ought not to forget that he is a member really of the Government of India, because, according to the Constitution of that Government, every member of the Legislative Council is really a member of the Government of India as every member of Parliament constitutes a part of the Government of England. So every member of the Legislative Council forms a part of the organic element in the

Constitution of the Government of India. But Mr. Gokhale said it was a theoretically perfect ideal; but not practically attainable. I don't understand an ideal that is theoretically perfect but which is absolutely unattainable practically. That which is not practically attainable, is not an ideal I beg to submit; it, is fancy, if is a figment of the imagination. It is a dream. It is poetry. It is a fairy abstraction; but it is not an ideal.

Modern thought does not recognise abstractions. The ideal is organically related to the real, the ideal is implied in the real, the ideal is involved is the real and the ideal is based on actualities of the real. It is not something that comes from the outside. Where do you find the ideal of the rose. Is it in the lotus? No. It is in the rose, the tiny little rose itself suggests the ideal of a full blown rose and it is in the rose, in the reality of the rose, that you find the ideal of the rose suggested but never exhausted by it; so the ideal of humanity you find in man or woman or the general human race and not any where else. It is in the realities of our human life and activities that we find the suggestion of the ideal of the human race; the ideal of humanity.

So, that which is not practically attainable is not an ideal, it is a fancy, it is a poesy. It is a dream, it is a fanciful abstraction and our ideal of *Swaraj* would not be an ideal if it were not practically attainable. Mr. Gokhale says that this ideal of *Swaraj* is not practically attainable. Why? because the English people will not understand it. They understand self-government within the Empire but they do not understand and will not understand, and will fight shy of his outlandish ideal of *Swaraj*. But I ask you gentlemen, to consider for one moment if self-government within the Empire is a really practically attainable ideal, what guarantee have we that the British people, those responsible British statesmen, would be willing to grant us even this practically attainable privilege of self-government within the Empire? What did Mr. Morley, Honest John, say last autumn in the course of his budget speech? I referred to it last night.

I will refer to it once more to night. 'As long as my imagination reaches, so long', Mr. Morley said, 'the Government of India must continue to be a personal and absolute Government'. What is a personal Government, Sir? What are the characteristics of absolute government? Is self-government consistent with the ideal of personal government, unless you refer to the self-government of the person who governs and not of those who are governed. Is self-government consistent with absolute government? Has Russia self-government? Why not, because the Czar is an absolute monarch there. Has Afghanistan self-Government? Why not?, because Habibulla is an absolute monarch in Afghan territory. Has Persia self-government? Only very recently and if she had not, it was because the rule that obtained in Persia was a personal and absolute rule.

Personal and absolute Government is dramatically opposed to self-government in any real shape or form and therefore how are we to know in the face of this open, this deliberate declaration, by the most distinguished, the most broad-minded, the most sympathetic, the most philosophical and the most literary of the English liberal statesmen? How are we to understand in the face of his broad open declaration, by a man like Mr. John Morley, the right-hand man of the late Mr. Gladstone? How are we to understand in the face of such a declaration that they would listen to our demands of self-government if only we shall keep it within the Empire more considerately and kindly than they are likely to listen to our demand for absolute autonomy or *Swaraj*.

Practically Attainable Ideals

Then again, Sir, is really self-Government within the Empire a practicable ideal. What would it mean? It would mean — I have to repeat once more what I said just now either no real self-Government for us or no real overlordship for England. Would we be satisfied with a shadow of self-Government? If not, would England be satisfied with the shadow of overlordship? In either case England would not be satisfied with a shadowy overlordship. We refuse to be satisfied with a shadowy self-government. (Hear, hear and cheers.) And therefore no compromise is possible under such conditions between self-government in India and the overlordship of England.

The fact of the matter is this; England will not think of granting us any measure of real self-government until she is compelled to do so. (Hear hear.) And when the compulsion becomes irresistible, when the pressure of Indian public opinion becomes absolutely irresistible and the alternative before England is either to give us substantial self-government or lead to the severance of India's connection with England, (Hear, hear.) when that alternative presents itself before English statesmen, it is then only that they will begin to consider any demands that you and I may make for a substantial measure of self-government in India; and if self-government is conceded to us, what would be England's position not only in India but in the British Empire itself. Self-government means right of self-taxation, it means right of financial control, it means the right of the people to impose protective and prohibitive tariff on foreign imports.

The moment we have the right of self-taxation, what shall we do? We shall not try to be engaged in this uphill work of Industrial boycott. But we shall do what every nation or almost every nation did, why, every nation has done. Under the circumstances in which we live now we shall impose a heavy prohibitive protective tariff upon every inch of textile fabric from Manchester. We shall impose a protective, prohibitive tariff upon every blade of knife that comes from Leeds. We shall refuse to grant admittance to a British soul into our territory. We shall make it impossible for Mauritius as well as for Australia and Belgium and France to carry our sugar industries by carrying cheap beetroot sugar from their territories here. And then England's trade with India would be a thing of the past (Laughter).

That is what we would do. Would England consent to it? This grand ideal of an Indian Parliament or an Indian Legislative assembly imposing a prohibitive tariff on Manchester, Sheffield, Leeds and other foreign British imports. It is more thinkable. Does it appeal better to the self-interest of Englishmen than *Swaraj?* then what, else. We would refuse admittance to Englishman within these territories. They would not be permitted to develop the natural resources of our country and convert us into a race of coolies. They would not be permitted to set up the Agricultural Institute at Pusa in Berar with a view to the exploitation of agricultural resources of that rich province. We would not allow British capital to be engaged in the development of Indian resources as British capital is now engaged, we would not grant any right to British capitalist to dig up the mineral wealth of the land and carry it to their own isle. We would refuse to do all these things. We shall want foreign capital. We must want foreign capital for the development of our own resources. But we shall apply for foreign loan in the open market of the whole world guaranteeing the credit of the Indian Government, the Indian Nation, for the repayment of the loan just as America had done and is doing, just as Russia is doing now, just as Japan has been doing of late; and England's commercial interest in India will not be furthered in the way these are being furthered now under the conditions of popular self-Government in this country, though it might be within the Empire? But what would it mean if within the Empire? It would mean that England would have to enter into some arrangement with us for some preferential tariff.

England would have to come to our markets on the conditions that we would impose on her for the purpose, and if she wanted to have an open door, an honest Swadeshism in India, we would also, perhaps not immediately, but after a while, when we have developed our resources a little and organised an industrial life, we would want open door not only to England but to every part of the British Empire. And do you know there is a British Empire growing in secret and silence on the African continent as a possible set off against the Indian Empire and we would almost occupy to the practical exclusion of England over the markets in the future African British Empire as England occupied every market in India today. And do you think it is possible for a small country like England with a handful of population although she might be enormously wealthy to compete on fair and equitable terms with a mighty continent like India, with an immense natural resources, with her teeming populations, with her labouring millions, the soberest and the moat abstemious labouring population known to any other part of the world.

If we have really self-Government within the Empire, if we have the rights of freedom of the Empire as Australia has, as Canada has, as England has herself today, if we, the 300 millions of people, have that freedom of the Empire, the Empire would cease to be the British. It would be the Indian Empire and the alliance between England and India would be absolutely an unequal alliance. It would be, as I have said elsewhere like tying a big brass vessel with a small earthen pot and throwing it at the breakers there. That would be if we had really self-government within the Empire. That would exactly be the relation as copartners in a co-British or the anti-British Empire of the future, and if the day comes when England will be reduced absolutely to the alternative of having us as an absolutely independent people or a copartner with her in the Empire, she would prefer to have us like the Japanese an ally and no longer a copartner, because we are bound to be the predominant partner in this imperial firm.

Therefore, no sane Englishman, politician or publicist, can ever contemplate seriously the possibility of a self-governing India like the self-governing Colonies forming a vital and organic part of the British Empire. It is, therefore, that Mr. Morley says that so long as India remains under the control of Great Britain, the Government of India must continue to be a personal and absolute Government.

It is for this reason that Lord Minto says that it would be a dangerous and mischievous thing for the Indian Government to be allowed to be controlled by public opinion in India. It is, therefore, that Lord Curzon said that as long as the Government in India continue to be British, the direction of the affairs of this Government, the direction and the control of its policy must entirely rest with the British and not with the Indian people. Therefore it seems to me that this ideal, the practically attainable ideal of self-Government within the Empire, when we analyse it with care, when we study it in the light of common human psychology, when we study it in the light of our past experience of racial characteristics of the British people, when we study in the light of past British history in India and in other parts of the world, when we study and analyse this ideal of self-Government within the Empire, we find that it is a far more impracticable thing to attain even our ideal of *Swaraj*.

Our Difficulties and Deficiencies

Now, Sir, when we talk of this ideal of *Swadeshi* we are told of our difficulties and deficiencies. We are reminded of our want of muscle. Mr. Gokhale reminded us of it at Allahabad or Lucknow.

Our want of muscle, the lack of the spirit of self-sacrifice in the country, our want of union, the Hindus being at war with the Muhammadans, and all these things are conjured up before the mind's vision with a view to scare us away from this glorious ideal of *Swaraj*, and gentlemen, the attainment of this *Swaraj* was no child's play. It will not be done by mere public meetings and enthusiastic demonstrations. I recognise, Sir, as fully and as clearly and as strongly as anybody else in this country the enormous difficulties that stand in our way. It would be the height of folly on the part of any man who really desires to realise the ideal of *Swaraj* to underestimate the difficulties that stand in our way.

It would be also an act of suicide to overestimate them. Let us take a proper measure of these difficulties and recognising these difficulties the question is, "Will the continuance of our present policy, the moderate policy of association with, and opposition to, the Government, will this policy, this policy of trying to appease the authorities with a view to secure small mercies, will this policy of moderate Indian politics help to remove these difficulties or will they help to increase and strengthen them". This is the question I put before you. You talk of the Hindu-Muhammadan difficulty. This difficulty was not in existence 30 or 10 years ago. This difficulty was unknown 50 years back, even during the turbulent times of the Sepoy Mutiny. How then these difficulties and by whom have they been created? It is not possible to answer this question, because no man knows the secret of the political movements in any part of the world.

So we do not know under whose inspiration and moved by what impulse the Muhammadans have fallen away in some parts of India from the Hindus, or why the Hindus have not been able to bring the Muhammadans to their own ranks. But this much I will say that this conflict between the Hindus and the Muhammadans is not industrial conflict. Our interests are identical. There is nothing in the agricultural life of the country which creates any conflict at the present time between the Muhammadan agriculturist and the Hindu agriculturist. There is absolutely no conflict between these two great communities in the trade-life of the land. The Mohamedan shopkeeper peacefully does his business side by side with the Hindu shopkeepers, and there is absolutely no conflict in trade matters between Muhammadan traders as a class and the Hindu traders as a class. There might be conflicts, rivalries between individual shopkeepers. Such rivalries exist between one Hindu shopkeeper and another Hindu shopkeeper. Such rivalries exist in some bazars of Hindus and Muhammadans. It is not in the commercial life or in the agricultural life that there is any conflict of interest.

In the industrial life there is no conflict of interest. Our trade is more in the hands of the Muhammadans than even in the hands of the Hindus where then is the conflict of interest. The conflict of interest is in the Government service, and in those honorary offices like membership of the Legislative Councils and Municipal and District Boards (cries of Bycott. That in no doubt a good suggestion, we shall come to that later on.) It is here in the competition for Government appointments, it is here in the rivalry in Municipal and District Boards or Legislative Council Membership, it is here that the interests of the two seem just now to stand in opposition to one another, and this opposition is due entirely to the fact that these offices are in the gift of the foreign administration. The English ruler throws out a bone in the form of a Sub-Registrarship between the Hindus and the Muhammadans and two fight for that bone.

He throws out a High Court Judgeship and the Muhammadan Barrister and the Hindu pleader fight for that bone in the High Court. He throws out a few bones of Legislative Council Membership and the Hindus and the Muhammadans try to fight over this. It is just in those matters that are in the keeping of the foreign bureaucracy, it is in regard to these matters and these matters alone that this new conflict has been treated between the Hindus and the Muhammadans in this country. And is it likely, my dear sirs, I want to know, that a continuance of the responsible authority in the politics in this country of this alien bureaucracy that will make for the amalgamation of the Hindu and Muhammadan interests.

I answer no. It is the system of the administration they have introduced that is responsible for this conflict and the effect cannot be removed as long as the cause exists. Therefore, it is impossible to hope for a solution of the Hindu-Muhammadan problem under existing conditions and even self-Government within the Empire will not solve it. You talk of the development of muscle. You talk of the physical powers of the people. We are emasculated. We have been awfully degenerated in our physique partly our poverty is responsible for it and partly the restrictive regulations of the Government in certain matters are also responsible for it. We are not permitted to form a Volunteer corps of our own. The Madrasis acquired half of India for the British at one time, but the Madrasi is not now admitted as he used to be into the British army.

As I was passing through the Northern Circars I happened to see in the way half a dozen men of the Raddiar caste. Finer specimens of physical humanity I had never seen in all my travels over three continents, and I wanted to take photograph of these men and write underneath this photograph — who sayest, mother, thou art without prowess or strength. These Reddiars might make the Guest army in any part of the world, but they are not allowed to enter the British army in India. Why? The answer comes neither from the Government nor is it possible for our moderate friends to render a satisfactory answer can muscle be developed without a national militia? Can muscle and muscular power be developed when a whole nation is disarmed by the outrageous Arms Act. Impossible. When we are deprived of the right of defending our own country by our own muscle, muscular development is a dream that can never be realised until the Government removed the restrictions of the Arms Act.

They are making the administration of that Act more and more stringent in every part of India. This Arms Act we owe to the administration of Lord Lytton. During the electioneering campaign that followed the dissolution of the Beaconsfield Cabinet in 1881 Mr. Gladstone attacked most strongly the Vernacular Press Act, the Arms Act and the Kabul war during the administration of Lord Lytton in India. When Mr. Gladstone got into power he sent out his chosen man Lord Ripon to this country to undo the evil that had been done by the Beaconsfield-Lytton administration.

Lord Ripon came and went away but the Arms Act remained and it remains even today. Lord Ripon did something. He repealed the Vernacular Press Act; why? Because it was necessary in the interests of the Government to repeal that pernicious Act for this reason. If we stop our newspapers today, if we stop our public meetings today, the Government, the foreign bureaucracy who know not the mind of the people and have no means of knowing their mind would run mad in twenty-four hours, under the weight of anxiety. They also admitted that the Vernacular Press Act was like sitting on the safety valve.

It lets out the gas which if accumulated might lead to the out burst of the boiler, and in whose interest I say has the safety valve to be kept open? Not in the interest of the valve itself but in the interest of the machinery which is saved by its being kept open. Who is injured? Grief and harm comes to him, in the matter of this safety valve, to the man who sits on it, and who was sitting upon it? The Government of India, through this Vernacular Press Act, therefore, in the interests of their own safety and salvation had to leave the safety valve and come out and sit elsewhere. That was how the Act came to be repealed, but the Arms Act was not a dangerous thing to the Government. It worked harm to the people, but it made the administration of the country easy and safe. Therefore, the Arms Act could not be repealed. That is the character, Sir, of the British policy, liberal or conservative. I do not blame that policy.

As I said last night, the British are a human people and the instinct of self-preservation is as strong in individuals as it is in nations, as it is also in organisations, whether social or political and the instinct of self-preservation in the Government of India compelled them to repeal the Vernacular Press Act, and the same instinct led them to continue the Arms Act and it leads them still now to continue it and increase its stringency. Therefore development of muscle or whatever else you may say is impossible as long as this Act is not repealed, and they will not repeal this Act simply because you and I want it. No nation, Sir, no Government has ever been known as yet to commit *harakiri* in the interests of political emancipation of its subjects. The Government of the Czar, has not committed suicide simply to emancipate the Russian people and the Foreign Government in India will not attempt by anything that we may say or do to commit suicide in our interest. That is a thing which you and I will have to bear in mind. Bearing this in mind we can dismiss without further consideration this plea of want of muscle as a plea for the continuance of the present order of things. From whatever point of view you look upon it, it is impossible not only to attain but even to advance towards your goal as long as the present order has not changed.

Mr. Gokhale talked of intellectual advancement. Is intellectual advancement really possible in India under present conditions? Don't you recognise what a large share every State has in the development of the intellectual life of its subject population? And is the Government of India run along such lines as are likely to develop the intellect of the nation? Colonel Du. Pre, a member of the Government of India Survey staff, in his evidence before the Public Service Commission made a significant declaration. He said "I never allow my native assistant to do any scientific work. I never allow them to touch the theodolite. I never allow them to do any real scientific work, because if we allow them to do it there will be no justification for our drawing the higher pay that we do now. This was what Colonel Du Pre said, and you will find it in the records of the evidence before the Public Service Commission. Does it not indicate the general Policy of British Government in regard to the intellectual life of your people? How can it be other wise, sir? We are so related to one another, the people of India and the foreign nation that rules them now, that our economic loss is their economic gain. Our economic gain is their economic loss. Every inch of textile fabric that is not tied out by our hand-looms means the exclusion of a corresponding inch of Manchester manufactured article from the Indian market. Every expansion of the industries of India means corresponding contraction of the trade of England with this country.

Every ounce of sugar that we grow and that we consume in India means an ounce less of imported sugar in out market. Every blade of knife that is turned by our blacksmith means the loss of the value of one blade of knife Sheffield and Leeds. Now, it stands almost as an open thing Our economic interests are in perpetual conflict under existing conditions with the economic interest of the British nation and the British Government, and our loss economically is England's gain. Our gain economically is England's loss. Similarly in regard to our intellectual life. You will remember, some of you at any rate, the important declaration made by Lord Curzon when he went out to England in the interregnum between one Viceroyalty and another. He made an important speech then in the Guildhall, London, and in that speech he put forward the claims of the Indian Government upon the attention of the British people, and what did he say then.

He said that the Government of India offered the best training ground for the intellect of England and the character of England. If it is so, it means so much loss of opportunity for the intellectual advancement and development of manly character to us, people of the country. Every high office that is in the keeping of an Englishman means not merely so much pay and pension, so much money, it means something far more valuable than pay or pension. It means so much intellectual or moral asset credited to England, and so much intellectual and moral loss credited to the people of India. Responsibility and opportunity are the two schools for the development of human mind and human character. So far as the Government of India is concerned, both these schools are crammed almost in every form by the foreigner, and we are excluded from these schools; and it means intellectual and moral loss. It means intellectual and moral gain to England.

Our intellectual loss is England's intellectual gain. Our moral loss is England's moral gain. Our moral gain is England's moral loss. Our intellectual gain is England's intellectual loss. They are as clear as daylight and when you consider this perpetual conflict of interest, economic, intellectual and moral between one nation and another, how can you expect that the nation which holds supreme authority over you now will, however good and generous, commit economic suicide intellectual *harakiri* and moral self-immolation with a view to advance your economic life, with a view to help the development of your intellectual life, or with a view to advance your spiritual and moral culture. No, Sir, Mr. Gokhale talks of his ambition to see the manhood of the nation fully developed.

I say under existing relations between this foreign bureaucracy and the people of this country, it is impossible for the manhood of India to reach this natural perfection. It is absolutely impossible; and therefore, this ideal of self-government within the Empire, this policy of association with, and opposition to, the Government, this policy of helping to smooth down the rough places of the administration will not do. They talk of British liberalism. They talk of a liberal policy and liberal sympathies. I say, Sir, our people had a clearer insight into the history of liberal politics. Before the Act of 1832 what was Liberal politics in England. After the Act of 1832 until very recently, what was the character of liberal policy, the policy of the Manchester School of British liberalism, the policy of Bright and Cobden? What was the liberal policy 50 years ago in England? It was the policy of *laissez faire*, a policy of not allowing Government to do anything more than giving peace and protection to the people.

There are certain primary rights inherent in every subject, under every Government. So there are certain primary responsibilities that rest with every Government, whether that Government be despotic or constitutional. And those responsibilities are the responsibilities of giving protection to the person and property of the subject population, and the policy of *Laisser faire* demands that the activities of the State shall be confined to this limit and limit alone, namely, that the State shall do nothing more than simply give protection to the person and property of the people, and leave the people to work out their own emancipation, their own progress, to work out their own problems, industrial, educational and political, themselves. That was the policy of British liberalism, and why that is the natural policy, because I say that is the natural policy under the conditions that, exist in England in those days.

What were those conditions? The main condition was the conflict between the prerogative of the Crown and the privileges of the people. The Crown wanted to appropriate to itself as ranch of the rights of Government as it could appropriate, and those who wanted to expand the rights of the people had necessarily to fight the authority of the Crown, and the authority of the Crown they knew would be so strengthened by the beneficent activities of the Crown among the people. If before 1832 there was free reduction in England, what would have been the condition of popular freedom in England? The Government in its own interest would educate people in loyalty and not in a democratic spirit. If 20 years back there was a talk of old age pension in England, it would have been fought outright by every Liberal Statesman in the country, simply because old age pension would incerease and strengthen the hold of the Government upon the people, and the objective of Liberalism in those days was not to strengthen the hold of the people on the Government but to weaken that hold; and, therefore, the activities of the Government had to be restricted. Therefore, their ideal was not to make for good Government.

Their ideal was not to make Government good but to confine the activities of the Government to the narrowest possible limits, and in view of this conflict of interests between the Government and the people in India our policy ought to be the policy, the old Liberal policy of *laissez faire*, restrict Government to their own primary responsibilities. Let the Government take care of the person and property of the people. Let them do nothing more, and let everything else be done by the people by their own exertions independently of the Government, because every beneficent work that a despotic Government does, increases the hold of that despotism upon the affections and the allegiance, if set upon the affections and the allegiance, upon the acquiescence of the people.

In that lies the strength of Governments and if a despotic Government has had its peculiar acquiescence of the general population of the country, Liberalism, freedom and progressive politics is impossible of attainment in that country (Hear, hear). Therefore our policy is a policy of *laissez faire* and by insisting upon this policy by restricting the Government to its narrowest possible limits to the discharge of those duties which it is bound to discharge, because it imposes taxes on us, by restricting the activities of the Government to the primary functions of granting protection to the people of this country, we hope some day to develop the spirit of self-sacrifice, the spirit of self-reliance, the spirit of self-determination in the people, and by this means we hope some day to attain the ideal of *Swaraj*.

[With a few remarks from the chair, the gathering dispersed.]

Swaraj: Ways and Means

Mr. Chairman and friends, Before I take up the thread of my last evening's address, I desire with your premission, Sir, to say one word in regard to a statement, I was going to say an accusation, that has been made against me by my old friend.

It has been said, that in interpreting Lord Minto's latest pronouncement and placing it on a level with the pronouncement of Lord Curzon, I have not been accurate, I have put an inaccurate and misleading interpretation upon His Excellency's words. I am a little careful about these charges, I am used to recognise, and I have been trained from my youth onward to respect differences of opinion, but I may claim it, I think, Sir, that even our rankest enemies, I mean of the Anglo-Indian Press, have not as yet found it easy to bring any charge of this kind against me. Whatever else I may be, I have never tried to do except the fullest justice to my political opponents. Therefore, I am compelled to take notice of this charge brought against me by a very friendly critic who says thus:

> "We must take exception, however, to a statement made by Mr. Pal with reference to His Excellency Lord Minto, which we think is an inaccurate, misleading statement which ought not, in our opinion, to be left uncorrected".

Then the writer quotes my words. What Lord Curzon said has been repeated by Lord Minto only two months back in his Budget Speech. What does Lord Minto say?' He says that it is absolutely necessary that whatever reforms are introduced by the Government of India they must be initiated by that Government itself, and it would be a mischievous thing for the British Government in India if the idea got abroad that the Government of India had on conviction of their own, that they initiated reforms under pressure of public opinion hero or under instructions from the people and the Government in England. That is what Lord Minto says.

The same thing has Lord Curzan said. It means that the control of affairs, the direction of the administration, the right of initiative shall always be with the British people and their representatives here and not with any one else. It means, Sir, an open declaration by the present Viceroy that they are not amenable and they will never be amenable to Indian opinion in these matters". This is what I said, and the writer quotes from Lord Minto, the portion of the Budget Speech to which reference was made by me and after quoting it, he says that "no farther explanation is required to show that the meaning attributed by Mr. Pal to the words contained in Lord Minto's speech is entirely foreign to the language used". I will appeal to you. I have interpreted Lord Minto's words according to the light that is in me, and I shall presently place the whole thing before you with a view to enable you to judge for yourself whether that interpretation has been inaccurate or misleading or otherwise. These are Lord Minto's words. "The Honourable Mr. Gokhale tempts me to foreshadow the future," and he goes on to say, "I have deemed it all-important that the initiation of possible reforms should emanate from us. I have felt that nothing would be more mischievous to British administration in India in the future than a belief that its Government had acted on no conviction of their own but simply in submission to agitation in this country and in accordance with instructions conveyed to them from Home. If there has been misconceptions as to this, I hope I may be allowed this opportunity of correcting if".

Now, I put it to you, gentlemen, did not I almost quote the words of Lord Minto? The only interpretation that I put upon these words is identifying the meaning with the purpose of Lord Curzon, and I think I am right in doing so. Lord Minto says that it would be a mischievous thing for the Government of India in the future if the impression got abroad that they undertook possible reforms under pressure of agitation here. Its means this. I put it to you if this does not distinctly mean that the Government have got a conscience of their own. They will listen to that conscience, not to your voice.

The Government have ideas of their own. They will govern you according to those ideas and not under pressure of agitation in India or England. What does it mean? Does it not mean that the control, the direction, the right of initiation shall always rest with the Government of India and not with any body else (cries of yes), and, if that is the meaning. I put it to you, was not that the meaning also of Lord Curzon, was not that the meaning of Lord Curzon's memorable declaration in which he said that the Government of India, as long as it continues, to be British, certain offices must necessarily be occupied by the British.

What are those offices, please? Offices in which is vested the right of initiative, offices which control the administration, offices which initiate reform, and offices which dictate the policy of the Government. It is these offices which shall always continue to be in their hands, in the occupation of the British; theirs is the controlling power, the power of dictating policy. These shall always rest with the Government, the foreign Government, with the representatives of the British people in India, with the Government as it is at present constituted and no part of this prerogative of the foreign Government in India shall be given to you (shame). I put it to you, Sir, (pointing to Mr. G. Subramania Aiyar), you presided on the last occasion (turning to the Chairman) you are the master of the meeting today, and I put it to you all, gentlemen, whether I mislead you (cries of no), whether I put an inaccurate interpretation upon Lord Minto's utterances.

Not even wit regard to Lord Minto, would I try to put an inaccurate interpretation upon his sayings, for the simple reason, that the truth itself is so ugly that no inaccurate interpretation is needed to be put. (cries of Boycott the *Hindu*) no, no, do not boycott always. No, no, respect the *Hindu,* because you are a Hindu. No, it is a well-meant thing. Do not take offence at it. It is a friendly criticism. The thing is this, journalists have to do their work at electric speed (cry of Boycott the *Hindu)* I regret very much if any disrespectful remark is passed against the *Hindu.* It has been the only paper that has contributed to the making of Southern India. *[Cries of Swadesamitran],* my dear friends, *Swadesamitran* is the *Hindu* in the new incarnation.

Swaraj Ideal

Last night, I considered the ideal of *Swaraj,* but I am often times told why do you talk of the ideal. *Swaraj* is an excellent thing but it is not within the range of practical politics. It is an excellent academic subject, but not a subject which need trouble us very much so far as the actual work that we have to do is concerned. I do not, Mr. Chairman, I cannot subscribe to this view, and for this simple reason, unless you are sure as to what you want, you cannot adopt now the necessary means, the instruments for securing that which you want. You are walking, but walking is not progression. Walking may be away from the goal as well as it may be towards the goal and you ought to know what your destination is with a view to determine what your work and duty, what your direction must now be. Practical politics means the adoption of practical measures for the amelioration of the political condition of the people. But unless you have always a clear conception of the ultimate end, you ran the risk of being carried away by the passions, the temptations, the prejudices, the difficulties, the obstacles of the hear, from your goal. Here is, for instance, a particular wrong that has to be remedied. Take, for instance, the misappropriation of a certain public fund by the Government — the misappropriation of the Famine Fund, the misappropriation in Bengal of the Road Cess Fund.

When the Road Cess was first introduced in Bengal, it was regarded by the people of the Province as a practical violation of the Permanent Settlement obtaining in that country. It was a cess imposed upon land, and according to the terms of the Permanent Settlement, the Government had given the undertaking that no further assessment would be 'imposed upon land and yet this Road Cess was practically an impost on land, and the Government said no, it is not a part of Land Revenue. It in a special cess levied for a specific purpose, and accordingly they defined these purposes. They said that sinking wells, digging tanks, keeping and repairing and constructing public roads, looking after village sanitation, establishing a system of proper drainage in the village areas. These are all the objects to which this fund shall be applied. Laterly, however, they refused to grant any money out of this Road Cess Fund for the removal of water scarcity in the rural areas of Bengal. They said, no, we will not give money for sinking wells or digging tanks.

We shall spend it on other purposes. Here was a distinct misappropriation of public funds, and you may do at once one thing. You may appeal to the Government, you may memorialise to Government. You may bring friendly pressure upon the Government with a view to induce them to take to sinking wells, digging tanks and grievance will be removed. If the Government sink wells, dig tanks, water scarcity will be partially removed, and so far as it is removed the lot of the people will be easy. It will be some relief to the people, but the question is, will this temporary relief contribute to your progress towards a particular goal upon which you have set your heart. A school boy is running to his school. He is feeling very thirsty. He has got only one minute's time during which he has to get into his school. He is feeling thirsty. A man offers him a cool-drink, and says here is a cocoanut tree. I am going to the top of it and I shall give you a drink of a tender cocoanut, wait here. If the school boy waits here, he will relieve his thirst, no doubt. He will find it very pleasant to have a drink of the tender cocoanut, but by going to enjoy a drink he will miss his lesson at his school; will he not? (cries of yes). Similarly, by seeking to relieve the present distress, you may be missing an opportunity of creating those forces in the community by the application of which, ultimately you may be able to attain *Swaraj* or autonomy.

If you do not care for *Swaraj,* yes, Sir, let the partition be removed, let the cess be repealed, let a few more seats be given to us in the Legislative Councils. These are palliatives. These are local applications, and he is a quack doctor who, when the disease is a constitutional disease, waste time by local application. In politics also, therefore, it is essential that you should know what it is that you desire to have. In the polities of free countries, the ultimate principles are well established. There the goal is kept in view, whatever party comes into power. The increase of the political power, the commercial prosperity of the British nation is the one end towards which Liberals or Conservatives both equally try to move and lead the country. Therefore, the goal being fixed at that point there being no chance of misconception in the public mind they are entitled to look after little things, to improve the details of the administration, to try palliatives, to make local applications for the removal of local maladies.

But, your malady is not a local malady. It is not the removal of one cess or another cess, it is not the securing of a few appointments here or a few honorary posts there. The evil under which you suffer is fundamental, a radical and a constitutional evil, and therefore it is the more necessary for you to keep this constitutional, this fundamental, this radical character of the problem that faces you, so that you may not run off from the right course by the passing temptations of the hour, this way or that way. I told you yesterday that when there is a conflict between the Government and the people, the right policy to follow for those who care for popular progress and popular freedom is to insist upon the Government, to adopt and follow the policy of *laissez faire,* to restrict the operation of the Government, to restrict the activities of the Government within the narrowest possible limits. But when you seek this isolated individual redress, the individual and isolated grievance, you do actually this.

You increase the hold of the Government upon the mind of the people. I should rather wish, Sir, that our people went without good drinking water for 2.5 years, if that is necessary, I should think it far more desirable that, like the Israelites of old, the Indian people shall pass through the desert, parched up desert, for 25 years together drawing water at the end of the Prophet's rod out of hard stone rather than, have wells sunk and tanks dug by this foreign authority, who by distributing this water to you will captivate your heart. What is the real objective of the conflict between the educated community in this country and the Government. What is it, Sir, what is the objective of this conflict, that has been going on for the last quarter of a century between the people, the representatives of the people, between the educated class, the enlightened class in India on the one hand and the foreign bureaucracy on the other.

What is that objective? What is the citadel which both, the parties are trying to capture and occupy? What is that top of the hold to which both the parties are trying to get up the soonest they can possibly do so? Is it merely the amendment of certain laws? Is it merely the removal of certain grievances? No. It is the heart, the mind of the people, of the masses that is the objective. Lord Curzon saw it, and all his measures were directed towards capturing the popular mind in India. He organised his pageants to appeal to the imagination of the man in the street. He has inaugurated Rural reforms, Agricultural Banks and other things with a view to captivate the mind of the teeming masses; and the intense scrupulousness with which he tried to do justice in cases of individual wrongs, is the punishment of the 9th Lancers, his desire to see British justice maintained in this country. All these things were directed towards one great end, if not the allegiance, at least the passive, the generous acquiescence of the general mass of the population (Hear, hear), and the battle must be waged around that citadel. The Government will try to capture the mind of the masses and he is a foolish politician in India who allows the Government to capture the mind of the masses to the exclusion of his own influence, of his own countrymen (cheers). And what do you do if you make the administration easy? What do you do if you cover the veil of the British administration with cotton and wool. It moves on and it grinds us small, but the padded wool makes it less painful to you. That is all. Good Government is not only no substitute for self-government, it is an exceedingly evil thing when the authority of the State rests in the hands of an irresponsible power.

Of all kinds of despotism, a benevolent despotism is the worst, because the benevolence makes people acquiesce in the despotism, and it is therefore necessary that you and I should have a clear vision of what we want. Do you want good government, Sir. If you want good government you can have it.. You will have it. Things will be made easy for you, but if you want self-government under existing conditions in India, good government would be absolutely opposed to the promotion of self-government, because, as I said last night, our trouble is with our selves. Our trouble is with our own mind. Our trouble is with our own sentiments. Our trouble is with our own wills, with our own inertia, and good government will help to continue if it does not increase the *Maya*. Pleasures of the world increase the hold of *Maya* on human beings, and it is therefore he who wants to get rid of *Maya* is asked to cultivate *Vairagya,* cultivate abstemiousness, cultivate disattachment. You talk of *Swaraj*.

The knowledge of *Swaraj* is absolutely impossible without a consciousness of the present *pararashtra.* The knowledge of self is absolutely impossible unless the self comes in contact and conflict with the Not-self. So the knowledge of *Swaraj* is absolutely impossible unless there is not a *pararashtra. Para* is directly against the *Swaraj.* It is in the conflict between *Swa* and *Para,* it is in the conflict between the self and the not-self, in political affairs, with the conception of the real. Self-Government grows and keen has become the conflict between the self and the not-self. In political matters as strong in proportion to this keenness becomes the desire of *Swaraj*. Therefore, the conflict must be kept up and good government helps to kill and not to keep up this conflict between the self and the not-self, in the political affairs of a country constituted as India is. Therefore you must have a clear conception of what you want. *Swaraj* your *raj*, your *Shastra*, and the first is, as in Vedantic culture the first thing is *nithaya vasthu vichara viveka*, improve the self and not improve the not-self. That is, discrimination is the very first thing in Vedantic culture, the very first thing in the culture of the ideal of the *Swaraj*.

Discrimination in political and civic matters between the national self and that which is not the national self. The ideal of *Swaraj* has been revealed to us only recently, and, why, because for nearly a hundred years and more we never looked upon the British Government in India as a *pararashtra*, as a foreign Government. When the Congress was started we looked upon this Government as our government, only it was not so good as we should like it to be. Before that we regarded this Government as our Government because we had been brought up under English ideals, brought up in English traditions. Not only have our territories been conquered by England, but by this English education even our mind, our mental ideals, our ethical ideals, our spiritual aspirations, all these had been got hold of by this foreign Government, this foreign culture, this foreign civilization. And because we found or we fancied that we found in this foreign Government until our better, our higher, our superior self, that which we ought to become tomorrow which we are not today, simply because we looked upon this Government and their institutions in this light, there was no possibility of the growth of the conception of *Swaraj* in our midst.

In proportion as there grew a conflict first in the political field, then in the field of religion, in the field of Social Reform, in the field of economics, all over the national life, in proportion as there grew in the consciousness of the Indian people the presence of a conflict between ourselves and those who govern the country, between ourselves and the British people, in proportion as this conflict grow in that proportion by slow degree grow this ideal of *Swaraj* until the conflict grew almost unbearable. The full revolution of the ideal of *Swaraj* came to as after the departure of Lord Curzon from this country and was proclaimed by Mr. Dadabhai Naoroji from the chair of the Congress last year (cheers). If this be so, if this be a fact, sir, that applying the principles of psychology to the consideration of our political problems, if we find that it is necessary that we should recognise this conflict between the people and the Government, it is also necessary that we should do nothing that will make this Government easy for us, because if the Government becomes easy, if it becomes pleasant, if it becomes good government, then our sense of separation from it will be gradually lost, and when the sense of separation is lost *Smrithi Brahamsath Budhi nasa, budhi nasath pranasyathi, &c.* You contemplate all the good things that this Government can do for you, you meditate on the honours that the Government can shower on you, you meditate on the high offices what the Government may give you.

You may get the High Court Judgeship here, a Membership of the Legislative Council there, an Advocate-Generalship in another part of the globe, a Legal Remembrancer in a third place, an executive membership of the Council possibly again. Now you think of all this, and thinking of all this you feel an attachment for this, and feeling an attachment for this, you desire to have this, and the feeling of this desire to have this, kills your consciousness of separation from this. And therefore good Government, pleasant Government, pleasurable associations with the Government, whatever else, however moderate or temperate, may be, they can never make for *Swaraj,* because the first thing in *Swaraj* is the perception of this, that there is an eternal, a natural conflict between the self and the not-self in political affair in this country.

It is for this reason that I always tried to impress the ideal of *Swaraj* upon my countrymen, because once you have the ideal before you it will be possible for you to judge of the particular methods or measures in the light of that ideal. Do you want an expansion of the Legislative Council? Let us see if it will help you for *Swaraj.* Do you want that a few Indians shall sit as your representatives in the House of Commons? Let us see if half-a-dozen, or a dozen, or two dozens or 40, 60 members in the House of Commons representing the interests of India elected by the

Indian leaders, will make or not make for *Swaraj*. Do you want a larger number of Indians to be in the Civil Service of the Government? Let us see whether 50, 60, 100, 200, or 300 Civilians will make the Government our Own. At one time we thought, Sir, that this was the method. At one time we thought that by slow degrees by participating in a small measure in the work of the administration with the Government of the country, with the foreign rulers of the land, we shall not only be trained in discharging rightly and properly the duties of the administration, but we shall also gradually oust them, replace the English agency by Indian agency. What, Sir, if you replace the agency? What about the principal? He is the primary factor and we, his agents.

The whole Civil Service might be Indian, but the Civil Servants have to carry out orders. They cannot direct. They cannot dictate policy. The policy is dictated by those who stand above them and you replace, as I have said, the agency, but the agency implies presence of an original, a principal, and if, instead of 200, 300, 2,000 Englishmen being the agents of the British nation and the British Parliament in India for the Government of India you have 2,000 natives, will that alter the state of things? (No) I know it will not. We have had a number of Indian civilians. Have they altered, at any rate, the character, the nature, the tradition of British Government in India? We have just now in Bengal an Indian Civilian who is the Senior Member of the Board of Revenue. But one swallow does not make a summer and one Civilian, 100 or 1,000 civilians in the service of the British Government will not make that Government Indian.

There are traditions, there are laws, there are principles, there are policies to which every Civilian, be he black, brown or white, mustsubmit, and as long as these traditions have not been altered, as long as these principles have not been amended, as long as that policy has not been radically changed, the supplanting of European by Indian agency will not make for self-government in this country. I doubt it very much whether it would make for good Government either. Why? You seem to think that a larger number of appointments in the Civil Service or in the Subordinate Service will improve the administration. I deny that it will be so, and it is for this simple reason. An Englishman, whatever else his fault is, is trained in the free atmosphere of England. An Englishman, whatever may be his attitude towards you and me, still knows this, he can stand upon his own rights. He never bends his knees unjustly, cringingly, after the manner of the sycophant even before the highest official superior; but can you say the name of your Indian Civil Servants? (No.) And why?, because the Indian Civil Servant knows there is no one behind his back to support him. The English Civil Servant knows there is behind his back the public opinion of England, the freedom of England, to stand him in good stead.

Our Police is corrupt, and they sometimes say, "Oh ! What a perfect officer the Policeman in London if". Transplant the London Policeman in India and see where his perfection goes; and what is the reason? Why is it, the London Police is so honest, so painstaking, so respectful to the rights and liberties of London? Because be knows that he is the servant of the public of London. In India every red turban knows and feels that he is not your servant but he is your master. And why does he feel it? Because he receives his *sannad* not from your hands but from the hands of the foreign rulers of the land. It is to him that the Policeman is responsible and not to you. It is to him the Civil Servant is responsible and not to you.

It is to him that the District Magistrate is responsible and not to you. It is to him that the Inspector is responsible and not to you; and therefore, the Inspector, the Civilian, the District Magistrate and the Police constable and every officer of the Government in fact looks to his own interest naturally, and looking to his own interest he sees that, if he can please the officials, his interest will be best served, and if he displeases you he will not in the least suffer in his own interest. Therefore, there is such weakness, inefficiency, such disregard of the rights, liberties and the privileges of the people in the service of the Government in this country. Therefore, I say, if you have a larger number of officials, native officials that may make things easy for a few families, get a few more coffers into their chest than otherwise, perhaps, they would get. It might make things easy for a few individuals, but for the nation at large it will not improve their lot.

It is, therefore, necessary, I say, from whatever point of view you look upon this question you will find that the consideration of the ideal, the creation of right conception, the creation of strong convictions in regard to the goal, is essentially necessary for the right conduct and management of what you call practical politics. It is said, Sir, are you fit for *Swaraj.* I put the question of fitness entirely out of Court, because I am not going to apply to anybody else for granting me *Swaraj.* It is only when you have to make an application to somebody else to give you a certain thing that you have to prove your fitness for getting it. When you have to make an application to the Registrar of the High Court for a clerkship in the High Court or to the Police Magistrate there for some office at his disposal, you have to say "Sir, Being given to understand that a clerkship is vacant, I beg to apply myself as a candidate for the same".

And then you have to say "as regards my qualification, I have passed F.A. or B.A. examination of the Madras University" but I say that when you want to open a shop with your own money, or the money left to you by your father or grandfather, do you in any application say you are qualified or not. Why not? Because you do it yourself. Therefore, you are not called upon to prove your fitness for the thing before you do it before anybody else, and those who ask us to prove our fitness for *Swaraj* forget that we have abjured a programme of petitions and prayers for good. They forget that we do not ask, nay, not even the benign Government of Britain in India, to grant as *Swaraj.* We do not pray to them for these things; and I would say more, Sir, if the Government were to come and tell me today 'take *Swaraj'* I would say, 'thank you for the gift', but I will not have that which I cannot acquire by my own hand, (cries of *Vande Mataram)* — because my dear friends, in real growth, which is organic growth, there is absolutely no room for gift.

Evolution whether in the case of individuals or of nations admits of no gifts from outside. We must grow from within, and I am surprised to find, Sir, that those eminently prudent and wise gentlemen, who, the moment we talk of social reform come up to us and say 'Oh, social reform muşt be a growth from within', when we talk of *Swaraj* they call as to prove our fitness. They take it for granted that we must get it from outside. If social reform is to be a growth from within, I accept it unreservedly. There can be no reform, social or economic or political, that can be got from outside. You must gradually acquire your rights and in the acquisition of your right you develop your character, you equip yourself with these forces and resources which will enable you to protect and to use those rights properly when you have got them. Lord Ripon's generous scheme of Local Self-Government has been a failure, more or less, I should say, out of regard for the tender susceptibilities of our Municipal Commissioners and Local Board Members. And why has it not succeeded, Sir? Simply because it was a gift from the Government. If we have grown into it, if we had acquired it by our own strength, if we had organised our village lives ourselves, if we had organised our Municipal life ourselves, if we had organised our *taluka* life ourselves, why, Local Self-Government would take its stand upon self-determination, self-exertion, self-recognition of the civic duties by the peoples themselves.

Such a Local Self-Government would not be a mushroom growth, would not be like an orchid that has no root on the ground but hangs on the tree of a foreign government. It will not be like that. The partial or complete failure of the schemes of Local Self-Government inaugurated by Lord Ripon proves my contention that for the exercise of civic rights it is essentially necessary that the people should desire to exercise those right, should acquire them, and in the acquisition of these rights they prove their fitness for the exercise of these rights. It is foolish politics, excuse me for that expression, to demand a *priori* reason and argument for proving the fitness of the people for Self-Government.

No man knows, no one can say, that a nation is fit for Self-Government or is not. The proof of the pudding is in the eating thereof, and the proof of the fitness of the people is in their capacity to achieve the institution of Self-Government by their own exertion, by their own strength, by their own combination, by their own determination and by their own sacrifice themselves (cries of *Vande Mataram).*

And because this is so, our programme is that we shall so work in the country, so combine the resources of the people, so organise the forces of the nation, so develop the instincts of freedom in the community, that by this means we shall — shall in the imperative — compel the submission to our will of any power that may set itself against us. Then, they ask, what you talk of *Swaraj*, would it be a Hindu *Swaraj* or a Muhammadan *Swaraj?* What would be the form of your *Swaraj?* My reply here, again, is this. It is impossible for any man to lay down beforehand what the particular form of a thing that is passing through a process of evolution will be. Evolution implies heredity and environment, certain original powers, capabilities and the possibilities in the organism that is being evolved, and the action and reaction of these capabilities on its environments, and as our environments will be, be our form also will necessarily be.

It will depend upon what lines the historic evolution of modern India takes to determine what will be the particular form of the *Swaraj* that will be established in this country. France started her revolution with the noble ideal of equality, fraternity and humanity. France raised the flag of democracy at the beginning of the Revolution, and no man held that flag more high than did Napoleon Bonaparte, and yet in the of a few months it was found out that France would not realise even her own ends through setting up a republic or democratic form of Government. When all the royalties of Europe, when all the European Powers combined together to crush this rising republic of France, France had necessarily to develop a dictatorship, had necessarily to develop an absolute and military form of Government with a view to meet the exigencies of the situation created by the combination of the European Powers against her.

France did not wish. It was of necessity imposed upon France by the circumstances of her case. Who knows what dire necessity may be imposed upon you and me by the circumstances of our case in the progress of the evolution of our political life in the future. We know it not, but so far as our ideal is concerned, we need not hesitate to make this declaration, that the *Swaraj* of ours is not merely the Hindu, not merely the Muhammadan, nor merely the Christian *Swaraj*, but the *Swaraj* of every Child of India, Hindu or Christian or Muhammadan, the *Swaraj* will be the *Swaraj* of the Indian people, not of any section of it.

The ideal of *Swaraj* that has revealed itself to us is the ideal of divine democracy. It is the ideal of democracy, higher than the fighting, the pushing, the materialistic, I was going to say, the cruel democracy of Europe and America. There is a higher message still: men are gods and the equality of Indian democracy is the equality of the divine original, the divine nature, the divine possibilities and the divine destiny of every individual being, be he Hindu, or Muhammadan, Buddhist or Christian. It is on account of this general training of the India people in the past whether they be Hindu or Muhammadan, it is on account of this spiritual emphasis of the Hindu character and the generality also of the Indian character that we have had the supreme privilege of seeing before us the revolution of a democratic ideal, superior to that which has as yet been revealed to the general consciousness of European humanity.

This is our *Swaraj*. Our *Swaraj* will not be Hindu or Muhammadan; it will be an Indian *Swaraj*. You, and I, the meanest of men, to whatever caste, to whatever community or denomination, the Indian may belong, we will form an organic element of the big *Swa* whose *raj* we desire to set up and attain in this country. But, Sir, though this may be our ideal, we know not under what particular historical Constitutions we may have to reach and realise this ideal. If it be so, that what happened in France is repeated in India also, I believe ours shall be a peaceful revolution, — absolutely peaceful. There is no parallel in the history of a people inhabiting such a vast continent as India and counting such a large number as 300 millions and more governed by a handful of representatives by a small country far across the seas whose whole population cannot bear any reasonable proportion to the population of the country that they govern.

History has not seen a nation of such a vast mass of humanity being governed absolutely and despotically by a handful of alien people, and therefore the Constitution being unique, unprecedented, history affords no help to as for our guidance. It will not do, my dear friends, for you simply to read history, you will have to make, to work out the history of India yourself; and, therefore, I believe what has never happened in the history of the world may yet happen, in the history of India, *viz.* that a popular revolutionary propaganda may attain its end absolutely by passive means and methods. But still no man knoweth which way the force of circumstances will lead his feet, that we know not, but if we are prompted by the Grace of God to work out a peaceful revolution in India we can picture to ourselves what the future form of our *Swaraj* will be. It will be as Sir Henry Cotton, — no doubt, in a slightly different, sense, because he is an Englishman and not an Indian, — declared at the Bombay Congress. It was a prophetic declaration, *viz.* that the future Government of India will be the United States of India.

All prophetic declarations are in their very nature unconscious. No declaration can be a prophetic declaration unless it is an unconscious declaration, and I am sure Sir Henry Cotton was not conscious of the implication in that declaration, the United States of India. But he made that declaration — under the aegis of Great Britain. We may leave the aegis for a while; the aegis is there and I told you last night, as long as it is there, United States of India will be a divided nationality of India. But whatever that may be our ideal is the United States of India. But the United States of India will not be like the United States of America. Some of our provinces themselves that are under British administration now will be republican.

Those that are under Native Chiefs will be constitutional monarchies. We cannot set up republics in Mysore. We would not try to set it up and create difficulties in our way. We cannot set up republics in the Nizam's dominions. We would not try it and create difficulties. We cannot set up republics in Baroda or Patiala. These Native States must remain as principalities, monarchical States, but the popular rights must be respected there; otherwise they would not form States of the great Indian Union. And this is our ideal. This is of course, a mere fancy. I am trying to consider the problem of historical possibilities and nothing else. What is the possibility before the country, and the consideration of historical possibilities.

I think there are lawyers here who will say it falls outside the range of Section 124A: not that I am afraid of that Section (Hear, hear) because I believe that, as in Ancient India, why ancient only 100 years back, when we had the customs of *sali* in our midst, no woman was permitted to ascend the funeral pyre of her husband until she has proved her capacity to be burnt without flinching, by burning one of her fingers in the presence of her relatives, as this test was necessary, the question of the fear of pain and burning was a precondition for the woman ascending the pyre, so the conquest of fear of Section 124. A and 153. A (cheers), is an essential precondition of the man who would step forward to lead the life of a publicist in India under existing conditions. But, gentlemen, whatever that may be, the historical possibilities that present themselves before us are not many. There is this possibility of an United States of India. But if there should be a conflict we do not desire it, we do not expect it, we will not create it (Hear, hear); but if there should be a conflict and a most inevitable one, between the forces of the people and the forces of Government, then who knows what will be.

Then, perhaps, we too may have to pass through some medium stage before we can reach the ideal of *Swaraj* because concentration of forces would be necessary, and in political life democracy is not best suited. Therefore we may not directly reach the democratic ideal. It may be that we shall have to work it out through some medium stage, and I refer to it for this simple reason to give an assurance to my Muhammadan friends, because if we fail to directly reach our democratic ideal, when the Muhammadan or Hindu will equally share in the rights of self-government, if we fail to realise this ideal directly, and if the necessities are imposed upon us of concentrating the forces of the nation and setting up a dictatorship us they did in France, then look about you and see if there is any man in India, or any possibility of any one in India, being found to undertake this dictatorship. I hope the necessity will not arise; but if the necessity arises there is a dreamer of dreams in the near neighbourhood of India and he is a Mussalman. I think Ameer Habibullah has got his head on his shoulders and he sees farther than many of our leaders seem to do.

And it is not merely out of love for the Anglo-Indian life that he proposes to pay a domiciliary visit next year to India (Hear, hear and laughter). He seems to be a politician of the first water as was proved by his declaration that the Hindus and the Mussalmans in India having lived together in peace and amity for so many centuries, they ought to live in the same peace and amity now. (Hear, hear). But these are vain imaginings. Let us not indulge in these fancies even though they be of historical imagination. The fact really in, my dear friends, that the condition of India is such that we hope to attain our *Swaraj* by the most peaceful methods possible. If you ask me what are those methods, I can only say that I cannot give you a cut and dried plan of our work. No man can do so. He who says that he can give a cut and dry plan of his work and methods in politics, especially in politics of the kind in which we are engaged at the present time in India, with all respect to that man, I will say he has not applied himself properly to a consideration of the actual problem before himself, and his country. Politics, Sir, is a game of chess.

It is a game of chess in international politics. It is a game of chess in national politics also; and what a fool is he who sitting down to play a game of chess with a powerful and acute and farsighted opponent can foresee and foretell every move that he makes without knowing the move of the other party. Our move shall be determined by their move; if they put forward a Pawn and make room for their Knight we shall have to put forward our Bishop and make it impossible to the Knight to come and occupy the place of the Pawn. Just as their move will be, so must our move be, and as we do not know what their move will be tomorrow, we cannot say what our move may be tomorrow. So far in Bengal we have been engaged these two years and more in a very beautiful game of chess. The partition measure was the first move of the Government (Laughter).

It was prompted by the desire to kill, nay, the King cannot be killed, to checkmate the growing political power of the Bengali people. First of all we prayed, we petitioned, we protested, but all to no purpose. And when we saw that the Government will not listen to our prayers we put forward our small proposal of boycott. (Laughter and cheers). They laughed at us. They had never known the Bengalis to possess the strength and determination and therefore they thought, it was mere gas; it will easily evaporate (laughter); it is like the explosion of the sodawater bottle which will harm nobody. Only you let out the gas confined in the bottle, but within two months they began to scratch their head.

On the lucky day, the 4th day of the Dushehra Festival and the last day of the Durga Puja, on that day it had been the custom in Calcutta for the Marwaris to enter into forward contracts with the agents of Manchester at Calcutta to the extent of many lakhs of rupees, but on the lucky day in 1905 October, not a single forward contract for Manchester goods was made. (Cries of *Vande Mataram).* That proved that the situation was more serious than gaseous; and the Government began to consider ways and means to meet this serious situation. They saw that the strength of boycott lay very largely in our young College-going population. (Hear, hear and cheers). They saw that it was these young men who by that persuasive eloquence which is the greatest strength of well-regulated youth, they saw that our young men by the strength of their natural persuasive eloquence compelled people to desist from buying foreign goods.

The story has been told that on one occasion a high class Bengali lady was going in her coach and pair to Whiteaway Laidlaw's shop. The boys got scent of the affair and they went and placed themselves before the coach and they were asked to get out of the way; they joined their hands and said, "Mother, you are like our mother. We are like your sons. Do not go to Whiteaway Laidlaw". She said — "No, No; Coachman clear the road". Then they said, "Madam, if you are determined to go and buy foreign things of Whiteaway Laidlaw, we are determined to be crushed under the wheel of your carriage (laughter and cheers) before we shall allow the carriage to pass near the door of Whiteaway Laidlaw". What woman, what mother could resist such an appeal and the lady asked her coachman to drive her back home, (Cheers).

This is the general method that our young men adopted for helping this boycott. This was the sort of picketing in which they engaged themselves for furthering this boycott. The Government saw it; the leaders had not the time; their age and the infirmities of the age would not allow them to do picketing work of this kind, and the Government saw that these young men contributed to the strength of the boycott and the Carlyle circular was moved out. (Shame). In that circular it was made penal for school and College-going young men to be engaged in picketing work; it was made penal for school and College young men to take part in political demonstrations; it was made penal for young people reading in schools and Colleges even to cry out *Vande Mataram,* (Shame).

The Government thought that by threatening our boys with expulsion from College and University, they would bring their leaders down to their knees (Cries of Never). The Carlyle circular was published in the *Statesman* on a Sunday morning. On Tuesday, within 60 hours of the publication of the circular, we called a public meeting in Calcutta. At that meeting the President, Mr. Rasul, of the Calcutta Bar, declared in reply to the Carlyle circular, that we would have a National University of our own. (Hear, hear and cheers). The Carlyle circular was their little Pawn and we placed before it the Knight of National University.

They actually punished our boys. In Rangpur the boys were fined, the whole school was fined. The boys refused to submit to this punishment, and the guardians of the boys supported them in this matter (Hear, hear). And within a week or so of the infliction of these punishments and the consequent expulsion of boys from the Rangpur School, the National school was established in Rangpur. The Government next saw that Carlyle circulars would not do. They brought out the Goorkha sticks (cries of shame), the Gurkha clubs, excuse me. (Cries of shame). Do not cry shame. They are doing exactly what is needed in their interest. Give them credit for common humanity. The Goorkha club was brought out, the Barisal outrage was committed, the earlier outrage.

Why, Sir? people scorn to have understood the inwardness of that policy. Many people opposed Fuller for it. I never opposed him for the simple reason that he was not responsible for what took place in East Bengal under his regime. In Barisal, what happened? Barisal had taken to boycott more earnestly than any other district in Bengal. In the town of Barisal there is an European, the Manager of the Nawab of Dacca's property. His name is Meyers. He wanted a piece of bleached Manchester cloth, a piece of mull. He sent his boy to the bazaar. No man would sell a piece of *belati* cloth in the bazaar of Barisal. Meyers appealed to the District Superintendent of Police. He sent his Constable to the bazaar to get a piece of mull, foreign mull, for Mr. Meyers.

The shopkeepers refused to sell foreign mull. The D. S. P. reported the matter to the District Magistrate. The District Magistrate wrote a letter to Aswini Kumar Dutta and the latter was something like this. He said, "My dear Aswini Kumar Datta.

What is it that Mr. Meyers cannot get a piece of foreign cloth in the Barisal bazaar? I am told that no man will sell a piece of foreign mull without a permit from you. Will you kindly give a permit to the bearer for a piece of foreign mull for the use of Mr. Meyers". He gave a permit because Meyers was an Englishman and Meyers had his mull, but what became, sir, of the prestige of British authority in Barisal. That proved that Aswani Kumar Dutta had become a greater power in the eye of his people than the representatives of King Edward himself. The situation was serious, exceedingly serious. If there be any landed proprietor here, he will understand the seriousness of the situation in Barisal so far as the Government is concerned, because every landed proprietor knows that if one man in his village becomes more powerful than his own agent he tries to check him, in order to prove before all the villagers that he is a man of straw.

So Government had to prove it to Barisal that Aswani Kumar Dutta and those leaders who had worked were men of straw. When this thing happened, Fuller was in East Bengal. He had some bad experience before also. I happened to be associated with one of these things. Fuller went to Dacca on Sunday and was met with great trouble. The students left the city and went on picnic 3 miles distant from the town with a view to avoid welcoming the Lieutenant-Governor. But the next day, on Monday, I happened to go to Dacca from Mymensingh, and when I arrived at the station, I found 5,000 men gathered there to receive me (cries of *Vande Mataram);* it showed the spirit of the people, the determination of the people of East Bengal, to give greater recognition to their own men than to a Governor that had been forced upon their heads. So Fuller when he had received intimation of the state of things in Barisal, he took down train to Agra.

Lord Curzon was in Agra then and they put their heads together and dictated the policy that Fuller carried out later on. It was from Agra that the telegram was sent to Assam calling up the Gurkha Military Police to Barisal, and at Barisal when Fuller went he invited Aswani Kumar Dutt to his board the steamer and there insulted the whole lot of them (Cries of shame). No, no. What is the meaning of it. The meaning of it was this. Sir B. Fuller had to prove it to the people of Bengal that the man on whom they depended, the man on whom they looked forward to was a straw before the breath of the governing power. That was what he wanted to show; and why were the Gurkhas lot loose upon inoffensive people. [Shame] No, no. It was clear it was a declaration to the people, it was a demonstration to the people of Barisal of their utter helplessness to protect themselves against the wrath of the Government. Every Gurkha outrage was a challenge to the people of Barisal to call upon their leaders to protect them. It meant this.

You boycotted British goods, because Aswani Kumar Dutta wanted you to do so. Call him and let him protect you from the outrage. Now, what was the meaning of what was done in Barisal, and what did we do; we gradually worked; we lay low for a while. These things had to be adopted in life and for a while we did lie low. But after a while what did happen. The Government had thought to demoralise the Barisal people by the application of Gurkha sticks. The nation refused to be demoralised. (Hear, hear). And then at Barisal daring the conference they played the same game. They tried to prove the utter helplessness of the whole leaders of Bengal and what happened.

They found that there was a strength in the people, the existence of which had never been dreamt of by them. We did not beat them; we did not mean to do them any harm, but I think there is proof of a greater strength in desisting to reply to an unjust outrage sometimes than in replying to that outrage. To beat a man when you were beaten is not always easy. But sometimes I think it is easy to allow yourselves to be beaten instead of beating them back, and it happened in Barisal. When the police applied their sticks upon the boys, not a man moved, every man kept to his place. I was coming back, because this outrage was started after some of us had gone a few paces ahead. Surendranath Bannerji led the procession, (laughter and cheers). We were moving out in three files deep leaving half the road absolutely free for the general traffic.

This was the object of the Police; this was the object with which it is required that people carrying or conducting a procession through crowded thoroughfares, should demand a license from the authorities so that the traffic in the streets may not be interfered with, and though we did not take out a license, we kept half the street free for ordinary traffic. But that was our offence — walking in quiet military order — that was our offence. But they did not touch us. The instructions were not to touch those, who were regarded more or less as leaders of the people. The instruction was evidently to beat those whose names were not known to the country, so that by leaving the leaders scot free and beating the following crowd, a sentiment would be created among the friends and relations against these leaders. That was the game that they were playing. And an assault was started when we had gone a few paces a head. When we heard, we turned our back.

I was going back; when I came near the culvert leading from the Rajah Bahadur Haveli, I saw the processionists standing shoulder to shoulder in the middle of the culvert. The Police made a charge before my eyes. A stick fell on the head of a man. He fell down flat upon the culvert. The others would not, but three men - one man stepped forward to hold the head of the man who had fallen down, another man got hold of his feet, and the third man got hold of his loins and carried him away, and the gap that was made was immediately closed. There was no cowardice, there was not the least desire to avoid being beaten. There was a bravery, a courage like the hidden powers of a volcano and the Government was taken aback. They thought that the sight of the stick would dispense a Bengalee crowd. But when a Bengalee crowd allowed itself to be beaten in this way without moving an inch, they thought there must be something behind the Bengalee nation. Are they manufacturing arms and ammunition somewhere? That was what some foolish official asked; but every one saw that there had grown up in the Bengalees a determination which it would not be easy to acquire.

After the Barisal incident we showed the strength of our determination to suffer. We openly declared that we would not suffer these outrages any more. In Mymensingh a public meeting was advertised. I was there then. On the day the meeting was to be held, the leader of the Mymensingh Bar sent for the Police Inspector to the Bar Library and told him we are having a public meeting today. If you come there as a respectable citizen you are welcome to do so. If you come with warrants to arrest any of us, no resistance will be offered to you or even without a warrant if you peacefully and lawfully come to arrest any of us, not the least resistance will be offered in the discharge of your public duty; but if you come in the name of law with your regulation stick to break our heads, heads will be broken on both sides. We had our meeting, and Babu Ananth Bandu Saho presided, and in his speech from the chair he repeated what I have said before the whole assembly. We did the same thing here and there. They had proscribed the cry of *Vande Mataram* in Bengal. They had by a circular prohibited and made it illegal to cry out *Vande Mataram* in public streets. What did our people do, and mostly young people. It was illegal and punishable to cry in a street.

All right! When a Policeman or an European officer passed by the street young people would jump out of the street, cross the drain and come to private ground and cry out *Vande Mataram.* That was absolutely legal. By this means we brought down the prestige of the Government in Bengal in the estimation of the people. I have recited all these things simply to tell you that our moves at every step had to be determined by the moves of the Government. I have told all these series of things that happened in Bengal during the past year simply with a view to prove that the game in which we are engaged just now is a game of chess and our moves are always determined by what move the Government makes, but a game of chess is played with 32 figures, and it is placed within the limits of 64 squares. The game of politics in which we are engaged will have to be played by 300 millions of figures and more, and the squares are almost infinite in number. Therefore, although it may be possible to figure before yourself every possible move that your Pawn may make, you can do so only when the possibilities range within 64 squares.

You cannot do it when the possibilities are almost infinite. Therefore, dear friends, our methods, our ways and means shall always be determined by the methods, by the ways and means adopted by those who are playing against us in this great national and political game. I cannot give you a cut and dry programme. I deem it the height of folly in any man to demand a cut and dry programme in a matter of this kind. I have presented to you the ideal in general terms. I have spoken to you of the possibilities of the future historic development of India. I have indicated to you briefly the nature of the game that the Government is playing, and I have also given you some idea of the way that we are playing our own part of the game as against our opponents. I cannot give you a clearer idea of our ways and means, but there are one or two general questions that may well be discussed, and if you ask me to state in general terms what are the methods, what are the means, what are the instruments by which you hope to farther this ideal of *Swaraj* in this country, my reply shall be that these means and methods are included under what is known in political science as methods of passive resistance.

Passive resistance is not the antonym of active resistance. There can be no resistance which is not an active resistance. Even the determination to allow a man to beat you is something of the activity of the will power in you. There can be no resistance which is not the act of something. What then does passive resistance mean. It means not resistance that is not active resistance, but resistance that is not aggressive resistance. Passive resistance is not non-active but non-aggressive resistance. We stand upon our own rights. We stand within the limits of the law that we have still in the country. We shall respect that law, as I said yesterday, as long as that law shall respect our primary rights which constitute the authority of every Government, whether that Government be a despotic Government or a constitutional Government, but rights which no Government can create, and which, therefore, no Government can destroy. As long as the laws of this Government respect our primary rights of life or person, property and other similar primary rights, so long we propose to keep ourselves within the bounds of law; and passive resistance means resistance offered by a people from within the limits of such law.

That is in general terms our method. The broad application of this method of passive resistance has brought out two or three special movements in India. One movement is the boycott movement. It is a movement of passive resistance. The other movement is the movement of National Education, and the third movement is the movement for the organisation of our public life, building it up from our village life, and by these three means, Boycott, National education and Swadeshi included in the boycott, and by the organisation of the forces and the resources of the people and by setting up a scheme of practical self-government running parallel to the officialised institutions of self-government in the country to find a school of civic duties for the people by this means we hope. God willing, to achieve our end without any serious trouble, without any serious discomforts to those who are placed in authority above us. These are, broadly speaking, our methods. The question of Boycott both as an economic movement and as a political movement, it will not be possible for me to consider at the close of an address which has extended, I believe, already to more than two hours. Neither can I consider tonight the question of National education, nor do I desire at the fag end of my address tonight to tell you what we are doing and how we are doing it with a view to organise the public life of Bengal, with a view to set up a system of real self-government independent of the Government institutions, of local self-government in the country. These things, God willing, I shall consider on another occasion.

Boycott

Mr. Chairman and Friends. — On Friday night in closing my address on the ways and means for the attainment of *Swaraj* I referred to general trends of the movement known as that, of passive resistance, and I tried to explain as briefly as I could, what passive resistance meant. It means this. I will repeat it briefly again. It means that we shall keep ourselves within the bounds of law in asserting the will of the nation against the great political wrong — why political — against the great wrong economically, politically, morally and even spiritually that the domination of one people over another universally inflicts. In carrying out a programme of passive resistance it should be our endeavour always to keep ourselves in the right and to place those who may be opposed to us at every step, in the wrong. That is a thing which will always have to be borne in mind, and it is this characteristic of the movement in Bengal that has sown consternation into the councils of the mighty.

Our boys, our youngman, our old men, they have always scrupulously been on the offensive. They have always kept themselves within the bounds of law. The Courts of law may have condemned them, but they are not always guided by considerations of law. Considerations of public policy sometimes in every country and not very rarely in India, control the verdict of our public Courts. No conviction, no promotion has been a notorious principle in the administration of Criminal justice by the subordinate Judiciary in more than one Province in India; and that being so it is not at all surprising that the Courts of law should have declared certain acts of our people here and there as trespassing beyond the limits of law, and they may have sent some of our men to jail for alleged breach of the law, but these judgements in many cases if they are published along with the records of evidence will not carry conviction to an impartial public.

So, sir, all through our campaign of passive resistance in Bengal it has been our earnest endeavour to keep ourselves within the limits of law, and by this self-restraint by this very regard in our determination to oppose the despotic will of the present Government, by this very regard for the laws of that Government we have to a very large extent made them powerless. This is a matter which you are always to bear in mind in carrying on a programme of passive resistance. An Anglo-Indian characterised the methods of the new party as are explained to you by me as unconstitutional. I wish the writer had either read or understood what I had said on this point in my previous address.

I have never either through the columns of my paper, *New India* or from the public platform advocated as yet any form of lawlessness, and yet this honest journalist (cries of shame and boycott it) says that I will have nothing to do with constitutional agitation in India, because as I said, India is not a constitutional Government (Hear, hear). But there are laws even in India, and I hold that our agitation should continue to be as it has been in the past. Our agitation should continue to be in the future lawful so far as the laws of the Government did not violate the primary rights of man (Hear, hear and cheers).

I know not, Sir, what more clear and definite declaration could possibly be made by any one in a matter of this kind, and if, after this declaration, the charge is repeated to mislead our moderate friends, I care not for others (Hear, hear); if the charge is repeated to mislead our moderate friends that we advocate lawlessness, it will be done no longer through ignorance or misconception, but through deliberate dishonesty. (Laughter and cheers and cries of shame). Keep then, my dear friends, keep yourselves within the right, and by being yourself in the right always, put those who oppose you in the wrong, and I say this especially, because it has been said here and there that there has grown up something like an offensive spirit in the people of Madras in consequence of my utterances (no, no, not at all). I do not ask you to sacrifice under any condition your national self-respect. But I do ask you to cultivate strength, determination, fixity of purpose, and when you have strength, cultivate self-respect (Hear, hear). There is no self-restraint unless there be strength. The self-restraint of the weak is an unreal something.

It is not a virtue. It is no self-restraint. It is cowardice pure and simple. It is selfishness, let there be no mistake on this point. We must cultivate strength, and when we are strong, we must apply the break to our strength. Keep it within the bounds of law, of decorum, of ordinary humanity, because, remember this, that patriotism is good, excellent, divine, only when it furthers the ends of universal humanity (Certainly), Nationality divorced from humanity is a source of weakness and evil and not of strength and good. Europe has committed a mistake. It has been committing this mistake for many hundreds of years past Europeans talk of humanity, but their humanity is not humanity, but white-inanity (Laughter and cheers); and what is needed for you and me is not to respect white-manity but to respect humanity, not to ask for brown-manity but to ask for humanity which includes within itself white, brown, black and yellow, all the races of the world.

In our campaign of passive resistance, we shall therefore keep always these two things in view just as I said, respect for the law, provided the law respect be primary rights of the individual and regard for the claims not of any particular section of the human race, nay not even our own section, but regard for the claims of the whole human race, irrespective of the creed and colour and climate. This movement of passive resistance includes, as it is, the most prominent and the correct feature or instrument, the boycott movement (Hear, hear). The boycott movement I told is an organic part of the real *Swadeshi* movement. We were asked by the Viceroy to cultivate honest Swadeshism, and Lord Minto under stood by honest Swadeshim non-political Swadeshism. He understood by it the movement for the promotion of the arts and industries of the nation, consistently with the open door in trade and commerce. Honest Swadeshism is Swadeshism within the limits of the free trade policy. That is one thing, and honest Swadeshism is Swadeshism without any political reference or motive behind it. We should have been glad, Sir, to follow the advice of such an august personage if he could altogether separate not only in India, but in any part of the world, the economic sphere of the people from their politics.

Honest Swadeshism is said to be economic Swadeshism, but every tiro in political economy knows that there can be no economics divorced from politics, economics and politics are organically related to one another, and India cannot consider the two apart, separated from and unconnected with one another. Economic Swadeshism may be possible in a free country. Not only in a free country, it may be possible in a country that has fully developed its manufacturing industries. It may be possible in a country which governs itself and has made considerable progress in the manufacture of commodities. Economic Swadeshism may be possible, for instance, in self-governing England which has developed manufacturing industries to so large an extent.

But the nation that comes low in the field of world competition, a nation that has at its command almost endless natural resources, a nation that is capable of producing almost infinite quantities of raw materials, but that has not the means and appliances of working out finished commodities from all these raw materials, for such a nation, specially when it is under the domination of another nation, — a commercial nation, a manufacturing nation which controls and regulates the fiscal policy of the people in the interest not unfrequently of the rulers, the manufacturing country (cries of shame), — for such a nation economic Swadeshism is an utter impossibility. England has something to do with the decay of indigenous industry in India, and that something, was it merely, Sir, an economic something or a political economic something. Did she not impose restrictions upon our own industries in the earlier days of the East India Company's rule with a view to help and farther her own industries (cries of yes)? And when our industries, though in those days could to a very large extent fairly compete with English' industries in certain matters were strangled by the application of political power (pity), is it fair, I ask (most unfair), to ask us now, to cultivate honest Swadeshism, non-political Swadeshism, mere economic Swadeshism (cries of no, no) Why, even now, are they cultivating the honest fiscal policy absolutely free from economic reference? If they had done it there should be some justification for asking us to divorce politics from economics. But what is this 5 per cent, excise duty on the coarse yarn that have been imposed on the product of the Bombay mills.

Is that honest economics? The Government of India must at least do this, must repeal this 5 per cent, excise duty before it can consistently with decency ask us to divorce our economics from our politics. There are, I believe, even in our midst our own men who advise us to separate economics from politics (cries of no, no, laughter). I must tell you one thing. If you allow any foreign matter to enter into your hand even if that matter be such an excellent matter as boycott, it will do good. Keep boycott in its own place. But there are our own people who advise us to divorce economics from politics, and they say that it is necessary to separate Swadeshism from politics, because if we do so, we shall be able to secure the support to this Swedeshi movement of large numbers of people who are in the Government service or who otherwise are afraid of doing anything, which the Government do not countenance; and with a view to secure the support by these means, practically of the whole nation on behalf of the Swadeshi movement they ask us to keep politics and Swadeshism apart from one another.

The argument seems to my mind to fail to recognise the psychology of the situation. No Government servant needs be afraid of using country products in preference to foreign imports (Hear, hear). No Government servant is prevented or can be precluded from buying shares in Industrial Companies except under certain circumstances, from setting up shops and stores in different places. So far as non-political Swadeshism is concerned, it can only promote the production of indigenous articles by organising Joint Stock Companies, by opening shops and stores, and by encouraging the use of indigenous products in preference to foreign imports. And this is all that was done under existing condition. This is the utmost that Government Servants can possibly do to further the cause of economic Swadeshism (Hear, hear). But what about the general population in the country. Economic Swadeshism before *Swaraj* aims at a stimulating production; increasing the quantity of native products, improving the quality of our industries and by larger production and better quality, honest Swadeshism helps gradually to push foreign imports out of the Indian market. That is the portion of honest Swedeshism.

I put it to you, Sir, is this a practical plan of Industrial development in India under her peculiar position? (No, no). Can you promote the production of manufacturing articles, manufacturing commodities, in the face of the killing competition with foreign imports. It is all well to say, lay out your money, bring out hidden treasures, (how many hundreds of crores it was, according to Lord Curzon, I just now forget). There is a good deal of hidden capital, unused capital lying idle in India, and Lord Curzon advised as to bring it out and to start machines to open factories, and by means of these factories, by a natural process through fair competition drive the foreign imports out of our markets. This is the recipe of those who claim to be eminently practical politicians.

Well, the hidden capital of India, if there be such a thing, will it come out at the bidding of the National Congress or of any body else, any more than the people will give up Government service at our bidding? They declared our boycott propaganda to be impracticable, because I believe they will not give up Government service at our bidding. I consider, Sir, that their programme is a practical programme, the programme of honest non-political purely economic Swadeshi. But I ask it in all seriousness, will the hidden Capital of India come out of its cover at the bidding of my moderate friends, while at their bidding has not risen in the country a spirit of Commercial cooperation. Can you start factories of the type of the dimensions and capacity of those the products of which are driving the products of your own hand-loom? Can you open factories like those of Manchester, Newcastle or Birmingham, all centres of manufacturing Industry, and if you can, would it be proper, would it be beneficial, would it be conducive to the highest good of the nation to set up an imitation of England, Germany, and America, huge-factories for the production of commodities?

Those who have bean to England and America, those who know something of the economic problems of the European countries, those who know something of the results of these large factories, they know it that in Europe and America, humanity is being ruthlessly sacrificed at every centre of manufacturing industry, for the production of commodity (Hear, hear). Are you to follow the same ruinous course and sacrifice Indian humanity for the production of commodity? Japan has taken many things from Europe but one thing Japan has refused to take from Europe; that is the European Factory system (Hear, hear). The strength of the nation lies in the moral stamina of the people.

But factories will kill that moral stamina. Huge factories concentrate population at particular centres, bring people away from their homes, detach them from their friends and family. Starting of big factories may or may not be able to solve the economic problem, but even if they do, it will be at irreparable risk to the moral, spiritual life of the nation and if your moral stamina is destroyed, if the spiritual ideals, the manhood of the nation, if these are killed, what will remain for you to fight the battle of life. Our industrial ideal should not be the ideal of England or America, our industrial methods should not be the method that has been followed, and not followed with complete success, either by England or America, because in every Western country this industrialism has created complex problems of capital and labour, economic and moral before which the wisest statesmen, the greatest thinkers of the nation are sitting down almost in despair; and will you create the same problems in this country also?

As in every other matter so in this matter of our industrial development, we will have to follow the lead of her own genius, follow the course indicated by her own past historic fallacy, draw inspiration and strength for guidance from her own past experience and above all keep before our mind's, eye, constantly this great fact, viz. that as man liveth not by bread alone, so nations also do not live and prosper merely by the production of marketable commodity. What then is the problem of economic Swadeshism?

Your market is being flooded by foreign imports and the cheapness of those foreign imports has already killed to a large extent (and the operation will be finished within a few years), is killing and will finally kill the indigenous arts and industries of the country. How to save yourself from this killing condition is the problem even of economic Swadeshism. If you had a state of your own, if you were a self-governing people, if the government so worked entirely and absolutely in the interests of the people, then this government would have imposed protective tariff upon such foreign imports as threatened to kill native industries. This is done in every part of the world. America has protected and by protecting has developed her arts and industries. Germany has been thriving under a protective tariff.

Australia and Canada though parts of the British Empire, and elements of the British race, they too have not accepted the doctrine of free trade from the mother country as the guiding principle in her economic advancement. But she, by means of a protective tariff, prevents the introduction of cheap foreign imports within her territories. India alone cannot do it, because India is not governed by herself, nor governed in her interest and in her interest alone. What then can we do? We can do one thing, we can organise a consumer's league. It is this, in economics there is production and there is consumption. The production is useless without consumption, it is consumption that regulates production and consumption and production are organically related one to the other. Production with a view to control foreign markets is absolutely impossible in India; but we can by regulating the consumption have some sort of protection to our indigenous arts and industries and the regulation of consumption is the economics principle that underlies the boycott movement.

I am bold enough to say and doubly declare this boycott to be a great economic theory. Boycott is protection, it is the imposition of protective tariff (Hear, hear) upon the people themselves not upon the foreign imports — indirectly upon the foreign imports also — and if protection be declared as of economic value, you are welcome to declare boycott also to be of economic value. But no economist, no economist outside Manchester has ever declared protection to be a wrong.

There are consumer's leagues in Western countries. I happened to be present when I was in New York at a meeting of Consumer's league there, 7 years back. The object of that league was to use the word boycott which meant the boycotting of the produce of certain firms who sweated their labourers. In America there are certain capitalists and combination of capitalists who do not treat their labourers properly, fairly and well. They sweat their labourers, they make them reduce the position almost of slaves; and the moral sense of the community rising up in arms against this sweating labourers by the producers of commodities, organised itself into a Consumer's league.

Those who joined this league took a pledge that they would not under any circumstances buy or use articles produced by such and such a firm who sweated their labourers. There is the boycott, the boycott of those who did not deal fairly with their operatives and I have not as yet heard that a Consumer's league is either an economic folly or a great moral evil. There the Consumer's leagues are organised in the interests of the oppressed labouring population. Here our boycott, our Consumer's league has been organised in the interests of the economic protection, economic advancement and the salvation of the whole nation. We cannot compel the Government to prevent the import of cheap articles into our market that kill by an unfair competition our own industries. But we can do one thing in the country. By our own determination, we can refuse to buy foreign articles, and by refusing to buy foreign articles, we can indirectly protect our own interests by this boycott movement.

It is an uphill work. If we had a State, a single law passed by the Legislature would have compelled you and me to buy country-made things, because foreign things could not be had cheaper. But though protection is economically an excellent weapon for saving weak industries from ruinous competition from foreign industries, boycott has got this advantage Boycott not only helps to protect native industries, but it helps to develop the manhood of the nation, the spirit of self-sacrifice in the people; it strengthens the will of the people and enables them to sacrifice immediate good in view of the ultimate good. Therefore though boycott is absolutely justified on economic grounds, it has a greater claim upon our attention, and our allegiance on account of the moral issues involved in it. You ask as to give preference to indigenous arts, indigenous commodities. Do not buy foreign articles, buy your country made articles when you can get them. When you cannot get it, go in for foreign things also. I want a piece of mull, things Swadeshi. I must have it by all means from one of your mills or one of your native stores. But if you cannot have it, buy the foreign thing from any shop that you like.

This is striking at the very root of the whole movement, because in these movements that depend for their success upon the determination of the people there is each a thing as *Nishta,* faithfulness, devotion, which must be cultivated and without which the determination of the people cannot stand. I pledge myself, (no) non-boycott gentlemen pledge themselves. I desire to be abstemious, not to drink intoxicating drinks. That is an excellent desire, is it not? And every one of you will ask me to cultivate it. Do not drink anything but pure water or soda — Brahmin soda. Drink any thing, do not drink wine. But you ask me, if a friend offers and if be is offended do not mind taking a sip; if you are present at a table with a European, and if you feel hurt, do not mind taking a glass of sherry.

If you say this it may be a good thing because you will say, why, you have not the strength of will to put a stop to drinking when you are not in the table of a European. You are a weak man, and you ought to be wise and in the presence of temptation you ought to rise above temptation. Therefore why do you din yourself, why do you pat such unreasonable restrictions upon yourself, that you will never drink a drop of wine. Now what will be the actual result? Has Temperance propaganda proceeded along these lines in any part of the world? Has *teetotalism* furnished in any part of the world reform on such humanitarian and tolerant lines. (No, no).

Touch not even a small dose of that which intoxicates the brain, that has been the injunction everywhere of temperance reform, and why simply because all these temperance reforms can only proceed upon the determination of the people to avoid the strong drinks and this determination can be kept up by a rigid law of exclusion and if once you allow a man to drink and yet call himself up a total abstainer, you open the floodgate of temptation, and you destroy the motive power, the strength of determination, by which you hope to carry out your programme of reform. Therefore in Boycott also, the psychological law must be applied; boycott must be absolute, not of all goods, that is impossible; but within certain limits it must be; absolute because with an absolute boycott, you cannot keep up the strong determination of the people, you cannot keep up the *Nishta* of the race. That is what is essential; we have not boycotted everything foreign, we do not propose to do so either.

They, who say, so misunderstand and misinterpret us. But if we had a state of our own we would have imposed protective tariff against such imports only as threatened to kill our indigenous industries; not upon all, nay, not even the picketed proposes to live isolated from the rest of the world. We have our natural resources to develop. We propose, God willing, to be not only an agricultural, but a manufacturing nation still, and we want to enter upon fair terms into competition with the other races in the markets of the world, and because we desire to do so, we must keep also our door open for the introduction of foreign made articles, because exports and imports are organically related one to the other. If you want to send your men to foreign countries you must leave the door open for foreign produce to enter your own country and your own market.

If we had a State organisation of our own, what we would have done is this, we would have taken a survey of our industries, we would have considered what industries have a chance of gaining entrance into the markets of the world, what industries in India had a large future before them, what raw materials we have available, raw materials within the reach of the labouring population within reach of being carried to the world of our own markets, to our own ports, by this means we would have to determine what thing is that we can produce or what are those things that we can produce best and cheapest, and we would have to concentrate our attention upon those things and exclude only those things from our markets that showed a tendency to destroy the chances of the protection of these native industries, not of others that would be the right thing.

No Government imposes all-round tariff unless it be for purely fiscal reasons, sometimes under exceptional circumstances, every country may have to taxed, but taxation there is not for the purpose of protection but for purely fiscal reasons, because Government want money to carry on the administration, to pay for the debts of the war and for such other reasons and therefore it must tax on all articles indiscriminately. They may possibly be taxed with a view to replenish its lean exchequer. That is a reason, but tariff is not imposed by any nation upon every kind of foreign imports. It is imposed only on those articles that are likely to enter into a dangerous and ruinous competition with the indigenous articles produced in the country.

That being so, if we had a state of our own we would have discriminated, we would have taken into consideration our industrial capabilities and we would have guided our protective tariff in the light of the capabilities of our native industries. But, we have not a government and therefore in our boycott we cannot altogether adopt that scientific method, here the method must be a little rough and ready, and what we have done is this. We have taken up three or four articles just for the present that appear to be affected by those foreign imports. We have taken the textile fabric. We produce cotton in this country, and this cotton goes out to England and comes back as yarn or textile fabrics. Now, our first boycott is the boycott of foreign clothing, and here the boycott is absolute, there is no exception. We have boycotted foreign salt. Here also the boycott is absolute. We have boycotted foreign sugar. Here also the boycott is absolute. We have boycotted enamelled articles that are killing, if they have not already killed, our brass and bell-metal industries.

These are the four things that we have boycotted, foreign cloth, foreign salt, foreign sugar and foreign enamelled articles, and in regard to these four-things the boycott is absolute. In regard to others the boycott is not of an absolute character. The general truth in fact is, so far as it is practicable, support home industries and give preference to home products even if they are dearer than foreign imports. That is the general principle of boycott, but in its application we have laid special stress upon 3 or 4 things, as I have indicated them already, *viz.* upon cloth, salt, sugar and enamelled wares, and partly also upon glass wares and generally upon all articles of luxury. This is the extent of our boycott. We never proposed to boycott every article. We do not propose to boycott English books, we do not propose to boycott scientific instruments. We do not propose to boycott machinery. We do not propose to boycott arms and ammunition (laughter.) We shall want them. We shall get them. We shall strengthen our material life with the help of all these. Wherefrom shall we get them.

Let it not be said if we are boycotters — why use Railways or trams, or why read English books or use electric fans and electric light. No, Sir, we cannot go back to barbarism. That will not be helpful to rational growth but we shall buy foreign goods always with an eye to this that by using foreign goods we do not injure the possibilities of the production of those goods in our own country. That is what must be done and in regard to three or four things the boycott must be absolute. Under no circumstances shall we any foreign textile fabric, under no circumstances shall take a pinch of foreign sugar or a pinch of salt; but we shall buy instruments and other things wherever we can get them. As regards books, in the domain of knowledge there is no trade such as we have in the domain of commodities.

All knowledge is divine; the sciences, the philosophies, the arts of Europe are not European. They are all God divine and every man who has a mind partakes in the general mental and intellectual life of the whole of the human race because all minds are and that mind is the mind of God. Every one who has the sense of the beautiful in him has a right, a native right upon every article of arts, upon everything that is beautiful because it is of God divine and all beauty is one. In the domain of learning, there is no distinction of race, and colour and clime. Knowledge is one. Science is one. Art in the higher domains is one. And every child of God has a natural right to all those things wherever they may be formed or grown. No, we do not mean to avoid these things. This, then, gentlemen, is our boycott movement. But the question arises about the political aspect of boycott. Industrially, this is what boycott means. But it is also a political weapon, a political weapon in this sense. It is a weapon of passive resistance.

It is a weapon that is capable of retaliating the iniquity that is inflicted upon us by the domination of another people. If the

English are: merely our political rulers as the Moghuls were, as the Pathans were before the Moghuls, the case would have been different. But unfortunately the British Government in India from the days of the Company has been like the mythical mermaids — half trader and half ruler. That ruler we may obey, but when the ruler enters the arena of trade he must submit to ordinary law of pushing and elbowing that is common to the commercial life. And yet one misfortune is that the present Government in this country uses its authority as a Government for the protection of its interests as a trader. Let it not be said that I am misconstruing and misinterpreting the benign purpose of the Government. I have my authority for this statement, an that authority in no less than the late Viceroy of India.

Lord Curzon himself, speaking to certain miners, declared, 'Your Work lies in exploitation. My work lies in administration and exploitation and administration are parts of the same duty the Government of India. What does it mean? It mean that the authority of the administration is to he applied for helping exploitation and the resources that exploitation placed in the hands of the exploiter, the Chambers of Commerce, are to be utilised for the purposes of administration. The Government House extends its hands across the streets to the Chamber of Commerce and the Chamber of Commerce takes it by one hand and stretches the other hand to the Government House, and between the two they manage to exploit for administration and administer for exploitation; and yet in the face of such a significant declaration from one than whom no greater authority over existed in this country for making such a declaration, yet even in the face of such a distinct declaration from the head of the Government of India, we are asked, Sir, to divorce politics from economics and economics from politics. What has happened in Eastern Bengal? We declared a boycott of British goods.

That was, as I have said, economically the organisation of Consumer's league. We are asked not to buy British goods. Is it not within the rights of every citizen to induce his fellow citizen to do or not to do something which in itself is not illegal. Is not to buy foreign goods illegal? Is not to use Manchester cloth illegal? Is it illegal not to use foreign salt or not to taste foreign sugar? Is it illegal for a man to persuade his neighbour not to use it (No. no). What do we do? Any thing more than what the temperance preacher does? That is picketing. Why? Not only in temperance; you do picketing work in our temple fairs. It is not illegal for the Christian *Padre* to stand in the front of a temple in fairs and call names and try to lower the religious ideals of the country in the estimation of the people. That is picketing, I dare say. The *Padre* says 'don't go and worship these gods'. Is it not picketing? The temperance preacher stands not far from the door of the grog shop, and he commences to preach against the use of liquors. He asks people not to drink. Is that not picketing? Does it not inflict injury on the poor man who sells liquor? and yet who ever heard that this picketing is condemned as criminal. But people were harassed and prosecuted, handed down by the Police, held up before the Magistrate and sent to jail simply because they asked their fellow men, there countrymen, their neighbours, their friends, their covillagers to desist from supporting foreign industries and articles. But it is due to this fact — administration and exploitation are parts of the same duty in the Government of India.

There is a very large and important mart on the banks of the river Magna which is really the Ganges in Eastern Bengal and a little over a year ago one flat loaded with Liverpool salt was sent to that mart. The coolies of that mart refused to unload the flat. The flat was sent by Turner Morrison & Co., Calcutta, and what happened? Possibly Turner Morrison & Co., when they heard that no cooly in Bhara Bazaar would touch their salt must have informed the authority of it. That is my inference.

I do not know the fact but the fact was that in the Course of three or four days the Sub-Divisional Magistrate of Kasargung within whose jurisdiction Bhara Bazaar is located came to that Bazaar and called for the chief officer of the zemindar who owns that Bazaar and asked him what it was. "What is it, Sir, that these coolies refused to touch foreign salt and will not unload the flat". He said, "What can I do". That Magistrate said, "You must be responsible for it, you must be working for it". He said, 'You call the coolies'. The coolies were brought. The Magistrate asked. "Why do you refuse to carry foreign salt from the flat to the godown". They said, "We are not to do so" "Ordered by whom," asked the Magistrate. "By our Biradhari, by our caste priest and if we touch it our *hookha* will be stopped, we shall be put out of caste". The Magistrate was non-plussed. He could not catch the Manager and Turner Morrison & Co, had to send a consignment of coolies from Calcutta to unload the salt at Bhara Bazaar. But the significant fact in this connection is the anxiety of the Sub-Divisional Magistrate to help the unloading of the foreign salt at Bhara Bazaar. Why? Was it a part of his duty to see that Turner Marrison & Co. did not suffer demurrage? Was he paid for it? (cries of no, no.) This same Sub-Divisional Magistrate had no time to go and make a local enquiry into a most pitiable case. It was the case of a young girl of 14 who had been one night when she went, out of her hut decoyed by a number of *gundas*.

After a week she was found in a wretched condition in a jungle, thrown away by them. She was brought. The case was instituted. It was a case of rape, inhuman outrage on that Hindu girl and the Sub Divisional Magistrate had no time to go and make a local enquiry (cry of shame). Does it not prove exploitation and administration are parts of the same duty in the Government of India? Let those of our friends who ask us to separate politics from boycott, politics from Swadesism, let them work out the separation of administration from exploitation in the policy of the Government of India (Hear, hear).

Let the Government of India refuse to utilise the powers of administration for purpose of exploitation, and then we may justly be asked by the officials and by our Moderate friends to work out a divorce between politics and pure Swadesism. The fact is, my dear friends that this Swadesism or boycott is not a mere economic movement. No economic movement is purely economic. Politics and economics are indissolubly bound up together in every country, so it is in India. There are special reasons which I have already placed before you why it is impossible to work out a divorce between politics and economics, politics and industries in India. Swadesism must associate itself with politics and when Swadesism associates itself with politics, it becomes boycott, and this boycott is a movement of passive resistance.

It is a movement of the determination of the people not only to save the industries of the nation but also to create those forces in the community which by passive methods work out the problem of *Swaraj*. Boycott in Bengal is not boycott of foreign goods. In it is included other than textile fabrics, sugar, salt. We have boycotted honorary offices to some extent. In East Bengal not a single popular man offered to stand for election to the New Legislative Council and the time is coming when they will boycott Municipalities and District Boards also. The meaning of this boycott is this. It desires to reduce the Government to Shylock's pound of flesh rule. You have political authority over us. We recognise that authority. You are entitled to all taxes. We shall pay them but nothing more than the taxes. We shall pay municipal rates but there our work is done. You shall have to look to the sweeping and the cleaning of the streets. We shall pay the taxes but nothing more than the payment of the taxes.

You shall have to carry on the administration yourself. A local Anglo-Indian paper finds a strange contradiction in my speech the other night when I said that we are people governing the country, and yet we have no share in the Government of the country; and he could not understand the Subtlety of the oriental intellect. He could not understand that both the things might be true. We might govern and yet we might not govern (laughter). I wonder if he understands the mystery of the Trinity. There are three Gods and yet the three are one. The Chinese could understand this arithmetic that one and one and one make three, they say. Yet what Indian ever said that this doctrine Trinity was a foolish doctrine? There is transcendental truth in this doctrine of Trinity; we have our own Vedantic conception of the Trinity.

We understand these things, but the *Mail* could not understand. How is it that we govern and yet we do not govern? The how is easily explained. We govern the country and yet, we do not know that we govern he country. *Maya, Maya* means this, want of knowledge; the removal of *Maya* creates no new factor. It simply gives a new meaning to the old factor, and it is the want of thin meaning in the factor that we govern the country that makes the difference between *Swaraj* and *Pararaj* and in this boycott and by this boycott we propose to create in the people consciousness of the *Pararaj* on the one hand and the desire for *Swaraj* on the other. It is by the assertion of the determination of the people against the despotism of the Government within absolutely legal bounds that we can hope to kill the *Maya* that has overcome us and that is the end of the boycott politically. We shall reduce the Government to the pound by the flesh rule. They say, 'Can you boycott all Government offices'. Who ever said that we would? Whoever said that there would be found not a single Indian to serve the Government or the European community here? But what we can do is this. We can make the Government impossible, without entirely making it impossible, for them to find people to serve them. We did it in East Bengal. Lord Minto admits it. In his letter to Sir Bampfylde Fuller in reply to his resignation letter, what does he say? He said that an organised attempt was being made in West Bengal to make the administration impossible and you have done well to resign.

Lord Minto recognised the possibility of the people by an organised attempt to make the administration impossible. The administration may be made impossible in a variety of ways. It is not actually that every Deputy Magistrate should say I won't serve in it. It is not that when one man resigns no body will be found to take up his place. Not that. But if you create this spirit in the country the Government service will gradually imbibe this spirit and they will occasionally strike work, and a whole office might go into strike.

That does not put an end to the administration, but it creates endless complications in the work of the administration and if those complications are created in every part of the country, the administration would have been brought to a deadlock and it has still made it nonetheless impossible and the primary thing is prestige of the government and the boycott strikes at the root of that prestige. This determination of the people to assert themselves within absolutely legal bounds against the despotic authority of the Government takes away naught from that authority, but that Magic, that illusory thing which they call prestige which is more powerful, more potent than the authority itself and we propose to do this, by means of boycott.

Boycott is not a great folly. There are people to whom the words of the Englishmen are as good as gospel truth and for their benefit it may be said that Professor Seeley, the author of the Expansion of England, himself confessed it that, if at any time the

Indian people became practically of one mind not to help our administration we would have to quit the country at once (cheers). This is what Professor Seeley said and boycott means an attempt to unite the determination of the people of India with a view to the application of that determination upon the Government of the country to cure their despotic character, and in this we are not moved by any hatred. We do not hate, Sir, the foreigner, we do not hate the British, nay not even the Government. We want to be indifferent to them. That is all (laughter and cheers), benevolently indifferent to them, and if there is such a thing as benevolent despotism I think there may be such a thing as benevolent indifference.

We desire to turn our faces away from the Government House, turn it to the hats of the people. We desire to stop our mouth so far as the appeal to Government is concerned and to open our mouth with a new appeal, a new petition or application to our own countrymen, to our own people, to the masses of our own people. This is the psychology, this is the ethics and this is the spiritual significance of the boycott movement. A boycott of all Government offices will not be complete. No body says it will be complete. But we can do one thing. The Government Service has extraneous value attached to it, a value which is more than the actual money that a Government servant receives from the Government. There are cases of men with an income of Rs. 1,00. a year giving security to the extent of Rs. 10,000 with a view to secure the post of a Treasurer on Re. 80 a month.

This man himself can keep two treasurers for his own *cutcheri* and yet he wants to become a treasurer in a Collectorate, simply for the sake of its prestige, the social position that goes with the Government service. We can kill that at any rate. We can induce Government service to its money value 'laughter; if we can't reduce it lower, not that no man shall serve the Government, but whoever serves Government social opinion may one day bring him down to the position of a *Vratya* who is not a Brahman but was having failed to pass through the ceremony of *Upanayanam,* falls short of Brahmanhood. We can reduce every Indian in Government service to position of a man who has fallen off from the dignity of Indian citizenship.

We can do something more by the application of our social opinion, drive those to Government service who do not find any other opening for earning a livelihood, reduce them to what is known in our *smrithi* as *apadharma.* Certain things are prohibited, but in times of famine when the alternative is to eat the prohibited food or death, the *Shasira* permits the use of prohibited food. That is *apadharma* and when the alternative before the man is death or Government service we shall allow him the Utter. We can reduce in this way the value of the Government service in this country and if we do it, it will be as good as boycott, because people who will go there are those driven by extreme necessity.

Social opinion will not encourage any man to go and seek Government service. No man shall receive social honours, because he is a *hakim* or a *munsiff* or a *bazar sheristadar.* These we can do and if we do it as I said, it will be practically as good as boycott. There was a time, and even now it is so in some parts of the country, a man would not sell shoes or leather goods if he was a Brahman. There was a time, and still it obtains in some parts, when no Brahman or Kshatriya would earn by selling shoes. Yet it is conceivable that a man might be reduced to the extreme necessity of opening a shop for the sale of leather goods and he will earn his livelihood thereby, but he will full in the estimation of his country and countrymen.

Similarly we may reduce the Government service to something that is not very desirable, and by those means we may make the administration impossible, because if we are able to create such a public opinion in our society, then the temptations of continuing in the Government service, even when the conditions of the service require men to sacrifice their conscience or self-respect, will have no effect. Now, a man cannot give his service, only for the money, the honour of the position, the estimation in which he is held by his people and he pockets his conscience with all the insults he receives from his superiors, because he knows there is ample compensation in the *Salam* that he receives from the people. The Deputy Magistrate pockets his conscience and pockets all the insults that he receives from the official, because these things are known to nobody else; but when he goes out of office he receives *salams* from every one.

Therefore he pockets this when he comes to know that nobody else will know it. But when he goes out of the office nobody *salams* him then the temptation for sacrificing his conscience, then the self-respect for keeping his office will be reduced to a minimum; and the fact of it will be endless difficulties in maintaining the discipline of the Government offices. This is what it will come to and this is absolutely lawful, because there is no law that compels him to prostrate himself before the feet of the *Hakim*. No law can compel him to give a chair to a man who comes to his house, he may give it to an ordinary shop keeper, he may refuse that honour to the Deputy Magistrate or a Subordinate Judge. He may give his daughter in marriage to a poor beggar he may refuse any marriage alliance with the son of a Deputy Magistrate, because it is absolutely within his rights, absolutely within legal bounds. Keeping ourselves within the bounds of law we may well hope to make the administration somewhat difficult if not impossible and that is passive resistance.

Passive resistance is recognised as legitimate in England. It is legitimate in theory even in India and if it is made illegal by new legislation these laws will infringe on the primary rights of personal freedom and will tread on dangerous grounds. Therefore, it seems to me, Sir, that by means of this boycott, we shall be able to negative the work that will have to be done for the attainmet of *Swaraj*. That is negative work. Positive work will have to be done and it may create a determination in the people to attain *Swaraj*. It may create the strength of the people to sacrifice their interest, immediate interest for the good of the country. Boycott may do all these things, but without positive training no self-Government will come to the boycotter.

It will have through the organisation of our village life, organisation of our talukas and districts. Let our programme include the setting up of a machinery, for popular administration and running parallel to, but independent of the existing administration of the Government (Hear, hear) is not illegal for the people of any village to combine their labour or their money and to dig a tank their own use or sink a well for their own use or to construct a road that will take them from their village to the ordinary District Board roads. Is it unlawful? No. Is it unlawful to combine for these purposes, to combine for purposes of medical relief, to combine for purposes of educational advancement, of industrial advancement, to tax themselves subject to a central organisation with a view to work out within local limits, to remove their own wants? I dare say no one will say it is unlawful, and yet we propose to start a practical scheme of self-Government running parallel to the District Boards and Municipalities and even the Provincial Government. (Cheers). We are doing it, we have done it partly in some districts in Bengal. We are organising our Arbitration Committees in our villages. Is it unlawful, Sir, for the people to refuse to go to Courts and be heavily taxed for seeking justice at their hands and for their civil complaints being heard by men of their own choosing who will adjudicate their claims? Is it unlawful. We are organising these arbitration committees and when our organisation is complete the Law Courts will be relieved considerably of their present pressure.

Our medical men appointed by us, by the funds collected on the principle of taxation by the people themselves, will distribute medical relief. Our minor Public works will be executed by the Cooperative labour of the villagers, because we cannot always command the cooperation in money. But it is easier to combine to work out Cooperative labour in Indian villages and by means of this Cooperative labour we hope to run our own Public Works Department parallel to the Public Works Department of the District Boards and Municipalities and we propose also our own police, our own volunteers who will not usurp the functions of the Police in the matter of criminal investigation, but who will help the protection of person and property of the people.

Can you prevent half a dozen young men properly trained, properly guided, who keep themselves absolutely within the law, but who go about every night in the streets of a village keeping watch and ward over the property of the villagers and prevent burglaries and other things which are often times done with the connivance of the Police? These are things which we propose to do and once we are able to organise the country in this way, then I think, we shall prove conclusively, we shall offer a practical demonstration to our opponents and to our friendly critics who always crow on the want of capacity in the people for self-Government. We shall offer conclusive 'proof to all these people for the capacity of the Indian population to organise their forces with a view to administer their forces themselves faithfully in few things. In the providence of God we shall then be made the rotors over many things. This is our programme. This, Sir, is the method by which we hope gradually to strengthen the manhood of the nation, to create in the community the determination to work out their own salvation themselves and to give them the training in the art of civic life, cooperative work for public good, in the art of self-government. We hope to do it by these means and we purpose to supplement, strengthen, the boycott by means of a system of national education which will undertake to train up the people, the youth of the nation in such a way as will enable them to earn an independent living, independent of the Government service or those professions which are under the control of the foreign Government. The subject of national education itself will demand a separate and exhaustive treatment. So I propose to take that question up some day next week (Loud cheers).

Contribution of Islam to Indian Nationality

Mr. Chairman and Fellow-Countrymen, — I am sincerely thankful to the Young Men's Muhammadan Association (Hear, hear) for this opportunity that they have given me of speaking upon the subject which concerns most vitally the future well-being of this great country. (Hear, hear). We hear often-times of the Hindu-Muhammadan problem. I will not tonight enter upon a consideration of the nature of this problem. I will not try to trace its history either. This much I may be permitted to say that in the days of my youth, not to go farther, before we had no Hindu-Muhammadan problem in any part of India, our religions were different, our social customs did not agree; we could not eat and drink with one another; but both the Hindus and the Muhammadans fully respected the conscientious scruples of the two communities (Hear, hear) and differences due to religions considerations or social customs did not create any ill-feeling between Hindu and Muhammadan neighbours.

Speaking of Bengal, I may say that, so far as my memory goes, and I am going close upon half a century of earthly life, we never had in our villages or in our towns until very recently any unpleasantness between the two communities. (Hear hear). In my own village we had a Muhammadan neighbour, a Muhammadan Zemindar. We had many Muhammadan friends, but I was referring to a Muhammadan Zemindar who was our neighbour; and in our village relations I remember that I used to call him my *chacha* or uncle as his son used to call may father as his *chacha* or uncle (Hear, hear, and cheers.) On the occasion of any marriage in my family we used to invite this Muhammadan Zemindar family and they used to make presents to the bride and bridegroom on those occasions (Hear, hear). In village life in Bengal in the olden times there was a great deal of exchange of social amenities which is falling into disuse and decay owing to the ingress of modern civilization. On marriage and other festive occasions we rarely bought fish in Bengal — we do take fish — we rarely bought fish from the bazaar.

We had our own tanks whence we could draw our own fish and on those festive occasions in my house the Muhammadan Zemindar would place his fish pond at our disposal and we would do the same when there was any festival in his house. During the Muhammadan festivals, on the occasion of *Eid* and other festivals we used to send presents to this Muhammadan Zemindar and strange to say, on the occasion of Durga Puja in my father's house we invited them. It is not they would send us any present but they would accept our invitation and come and exchange social amenities apart from the religious worship.

In my part of the country it was a custom in the days of my youth when there was any death in a family and there was a *Sradha* ceremony to be performed, friends and relations from distant parts of the country used to send special contributions. These contributions were regulated by the relative position and respectability of the people making them and receiving them. With regard to some the regulated fee, so to say, was Rs. 4. That is in the case of a *Sradha* in a family, they would send Rs. 4 and a piece of cloth and in the case of *Sradha* in their families my parents would send Rs. 4 and a piece of cloth in return. In others the regulated fee was Rs. 2, with some Re. 1, with some half a rupee; and this relation existed between my family and this neighbouring Zemindar family. When there was any mourning in their family we used to send them this money and this present and when there was any *Sradha* in our family, they used to do the same. This, Sir, was the relation that existed even in East Bengal 25 and 30 years ago, 15 years ago, 10 years ago between the Hindus and Muhammadans of that Province. About this time last year I was in Comilla and I was invited by a dozen respectable Muhammadans of that town to address a public meeting specially organised by them over which a Muhammadan Zemindar of the town presided, and on the day when this meeting was advertised, as I was taking a little rest in the afternoon, I received a surprise visit from a member of that Muhammadan Zemindar family who was my father's neighbour, who had married in Comilla and by marriage was connected with one of the highest Muhammadan families in that district.

I had left my village almost when I was in my teens. My connection with my village had practically ceased for quarter of a century and I did not know that this young man belonged to a family, which was one of the families that stood in friendly relations with my family; I did not know that this youngman watched my movements; I did not know that he would care to know me and I was surprised to find him coming to see me at a time that was significant, at a time when some attempts were being made in Comilla itself to influence the aristocracy among the Muhammadan population to keep themselves away from the Hindu movements. This visit was significant; it had no political reference. It was significant as the evidence of the old friendship that existed between my family and this respectable Muhammadan family in my village. (Hear, hear.) This was the state of things quarter of a century ago. This was, as I said, true of many parts of Bengal 10 year ago.

This was true almost I was going to say 5 years' back. It is therefore that I say, Sir, that we have not known really any Hindu Muhammadan problem; yet it must be said that since difference have commenced to arise between the two communities due to whatever causes it may be, it is necessary that those who wish well of the two communities and of the country at large should put their heads together, (Laughter and cheers) and devise some means by which this estrangement may at once be put a stop to; (Hear, hear) for let us remember this, that, though the Muhammadans came to India originally from another land and were originally alien conquerors, they have lived in the country among its people for nearly more then thousand years now (Hear, hear) and they have become part and parcel of the great Indian nation. (Hear hear). And they followed the example that the Hindus themselves had set, because this country at one time did not belong to the Hindus either. They came from another country, conquered the aboriginal races, established and spread their civilization and culture and became in process of time the inhabitants of this country.

So the Muhammadans also coming from another country to conquer those that had come before them, gradually established their rule over them and in course of a few centuries they became organically a part of the nation, which they had originally conquered and come to live among. (Cheers.) The Indian nation is not a Hindu nation. The Indian nation is not a Mohamedan nation either, nor is the Indian nation composed of Hindus and Muhammadans alone. There are others, Christians and they form a large proportion indeed of the Indian Nationality. There are others though smaller in number, but great in wealth and considerably advanced in culture — the Parsees. (Cheers) There are also the followers of Gouthama Budha and these different cultures. All these different communities constitute the new Indian nation. (Laughter and Cheers). When I was talking of *Swaraj,* when I talked of India and Indian Nationality I did not, I beg to assure you, talk either of the Hindu or of the Muhammadan, Budhists or Parsees.

But I talked of all those, who belong to this land who, where-ever they may live, have their life-desire to spend the evening of that life within these shores, who earn money elsewhere but desire to contribute their earning to the economic advancement of this nation (Hear, hear and cheers), who gather the wisdom of the world with a view to replenish the culture of the East — the civilization of this land. It is this land which to them is dearer then all lands. (Cheers) It is this land which has borne on its lap their forefathers and this land it is wherein they hope and pray that their children, and their children may grow and develop and be happy and wise, and advance in every department of human culture from generation to generation. (Cheers). The Hindu Muhammadan problem to whatever cause or causes it may be due desires therefore our most serious consideration. And I believe it, Sir, that this problem can be best solved by an understanding on the part of the Hindus of the excellence of Islamic culture and Islamic civilization and by similar appreciation on the part of my Muhammadan friends of Hindu culture and Hindu civilization. (Hear, hear).

The problem, if any problem exists at all, exists as I said the other night, not among the lower orders of the two communities. The conflict is among the higher classes wherever there is this conflict, and if the higher classes who alone are able to study, to understand, to appreciate and to honour the universal elements of their respective cultures, if the higher classes will apply themselves, the Hindu to the study of Islamic culture and civilization, and the educated Muhammadan to the study of Hindu culture and civilization, I believe it will be impossible for either of them not to respect one another, and where the classes are trained and led to respect one another, then the masses who are already living in amity will grow in community of interest, mutual respect and friendship more and more. (Hear, hear.)

It is for this reason, gentlemen, that I want to draw your attention just for a few moments and very briefly to the contributions that have been made by Islam to the general progress of Indian life, since Islam became a political factor in this country. (Hear, hear). In the first place you, Gentlemen, who are Hindus are proud of your religious ideals, and there are two ideals that stand out above the rest in the whole religious culture of Hinduism. These two ideals are the ideal of Yoga or concentration and the ideal of Viraigya or renunciation and disattachment. But do you know that, as you had your Yogies and your Viragies, the ideal of Yoga and Viragya flourished as much among the founder?, among the teachers, among the saints and sages of Islam, as it flourished, and as it is to be found among your own prophets and teachers, and saints and seers? You know of the great Viraigya of King Janaka who, though King of Kings, never felt any attachment to the earthly things.

But do you know that the world has not as yet known of an example of absolute disattachment, grander, nobler, diviner than that which was by the founder, the prophet of Islam. (Cheers.) When he died what did he leave? He the first founder of Islamic Empire, he, who had fought many battles, conquered many peoples and received, according to the custom, his share of the booty in many wars, what did he leave? A torn mat and an earthen chetty. These were all the earthly effects of the first prophet, Emperor of Islam, Muhammad (Pbuh) himself (Cries of Allaho Akbar.) The story is recited of Muhammad (Pbuh) and his daughter, and his son-in-low Hazrat Ali. Hazrat Ali one day became victorious in a battle and had his part of the booty, he got a large number of gold coins. Muhammad (Pbuh) had nothing to eat that day.

But thinking that his son-in-law having received a large booty would be able to feed him and his friends, Muhammad (Pbuh) with his disciples went to Hazrat Ali's house and he called out to Hazrat Ali. Hazrat Ali was not at home but his wife Hazrat Fatimah, Muhammad (Pbuh) daughter was there. She answered to the call of her father. Muhammad (Pbuh) asked his daughter to come out. She said, "Father, are you alone or are there others with you? He said "yes — I have got my friends". I cannot come out. Why? I have no decent garments to appear before anyone except yourself. Then, he said, we have come to have a good dinner at your house. Where is Hazrat Ali? She said "Hazrat Ali has not returned". 'But give us then a good dinner'. 'Father, my little baby had not had milk to drink this day'. 'What, your baby had no milk to drink; how can it to be? And the lady replied: 'What Hazrat Ali received as his booty, he distributed on the spot to the fakirs'. Is this not an example of Viraigya? You talk of Yoga, of concentration but do you know that there was Samadhi even in the Muhammadan prophets, Saints, and Seers.

This incident is related of Hazrat Ali. Hazrat Ali was wounded in the battle and the spear that wounded him entered his flesh just underneath his knee and it was so painful that he would not allow any body to touch it. His disciple came to Muhammad and said, "We are in a fix, a broken spear has got into the thigh of Hazrat Ali, but Hazrat Ali will not allow us to touch it. How are we to bring it out? Then Muhammad (Pbuh) said, "Do not do anything now. When the time of prayer comes, and when Hazrat Ali sits down to pray, draw it out and he will not feel it". And when the time of prayer came, and Hazrat Ali sat down to pray, the spear was drawn away by force, out of his flesh, and he did not feel that it was drawn. (Cries of Allaho Akbar.) Talking of

Yoga and Samadhi, I am reminded of another anecdote concerning the Hazrat himself and it is this. You know that his beloved wife was Hazrat Ayesha and it often happened that if when Muhammad (Pbuh) was in the company of Ayesha, talking to her completely forgetful of the whole world, engaged in mutual conversation, when there was a flow of heart and a feast of soul between husband and wife, at that moment if the *Muazzin's* call to prayer went out, Muhammad (Pbuh) could not recognise Ayesha who was sitting before him. The call to prayer at once took the soul of Muhammad (Pbuh) to his God and he became absolutely forgetful of all his earthly surroundings including the presence of his beloved and beautiful wife herself.

If you read the Holy Quran, if you read the holy traditions, if you read the lives of Muhammadan saints, you will find underneath all this divergence of ritual and ceremonial and dogma and custom, there is the spirit of devotion to God, there is the spirit of concentration and meditation to God; there is the spirit of disattachment as much in Islam, as is found in Hinduism or in any other religion. (Hear, hear.) But it is not merely the general unit between the highest religious ideal of Islam and the highest ideals of piety of the Hindus, upon which our mutual appreciation and understanding must be based. Islam as an Empire as a governing power as a political authority has made contributions to the general life of India, which is not as yet made perhaps by any political power.

We seem to think that the idea of Empire in India is a new idea imported from the West, but long before the British raised up the Standard of Empire in India the Mogals had done it. The process of Indian unification though it has received considerable impetus from the present British administration did not start with the establishment of this administration. The process of Indian unification had commenced with the establishment of the general authority of the Mogals all over Indian Continent. The idea of Indian Nationalism though it has been considerably developed by the contribution of European thought and culture did not originate with the establishment of British Rule. It grew with the growth and expansion of the Mogal Empire (Hear, hear.) The growth of an Empire always everywhere helps the growth of national unions and under the proper ideal of Empire, nations grow more rapidly than they are able to grow within isolated Kingdoms and small principalities.

I am, Sir, an imperialist, an imperialist of an imperialist, but it must be an Empire of a right sort. It must be an Empire where all the component parts shall enjoy equal liberty and equal freedom. It must be an Empire which will be an Empire of the people or, if it be an Empire of any particular dynasty at least among the people themselves, there shall run a practical equality and practical rights equal rights and equal freedom (Hear, hear) and thought here were differences recognised by Muhammadan administration in certain matters between the Hindus, between the non-Muhammadans subjects of the Emperors of Delhi and elsewhere, those differences I make bold to say, were not political differences but they were more or less exclusively religious differences.

Under the Muhamadans, the Pattans and the Moghuls, had the Hindus not a right of using arms? Were the Hindus deprived of that right? Under the Moghuls, the Muhammadans could not claim the privilege of being tried by a special Court while the Hindus had to be tried by another Court. Under the Moghuls the Muhamadan prisoner did not live in storied building while the Hindu prisoner lived in the first floor. There were distinctions but as I said, they were religious distinctions and the idea of equality before law, the fundamental idea in the growth of nationalities was received first of all from our Muhammadan friends. Before the advent of the Muhammadans we, Hindus, had no rights apart from that which was determined by our status. Before the Muhamadans our civil rights and even our criminal rights were all determined by our caste itself — by the status of the individual.

That is decidedly, Sir, a lower stage in the growth of civic life a lower stage in the evolution of jurisprudence and it is the Muhamadans who gave us a right, a political right in India apart from and independent of, our status as members of particular castes and communities. There lies the foundation of democracy, there lies the foundation of real national life, there lies the foundation of true civic equality and this foundation was laid by the Muhamadans. Our law, the Hindu law received material contributions from the Muhamadan law and administration, our fiscal system grew out of our old Village limitation to a more or less extent into a general fiscal system under the Muhamadans and the fiscal system of the Muhamadans especially so far as the laud revenues are concerned, has not bean improved if it has at all been improved by the advanced and civilized administration of Great Britain. A great deal is said now and then by ignorant men even among my own people about *Jezia,* the tax that was imposed by Aurangzeb upon Hindus and from which the Muhammadans were free. But I have a suspicion, Sir. If I am wrong, you will correct me that the *Jezia* is it-ally a war tax. It was a tax levied upon those who did not belong to Islam but who were subject to the rule of Islam.

It was a tax levied upon subjects of Islam who did not follow the rules of Islam, because every member of the Islamic brotherhood, every subject of the Islamic common wealth had to render military service in the wars of Islam, but those who did not belong to the Islamic commonwealth could not be compelled to render this military service and in lieu of this military service which every member of Islam had to render to the commonwealth of Islam, those who did not belong to Islam but who were subject to this common wealth had to pay this special tax of *Jezia.*

It was not therefore a special tax that was levied upon the Hindus by the Muhammadan rulers of India, but it was a tax levied upon every one who did not render and who could not be called upon to render personal military service for the execution of religions wars of Islam. Hear, Now, Sir, briefly speaking, in politics, in administration, those have been the contributions of Islam to the general growth of Indian National life; but far more valuable have been the contributions of Islam to the social and religious life of India. All our great reforms in the sixteenth and fifteenth centuries were really the product of the influence of Islam upon Hindu thought. Nanak owed his monotheism and a good deal of his religious ideals to Islamic culture and Islamic tradition. In the scripture of Sheikhs you will find quotation from the Vedas the Upanishads, the Puranas, standing side by side with citations from the life and teachings of the Muhammadan saints and sages, men like Shiek Farid and others. The movement of Muhammadan influenced. Even the movement of Kabir owed something to our contact with Muhammadan thought and culture. I am not aware, Sir, of the Bhaghavatars of Southern India who lived and flourished 400 or 500 years back who were contemporaries of Nanak in Punjab, of Kabir in Upper India, of Chaitanya in Bengal and of Thukaram on the Bombay side.

But we know there was a great spiritual upheaval four or five years back in India, the upheaval that tried to raise socially and morally the lowest classes of the Indian community, an up heaval that declared more or loss openly a war against the system of caste, an upheaval that sought to raise in virtue the spiritual excellence and character the lowest Pariah to the position of the saint and the seer and this upheaval which on the political side again contributed to the effort at nation-building of Sivaji in the Maharatta country, of Gurugovind, in the Punjab, of Prataparudra in Bengal. All this political, spiritual, religious, and social upheaval were due to the influence of the ideal and culture of Islam upon Hindu thought, Hindu life, Hindu culture and Hindu ideals (cheers); and keeping all this in view, is it at all surprising that we who have come now under other influences seek to combine our forces and resources and try to work out a larger, a deeper, a wider union between the different Indian communities than had been known in the past.

The Indian nation which we desire to build up in this country will differ from other nations in the world. Nations grew in the past by the accretion of small tribes, tribal organisations that were more or less in their fluid state coming together under the stress of political circumstances, formed themselves into larger nations. But, in India the problem of nation building stands on a different plane.

In India it is not as it were of old in other countries and even in this country is it not with a few fluid tribal organisations that met together under stress of common political circumstances and are trying to form themselves into a compact nation. No. In India, not fluid tribal organisations but developed cultures fully developed communities with a past history of their own, with a special characteristic of their own, with religions of their own, with traditions of their own, such nations, grown up nations, who have developed cultures have come together in India in the present day and the nation that will have to be built up in India, therefore, will have to be built up by the union of fully developed cultures, fully developed nationalities and not by the union as of old, of the tribal organisations and when fully developed, nationalities come together in one territory, and commence to live one common civic and commercial life. The nation that most grow out of that must be a federated nation, and a nation that will respect and recognise the individuality of the different parts of it, the nation that will present to the world a miniature ideal of a federated humanity, the dream of the poet, the hope of the man of God.

When the great world cultures meet together they shall contribute that which is best and highest in them for the general uplifting and advancement of humanity, when each culture will receive from other cultures that which it lacks in itself and will contribute to those cultures things that it has developed specially in itself and which they may be lacking in; that is the problem of nation building in India. The future Indian nation will not be a nation that will profess one religion. The future Indian nation will not be a nation that will accept one social code, the future Indian nation will not be a nation that will submit itself to one particular set of spiritual or ethical discipline. We cannot obliterate the past, neither can the Hindu cease to be a Hindu, nor can the Muhammadan cease to be a Muhammadan; for the Hindu to cease to be a Hindu is to forego his claims to the service of humanity; for the Muhamadan to cease to be a Muhamadan is similarly to forego his claims to render his own service to universal humanity. The Hindu must continue to be a Hindu, must grow as a Hindu along his own line, following his own historic evolution towards his own ideal.

The Muhammadan must continue to be a Muhammadan, must develop Islamic feeling, traditions of Islamic history and Islamic culture and the Christian shall continue to be Christian following the line of Christian civilization, Christian culture and Christian tradition. The Parsee similarly shall continue to be a Parsee, grow in his own special life and culture all these shall contribute their best and their highest to the common life of the nation and shall exchange one with another best and the highest that they have in them. (Cheer) That being our ideal of nationality it in almost foolish for any one to think that if the Indian people grow into a nation the minority shall go to the wall; if the Indian people grow into a nation it will not be a Hindu nation nor it will be a Muhammadan nation nor will it be a Christian nation. No. Sir, it will be a federated nation. We have had our own history, our position is unique in the world, our history has been unique in the world and in God's Providence, as I read this history and as I read the position, our destiny will be a unique destiny among the nations of the world. We shall work out in India the problem of the federation of the human race.

And in working out this problem the Hindu, the Muhammadan and the Christian shall make their highest and best contribution to the common culture, first of the Indian nation and then through the Indian nation to the common culture of the wider, the universal life of humanity. And in this work my young Muhammadan friends you must join the Hindus and the Hindus must join you; because let us remember this that our interests have been indissolubly bound up together by God. You belong to this land, our weal is your weal, our ill is your ill (Hear hear); our weakness is your weakness, your weakness is our weakness and our strength, you shall grow strong and in your strength, we shall grow strong (cheers) and in our mutual combination and strength we shall be able to solve the most complex problems of Indian civilization and India politics far more easily and with the least disturbance to the present order than our enemies desire us or wish us to do.

(Prolonged cheers and loud shouts Vande Mataram)

National Education

[*Mr. Pal continuing his address on the above subject on Thursday evening, said:*]

The next question is, 'Is the education that we received, that we have been receiving for the last 50 years and more, the education that has been established in this country by the present alien Government, is that education conducted along National lines?' (Cries of no, no.) No! Why not, because those who control and direct this education are not competent to direct it along our National lines. (Cheers.) Even if they desire it they have not the adequate knowledge for doing it. They may translate our ancient scriptures and they may win the reputation of being superior orientalists by translating a chapter of the *Ramayana* or one or two *Sutras* of the *Vedanta*, but a study of Sanskrit grammar or translation of a few sutras of the *Vedanta* or a few chapters of the *Nyaya* does not entitle a foreigner to get into the spirit of the consciousness of our race, and as foreigners having a different cast of mind, having different traditions, having had a different training, the foreign Government and those whom that foreign Government imports from its own country are utterly unfit to guide and control education in India along National lines.

No man knew more intimately of India than did the late Professor Max Muller and yet when an Indian reads the voluminous works of Max Muller what does he find. He finds there that at every step the great orientalist has translated the words but has failed to convey the meaning. When I first read his translation of *Dharmapada*, the great Buddhist scripture, I read it comparing it with the original; and even without any intimate acquaintance with *Pali*, a man who knows a little of Sanskrit and Prakrati, as these Prakratis are found in Sanskrit may help understand Pali scriptures. I was reading *Dharmapada* and I took Max Muller for help. I found there one word in *Dharmapada* which is a significant word describing the discipline of Buddhism. There is used this word *Nirudha Veerya;* I needed no translation to understand what it means, — holding of the *Veerya, Sutra Dharma, Brahma Charya.* These are all common things in our country. *Nirudha Veerya.* I looked in to Max Muller.

What did I find He says it means strong, Sandow is a strong man, but can the qualification of *Nirudha Veerya* be applied to Sandow. Now, this is just the sort of insight that we find into our literature, our thought, our life, our habits, our custom, our culture and our civilization in the oriental scholars. And if Max Muller could go to further in *Nirudha Veerya* than Sandow's strength, how can you expect a raw graduate or for the matter of that, ripe graduate from Oxford or Cambridge coming out to India and directing Indian education along Indian National lines. No, Sir. The present Government stands incapacitated, because it is a foreign Government directing the education of the people along National lines. And what is the sort of education that you have been receiving all these years. It has had precious little reference to your own life, to the actualities of your own National history, not even had it any reference. An attempt is being made now only recently. It had very little reference even to your physical surroundings. You would learn Botany by British specimens and not by Indian specimens. Indian Botany is of recent growth, if it has grown at all. Even now in your book you learn words, but the things that these words signify are more or less absolutely absent from your actual life and environments.

In the days when I was a boy we read many excellent things. The smell of hay is sweet. And every Indian boy wonders why should, of all things on earth, the smell of hay be sweet. He does not know what hay is, and the teacher, at least my teacher did it, he said it was straw, and when going through a straw field in

December or January, I have tried to smell the roots of dried straw to see what sweetness there was in it. Gradually the revelation came to me (laughter) that the sweetness was not to be found by human nose, but the Britisher being represented by John Ball, race of Balls, naturally must have some perception of sweetness in straw. (Laughter.) I read, as some of you must have read also, of the swallow, my fourteen generations upward have never seen and I believe my 14 generations down shall never see swallow unless they go to England like me. And yet I have learnt swallow, swallow, swallow to swallow the whole without getting any idea whether it was a big thing or a small thing, whether it was white, brown or black, and what was its formation and what was its colour. Sometimes they give us pictures of swallow and other things but what physiologist is there who teaches physiology to his students from physiological charts.

They are helpful to a certain extent, with a view to revive the memory of things that have not been seen in their original actualities. The education that you have been receiving all these years has been shallow and because of this fact, namely, that this education has been verbal education, it had no reference to things but words. It helped to develop our memory but never our sense or our understanding as it ought to have done. And the result is not only we have suffered in intellectual life, but we have suffered in our ethical, our artistic and our spiritual life as well. Our character has grown on foreign tubs, not even in tubs but in orchids, our manhood has been hung up on the veranda having no roots in the actualities of our nation and our life in the past traditions of our race, we have grown like orchids — orchids grown on the verandas of European Government. That is what our education had been and the greatest pity of it is this, that it has divorced our minds, our heart, our spirit, our character, and our manhood from our National life. We have been taught to botanise the oak, to botanise the elm, to botanise the beech to the neglect of our banyan, our mango groves, our chanpaka tree, to the neglect of the flora of our own country.

We have been taught to investigate into the habits and customs of foreign animals and birds and this teaching has blinded our eyes to the beauties of the ornithological kingdom in India. Our birds that resound in the morning in mango groves with their thousand notes, do not form any part of our intellectual life. The grass covered fields, the paddy fields, the mango groves, the flowering chanpakas, asoka, the flowering vakula, all these things do not awaken in us any intellectual, do not create in us any intellectual quickening or emotional movement, because from our childhood onwards we have lived apart from these actualities of our life.

Open an English textbook and what do you find then? Those textbooks are not meant for you, they were made for European, English boys and they described the surroundings in the midst of which an English boy lives and grows and therefore from his infancy onwards every English boy is placed in vital contact with his own surroundings, with his social surroundings, with his National life. Why, on account of this outlandish education, you are divorced from your actual surroundings and your actual National life. Patriotism has suffered in India in the past on account of this divorce between education and Nationalism. There has been patriotism in India among the educated classes of a type, I admit. In the days of my youth we also dreamt divine dreams in regard to the glory of our country.

We sang also then National songs, but this partriotism of 25 years ago was an airy, fairy something, absolutely unrelated to the reality of our life and surroundings and this is due, this starvation of the patriotic sentiment in India, this weakening of civic aspiration in the people, this dependence upon the alien bureaucracy for the attainment of personal ambition or National advancement — all this is due entirely to the outlandish, the rootless education that we have been receiving all these years. Since sometime past open attempts have commenced to be made by the Government to impart a particular kind of education in this country, an education that creates hot-house loyalty among the people of the land. (Cries of shame). Lord Curzon started University and educational reform with a view to the cultivation of loyalty to the present Government in India. Bishop Weldon, when the University reform was under discussion in India, writing to the *London Times* distinctly declared, and Bishop Weldon ought to know what was in the mind of his old classmate, the Viceroy of India in those days, that educational reforms were needed for the cultivation of loyal sentiments among the people of the country.

Lee Warner's Bible has been made a textbook, specifically for these purposes and the recent circulars indicate what is the trend and tendency of the officialised system of education among us.

This education was introduced by the English Government more than 50 years ago, specifically for their own benefit. English education was not introduced haphazard. So far as Bengal is concerned, we know that a great controversy arose between the supporters of English education and the advocates of oriental learning before English Schools and Colleges were opened. Among those who advocated the introduction of English and western education was Lord Macaulay. There were others opposed to him who wanted to introduce the old, to reintroduce the old, oriental system of education. Their idea was to teach us *Ghatathwa* and *Patathwa* as I said once with a view to perpetuate our Dasathwa through *Ghatathwa* and *Patathwa* and once you devote yourself to *Ghatakasa* and *Patakasa* the political Akasa would be free of all disturbances.

The orientalists wanted to keep the light of modern education and science away from this country and why, because they were afraid lest the Indian people, educated in Western science educated in Western literature, brought up in Western history, might gradually demand to quote Lord Dufferin "to ride in the chariot of the sun" might be led to demand those free political institutions that are the most glorious heritage of Western nations. And Macaulay in reply to these forces declared that it would be a glorious day for England if the people of India, educated in Western science, brought up in Western history and literature, demanded those free political institutions for themselves in their country which exist in the land of their rulers. (Cheers.) And this declaration of Lord Macaulay was only an argument used against his opponents. It was not, Sir, as I read it, a declaration of original policy, should this thing happen then we shall enjoy the supreme satisfaction of having raised a fallen nation to such and such an object of National glory, not that we desire it to happen, but if the contingency should happen as your orientalists say, then this will be our consolation. The consolation, the consolation, twice will be the uplifting of a fallen nation.

That what Lord Macaulay's words meant and the policy that guided Lord Macaulay was this. He saw that the British Government in India was a despotic Government and no despotic Government can exist in any country unless it is able to secure the support of the people of that country. Even Russian despotism depends for its continuance upon the support that it has been receiving from the royal duties and from those who are dependent on the royal duties in Russia. The despotism of the unspeakable Turk, as he is called, the hidden Turk, of the Sultan of Turkey, that is also an unmitigated despotism. It is supported by the Pasha. The power of the priest and the power of the aristocracy stand as a bulwark around the throne of the Sultan of Turkey protecting it from all insults from within and from without. Every student of political history knows that no despotism can exist anywhere unless it is able to create about itself a citadel of interest, popular interest, in the perpetuation of its own authority and the English Government in India having established itself as the supreme political authority in the country, looked about for the creation of such a citadel.

It looked about and saw the native Princes but they were unthinkable as a support of British rule which is established to the loss of their own power. They looked upon the middle classes, the real aristocracy of the country, the Brahman and the other higher castes. They had been to some extent greatest sufferers under the preceding administrations and the British policy saw in this middle class the possibilities of a bulwark that might be raised round itself for its own protection. English education was imparted with a view to create this bulwark. It had to be imparted, because the Government of such a large people could not be conducted by importing alien officers from their island home. Native agency had to be employed. It was essential that it should be employed and an agency had to be created, because the Government that these foreigners established in this country was their own Government and not the Government of the people themselves. The system was their own.

English education had to be imparted, imparted with a view to raise up a class of men who would be able to serve the Government, that was one object. It had to be imparted, secondly, to create a class of men whose interests would be indissolubly bound up with the interests of the Government, which would receive their living from the hands of the Government as Government servants, who would receive honour and distinction from the Government, whose temporal interest would be bound up indissolubly with the Government, and more than that, if these people are trained in European history in English literature not only their temporal interests but their intellectual, their moral, their ethical ideal, nay even their civic ideal, may be bound with the perpetuation of the foreign authority in this country. Policy demanded that you should be educated in Western science and English literature, and for a long time the Government of India looked upon you as its greatest help and support.

Until very recently, before a quarter of a century even, I might say, the Government in India looked upon the educated classes as those who would interpret their wishes to the people and stand between the people and the Government gaining the allegiance of the people for the Government and gaining the good offices of the Government or the people. That was the ideal even of British statesmen in India 25 years ago. The creation of an educated aristocracy so to say in India was thus of the Government in this country. But gradually you refused to discharge the functions which they wanted you to discharge, you claimed more than they thought you would even claim from them Lord Dufferin said that you wanted to ride in the chariot of the sun and then gradually when you became restive, when you became discontented, when you began, instead of helping to strengthen the authority of the Government, to place yourself over the head of the people and set up a permanent opposition to that Government, the educational policy had to be changed, and it was changed.

At first gradually, at first secretly, at first insidiously and then, as your opposition became violent and open the policy of the Government also became violent and open until in the last University Act, we find the culmination of that policy whose object is, has been, to curtail to some extent, in the name of depth of learning, an extensive cultivation of European literature and European art by our people. I have been told and I believe it is true, but, I speak open to correction, that Burke had been tabooed by the Calcutta University, the old books would be tabooed more and more, and in place of Burke you have Lee Warner's Bible (Laughter). The time therefore has come when in the interests of the intellectual life of the nation, nay, more than that, in the interest of the preservation of the nation itself, you and I should take up the charge of educating people in our own hands, so that we may direct the mind of the nation, the will of the nation, the heart of the nation, the energy of the nation with a view to the realisation of the destiny of the nation. In the system of education that we propose to start in this country, liberal and scientific culture will be combined with technical education. In the system of education that we have formulated already in the National Council of Education in Bengal we have sought to combine scientific and liberal education with technical training. Whatever else might be done in other countries, in India it well be suicidal to set up wholly technics independently or apart from liberal and scientific training.

We are essentially Sir, an intellectual race and we cannot sacrifice the intellectual life for the earning of bread. Man liveth not by bread alone. No, as I said the other night, neither do nations live by bread alone and National destiny could not be realised by setting up soap factories or cotton mills. Indeed, even in the interest of the economic life of the nation, liberal and scientific education is essential, because what is technical education? Technical education is that education which helps a man to produce marketable commodities by the application of trained intelligence on the knowledge of the material that he possesses. In the application of trained intelligence to the knowledge of material for the production of marketable commodity, that is technical education, the intelligence must be trained for technical education and intelligence can only be trained by a liberal training, by a liberal culture, and knowledge of material must be gained for the purpose of technical education; and knowledge of material can only be gained by scientific education, because it is the science which gives you a knowledge of material, and technical education being the application of trained intelligence to knowledge of material for the production of marketable commodity, it is impossible to divorce this education from general, liberal and scientific culture.

Therefore in our system of National education we had combined as compulsory branches in the lower school standards liberal and scientific education with technical training up to 12 years of age. Up to the class which an ordinary boy may get to by the time he is 12 years, we teach no technical arts. It is the period which is devoted to the cultivation of the natural intelligence of the boy, of the development of his powers of understanding, to the development of his eye and hand, the training of his senses and of the imparting of ordinary knowledge of material for the training of the senses. From the 13th to 14th, two years this trained, intelligence develops this knowledge of materially advancing and we teach him to apply this intelligence to the knowledge of material that he gains during these two periods by a specific scientific culture for the production of some marketable commodity and this goes on advancing from step to step.

For instance, let as represent the degree of; intelligence that a boy receives, attains when he is 14 years old, by *a*, let us represent the knowledge of material that an average boy gets in the class where a boy of 14 may get to in our college or school by b; *a* applied to b will produce the commodity *c*. In the next year his intelligence grows let as indicate the growth of this intelligence by a raised to the power of 1. His knowledge of experience as *b* raised to the power of 1 and the commodity that be produces also *c* raised to the power of 1. In the next year it will be raised to the power of 2, and a corresponding improvement in the commodity, c raised to power of 2 and in this way we go up to the end of our school career and if the school career is finished, when the young man goes to the National College there are three branches. One is the general liberal branch wherein he is taught language, history, philosophy, arts. All these things are taught in one branch. There is a middle branch wherein pure science is taught. There is a third branch wherein higher technical studies are encouraged and held for the production of higher kinds of materials and commodities. Those who have not to earn a living, sons of rich men, men with independence, they may go in for pure literary or humanitarian studies. Those who, though not rich, desire to devote themselves to literary work may go in to that and devote themselves exclusively to the cultivation of the arts. In this department we shall train up others, historians, philosophers, poets, journalists, painters, sculptors, artists.

Then in the middle branch of science pure, our aim shall be to produce men of science who shall devote them selves to original scientific investigation, men the of type of Jagadees Chandra Bhose, or Prafhulla Chandra Bhose, and in the third branch there will be men who will apply the principles of science as attained by the researches of the scientific students and savants for the production of ordinary commodity. This Sir, briefly is the sketch of the system of National education that we propose to impart in our National Schools and Colleges in Bengal. We have already a number of schools, one in Rungpur, one in Dinajpur, one in Dacca, two in the Mymensingh District, two in Comilla District, one in Jalpaigiri and a school and college in Calcutta. The income from endowed funds of the National Council of which I have the honour to be a member is just now Rs. 60,000. It is not a large sum for a National University, but we hope, in course of time as we are able to prove by results the superiority of the education that we seek to impart to our youths, funds will be forth coming.

We have got now 2,500 to 3,000 students reading in our different colleges and schools. (Cheers.) It is not a large number and yet we are not disheartened because we are working against great odds. This present system of education, officialised education, has created a hankering in the people for the Government service and the so called learned professions and the education that we offer can hold out no temptations in those lines. (Hear, hear and cheers.) Our certificates of degrees will not help any one to get into the Government service. (Cheers.) I shall be sorry, Sir, if at any time it is regarded as a passport of Government service until the Government becomes our own (cheers). We may teach law, we have not started any legal faculty as yet, but our legal degrees will not entitle one to plead before these foreign Law Courts (Cheers.) We are working against great odds, but still we are thankful for these 3,000 students.

There were not as many when they first started English education in this country and I believe, Sir, that in proportion as the repressive measured of the present Government advances and persecution is started against the student population and an attempt is made to stifle their newborn love for the motherland (cheers), in proportion as this is done, in proportion as an alternative that the officialised institutions will place before the people, becomes this, either to serve the motherland (cheers) or to attain a livelihood by following the service of the foreign Government; in proportion as this is done, in that proportion, I believe, with the help of God, the enthusiasm for National education will increase (shouts of *Vande Mataram)* and both guardians and boys, as they are doing in Bengal, will in every part of India consider it their sacred duty to give their go-by to the officialised educational institutions and the chances of earning a livelihood by slaving under this Government and take to National education (cheers); and this much, I can assure you, my dear friends, that whoever will come to our schools and colleges will have a greater chance of earning a decent livelihood than what is offered by the present officialised University. (Cheers.)

How many of those, I say, who are sent to school by their parents with a view to pass their examinations, and passing their examinations, to get into some honourable post under the Government, how many, what percentage of those do attain their goal? (A voice 5 per cent.) Yes. Out of every 100, five or six at the utmost (cries of yes, yes). A number fall off at the matriculation and they cannot go further; a number fall off at the F. A. and they cannot go to the B.A.; again a number fall off at the law degree and they cannot pass and it is just like the *Mahaprayana* of the *Pandavas* and ultimately the *Yudhishtira* reaches the position of a Deputy Magistrate. That is what becomes and the boy that falls upon the way, the young man that falls off at the Matric, at the F.A., the young man that is expelled from the gate of the B.A., what are they worth? What can they earn? (A voice Rs. 7.8-0 another Re. 10.) (Laughter and cheers).

In Madras a B.A., as I understand, earns on an average Rs. 15 or Rs. 20 a month (cries of shame and not even that.) I am glad to learn that it is true, because if you realise that truth of it the temptation to follow this University will not be so strong as it otherwise might have been and what we can offer for you in our education, you must have seen from this brief sketch that I have given you, all prizes, no blanks. (Cheers.) Ours will not be merely an examining body. We to some extent are an examining body, but it is due to an example set by the University. If we are left to ourselves, we would not be an examining body, but we would be a teaching body (Hear, hear); and gradually I hope that these Universities rather filled to their utmost capacity by the son of Tahsildars and Deputy Magistrates and other Government servants, (laughter and cheers) the general population leaving it altogether.

When that day comes, as I hope it will be, we shall be able also to considerably modify our present examination system in the National University. But, as I said, our system offers all prizes and no blanks; because the boy that leaves our National Schools at the age of 14 is good for doing something, perhaps he can turn out some work as a carpenter, as a blacksmith, as a goldsmith, as a weaver, something he can turn his hand to; we take care to teach every boy that which he is best fitted to learn, we teach every boy something, be he the son of a Zemindar or a peasant. Compulsory technical education in the school department (Hear, hear) he must have if not for earning bread, at least as a part of the general liberal culture, because making of things is regarded now by moderate Pedagogues in America and other places as part of the liberal education of every boy. Therefore whoever goes out of school will have learnt something from us by which he can earn something say 15 to 20 if he cannot earn more, but will have the consolation, the supreme satisfaction of feeling that he is a free man and independent man.

If he cannot provide himself and his family with luxurious food he will at least have the satisfaction of dining upon his rice and *rasam* or *charu*, but consistently with the preservation of his self-respect. (Hear, hear and cheers) This, then, is the sort of education that we have schemed in our National University. This is the ideal of the realisation of the National destiny; and say last word to you is this unless you accept this ideal of National education and not only accept it intellectually but unless you make a strong realisation, the rich to lay out their money, those who have not money to place their boys and their youths for tuition in these schools and the general public to offer the best that they can towards the furtherance of this object, unless you do it, the time would come when all this new spirit will fail to attain its purpose because of the repressive measures that are being introduced in the Educational Department of India by that Government (Cries of shame.) The recent circular, I do not know what effect it will have upon the conscience and consciousness of the people in Madras. (Cries of It will have).

Need I say that henceforth it will not be possible not only for our school boys, but it will be difficult, if not impossible for our teachers and professors and the educated community in general to participate in the present National upheaval. Why, Sir, why should politics be tabooed from our University and our schools. Do they do it in England? (Cries of no, no.) Is politics condemned even in the public schools of England; in the Universities do they not discuss patriotic and academical problems, but actually deal with the burning political questions of the day. In the Oxford and Cambridge unions they discuss politics and in the schools they bring up boy brigades, do they not sing the National Anthem in the public schools in England, Rule Britannia rules the waves, Britain shall never be slaves, is it tabooed in any public school in England, and if not, how can you say that the singing of *Vande Mataram* is not consistent with the advancement of real culture and education among the people of this country. (Shouts of *Vande Mataram.)*

The Principal of a College in Madras, it is reported, wanted to amend the objects of Young Men's Association which declared that the cultivation of the patriotic sentiment was its end and aim and be wanted to amend it. Cultivation of the patriotic sentiment consistently with loyalty to the present Government, would it be impossible, would it be thought of or would it be dreamt in any part of England. (Cries of no, no) Patriotism in an absolute virtue and if it is to be limited by at consideration it is to be limited by a consideration of universal humanity and by no other consideration patriotic sentiment must be cultivated consistently with the cultivation of love for universal humanity.

That is what one can understand. Therefore, it seems to me. Sir, that this new circular and the repressive measures that are presaged in this circular, all these will either kill National education, not in every Province, but in some Provinces. (Cries of "not in Madras".) I thank you; but it will, I hope, it will not be able to kill it; on the contrary it seems to me that this circular of the Government of India well help the growth of National education (cheers) and I hope and trust that the patriotism and public spirit of Madras (shouts of *Vande Mataram)* will give a practical reply to this circular by organising now at once a National College and School here. (Shouts of *Vande Mataram.)*

If this is done, you will solve the problem of education in India such as it is not as yet been solved by the British, our Universities and officialised agencies of public instrument in this country. (Loud shouts of *Vande Mataram* and loud cheers.)

8

Golden Words of Pal

- Religion is not a part of life, but the whole of it.
- The unity of India was, thus, neither racial nor religious, nor political nor administrative. It was a peculiar type of unity, which may, perhaps be best described as cultural.
- Those who so persistently deny any fundamental historic unity or any real national individuality to our land and our people, either do not know, or do not remember the fact that we never called our country by the alien name of India or even by that of Hindustan. Our own name was, and is still today, Bharat Varsha.
- The central aim of the Maha Bharata war, which Shri Krishna in some sense himself brought about, was not to acquire territory, but to work out a great socio-political synthesis in India on the basis of dharma, and thus to combine the numerous races and divergent cultures of the continent into one organic whole.

9

Great Life at a Glance

1858, Nov. 7: Bipin Chandra Pal was born in Sylhet in a wealthy Hindu Kayastha family. His father Ramchandra Pal, a village zamindar and a prominent member of the Sylhet bar was influenced by both Hindu rituals and Islamic thought, though, he was a follower of Vaishnavism. The only son of his parents, Bipin Chandra Pal took his early education from a Maulvi in Sylhet town.

1873: A philanthropist, Rao Bahadur Arcot Narayanaswamy Mudaliar, started a school, the forerunner to the later RBANM Institutions, where the revolutionary Bipin Chandra Pal served as principal.

1881: Sardar Dayal Singh Majitha on the advice of Surendra Nath Bannerjee brought out 'Tribune' under the editorship of Sheetala Kant Chatterjee. Bipin Chandra Pal edited this paper for sometime.

1886: Bipin Chandra Pal joined the Indian National Congress and was also one of the key members of revolutionary India House.

1905, Nov.: Bipin Chandra Pal, along with Pramathanath Mitra, visited Dhaka where, at a political meeting, Pal called for volunteers, ready to sacrifice their all for the Motherland.

1906, Aug.: Bipin Chandra Pal decided to start a patriotic journal. He named it *'Vande Mataram'*, after the popular song.

1907: Bipin Chandra Pal gave lectures in Madras, he stayed in Gautamsarama for a week.

1909, Jul 29: Savarkar asked Gyan Chand Varma "not to leave London and to attend the function at Imperial Institute". Dhingra finalised his plans. He met Savarkar that evening in Bipin Chandra Pal's house. Niranjan Pal was also present at the meeting.

1910, Jan. 22: Bipin Chandra Pal became active in Paris, Geneva and Berlin.

1919: Bipin Chandra Pal broke away with Mahatma Gandhi, when the non-cooperation movement was launched.

1920, Sep.: The special Congress session which met at Calcutta, marked a turning point in Indian politics. Gandhiji's resolutions on Hindu-Muslim unity and the policy of non-violent non-cooperation for the attainment of Swaraj, were passed by the session. Bipin Chandra Pal and C.R. Has strongly opposed them, considering them to be disadvantageous to the country.

1923: Bipin Chandra Pal became an active participant in Bengal partition movement, Non-cooperation Movement and Swadeshi Movement.

1932, May 20: Bipin Chandra Pal died, after he had for almost fifty years, roused the country from one end to the other to a new height—unknown, unsung and almost unnoticed.

Bibliography

Aditya Mukherjee, Sucheta Mahajan, Panikkar, K.N.: *India's Struggle for Independence*, Penguin Books, New Delhi, 1989.

Bakshi, S.R.: *Indian Freedom Fighters: Struggle for Independence*, Hardcover, 2002.

Bhagwan, V.: *Indian Freedom Movement and Constitutional Acts*, Atma Ram, 1999.

Bhattacharya, B.K.: *India's Freedom Movement: Legacy of Bipin Chandra Pal*, Deep and Deep, New Delhi, 2007.

Brown, Giles: *The Hindu Conspiracy, 1914-1917: The Pacific Historical Review*, University of California Press, 1948.

Brown, Judith M.: *Civil Resistance and Power Politics: The Experience of Non-violent Action from Gandhi to the Present*, Oxford University Press, New York, 2009.

Chandler, Malcolm; Wright, John: *Modern World History*, Heinemann Educational Publishers, 2001.

Chandra, Bipan: *India's Struggle For Independence*, Penguin Books India (P) Ltd., New Delhi, 1989.

Collett, Nigel: *The Butcher of Amritsar: General Reginald Dyer*, Hambledon and London, 2007.

Collins, Larry; Lapierre, Dominique: *Freedom at Midnight*, HarperCollins, London, 1997.

Forest, G.W.: *The Indian Mutiny 1857–1858*, Low Price Publications, Delhi, 2000.

Fraser, Thomas G.: *Germany and Indian Revolution, 1914-18: Journal of Contemporary History,* Sage Publications, 1977.

Gandhi, Mohandas: *An Autobiography: The Story of My Experiments with Truth,* Beacon Press, Boston, 1993.

Ganjoo, S.: *Muslim Freedom Fighters of India,* Anmol Publication, New Delhi, 2002.

Goyal, P.K.: *Battle of India's Freedom Movement,* Vista International, 2005.

Gupta, Shantinath: *Great Freedom Fighters of India,* Anmol, 2006.

Hari Hara Das: *The History of Freedom Movement in India (1857-1947),* National, 1998.

Heehs, Peter: *India's Freedom Struggle: A Short History,* Oxford University Press, Delhi, 1998.

Hoover, Karl: *The Hindu Conspiracy in California, 1913-1918: German Studies Review,* German Studies Association, 1985.

Hopkirk, Peter: *Like Hidden Fire: The Plot to Bring Down the British Empire,* Kodansha Globe, 1997.

Indu Dave: *Indian Personality in Its Developmental Background,* Himanshu, 1991.

Iyengar, A.S.: *Role of Press and Indian Freedom Struggle: All through the Gandhian Era,* APH, 2001.

Kailash Khanna: *History of Indian Freedom Struggle,* Commonwealth Publication, 2004.

Kaushik, A.S.: *Great Freedom Fighters of India,* Indian Publication, 2007.

Khairul Anam, Md.: *Indian Freedom Movement and Murshidabad District 1905-1947,* Bagchi, K. P., 2008.

Krishan Mohan: *Encyclopaedic History of Indian Freedom Movement,* Book Enclave, 1999.

Kumar, Raj: *Essays on Indian Freedom Movement,* History and Culture Series, Discovery, 2003.

Kumar, Ravindra: *Champaran to Quit India Movement,* Mittal, 2002.

Kumar, Sirisa Shadangi: *The Prisons of South Orissa and the Freedom Fighters in Incarceration, 1900 - 1947*, Punthi Pustak, 2005.

Lion Agrawal, M. G.: *Freedom Fighters of India (4 Vols-Set)*, Isha Books, 2008.

Lovett, Sir Verney: *A History of the Indian Nationalist Movement*, Frederick A. Stokes Company, New York, 1920.

Majumdar, R. C.: *History of the Freedom Movement in India (3 Vols-Set)*, Firma KLM, 1997.

Majumdar, R.C.: *History of the Freedom Movement in India.*

Malhotra, Sumiti: *Thoughts of Great Personalities in 20 Century*, Raj Publishing, 2003.

Manju Verma: *The Role of Women in the Freedom Movement in Punjab (1919-1947)*, Abhijeet, 2003.

Maulana Syed Mohammad Mian: *The Prisoners of Malta (Asira'n-E-Malta): The Heart-Rending Tale of Muslim Freedom Fighters in British Period*, Manak, 2005.

Mazhar Kibriya: *Gandhi and Indian Freedom Struggle*, APH, 1999.

Muthaiah, S.: *Women Freedom Fighters*, The Hindu, 2004.

Nanda, S.P.: *Freedom Movement and Constitutional Development in India*, Dominant, 2004.

Nehru, Jawaharlal: *Discovery of India*, Oxford University Press, Delhi, 1989.

Om Prakash: *Encyclopaedic History of Indian Freedom Movement*, Anmol, 2003.

Omesh Saigal: *Shaheed Bhagat Singh: Unique Martyr in Freedom Movement*, Gyan Publication, 2002.

Owen, N.: *The British Left and India*, Oxford University Press, Oxford, 2007.

Parashar, Parmanand: *Kashmir and the Freedom Movement*, Sarup, 2004.

Popplewell, Richard J.: *Intelligence and Imperial Defence: British Intelligence and the Defence of the Indian Empire 1904-1924*, 1995.

Pradhan, K.B.: *Freedom Movement in India*, Arise Publication, 2007.

Rafiya, Nisar: *Shaikh-Ul-Hind Maulana Mahmud Hasan and Indian Freedom Movement*, Manak Publication, 2008.

Ram Sharma, S.: *Education of Women and Freedom Movement*, Discovery, 1996.

Ram, S. and Kumar, R.: *Encyclopaedia of Indian Freedom Struggle*, Commonwealth Publication, 2008.

Ram, S. and Kumar, R.: *Quit India Movement: 1942-1945*, Commonwealth Publication, 2008.

Ramanathan, K.V.: *The Satyamurti Letters, Vol. II: The Indian Freedom Struggle Through the Eyes of a Parliamentarian*, Dorling Kindersley for Pearson Longman an Imprint of Pearson Education, 2008.

Ramu, P. S.: *Azad Hind Fauj (I.N.A.) and The Freedom Movement*, Freedom Movement Memorial Comm, 1998.

Sarkar, B.K.: *Political Science Quarterly*, The Acedemy of Political Science, 1921.

Sarkar, Sumit: *Modern India: 1885-1947*, Macmillan, Madras, 1983.

Sharma, S.K.: *Eminent Indian Freedom Fighters*, Anmol Publication, New Delhi, 2004.

Sofri, Gianni: *Gandhi and India: A Century in Focus*, The Windrush Press, Gloucestershire, 1999.

Strachan, Hew.: *The First World War: To Arms*, Oxford University Press, USA, 2001.

Sundaram, V.: *Great Crusader for Women's Emancipation*, News Today, 2005.

Sundararaja, Saroja: *March to Freedom in Madras Presidency, 1916-1947*, Lalitha Publication, Chennai, 1989.

Taneja, Anup: *Gandhi, Women and the National Movement, 1920-47*, Har-Anand Publications, Delhi, 2005.

Tinker, Hugh: *India in the First World War and after Journal of Contemporary History: From War to Peace*, Sage Publications, 1968.

Index

E

F

G

P

Q

R

S

T

U

V

W

Z

❑❑❑